SCM PELICAN COMMENTARIES
EDITED BY D. E. NINEHAM

Saint Mark

SCM PELICAN COMMENTARIES

Saint Mark

D. E. NINEHAM

SCM PRESS LTD

0 334 02168 5

First published 1963 by Penguin Books Ltd
This edition first published 1977
by SCM Press Ltd
56 Bloomsbury Street London WC1
Printed in Great Britain by
Fletcher & Son Ltd, Norwich

Contents

Editorial Foreword

Biblical commentaries are of various kinds. Some are intended solely for the specialist; others are devotional commentaries meant simply to help the Christian believer in his prayer and meditation. The commentaries in this series belong to neither class. Though they are based on full scholarly study and deal with technical points wherever necessary, the aim throughout has been to bring out the meaning the Evangelists intended to convey to their original readers. Since that meaning was religious, it is hoped that the commentaries, while being of interest to readers of any religious persuasion or none, and giving a fair indication of the current position in Gospel study, will help Christian readers to a deeper and more informed appreciation of the Gospels.

Technical terms have been avoided wherever possible; where used, they have been fully explained in the Introductions, and readers are advised to read the Introduction to each volume before beginning on the commentary proper. The extended Introduction to the volume on Mark is in some degree intended as an introduction to the series as a whole.

Preface

A book such as this, which comes out of many years' reflection on the Gospels, owes so much to so many that it would be impracticable to give a complete list of all my obligations, even were I consciously aware of them all. My chief obligations to previous writers and commentators on St Mark are acknowledged in the Introduction and notes, but certain more personal obligations it is a pleasure to record here. First, there is my incalculable debt to the late Robert Henry Lightfoot, for two years my tutor and many more my friend; then, while the book was actually being written, three friends helped me a great deal in various ways – more, perhaps, than they realize: my colleague Professor C. F. Evans, the Reverend J. C. Fenton, Principal of Lichfield Theological College, and Canon S. H. Evans, Dean of King's College, London. Mrs H. G. Grainger and my father-in-law, the Reverend A. P. Miller, have relieved me of most of the burdensome work of preparing indexes. My former secretary Mrs Robin Wilkinson and her sister-in-law Mrs Alan Wright did the typing, and my present secretary Miss Dorothy Williams has worked indefatigably and with an eagle eye on the proofs. Dr G. B. Caird read the whole book in typescript and helped me by a number of characteristically penetrating comments. To my wife my debt, in this as in all other things, is far too great to be expressed; but she knows how grateful I am.

I should like to end my task, as more than one previous expositor of St Mark has done, with these words from St Augustine: *Domine Deus . . . quaecumque dixi in hoc libro de tuo, agnoscant et tui; si qua de meo, et Tu ignosce et tui* (*De Trin.*, XV, 28: O Lord, whatever I have said in this book that comes of thy prompting, may thy people recognize it; for what I have said that comes only of myself, I ask of thee and of thy people pardon). D.E.N.

References, Abbreviations, and Technical Terms

As most readers will know, when St Matthew and St Luke were writing they both had copies of Mark in front of them and incorporated almost the whole of it into their Gospels. They did not copy slavishly, however, and it is often instructive to compare their versions of a passage (which sometimes drew on additional sources) with the Marcan original. In such cases the passages from Matthew and Luke are known as the 'Synoptic parallels', or as the 'Matthean' and the 'Lucan' parallel respectively. In the commentary this is abbreviated as Matt. //, Luke //.

St Matthew and St Luke also appear to have used another common source, in addition to Mark, which is usually known as 'Q'. The relationship of this hypothetical document to Mark is quite uncertain; if it was earlier than St Mark he may have drawn on it to some extent, though in places it appears to give accounts of incidents parallel to, and independent of, Mark's. In the commentary, when reference is made to passages from Q in Matthew and Luke, they are cited as Matt. a^{b} // Luke x^{y}.

Readers will also realize that the Gospel was originally written by hand and that for centuries all copies had to be made by hand. Inevitably changes, both intentional and unintentional, crept in, and, of the hundreds of manuscripts (that is, hand-written copies) of Mark that have survived, no two agree exactly. When manuscripts differ we speak of 'variant readings' and in a certain – limited – number of cases it is not easy to be sure which 'reading' reproduces what Mark originally wrote; in these cases the Revised Standard Version often gives one or more alternative readings in a footnote – these are referred to as 'marginal readings'. Such passages are briefly discussed in the commentary; in such discussions

version = an early translation (also hand-copied) into some language other than the original Greek, e.g. Latin or Syriac;

witness = a passage from some ancient book which quotes a text from the Gospel and so shows the form in which the ancient writer was familiar with it.

Frequent reference is made in the commentary to the *Greek* version of the Old Testament, which differs considerably from the Hebrew text on which our English translations are based. The standard Greek translation came to be known as the Septuagint, because it was believed to be the work of seventy-two translators working independently, and by a miracle producing an identical version in seventy-two days. The standard abbreviation for Septuagint is LXX.

As far as possible the units into which the Gospel has been divided for comment are the units of tradition from which it was originally made up.

Certain modern works dealing with St Mark which have been referred to very frequently are cited by initial letters. The great modern English commentary on the Greek text, to which every page of this book is indebted even though the general approach and conclusions are rather different, is that by Dr Vincent Taylor – cited as V. T.

Other important commentaries – all on the English text – are those by:

A. E. J. Rawlinson (Westminster Commentary) – R.
B. H. Branscomb (Moffatt Commentaries) – B.
C. G. Montefiore, *The Synoptic Gospels*, I – Montef.

Two German commentaries are so important that they must be mentioned: one by J. Wellhausen, which though very brief and now sixty years old is full of suggestive insights; and one by E. Klostermann, which succeeds in packing a mine of information into a single, handy volume.

Two very valuable books on the theological ideas of the Gospel are:

History and Interpretation in the Gospels by R. H. Lightfoot – *H. & I.*
The Gospel Message of St Mark by R. H. Lightfoot – *G. M. M.*

Also frequently cited are:

From Tradition to Gospel by M. Dibelius – *F. T. G.*
The Message of Jesus by M. Dibelius – *M. J.*

The Parables of the Kingdom by C. H. Dodd – *Parables*
The Parables of Jesus by J. Jeremias – *P. J.*
The Eucharistic Words of Jesus by J. Jeremias – *E. W. J.*
The Sayings of Jesus by T. W. Manson – *S. J.*
The Teaching of Jesus by T. W. Manson – *T. J.*
The Holy Spirit and the Gospel Tradition by C. K. Barrett – *H. S. G. T.*
Jesus and the First Three Gospels by W. E. Bundy – Bundy
Die Geschichte der synoptischen Tradition by R. Bultmann – Bultmann
Kommentar zum Neuen Testament aus Talmud und Midrasch by H. L. Strack and P. Billerbeck – S.–B.

Other abbreviations frequently used are as follows:
Manuscript(s) – MS(S).
English translation – E. T.
Journal of Theological Studies – *J. T. S.*

Permission to quote from the following works is gratefully acknowledged:

B. H. Branscomb, *Commentary on St Mark's Gospel*, Moffatt Commentaries, Hodder and Stoughton.

R. H. Lightfoot, *History and Interpretation in the Gospels*, Hodder and Stoughton; *The Gospel Message of St Mark*, Clarendon Press. (Thanks are also due to the Reverend Philip M. Haynes for permission to use these last two books.)

C. G. Montefiore, *The Synoptic Gospels*, volume I, second edition, Macmillan.

A. E. J. Rawlinson, *Commentary on St Mark's Gospel*, Westminster Commentaries, Methuen.

Vincent Taylor, *The Gospel According to St Mark*, the Greek text, introduction, notes, and indexes, Macmillan.

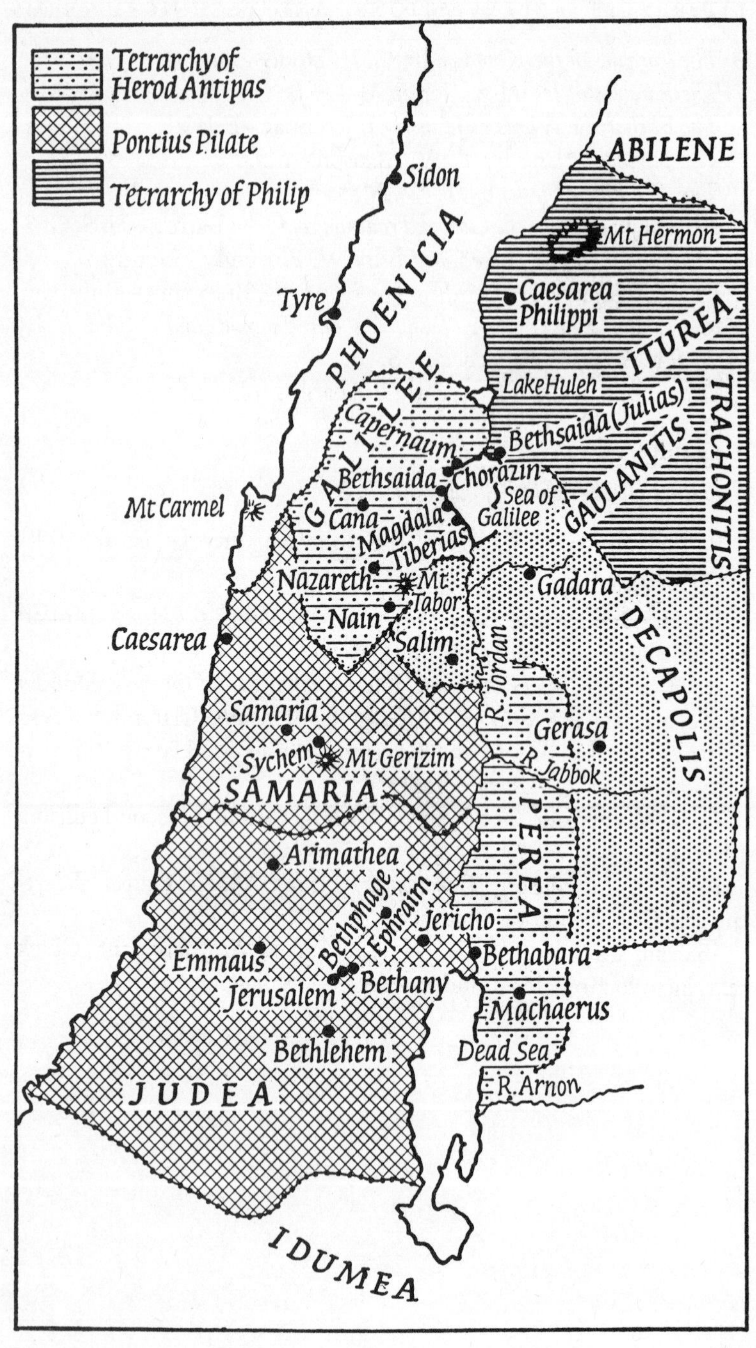

Tetrarchy of Herod Antipas
Pontius Pilate
Tetrarchy of Philip
ABILENE
Sidon
Mt Hermon
PHOENICIA
Tyre
Caesarea Philippi
ITUREA
Lake Huleh
TRACHONITIS
GALILEE
Capernaum
Bethsaida (Julias)
GAULANITIS
Chorazin
Bethsaida
Sea of Galilee
Mt Carmel
Cana
Magdala
Tiberias
Nazareth
Mt. Tabor
Gadara
Nain
DECAPOLIS
Caesarea
Salim
R. Jordan
Samaria
Gerasa
Sychem
Mt Gerizim
R. Jabbok
SAMARIA
PEREA
Arimathea
Bethphage
Ephraim
Jericho
Emmaus
Bethabara
Bethany
Jerusalem
Machaerus
Bethlehem
Dead Sea
R. Arnon
JUDEA
IDUMEA

Introduction

The function of a commentary

Why should a Gospel be supposed to need a commentary? Certainly no one doubts that it is possible to read the Gospels with both profit and pleasure without the help of any commentator. Yet many readers of the Gospels are rather like modern visitors to an ancient building. Such visitors can get a great deal out of going round by themselves without any guide or guide book, but if they have a guide who knows his job they are sure to get much more profit and pleasure from their visit. Things will be pointed out to them which they would never have noticed for themselves and they will be shown the significance of things which otherwise would not have seemed to have any significance. A guide can help in this way largely because he has a background knowledge not shared by those he is taking round. He knows the history of the times when the building was first put up and subsequently enlarged and rebuilt; he knows about the social customs, religious beliefs, and methods of building which prevailed at those periods and so, by passing on some of this knowledge to the visitors, he can help them to set the building in its true perspective, to understand why it was built, and to appreciate the significance of the various features and the reasons for the different alterations and additions.

In some ways a commentator on the Gospels is like such a guide. He must know something of the background against which the Gospels were written and against which the events described in them took place, and in the light of that knowledge it is his function to point out to non-specialist readers things they might not notice for themselves and to help them to see the significance – especially the religious significance – of passages where otherwise they might not detect any significance at all or might even impose on the text a meaning it was never meant to bear.

But we all know the sort of guide who is little better than a licensed gossip; he produces masses of chatty historical information, which, even if it is accurate, contributes very little to our real appreciation of the building we are visiting. There is a suspicion in some quarters that biblical commentators are rather like that: people who constantly comb the text for references to obscure social customs or events in secular history, and then write voluminous notes about the origins of the customs and the accuracy of the dates, concluding more often than not, that the biblical writers have got it all wrong. And so, since most readers of the Bible come to it for its *religious* message, they are apt to regard commentators as at best an unnecessary luxury and at worst a positive hindrance.

About that two things may be said. On the one hand it is certainly true that a commentator should always be concerned with the central and primary theme of his text; and since the Gospels are essentially religious works, the aim of the Gospel commentator must always be to elucidate their *religious* meaning. On the other hand it is a complete, though no doubt widespread, misconception to suppose that the religious, or devotional, study of the Gospels can be kept separate from the study of critical, historical, and linguistic questions to which they give rise. The justification of that statement must be left to emerge as the commentary proceeds, but one signal example of the principle arises at once, for it must be shown at the outset that no full understanding of the Gospels is possible without some knowledge of the long and rather complicated process by which they came into being.

At first sight the modern reader will probably find such a statement hard to appreciate, for he is used to books which can be fully understood and enjoyed without any knowledge of the way they came to be written. You can enjoy the Sherlock Holmes stories, for example, without knowing anything about how Conan Doyle came to write them; and you can perfectly well learn the principles of geometry from any reputable text-book on the subject without having the faintest idea how the book in question came into being.

But with the Gospels it is different; without some knowledge of the various stages in their long growth, it is impossible to appreciate them fully, from either the religious or the historical point of view. Indeed, the point might be put more strongly: if the Gospels are read by a modern reader without any knowledge of their origins and consequent character, positive misunderstanding is likely to be the result. For the nearest analogy to a Gospel in the experience of the modern reader is the biography, and so it is natural for him to approach and interpret the Gospels as if they were so many biographies, or memoirs, of Jesus.* But, as the following pages will show (see especially pp. 34–8.), Gospels are in fact very far from being biographies, and anyone who treats them as if they were will almost certainly misuse them, discovering in them all sorts of information which in fact is not there, and at the same time missing a great deal of the religious insight and historical information they can, and ought to, afford.

Accordingly, the aim of this commentary is first – in the Introduction – to give some account of how the Gospel according to St Mark came into being, and to discuss briefly its character and purposes in the light of its origins; and then in the body of the work to show some of the implications of all this for the understanding of the successive sections of the Gospel. It will be apparent, therefore, that the Introduction is an integral part of the book, apart from which the commentary proper can hardly be understood.

THE ORIGINS AND CHARACTER OF THE GOSPEL

The story begins in the period immediately after the lifetime of Jesus when as yet there were no written accounts of any sort, but the tradition about him was preserved entirely by word of mouth. So far as the material in our Gospels is concerned, it was preserved during this period exclusively by Christians.† This is a fact of the utmost significance for the understanding of the Gospel tradition, for it means that during this period the tradition about

* There is nothing new in this. The second-century writer Justin Martyr refers to the Gospels as 'the memoirs of the apostles' (1 *Apology* 66, *Dialogue* 106).

† The information we possess about Jesus from non-Christian sources is exceedingly slight, though it is sufficient to establish the fact of his existence, and his character as the founder of a new religious group among the Jews of the first century. Cf. especially Suetonius, *Claudius*, 25; Tacitus, *Annals*, XV, 44; and Josephus, *Antiquities*, XVIII, 63f. – conveniently collected and discussed in C. K. Barrett, *The New Testament Background*. See also the articles by T. W. Manson, in *The Bulletin of the John Rylands Library* for 1942–7.

Jesus was preserved by people to whom he was not a dead figure of the past, but a living contemporary with whom they were in constant and intimate relationship.

The Risen Christ in the thought of the early Church

For them the Jesus of whose earthly life the tradition spoke was the same person whom they now knew as Lord and Son of God, and whom they believed to be sitting at God's right hand in glory, governing the universe on his behalf, and soon to come to earth again to judge and wind up the universe, and usher in a wholly new world-order.

This last belief is particularly important; the earliest Christians confidently expected Christ's return and the complete establishment of God's kingdom within one or two generations at most, so from their point of view it was natural to regard the three stages of Christ's work, his earthly life in the past, his present lordship in heaven, and his future coming, as three acts of a single – and quite compact – drama, three stages in one continuous operation by which the salvation of man was to be secured and the kingdom of God established. And since the first Christians were all Jews, they naturally set this three-act drama against the background of the Old Testament and saw it as simply the final phase of God's age-long working towards man's salvation, of which the Old Testament revealed the earlier stages.

Since the early Christians thus believed themselves to be living in a comparatively short interim period before the end of the world, their energies were naturally concentrated on practical tasks, on bringing others to a realization of the situation and on the attempt to maintain and deepen their own relationship with the exalted Lord so that when he came to establish his kingdom finally, they would be worthy to be members of it. Consequently, they will have had little leisure, even had they had the aptitude, for antiquarian research into Christ's earthly life;* nor would they have thought it worth while, seeing that they did not look forward to any posterity who might be expected to profit from the result of it.

* It is worth remembering throughout this discussion that at this early period 'not many wise [by human standards], not many mighty, not many noble' had been called. St Mark himself, as we shall see, was probably a man of comparatively poor education.

Such interest as they had in the earthly life of Jesus was of a quite different kind; as we have seen, they understood his earthly life as one stage in the total comprehensive drama of salvation, and consequently their curiosity about it was directed not to the precise biographical details, but to the question of what contribution it made to the total action of the play; in what way exactly had Jesus' earthly life contributed to the achievement of man's salvation and the establishment of God's kingdom? In St Paul's Epistles – all written during this period – we can watch one early Christian wrestling with this problem and concluding, on the whole, that it was the *death* of Christ – interpreted as a sacrifice for sin – which was the decisive contribution of the earthly phase of Christ's activity to the total action of the drama. Similarly in the finished Gospels, the events surrounding Christ's *death* are treated more fully than any others and treated, as we shall see, in a way which suggests that they had been studied and pondered in the Church longer and more deeply than earlier events in the earthly life. Indeed, so far as the evidence of the Epistles goes, St Paul shows practically no interest in any aspect of Jesus' earthly career *except* the death.* But then in the Epistles St Paul was writing to convinced Christians. When trying to convert those who knew nothing of Jesus or Christianity he must surely have spoken rather differently; he must have given at least sufficient information about the earthly life to provide the answers to certain obvious questions. Who was this Jesus to whom allegiance was being demanded, and did he merit such allegiance? How had he come to his present exalted position? Had his earthly life been such as to make plausible the very high claims that were now being made on his behalf? And when converts were won, they would have further needs. They would require a living concrete picture of the one to whom they were now committed. If they were to enter into relationship with him they must be able to envisage him, his demands, his attitude towards them, the attitude he expected from them, the way he wanted them to live, and so forth.

The early Christians thus had very definite motives for preserving memories of Jesus' earthly life, but only for preserving memories *of certain special kinds* – memories which would persuade non-believers of his supernatural status and help converts to realize him fully as a

* Some scholars would perhaps regard this as a rather sweeping way of putting it, but broadly speaking the point would be generally conceded.

living person and discover the implications of their discipleship to him. In the earliest period, when converts were sought exclusively among the Jews, this will have had one particular corollary. No Jew could be expected to accept the claims made for Jesus unless it could be shown that his work was all of a piece with the saving work of God outlined in the Old Testament, and that it fulfilled the expectations there set out. In this connexion the Church would need memories of Jesus which showed how his life had conformed to Old Testament predictions, especially at the moments for which decisive religious significance was claimed.

It will now be clear that the circumstances in which the tradition about Jesus was preserved *exercised a strong selective influence upon the character of what was preserved* – in a negative, as well as a positive direction. Viewing the life of Jesus as they did, there were certain things about him – for example, his sinlessness, or the complete truth of all he said – that the early Christians would never have dreamed of questioning, let alone attempting to prove; they would therefore have had no interest in preserving material relevant to such issues. More important, since they thought of him as essentially a supernatural figure, even in the days of his flesh, his humanity would not in itself interest them very much. They recognized it of course as the means through which his work had been accomplished, but it never occurred to them to think of him as receiving anything essential from his human environment; and so they made no attempt to trace the effects of his environment upon him or the working of his mind – what led him to the conclusions he arrived at or what influenced him in forming his plans. Indeed, if they could have understood the term at all, they would no doubt have denied that the Son of God, for all his humanity, had any 'psychology' in this sort of sense at all.* Hence all our questionings about Jesus' self-consciousness and his understanding of himself and his mission were entirely foreign to their concern.

Two further corollaries of the early Christians' attitude need to be noticed.

* One is reminded of the hyper-orthodox student, described by H. J. Cadbury, who, 'when asked of a certain narrative in the gospels what Jesus had in mind, replied simply that Jesus had no mind' (*The Peril of Modernizing Jesus*, p. 50).

They took it for granted that the heavenly Christ was continually revealing further truth about himself to his followers in various ways (cf. e.g. 1 Cor. 2^{16}, 7^{40}, John $16^{12\text{ff.}}$); and since the Christ who was thus revealed was the same person as the Jesus of the earthly life, it was only natural that the memories of his earthly life should be interpreted, and on occasions even modified and added to, in the light of these subsequent revelations. For example, to take a rather extreme case which will be discussed further on pp. 24–5, it is at least possible that it was only when the heavenly Christ came to be recognized as Son of God that the idea arose that he had claimed to be such, and been recognized as such, in the days of his flesh, no explicit tradition to that effect being known.

The second corollary arises from the fact that they regarded Christ's activity as the final saving act of God to which the Old Testament had pointed forward. Since the Old Testament was regarded as completely accurate down to the last detail, it followed that everything it predicted concerning this final event must have found fulfilment at some point in Christ's ministry. Hence the Old Testament could become a source of information about the events of Christ's earthly life; and to the early Christians, with their deep conviction of its inerrancy, it may well have seemed a safer guide than the fallible memories of human witnesses, however well informed. There are, as we shall see, passages in Mark where it is impossible to be certain whether a particular story rests on a tradition derived from witnesses or whether it represents a deduction from Old Testament prophecy about what 'must have' happened when the Messiah came. (For example, see the commentary on 15^{24}.)

Effects of the way the oral tradition was handed on

If the tradition about Jesus was thus influenced by the beliefs and motives of those who preserved it, its character was also determined by the particular circumstances in which it was handed down. No doubt, at first, disciples of Jesus told stories about him to audiences of all kinds, both private and public, just as need and opportunity suggested; but it appears that the tradition on which the Gospels are based was handed on during the greater part of the oral period *in the context of public and formal occasions*;*

* The grounds for this important claim cannot be set out here: those interested should consult such works as *H. & I.* especially Chapter II.

that is to say, the people by whom it was passed on were preachers and teachers, speaking at meetings for public worship or addressing groups of catechumens and the like. This had at least two very important effects on the tradition.

(i) The natural thing would be for the preacher or catechist to repeat *one* story, or parable, or group of sayings, at each meeting and then go on to expound its significance for his hearers. Naturally he would choose his story or parable on each occasion in accordance with the particular needs of his audience; if he thought they needed a lesson in good-neighbourliness, he would tell the parable of the Good Samaritan; if he knew they were in doubt whether to pay their taxes to the Roman authorities, he might describe how Our Lord had been questioned on that subject (see Mark 12^{13-17}), and so on. Consequently, the order in which the incidents were recounted would vary from church to church, in accordance with local needs; and there would be no compelling motive for preserving, or even remembering, the order in which they originally occurred during Our Lord's lifetime.* The tradition about Jesus would thus assume the form of a variety of separate stories with no fixed or generally agreed order. No doubt particular individuals or groups sometimes made collections of some of these stories, and even had them committed to writing, but their motives in doing so were always practical and led them to select stories of a particular kind and arrange them in an order which served some practical purpose. One group, for example, might collect for controversial purposes stories of Our Lord's arguments with his opponents (see Mark 2^{1}–3^{6}), another group might be led by the needs of uneducated catechumens to collect all Our Lord's sayings about 'stumbling' or 'salt' or 'watchfulness' in an order that could be easily memorized (see Mark $9^{38\text{ff.}}$ and 13^{28-37}, for example); but in such cases there would be no attempt to recover, or preserve, the original *historical* order of the incidents or sayings in question.

A partial exception to the last statement must be made in favour of the Passion narrative (for this term, see further p. 365), to which several

* See further p. 28 n. Even a modern preacher, when he is expounding the 'gospel' for the day, does not begin by relating it chronologically or geographically with the incident which formed the 'gospel' for the previous Sunday.

special considerations applied. Not only were the events of Christ's death the centre of the whole ministry, as we have seen, but in the interests of its missionary work the early Church was bound to have its own more or less coherent account of the last few days of Jesus' life. It claimed divine honours for a young man who had shortly before suffered capital punishment at the hands of the Romans, after due processes of Roman Law, the accusers being the accredited leaders of the Jewish faith. If the Church was to have any hope of sustaining this astonishing claim in the eyes of people with a Jewish background, it must be able to show, not only that the charges on which Jesus had been condemned were false accusations, inspired by the pride and jealousy of the Jewish leaders, but also that what had happened corresponded exactly with Old Testament prophecy and was all part of God's predetermined plan for his Son. In that connexion the need for a circumstantial account of Christ's last days from the Christian standpoint will fairly soon have made itself felt; and so, as we have seen, the incidents of the Passion appear to have been the first to be collected together in anything like a historical narrative. Even so the account was some time in coming into existence, and it can only be called 'historical' with considerable qualifications; the aim was not an objective historical report as those words would be understood today, but a selective account, such as would support and justify the Christian understanding of Christ's death. (See further pp. 365ff.)

Exceptional nature of the Passion narrative

Before we consider the significance of all this for the Gospels, we must look briefly at the other result of the tradition's being handed down in the context of public worship and instruction. This touches the form and content of the individual units of the tradition.

(ii) We have seen that the various incidents and sayings were handed on in a *public* setting. This in itself would mean that all purely personal detail would be out of place; but we must also remember that the stories were normally recounted in order to form the basis of a lesson or sermon in which their particular application would be drawn out. Naturally, therefore, they would be told in the way best calculated to lead on to the subsequent exposition or application; if the point to be brought out in connexion with some incident was the comment Our Lord made upon it, then, in the telling of the story, the comment itself would be reported in full and given prominence, while the rest of the incident would be related as briefly as possible, just the minimum being retained that was necessary to provide the Lord's words with an intelligible setting.* If, on the other hand, the aim was to stress the remarkable nature of some action of Jesus, as evidence of his supernatural power, then any words that might have been spoken in connexion with it would be briefly reported and little emphasized, and the emphasis would be concentrated entirely on those features of the incident which underlined its supernatural character – for example, in the case of a healing, the chronic and deep-seated nature of the illness, the ease with which Jesus cured it, the impression of amazement made on the bystanders and the completeness of the cure as evidenced by the healed man's ability to run or shout or carry his own bed.† (See e.g. Mark 5^{25-26}, 9^{20-22}, 2^{12}.)

What we have just been describing can have been no more than a tendency, and it will have taken some time to make itself felt. No doubt, in the earliest days, stories about Jesus were told by his disciples with all the wealth of detail, often strictly irrelevant detail, we associate with the eyewitness; but as time went on, and the stories were more and more told by local Church leaders who had not personally known Our Lord and were not even Jews with a first-hand knowledge of Palestine, sheer ignorance of the details must have combined with the other factors just mentioned to produce increasingly 'streamlined' versions of the various incidents in which little or nothing was retained except what was of practical religious significance. And naturally, when once a story had attained its most 'economical' form in this way, there will have been a tendency for it to become more or less stereotyped and to circulate in that form with relatively little further change.

At this point we must take account of another consideration which modern readers are apt to find rather surprising. People's attitude towards history in the ancient world was often rather different from our own. If, for example, an ancient writer was convinced that

* A story of this kind about Jesus is usually referred to in English as a 'pronouncement story'.

† Such stories are usually referred to as 'miracle stories'.

Jesus was, as a matter of fact, Christ and Son of God, he might well tell the story of his earthly life in terms of his having claimed, and been accorded, those titles, even though there was no explicit tradition to that effect. Indeed he might well feel that it would be wrong to do otherwise; for if Jesus was in fact Son of God, then any account of his earthly life which did not make that clear would be misleading and would not convey the true meaning of the events it professed to describe.

The early Christians' attitude to history

Probably such feelings seldom attained the level of full consciousness, but their influence on the development of the tradition could be all the greater for being unconscious; and another, parallel influence may have worked equally unconsciously. If Jesus was Son of God, it was felt, his words must have had universal significance; they must have something to say to his followers in every time and place. In practice, words which Jesus had spoken in early first-century Palestine, often in very special circumstances, did not always seem to apply without modification to the conditions of, let us say, a Hellenistic congregation some decades later, and so it was only natural for people to feel that what he must 'really' have meant, or said, was something which had a direct lesson for them. Here then is another factor which will have worked, largely below the conscious level, in the direction of modifying the various units of tradition in accordance with the circumstances and preoccupations of the various little communities scattered over the Mediterranean world.* As the body of the com-

* If all this still seems strange to a modern reader, it should be kept in mind, first that: '"The formulation of the tradition regarding Jesus was a work of enthusiasm and devotion, carried on by men on whom he had made an overmastering impression, and in whom his spirit was alive and active. . . . Their heart was in their work of making their Master live and act again in the world, as they now knew that he had lived and acted when in the flesh." It was in this enthusiasm that the preacher or teacher could not be restrained from adding his own comment to the narrative.' (H. A. Guy, *The Origin of the Gospel of Mark*, pp. 109–10, quoting A. Menzies, *The Earliest Gospel*, p. 24). Cf., to the same effect, M. Dibelius, *A Fresh Approach to the New Testament*, pp. 34–5, who stresses the remoteness of such enthusiastic, uncultured preaching from 'the critical conscience of a historian guarding with meticulous exactness the very words that had been spoken'. In the case of Jewish-Christian preachers, all this would be reinforced by their familiarity with a type of scriptural exegesis traditional among the Jews, known as *Haggadah* or 'narration'. This

mentary will show, this factor influenced particularly the accounts of Our Lord's parables; but meanwhile we must pass to the question how all these factors, and the character of the tradition they produced, affected our written Gospels. What does it mean for the Gospels that this sort of tradition was the material from which they had to be composed?

Before that question is discussed, however, there is a prior question. Readers of the Gospels usually assume that the authors were themselves present at the events they describe, or at any rate that they

Papias

knew people who were, so that their accounts give us direct eyewitness testimony, unaffected by the processes described above. How far is this true? Certainly it was believed to be true in the second century, particularly so far as St Mark was concerned. Papias, a second-century bishop of Hierapolis, is reported as having said, on the authority of an 'elder': 'This also the presbyter used to say: Mark indeed, who became the interpreter of Peter, wrote accurately, as far as he remembered them, the things said or done by the Lord, but not however in order. For he had neither heard the Lord nor been His personal follower, but at a later stage, as I said, he had followed Peter, who used to adapt his teachings to the needs [of the moment], but not as though he were drawing up a connected account of the oracles of the Lord: so that Mark committed no error in writing certain matters just as he remembered them. For he had one object only in view, viz. to leave out nothing of the things which he had heard, and to include no false statement among them' (R., pp. xxv–xxvi). In view of this and of the fact that much of the information in the Gospel is of a kind that seems unlikely to have come from anyone but Peter,* the Gospel is often

* The grounds for this statement are of two kinds. (1) Much of the information in the Gospel is about things which were not witnessed by anyone except Peter (and sometimes one or two others) – cf. e.g. 14^{66-72}, $14^{32ff.}$, 1^{29-39},

---

is described by Professor G. D. Kilpatrick as follows: 'the exegesis of Holy Writ for edification in a free manner. . . . The text of Scripture provided a starting point, it was often embellished with additional details which might be expanded into full-length narratives on their own. As the exposition advanced it would be buttressed by other citations from Scripture and other enrichments until the text of the sermon appeared only a kind of peg on which to hang a discourse that soon went its own luxuriant way' (*The Origins of the Gospel according to St Matthew*, p. 61).

described as 'the Petrine source' and much of it is taken to come almost direct from the apostle's lips. It may well be that some of the material in the Gospel does derive ultimately from Peter, but in the last forty years or so Papias's statement has come in for a good deal of criticism,* and most contemporary scholars agree that in places St Mark's material *bears all the signs of having been community tradition* and cannot therefore be derived *directly* from St Peter or any other eyewitness. But once that admission has been made about some of St Mark's material, it seems only logical to go on and make it about *all* his material, for, as will be shown in the body of the commentary, all of it, without exception, seems to bear the characteristic marks of community tradition. Since this fact is equally against the supposition that the Evangelist is reporting what he himself had seen, the safest conclusion seems to be that, whatever its ultimate origins may have been, St Mark's material *as it reached him* had been transmitted in the sort of way outlined in the previous section.† If so, what are the implications for his Gospel?

Unit structure of the Gospel

In the first place it means that what the Evangelist had to work on, apart from an outline Passion narrative and perhaps one or two short collections of material relating to special subjects,‡ was a series of essentially disconnected stories. This at once explains an otherwise puzzling feature of the Gospel, the way it consists of a number of unrelated paragraphs set down one after another with very little organic connexion, almost like a series of snapshots placed side by side in a photograph album. These paragraphs are sometimes externally related to one another by a short phrase at the beginning or end, but

* See for example A. M. Farrer, *A Study in St Mark*, pp. 10ff.

† It is only fair to add that many scholars, at any rate in England, would allow a greater element of Petrine reminiscence in the Gospel than this suggests.

‡ See on 2^{1}–3^{6} and $9^{33\text{ff.}}$.

9^{2-13}. (2) Not only is there a disproportionately large amount of material about Peter himself, but much of it is of so unflattering a kind that it is felt unlikely to have been reported about the prince of the apostles by anyone except himself – cf. e.g. 8^{32-33}. As far as the amount of Petrine material is concerned, however, other Evangelists in fact give him even greater prominence, and for an alternative explanation of its unflattering character, see pp. 31–2.

essentially each one is an independent unit, complete in itself, undatable except by its contents, and usually equally devoid of any allusion to place.* By the same token, the minor characters in these stories, unless they had some special significance for the early Church, are very summarily described and hardly ever named (see on 2^{18}, 5^{22} and 10^{46}). All this is well exemplified, for instance, in Chapter 3, where the successive paragraphs are so essentially separate that their order could easily be interchanged without doing any violence to the chapter as a whole.

On what principle, then, are the units arranged, here and in the rest of the Gospel? In the light of what has been said earlier (see p. 22) it seems clear that the ordering of the units will have been something for which the Evangelist himself was responsible; and although it is just possible that he could rely on an outline account of Christ's ministry preserved in the early Church,† it seems clear that by the

* Some stories, it is true, contain specific notes of time or place – e.g. a reference to the sabbath or the night, the mountain, the sea, or the temple; but it will almost always be found that in such cases the reference serves a *practical* purpose; it is necessary for the full understanding of the contents of the paragraph.

All the characteristics of the Gospels mentioned in the text have been recognized for some time, but the credit for realizing their true significance, and so uncovering the prehistory of the tradition, belongs mainly to a group of scholars, known as *form-critics*, of whom the most notable are four Germans, H. Gunkel, R. Bultmann, K. L. Schmidt, and M. Dibelius. The name *form-critic* is derived from the fact that these scholars attempted to classify the various units, or pericopae, as they called them (the Greek *pericope* = 'section' or 'paragraph') according to their form, and to show the practical religious purpose for which each form of pericope was designed. Although the work of these four scholars was complete in essence soon after the First World War, only one major work of theirs on the subject has so far been translated into English, viz. M. Dibelius, *From Tradition to Gospel*. Bultmann's big work is shortly to appear in an English version; as will then be seen, its rather radical conclusions have led to its being somewhat undervalued in England. An English book on the subject is V. Taylor, *The Formation of the Gospel Tradition*.

† Dr C. H. Dodd has argued for the existence of such an outline, and for St Mark's use of it, in Chapter 1 of his *New Testament Studies*, which should be consulted. On the other hand: (*a*) To the present writer Dr Dodd's argument does not seem entirely convincing; see his discussion in *Studies in the Gospels* (ed. D. E. Nineham), pp. 223ff; and (*b*) even if Dr Dodd is judged to have made out his case, the outline he has in mind is so very brief and general that it hardly affects the view taken in the text above.

time he wrote it will no longer have been possible to recover the *historical* order of events, except in the most general terms. What is more, the earlier history of the material, as we have traced it, suggests a doubt – surprising perhaps to a modern reader – whether St Mark was *interested* in the historical order. The handling of the tradition before his time seems always to have been governed by practical, religious considerations, and it is being increasingly realized nowadays that the same is true of the Evangelists' handling of it. The older view that the Gospels were attempted biographies of Jesus, as adequate as the education of the Evangelists and the circumstances of the time would allow, has given place to the recognition that each of them was produced to meet some specific practical and religious needs in the church of its origin, and that it is those needs which have very largely controlled each Evangelist's choice, arrangement, and presentation of material and distribution of emphasis.

So far as St Mark is concerned, it would not be too much to say that the basic quest of Marcan scholarship in recent years has been to discover what precise *religious* needs St Mark wrote to satisfy and so why he chose and arranged his material in the particular way he did. This is easier said than done. The only evidence we have to go on is the internal evidence of the Gospel itself, and although it has been minutely studied in the last few years by various scholars, each trying to show that it was arranged in this, that, or the other way in order to produce a particular effect on the community,* it cannot be said that any of the suggested solutions has met with really widespread acceptance. The very fact that such widely differing principles of arrangement have been attributed to St Mark perhaps suggests that in searching the Gospel for a single and entirely coherent master-plan, corresponding to a set of clearly formulated practical purposes, scholars are looking for something that is not there and attributing to the Evangelist a higher degree of self-conscious purpose than he in fact possessed. Dr H. J. Cadbury is perhaps guilty of overstatement when he writes that St Mark 'does not betray any subjectiveness of his own',† but a useful corrective to some current

St Mark's purpose in writing

* Two such studies are A. M. Farrer, *A Study in St Mark*, and P. Carrington, *The Primitive Christian Calendar*.

† *The Making of Luke-Acts*, p. 79.

exaggerations is contained both in that statement and in his further statement that 'there is scarcely any thorough-going theological theory that permeates the whole narrative, and many things remain that a single unified theory would hardly have selected or left unexpurgated. The material was already miscellaneous, and St Mark tried as little to bring it into theological as into biographical articulation.'*

But if we are not to think of St Mark as having conceived some single overriding purpose, whether practical or theological, and then organized the whole of his material in accordance with it, that does not prevent us from recognizing that certain beliefs and attitudes seemed to him particularly vital in the situation in which he wrote, and that at various points in the Gospel he selected and arranged his material so as to give them prominence, perhaps without always being fully aware of what he was doing. Indeed, it was presumably his feeling that these points needed making about Our Lord's life and work that led him to break with the previous custom of the Church and commit a number of the oral units to writing.†

Some of the more obvious and undisputed of these concerns of the Evangelist may usefully be listed here:

(1) St Mark was not primarily concerned to prove that Jesus was

* ibid., p. 80.

† The question of what led St Mark and others to break with the custom of transmitting the tradition orally and to commit some of it to writing is one which has not been satisfactorily answered, and perhaps on the basis of our present information never can be. A motive sometimes suggested is the growing recognition in the early Church that there were to be many generations in the future for whom information needed to be preserved in permanent form; but St Mark still seems to expect the end of the world within a generation or so (see on 9[1]). That fact, and the general character of his Gospel, also tell against the suggestion that he was seeking to preserve for posterity the testimony of the eyewitness generation, which was beginning to die off in his period. Most probably his motives were connected with particular circumstances and needs of his local church, and the production of his Gospel was very much a local affair, which at the time attracted very little attention in other Christian communities. It is a mistake to import the language of modern printing and publishing, and talk of the 'publication' of the Gospel. This of course is not to minimize the *ultimate* effects of St Mark's action. Not only is he the first of the Evangelists but to the best of our knowledge he is the founder of the Gospel as a type of writing – a type which has had incalculable influence.

Messiah;* in the circles for which he wrote that was by this time taken for granted. But the fundamental conception of the Messiah in all its many forms was of a victorious figure; how then, outsiders might ask, could Jesus' Messiahship be reconciled with the fact that his career had ended in complete disgrace and a criminal's death? A good deal of the material St Mark has chosen to include is relevant to this issue, and in dealing with it he uses two methods. The one is historical; he strives to show, by reporting various phases of it (cf. especially Chapters 2 and 12), the true character of the quarrel between Jesus and the Jewish authorities who were responsible for his death, and so to present Jesus as innocent of any charge except – in the later stage – the charge that he claimed to be the Messiah. The other method is theological; he seeks to show that it is often God's way to produce great and glorious results from inconspicuous and unpromising beginnings (this is the point of the parabolic material in Chapter 4, and cf. introductory note to 8^{27}–9^{1}). In the particular case of the Messiah he endeavours to prove, on the basis of Old Testament prophecy, that his suffering was all part of God's appointed plan and only the prelude to his present glory and his speedy return in power. This concern of the Evangelist seems to lie behind the inclusion, not only of many of the parables, but of such teaching as that in Chapter 13 and also of the many verses designed to show that Jesus' suffering was in accordance with Old Testament prediction.

(2) St Mark's second concern is more problematic. The question had apparently been raised: if Jesus was indeed the Messiah, why did he not claim the title earlier and more outspokenly, and why was his Messiahship not more fully and enthusiastically recognized during his earthly life, at any rate by his disciples? According to St Mark the answer was twofold; partly it was that Jesus had deliberately sought to keep the fact of his Messiahship secret, at any rate until just before his death, and so had promptly silenced any demons or human beings who recognized him (cf. e.g. 1^{34} and 5^{43}); and partly that the crowds – and even the disciples – had displayed an almost incredible

* Of course some of the stories he has incorporated may have had that purpose in their pre-Marcan form; but, as we have already seen, a story might be used at different stages in the history of the tradition to bring out different points.

For the meaning of Messiah and similar Jewish terms, see pp. 46–8.

obtuseness with regard to what they heard and saw (cf. e.g. 8^{17-18}), an obtuseness which St Mark, following a common Old Testament idea, regarded as divinely ordained (cf. Isa. 6^{9-10} and notes on 4^{10-12}). It is no doubt this concern which accounts for the Evangelist's theory that the parables were intended to conceal the truth (see on $4^{10ff.}$) and also for his including so much very unflattering information about the twelve; which makes all the more interesting the question how far his account in this respect is true to the historical facts.

Some scholars have regarded the whole idea of the 'messianic secret' as an invention of the Evangelist for apologetic purposes, and certainly some of the narratives which incorporate it raise acute problems (see e.g. on 5^{21-43} and 8^{22-26}). Others, however, have argued for a historical basis to St Mark's theory; St Mark himself suggests no motive for Our Lord's secrecy, but it is often suggested that a possible motive might have been fear lest his messianic claims should be misunderstood in a nationalistic or crudely political sense. Some such theory is frequently put forward, especially by English scholars, but, as the commentary will show, it will by no means cover all the relevant passages, and it may be doubted if it is entirely plausible in itself; if Our Lord feared that the character of his Messiahship might be misunderstood, could he not have forestalled such misunderstandings by patient and unambiguous teaching on the subject? We cannot therefore rule out the possibility that the whole theory of secret Messiahship is the product of the Evangelist, though that does not necessarily commit us to the view of Wilhelm Wrede, who thought that the whole idea of any messianic claim on the part of Jesus was an invention of the early Christians who wanted to ascribe to him messianic claims, but had to represent them as secret because it was remembered that he had made no such claims publicly (see also p. 51).

(3) St Mark's third concern is of a rather different kind. As we have seen, the various primitive communities each had their own problems and concerns; it would seem that St Mark wrote in and for a community* which was already beginning to suffer unpopularity, persecution, and perhaps even in some cases death, for the sake of Christianity. Naturally this would give rise to some heart-searching among the

* On its locality, see pp. 42–3.

members, and one of St Mark's aims was clearly to meet the resultant situation. This he did by emphasizing three things:

(*a*) That Jesus himself had suffered exactly as his followers were now being called upon to do.

(*b*) That Jesus had clearly warned his disciples that following him would involve sharing in his sufferings.

(*c*) That he had promised great and sure rewards to those who endured such sufferings without loss of faith. (Cf. e.g. 8^{34-38} and 10^{28-30}.)

St Mark sought to produce in his readers the conviction that nothing was happening to them which lay outside the providence of God or the predictions of their Master. If they 'had' to 'suffer' so had he 'had to suffer'. St Mark's has been described as 'the martyr Gospel' – that is, the Gospel designed for the strengthening and encouraging of Christians facing martyrdom.

It must be admitted that the Evangelist has little to say which *explains* the suffering, either in the case of Christ or of the disciples. So far as Christ is concerned, he believes that he *had* to suffer – a necessity which lay deep in the counsels of God (see 8^{31} and notes); he allots a high proportion of his space to the description of Christ's suffering and death and reproduces one or two sayings which suggest in a general way that forgiveness is promoted, if not conditioned, by it (10^{45} and 14^{24}). But there is no emphasis on the central Pauline doctrine of 'atonement' or 'reconciliation' (a fact which tells against the deep Pauline influence that some have detected in the Gospel); probably, so far as St Mark had any formulated opinion on the matter, it was along the lines of the widespread Jewish belief in the vicarious efficacy of innocent suffering (see notes on 8^{27}–9^{1}), but as we shall see, his understanding of Christ's work lay at least as much along other lines (see the next section).

(4) Another belief of the Evangelist was a potent, though probably less conscious, factor in the formulation of his Gospel, and this was a belief which reveals him as fully a man of his own day. The Jews and others in the ancient world held that the act of creation had involved God in a tremendous struggle against the supernatural forces of evil and chaos. In this struggle God had been victorious, but in the course of time the evil powers had to some extent reasserted their sway over God's creation; and so, before God could bring

creation to the perfect consummation he planned for it, it was expected that he, or some representative of his, would have to engage in a further, and this time finally decisive, struggle against the evil powers. It was largely in terms of this expectation that St Mark understood Our Lord's life and work, regarding him as God's agent sent to begin the great final battle against the powers of evil and endowed with power to carry through the first stages of it to a victorious conclusion. (See also pp. 44–5.) This comes out most clearly in $3^{23\text{ff.}}$ (see commentary on that passage), but it also lies behind St Mark's account of the Lord's 'temptation' (see on 1^{12-13}); and, as Dr J. M. Robinson has recently shown,* it has shaped St Mark's account not only of Our Lord's exorcisms and acts of power over 'nature', but of his successful disputes with his *human* opponents, who are themselves regarded by the Evangelist as agents of the evil powers.

Other concerns of the Evangelist could be enumerated,† but perhaps by now it is becoming clear what sort of work St Mark's Gospel is, and why it was claimed earlier that a knowledge of its origins helps greatly towards the understanding of it. Being familiar with a large number of separate stories about Our Lord, St Mark selected those which were specially relevant to the circumstances of his particular community, and he arranged and presented them so as to bring out the truths about Our Lord's life and work which he felt it most vital for his fellow-members in the community to grasp. The description of the Gospel as 'a kind of theological pamphlet' (J. H. Ropes, *The Synoptic Gospels*, p. 10) perhaps overemphasizes one side of the truth, but it at least makes clear that the Gospel is not a biography. It should now be clear why the people in the early Church were right who called a work like St Mark's not 'memoirs' but a gospel, i.e. a setting out of the facts of Christ's ministry so as to show that they constitute *good news*, which is what the word *gospel* means.‡ The character of the material and the interests of the Evangelist

* In his short but very important book, *The Problem of History in Mark.*

† In particular, many scholars would endorse the statement of J. Knox that: 'One of the principal purposes of this Gospel was to make clear the messianic significance of Jesus' whole career, from the baptism on, as over against an earlier belief that Jesus really became the Messiah only with, or after, the Resurrection' (*The Death of Christ*, pp. 102–3).

‡ It is not certain when the word Gospel was first used for works of this type, but it was probably not until after St Mark's lifetime.

both precluded him from even attempting to write a 'life' of Jesus.

A Gospel not a biography

To write a biography in the modern sense you need to know how the various incidents were related externally, in space and time, and also the internal connexions between them in the mind of the subject – how one incident led him on to the next and made him think and react in the way he did. Of all this the tradition and the Evangelist were alike ignorant. Moreover, a biographer must tell us about his subject's constitution – both physical and mental – and show how it made him the man he became – he must explain what made his subject 'tick'. But on all such matters St Mark and the other Evangelists are completely silent. It is a striking fact that they tell us nothing whatsoever about Our Lord's appearance, physique, and health, or, for that matter, about his personality – whether, for example, he was a happy, carefree, placid man or the reverse. They do not even think to tell us definately whether or not he was married! Likewise they give us no definite information about the length of his ministry or his age when he died, and there is no hint of the influence of his early environment upon him or of any development in his outlook or beliefs. From the point of view of the biographer the sheer *amount* of information the Evangelists give us is quite inadequate. It has been calculated that three or four weeks would suffice for everything related in Mark, except 1^{13}; as B. H. Streeter remarked: 'the total number of incidents recorded is so small that the gaps in the story must be the more considerable part of it' (*The Four Gospels*, p. 424). On some of these matters it is of course possible to 'read between the lines' to some extent; but there is a strict limit to what may be learned in this way, and anyone who has looked critically at the various modern 'lives' of Jesus, with their widely different pictures of him, will realize how largely their authors have had to draw on their own imaginations. The fact is that, for reasons which should now be clear, the Gospels are not themselves 'lives' of Jesus and scarcely provide the basis on which other people can write such 'lives'.

Two further points deserve notice in this connexion. A biographer assumes that his readers will, to start with, be ignorant about the subject-matter of his book. St Mark, on the other hand, is writing for fellow Christians who already know the story as well as he does; he has no need therefore to 'introduce' such figures as John the Baptist,

Herod, and Pilate or to explain where 'the wilderness' (1[4]) or 'the Jordan' and such places are to be found.* He wrote, as Johannes Weiss put it, 'from faith to faith'. The second point to notice is that the typical biographer has his own individual interpretation of his subject's life and writes to commend it to others. St Mark, although, as we have seen, he has his distinctive preoccupations, as compared with the other Evangelists, remains completely anonymous; he makes no attempt to 'push' his interpretation explicitly and it has to be discovered by reading carefully between his lines. This was no doubt because his understanding of Christ was for the most part simply that of the Church to which he belonged, and he was not conscious of doing anything more than commit the 'gospel' of that Church to writing.

But although St Mark was no biographer, by linking together the various separate stories and groups of stories with summary passages of his own composition,† he has produced what is, so far as its *form* is concerned, a connected historical narrative. It tells of the Lord's baptism by John the Baptist, of a subsequent varied ministry in Galilee, of some journeys outside Galilee ending with a journey to Jerusalem, and finally of a series of events – the entry upon the ass, the cleansing of the temple, the scene in the treasury, and the like – which must obviously have taken place in Jerusalem.

This arrangement by place naturally suggests a corresponding chronological sequence – a 'chronological outline of the ministry' – but this, though not impossible, is by no means inevitable, as one example may help to show. St Mark has chosen to group together at the end of his Gospel all his stories relating to Jerusalem, thus giving the impression that Our Lord paid only one final visit to the Holy City. In fact, however, scholars are agreed that Our Lord visited Jerusalem on a number of occasions and thus many of Mark's Jerusalem incidents may really date back to one of the earlier visits.‡ When we remember that many of the stories reached St Mark without any indication of the time or place at which they occurred, we shall learn

* It may be doubted whether St Mark or his readers could have given an account of all these people and places such as would satisfy a historian or geographer – but then neither could most members of a modern congregation; then, as now, these were simply familiar items of the sacred story.

† For these 'summary passages' see pp. 112 and 185.

‡ St John dates the cleansing of the Temple, for example, to a stay in Jerusalem right at the outset of the ministry as he describes it.

not to place on Mark's order a weight it was never intended to bear, and our question about each incident will be: 'what is the significance of St Mark's having placed it here *in his Gospel*?' not: 'what is the significance of its having happened at this point *in Our Lord's original ministry*?' J. H. Ropes makes the point admirably when he writes:* 'The form of the Gospel of Mark is, to be sure, that of narrative, but the important question is not of its form, but of its purpose; and that is theological.' That means that the location of incidents to particular points in the Gospel is likely to have rested on theological and devotional considerations quite as much as on biographical information; though of course certain incidents locate themselves *by their content* at the point where St Mark has placed them – for example, the baptism at the beginning of the ministry and the arrest, trial, and death in Jerusalem at the end.

All this has one particularly important application. The Gospel divides fairly sharply into two parts, each with its own clearly marked characteristics. Down to 8^{26}† the emphasis falls very largely on the miraculous deeds of Jesus, and such teaching as is recorded is mostly (*a*) directed to the crowd, (*b*) couched in parables, and (*c*) concerned with the coming of God's kingdom. Jesus strives to prevent recognition of his Messiahship and there is practically no teaching about it. After 8^{31} we notice a change in all these respects. Miraculous healings become very rare and the emphasis falls far more on Jesus' teaching; this is now for the most part directed only to the disciples, and it assumes knowledge of Jesus' Messiahship, being in fact very largely concerned with its character. God's will is not that the Messiah's work should be carried out by an effortless exercise of power, as the Jews had expected, but that it should involve grievous suffering, both for the Messiah himself and for his followers, though the upshot of this suffering is to be the glorious triumph of God's cause which the Messiah had traditionally been expected to usher in.

Between these two parts of the Gospel comes the story (8^{27-30}) of an incident when the twelve were alone with Jesus near Caesarea Philippi and Peter expressed, on behalf of them all, the conviction that his Master was the Messiah (8^{29}). This has generally been regarded by modern commentators as the *first* recognition of Jesus' Messiahship

* *The Synoptic Gospels*, p. 10.

† Or possibly 8^{21}, see notes on 8^{22-26}.

by human beings, and the change of tone after 8^{30} has been taken as reflecting a historical fact, namely that Our Lord changed his tactics when at last he had been recognized for what he really was. Anxious that eventually his Messiahship should be known without being misunderstood, he continued to hide it from outsiders who were likely to misunderstand it, and concentrated on teaching its true character to his disciples who had penetrated the secret, and, being constantly with him, might be made to understand. When 8^{27-30} is so interpreted, the twofold division of the Gospel can be (and often is) made the basis of an historical reconstruction of the broad lines of development of Our Lord's career.*

This understanding of the Gospel may well be the right one, but in view of all that has been said earlier, it will be clear that we cannot by any means be sure that it is. In itself St Mark's account of the incident at Caesarea Philippi contains nothing to suggest that this was a *first* recognition. In fact, it suggests that he was thinking, not so much of a contrast between previously unenlightened and now suddenly enlightened disciples as of the contrast between those who perceive and confess Our Lord's divine status (however and whenever they come by this discernment) and those who see him only as a human figure, however good and wise. St Mark appears to be contrasting the *opinion* of the world about Our Lord with the inner *knowledge* of his disciples; and through his careful phrasing of the story he seeks to show how such inner knowledge is arrived at. (See the commentary ad loc., and R. H. Lightfoot, *The Gospel Message of St Mark*, pp. 33–4.) But the biographical interpretation of this story is the linch-pin of the historical interpretation of the twofold division of the Gospel as a whole, and it may well be that the understanding of the two halves of the Gospel as reflecting successive stages in the historic ministry is just one more example of the modern reader's almost irresistible tendency to attribute biographical intention to the Evangelist and to try to turn his Gospel into a life of Jesus.

AUTHORSHIP, DATE, AND PROVENANCE

In view of all that has been said, it is now perhaps possible to suggest

* See e.g. Vincent Taylor, *The Life and Ministry of Jesus*; A. M. Hunter, *The Words and Works of Jesus*; H. E. W. Turner, *Jesus, Master and Lord.*

without fear of misunderstanding that the question who precisely wrote the Gospel is a *comparatively* unimportant one. Whoever the Evangelist was, we know what sort of material he had at his disposal and what sort of use he made of it; what more should we learn if we could discover his name?

In fact there is little reason to doubt the tradition, which goes back, as we have seen, to Papias and perhaps beyond him to the 'Elder' whom he quotes,* that the Evangelist's name was Mark. No one of that name is known to have been in specially close relationship with Our Lord or to have been particularly prominent in the early Church, so there would have been no good reason for attributing the Gospel to Mark unless he had been known to have written it. It is less certain that the tradition is right in identifying the Mark who wrote the Gospel with the John Mark of Acts (e.g. $12^{12, 25}$, etc.) and the Mark of 1 Pet. 5^{13} (cf. also Col. 4^{10}, 2 Tim. 4^{11}, Philem. ^{24}). The early Church was in the habit of assuming that all occurrences of a given name in the New Testament referred to a single individual, but when we remember that Mark (Marcus) was the commonest Latin name in the Roman Empire† and that the early Church must have contained innumerable Marks, we realize how precarious any assumption of identity is in this case. In favour of identifying the Evangelist with the Mark of 1 Pet. 5^{13} it is often pointed out that the Mark there referred to is expressly associated with Peter, as the Evangelist is by Papias, and that the two are said to be together in Babylon, the code name often used by early Christians for Rome, the traditional

* Nothing can be based on the title 'according to Mark' which the Gospel bears in surviving manuscripts, for such titles are known to have been added long after the writing of the books themselves; likewise the testimony of early Christian writers subsequent to Papias, such as Irenaeus, Clement of Alexandria, Origen, and Jerome, need not be discussed at length; for it is not clear that these writers had any trustworthy source of information other than the Papias tradition. Where they add to it their statements frequently conflict, and are often clearly influenced by the desire to associate the Gospel as completely as possible with Peter. Thus Irenaeus (like Papias) appears to think Mark wrote after Peter's death; later, however, the composition of the Gospel is placed in Peter's lifetime – without his sanction (Clement), with his approval (Eusebius), at his dictation (Jerome). The relevant passages are usefully assembled and discussed in V. T. pp. 1–8.

† Cf. *Marcus* Tullius Cicero, *Marcus* Brutus, *Marcus* Aurelius, *Mark* Antony, etc., etc.

birthplace of the Gospel. For its full force this argument rests on the belief that 1 Peter was written by Simon Peter, a belief not shared by many scholars; and even if it was, we must reckon very seriously with the possibility that the Papias tradition is itself a deduction from the verse in 1 Peter taken together with the fact that the Gospel was known to have been written by someone called Mark.* In favour of the Evangelist's being the John Mark of Acts it is pointed out that the latter was a native of Palestine and so his authorship would account for the knowledge of Palestine and its conditions which the Gospel betrays. Certainly, as the commentary will show, the general picture in the Gospel is remarkably true to the conditions of Palestine in Jesus' day, and from time to time Aramaic expressions are quoted in the original; but it is not clear how far all this is due to the Evangelist and how far to the tradition; and numerous vaguenesses and inaccuracies are most naturally explained if the Evangelist was *not* directly acquainted with Palestine. (See the commentary on e.g. 5^{1}, 6^{45}, 7^{2-4}, 7^{31}, 8^{22}, 10^{1}, 11^{1}.)

Certainty with regard to the author is clearly unattainable. Even the limited information afforded by the internal evidence of the Gospel has been very variously estimated; some have thought that the rather rough Greek, far removed from the polished style of the rhetorical schools, points to the Gospel being a translation of a document originally written in Aramaic;† others have taken it as

* See H. J. Cadbury, *The Making of Luke-Acts*, pp. 85ff., who rightly points out how largely second-century statements about the authorship of biblical books were based on conjecture.

† Judgements about an author's style will naturally vary from person to person, and it is almost impossible to convey a fair impression to those not acquainted with the original language. However, the following quotation from Rawlinson would probably command fairly general assent: 'The writing all through is vulgar [i.e. popular, uncultured], colloquial, unpolished, and is characterized by a singular monotony of style. There are hardly any connecting particles (*de rigueur* in literary Greek): the sentences and paragraphs follow one another in rapid succession, linked in the majority of cases by a simple *and*, or by the curiously frequent *and immediately*. Stereotyped phrases and ideas recur constantly. There is a tendency to redundancy of expression (e.g. 1^{32}, *At even, when the sun did set*). There is a frequent use of parenthesis, a tendency to accumulate participles. The Greek of Mark is essentially a non-literary Greek, full of roughnesses and semitisms – the kind of Greek which might be *spoken* by the lower classes at Rome' (*The Gospel according to St Mark*, xxxi–xxxii). It may well be that the last sentence provides all the explanation that is

evidence of an author who wrote in Greek but thought in Aramaic, while others, perhaps with greater probability, have been led to think of a Gentile author, deeply Christian, soaked in the tradition, by no means lacking in intellectual ability but without the formal education to express himself in better Greek or to impose on his material the completely consistent arrangement achieved by the fourth Evangelist.

In a commentary of this limited size nothing more can profitably be said about the Evangelist, except perhaps with regard to the date and place at which he wrote.

(*a*) *Date*. Though we have no explicit evidence we can fix the date within quite narrow limits; there has been considerable scholarly discussion of the matter, but it has been almost entirely concerned with the fixing of a precise date within these limits.

The statements of Papias and Irenaeus are generally taken to mean that Mark wrote after Peter's death; if, as is generally agreed, Peter perished in the Neronian persecution of A.D. 64, and we allow a minimum of a few months for the work of composition, that sets a lower limit in about A.D. 65. Those who are cautious about accepting the Papias tradition can hardly put the lower limit much earlier, for they must allow time for the oral tradition to have developed in the way described above.

As far as the upper limit is concerned, there are good grounds for thinking that the Gospels of Matthew and Luke were written before the end of the first century. By the time they were written Mark's Gospel was not only well enough known to have been available to both of them, but it had attained sufficient authority for both of them to follow it fairly closely. We can hardly date its appearance, therefore, after about A.D. 75.

Attempts to be more precise depend very largely on the interpretation of Chapter 13. A Jewish revolt which began in A.D. 66 led

necessary; the conclusion, based on the Greek style, that the Gospel as a whole is a translation of an Aramaic original has not generally commended itself, though it is another question whether in particular pericopes the Aramaic diction may not still show through the Greek. See the commentary and cf. M. Black, *An Aramaic Approach to the Gospels and Acts*. Aramaic is the name by which modern scholars refer to the semitic dialect, akin to Old Testament Hebrew, which was current in Galilee and Judaea in the time of Our Lord, and which, in all probability, he himself habitually used.

to the capture of Jerusalem and the destruction of the Temple by Titus in A.D. 70. It is generally agreed that these are among the events prophesied in Mark 13 and a comparison of Mark's version of the prophecy with the versions of Matthew and Luke has led many scholars to think that, whereas their versions were written after the event and were to some extent modified to fit the known facts, Mark's version suggests a genuine prophecy recorded before the event. Accordingly, the Gospel is frequently dated to the earlier part of the period A.D. 65–75, often to A.D. 65 or 66. However, as the commentary will show, the interpretation of Chapter 13 is no easy matter, and many scholars feel that what Mark wrote there could well have been written after A.D. 70. (See especially pp. 351–4.) The present writer is inclined on balance to favour a date in the latter part of the decade from 65 to 75; if the Gospel was not so closely connected with Peter as Papias supposed, there is no compelling reason why it should have been written immediately after his death, and a later date allows more time for the various stages through which, as we have seen, the tradition passed before its incorporation in the Gospel.

(*b*) *Place of composition.* About this early Christian tradition gives little help. Papias and Irenaeus say nothing (though perhaps implying Rome), the anti-Marcionite prologue (about A.D. 180?) says 'the regions of Italy', Clement of Alexandria and Origen say Rome, and rather later, Chrysostom, with equal assurance, says Egypt. In the absence of a clear lead from tradition, scholars have searched the Gospel itself for evidence.* On this basis, several suggestions have been made – e.g. Antioch;† but of all the places suggested Rome has been by far the most popular, and, so far as the evidence permits of any conclusion, it is perhaps the most likely. The Gospel was clearly intended for a church consisting largely of Gentile members (see e.g. $7^{3f.}$, 11^{13}, 12^{42}), and one which had known, or was expecting, persecution for faith (cf. 8^{34-38}, $10^{38f.}$, 13^{9-13}); all this is compatible with Roman

* As often happens when evidence is not really sufficient to form the basis of a definite conclusion, it is pressed to yield more than it really contains. For example, the occurrence in the Gospel of a number of Latin words in Greek form has been taken as evidence of a Roman origin. But, as H. J. Cadbury shows, if this is a pointer at all, the particular type of Latinism Mark employs 'tells perhaps more against than for that gospel's Roman provenience'. For details see *The Making of Luke-Acts*, pp. 88–9.

† See e.g. J. V. Bartlet, *St Mark*, pp. 36ff.

origin, and if the Gospel circulated from the beginning with the authority of the Roman church it is easier to explain how it so soon won an authoritative position. However, the arguments for Antioch are not lacking in weight, and dogmatism is out of the question; fortunately for the exegesis of the Gospel, while it is helpful to know the *kind* of community addressed, we do not need to know its precise location.*

JEWISH IDEAS AND BELIEFS PRESUPPOSED IN THE GOSPEL

Before all these data can be summed up and evaluated, one further section must be added to the Introduction. For the Evangelist assumes in his readers a familiarity with many of the terms and categories of late Judaism which are quite unfamiliar today.

First of all, the early Christian view of things, like the late Jewish view, on which it was largely based, was *eschatological*; that is, it held:

that the universe had been brought into being, and peopled, by a single creative act of God;

that in creating it God had a definite purpose for it;

that throughout its history he had exerted pressure on it to bring it into conformity with that purpose;

that nevertheless, under the influence of various powers opposed to God, it had diverged widely from his purpose for it;

that at some definite point in the future God would intervene decisively to overthrow the forces opposed to him and bring about finally the state of affairs he had originally intended at the time of creation;

that this state of affairs would involve for certain chosen human beings a life of unending bliss in God's presence, often symbolized under the picture of a glorious Banquet at which God would be host and his elect the guests.

For a variety of reasons, many Jews of Our Lord's time had come to expect that the final intervention by God would occur in the

* The suggestion has often been canvassed that the original Gospel was a shorter work (*Ur-Marcus*) of which our present Gospel is a revised version. No form of this idea has universally approved itself, and since the question is a highly technical one, and one which does not often affect the exegesis of the *present* text, it has not been very fully discussed in the commentary.

fairly *near* future, and in certain circles there was a good deal of speculation about its precise date and the form it would take.

Although the writers responsible for such speculations usually believed their accounts to have been revealed to them by God (hence the name *apocalyptic* for their writings, meaning, literally, 'uncovered' or 'revealed'), the pictures which they painted of the future differed widely. Some, for example, believed that God would make his intervention by direct action, but the greater number believed that he would act through an intermediary of some sort. Some pictured the final state of affairs which God would introduce as a kingdom of the blessed here in this world, while others felt that this whole world-order was so far gone from God's plan that he would have to replace it by another, and create 'a new heaven and a new earth' for his elect. Yet others combined both views and thought of a period of bliss in this world followed by an eternity of glory in another. According to most apocalyptic schemes, the dead of past generations were expected to be raised in their bodies at some stage, to face judgement and consequent assignment either to eternal bliss or to eternal torment.

Among the Christians at least, God's decisive act, and the state of affairs it would bring about, were referred to as the kingdom of God – or, to translate the original Aramaic more exactly, the king*ship*, or sovran rule, of God. The phrase connoted not primarily a place – a 'realm' as we might say – nor even a group of people, or 'subjects'; the emphasis was on the autonomous sovran action by which God would assert his authority and bring everything into conformity with his will for ever.

The kingdom of God and God's final battle against the forces of evil

It cannot be too strongly emphasized that in the New Testament the kingdom is something whose coming and existence will depend exclusively on *divine* power.

As we have already seen, it was not to be expected that the powers of evil would give up their hold over the world without a struggle, and so it was widely believed that God's assertion of his authority would involve a bitter battle between him and them, in the course of which men and nature would suffer most terribly.* It was pointed out earlier that St Mark's understanding of the ministry of Christ is

* This suffering was often referred to as the 'birth-pangs of the Messiah' – i.e. the pains through which the new age would come to birth; see on 13[8].

very largely in terms of this fight between God and the evil powers, and the commentary will show that the thought of Chapter 13 moves in the same circle of apocalyptic ideas. (Indeed Chapter 13 is often referred to as 'the Marcan apocalypse'.)

The evil powers were believed to be of many different kinds, among them being the 'demons' and 'unclean spirits' of whom St Mark constantly speaks; these were thought to have the power of causing storms and other natural phenomena injurious to men, and also of entering the bodies and minds of men themselves and causing disease, accidents, madness, moral blindness, and disobedience to God. Epilepsy and allied conditions lent themselves especially to interpretation in such terms. At the head of the evil powers stood their leader, often known as the devil, but referred to by St Mark as Satan or Beelzebul – titles which are explained in the commentary at 1^{12-13} and 3^{22}. St Mark's view of these demonic forces was entirely realistic; where we, if we had been there, should have heard simply the half-inarticulate cries of a man in an epileptic seizure, St Mark thinks of a demon inside the man who, because he belongs to the supernatural world, is aware of Our Lord's true identity and tries, by giving expression to his knowledge, to rob Our Lord of his power;* these wordy battles of Our Lord with the demons, and even with the demon-possessed Pharisees, were, for St Mark, very much a part of his total battle against the powers of evil† and his repeated success in them was further evidence of his mission from God. So far as we can tell, St Mark took an equally realistic view of angels (cf. 1^{13}, etc.). In thus accepting the existence of innumerable supernatural beings other than God he was only typical of the great majority of his contemporaries, both Jews and Gentiles; and not only was it universally believed that men could fall under the power of such supernatural forces, it was equally widely believed that certain individuals were granted the power to expel or exorcize‡ these powers. (Cf. e.g.

* It was commonly believed that knowledge of a person's identity and the use of his name conferred magical power to harm and defeat him; hence the point of such verses as 1^{24}.

† As is brought out in the original by the stridency with which they are conducted; in the Greek the words translated 'cry out' and the like (cf. e.g. 1^{24}) are very strong and express deep emotion and a sense of great urgency.

‡ A word meaning literally: to expel a demon by invocation of a holy name, and so generally to cure those possessed by a demon or demons.

Matt. 12^{27} // Luke 11^{19}.) As the commentary will show, the techniques by which Our Lord is said to have dealt with them are often closely similar to those known to have been used by other exorcists (see e.g. on 7^{33-34}); indeed, it is probable that one of the motives leading the Church to preserve the details of the techniques employed by Jesus was the desire to afford guidance to Christian exorcists attempting to deal with similar cases. For St Mark, however, the connexion of Our Lord's exorcisms and other 'mighty works' with the coming of the kingdom of God* gave them a unique status.

The Messiah or Christ

Just as different apocalyptists had different pictures of what the kingdom of God would be like, so they pictured in very different ways the intermediary (if any) whom God would send to bring it into existence. If their picture of the kingdom was of an essentially earthly kingdom, they naturally tended to think of an earthly king raised up by God to found it, possibly by force of arms. As the great days of their nation had been under David and his sons, they often (though not always) pictured the future king as a descendant of David; and since the token of God's choice and appointment of a king was a solemn anointing with oil, they often referred to the future king as *the* Anointed One, the Messiah or Christ.† Even in circles which held a less worldly conception of the king and the kingdom, the title Messiah was frequently retained, so that by Our Lord's time it could be used quite generally for the one who was to be sent, or raised up, to introduce God's kingdom, by whatever means he was expected to accomplish his task.

Son of Man

Those, however, who looked for more radical action on the part of God and a purely supernatural kingdom, tended to have their own nomenclature. They usually believed that the agent through whom the kingdom would be brought in would be a transcendent figure, specially sent from heaven, where he had previously existed at God's side, and possessed of power to carry through his work by purely super-

* According to St Mark many of them had been foretold in the Old Testament as part of what would happen when the kingdom of God arrived – see, for example, on p. 202.

† These two adjectives, *Messiah* and *Christ*, are simply the Hebrew and Greek respectively for 'anointed'.

natural means; for complicated historical reasons* they referred to this figure as *bar nasha* which really means 'The Man' but was over-literally translated into Greek as 'the Son of the Man' and so has found its way into our English versions as 'the Son of man'.

This short survey is designed only to *introduce* the main titles by which Jesus is described in the Gospels; of course it does not reveal the full meaning that St Mark found in them. Meanwhile, one other title must be mentioned, namely, Son of God.

Son of God

Although it occurs only some five or six times in the Gospel its occurrence is almost always at key points, and the Evangelist clearly attached great importance to it. Unfortunately, it is not possible to be certain exactly how he understood it. In Jewish usage it was applied to the whole Israelite people from the time of their election by God, and to individual kings from the moment of their anointing, apparently with the meaning that they had been chosen by God as his representatives, and that he had adopted them, as it were, and could be relied on to give them the love and protection that a son can always expect from a father (cf. e.g. Hos. 11^{1}, Exod. 4^{22}, Pss. 2^{7} and $89^{26f.}$, 2 Sam. 7^{14}). It is possible, though we have no direct proof, that the term was already used in Our Lord's day as a messianic title. In any case, such a passage as 1^{11} shows clearly that these Jewish ideas lay behind St Mark's use of the term. On the other hand, the phrase was also current in the Hellenistic religions of the day to describe great rulers and other 'divine men', or 'spirit-filled men', whose remarkable deeds were thought to betoken a divine origin, and this usage also seems to lie behind St Mark's understanding of the term, perhaps without being completely integrated in his mind with the Jewish usage.† To fuse these various terms, with their different backgrounds, into a wholly consistent

* Those interested should consult S. Mowinckel, *He That Cometh*, J. Klausner, *The Messianic Idea in Israel*, and A. Bentzen, *King Messiah*.

† B. W. Bacon, *Is Mark a Roman Gospel?* pp. 87ff., suggests that in $1^{9ff.}$, following a Hebrew line of thought, St Mark appears to think of Jesus as being *appointed* Son of God at a particular moment of his life, whereas elsewhere, working in the Hellenistic tradition, he takes Son of God to mean a superhuman figure who was divine by origin. There may be an element of truth in this, inasmuch as some of St Mark's material, which had been transmitted through Jewish-Christian channels, took one view of Our Lord, while some of it, reaching him from Hellenistic communities, took another. It is doubtful,

account of Jesus, in the light of the facts of the ministry, was clearly the work of centuries. But though St Mark's use of the term Son of God may not be entirely consistent, and perhaps he could not have defined his precise understanding of it himself, it certainly betokens for him something more than Messiah – a supernatural being of divine origin, uniquely related to God, whose endowments enabled him to silence the claims of the Law by an act of supernatural power and to impose obedience on the wind and the sea as well as on unclean spirits; and whose unmerited death was marked by unheard-of portents which revealed his true status. Anyone who reads the Gospel straight through will recognize that it is as Son of God rather than as teacher or prophet that St Mark presents Our Lord. Jesus, in Mark, comes before us not primarily as a teacher, but as the mysterious Son of God – a numinous and rather aweful figure whose work is to bring home to his generation the conviction that the end of this dispensation is imminent, and by his ministry and death to hasten the coming of the kingdom. It would be quite in keeping with all this if the Gospel originally ended, as it does in our best manuscripts now, at 16^8. (See commentary ad loc.)

THE GOSPEL AND THE MODERN READER

To those unfamiliar with New Testament scholarship a good deal in this Introduction will probably have come as something of a surprise. The suggestion is that a Gospel is not a photographic panorama of the whole of Christ's life, based on the personal recollections of eye-witnesses, but a series of essentially independent stories, each one of which was preserved, and to some extent modified, in the context of the Church's life and worship before its inclusion in the Gospel. In selecting, presenting, and arranging his stories the Evangelist's aim was practical, rather than directly biographical, and was related to the special problems, needs, and aspirations of the particular, persecuted, Gentile-Christian community for which the Gospel was

---

however, whether St Mark himself thought of Our Lord as being Son of God in the adoptive sense, either in the baptism narrative or elsewhere. See the commentary and Johannes Weiss, *The History of Primitive Christianity*, II, p. 698.

produced about three-quarters of the way through the first century. The Evangelist, and those who handled the tradition before him, have interpreted the material in terms of the outlook and thought-forms of their own time, and the possibility is not excluded that the Evangelist himself may have introduced certain modifications into the tradition in the process of writing it up into a Gospel. These conclusions, which, be it said, the great majority of scholars, at any rate outside the Roman obedience, would now accept in greater or lesser degree, clearly raise questions too far-reaching to be discussed adequately here;* we must

* It may be expected that any surprise occasioned by the Introduction will be deepened by the commentary proper, particualrly in two respects. It will become clear that the inspiration of the Bible – however exactly it is to be defined – did not exempt the Gospel writers and those from whom they derived their material from being fully men of their own time and cultural outlook. Their attitude to historical and biographical accuracy was, as the commentary will show, that of their own day rather than of ours, and even by the standards of their own day it was 'popular' rather than scholarly. And likewise the categories of thought in which they understood their Master and his work were essentially those of the first century; for example, they expected the end of the world very soon and they believed, as did the great majority of their contemporaries, both Jews and pagans, in the presence and evil activities of demons everywhere, and the possibility of overcoming them by miraculous means. This last point comes out most clearly in St Matthew's Gospel, and, although it is dealt with to some extent in this commentary, a much fuller treatment will be found in the commentary on St Matthew in the present series by J. C. Fenton.

With regard to the question as a whole, the reader is reminded that what may seem new, and somewhat startling, to him has been fully recognized by professional students of the New Testament for many years. Many of the Christian leaders of today are men who have long been well aware of these questions, and a lively debate about the theological implications of them has been in progress for some time. The matter is dealt with in a number of the books referred to in the remaining part of the Introduction, and perhaps the present writer may also refer to his own brief discussion in *The Church's Use of the Bible*, pp. 145ff and to that in J. Knox, *Criticism and Faith*. That many readers should be as surprised as they probably will be is a sad reflection on the extent to which all denominations do so little to keep an increasingly educated laity informed about the progress of biblical study.

The other respect in which the commentary may occasion surprise concerns the extent to which the Evangelist will emerge as a distinct individual – and a theologically very important individual – whose personal activity in selecting, moulding, and presenting the material, even though it may do little more than reflect the Church opinion of his day, must be recognized and thoroughly understood, if the full meaning of his Gospel is to be grasped. Subject to the content ourselves with making just one or two immediately relevant points.

First, it is certainly true that what Mark's Gospel *directly* attests is the beliefs about, and understanding of, Christ's ministry in the Christian Church of about A.D. 75, and particularly in that (? Roman) branch of it where the Gospel was produced. And in view of what we have seen of the way the material was transmitted, it would clearly be hazardous to press some of the details of the story or to base doctrinal constructions or devotional practices upon their historicity.

But these conclusions, significant though they are, need to be seen in perspective.

Historicity of the Gospel

We know a good deal now about the life and conditions of Palestine in the time of Our Lord, and, as the commentary will show, the general picture presented by St Mark fits very well into that background. Whatever qualifications have to be made, the Jesus of Mark, with the language he uses, the traditional parabolic method of teaching he employs, the claims he makes, and the hostilities he arouses, is beyond any doubt basically a figure of early first-century Palestine and not an invention of late first-century Rome.

That conclusion is borne out by what we can learn from the study of the history of the material. As we have seen, it is possible to some extent to reconstruct the units of tradition on which the Gospels are based. When we do reconstruct them, not only do we find that the units on which Mark is based presuppose *broadly* the same Christ as the finished Gospel, but we find that other units, preserved independently in other places and used by the other Evangelists, also presuppose a fundamentally similar figure.* Our basic picture of Christ is thus carried back to a point only a quarter of a century or so after his death; and when we bear in mind the wonderfully retentive memory

* See especially C. H. Dodd, *History and the Gospels*, which also deals with some of the other questions raised by this Introduction. And cf. Hoskyns and Davey, *The Riddle of the New Testament.*

---

caution sounded above (pp. 29–30), this modern rediscovery of the Evangelist as theologian and preacher – evangelist in both senses of the word – is thoroughly to be welcomed. A Gospel, it is increasingly recognized today, is a literary genre quite on its own, designed among other things to challenge the reader with the necessity of a definite decision about the claims made by and for Jesus.

of the Oriental, who, being unable to read and write, had perforce to cultivate accuracy of memory,* it will not seem surprising that we can often be virtually sure that what the tradition is offering us are the authentic deeds, and especially the authentic words, of the historic Jesus.†

However, passages in which all competent scholars would agree in recognizing that that is the case are rare, and it is important not to claim too much. What the Gospels give us, inextricably fused together in a single picture, is the historic Jesus and the Church's reactions to, and understanding of, him as they developed over half a century and more. Seldom, if ever, can we distinguish with certainty and say: 'This is pure history' and 'that is pure invention or interpretation'. Indeed it is not at all clear what 'pure history' would be, for the history of any man comprises what he did and said and the impression it made upon those with whom he came into contact. If the early Church was led to see in Christ's life more than the first disciples saw, even perhaps more than he saw himself, that is not to say that they were wrong. If they were led to assign to him titles to which he himself laid no claim in the days of his flesh, those titles may still point to the truth about him.‡ Even when all the Gospels had appeared the Church still had further truth to discover about Jesus; what the Gospels give us is a picture of his ministry which incorporates the insight that had been vouchsafed to the apostolic and immediately

* It would be quite in keeping with Jewish habit if some of the tradition, especially the tradition of Our Lord's words, had been formally committed to memory by groups of Christians and later reproduced with remarkable accuracy. Our Lord may even have couched his teaching in deliberately memorable form. This aspect of the matter is interestingly discussed by Professor H. Riesenfeld in his little book *The Gospel Tradition and its Beginnings*, where, however, quite exaggerated claims are based upon it.

† It must be left to the commentary proper to show in practice the criteria by which we may attempt – always tentatively – to assign material to the Evangelist, the pre-Gospel tradition, or the historic Christ.

‡ Not all scholars are convinced that Our Lord in fact claimed to be Messiah, Son of man, or Son of God. For different points of view see V. Taylor, *The Names of Jesus*, and J. Knox, *The Death of Christ*, *Criticism and Faith*, and *Jesus, Lord and Christ*. And on the general principle at issue see L. Hodgson, *For Faith and Freedom*, vol. II, especially pp. 69–70; cf.: 'The developed doctrine is not simply concerned with what He thought of Himself while on earth, or what His disciples thought of Him, but with what He was.'

post-apostolic generations. Christians, who regard the books of the Bible as in some sense inspired by God, will treat that insight with corresponding seriousness and not simply try to elbow it out of the way.* They will not, however, expect it to provide them, just as it is expressed in the Gospel, with the truth about Our Lord in the form in which it can be grasped and expounded in our own day. Rather they will seek, with the aid of all the historical and critical enlightenment they can get, to grasp the meaning of the Gospel considered as a spiritual message *addressed to the church for which it was originally written*, and only then will they expect to be able to find in it a spiritual message for the Church of today.† Nor will the approach of the non-Christian be very different. For the first step in the understanding of any book is to enter imaginatively and sympathetically into the world and intentions of its author; the Gospels are essentially works intended to convey a religious message and demand a religious decision, and the only fruitful approach to them, even for historical purposes, is by way of entering into their understanding of Christ's ministry and the truths about it they were intended to convey. The aim of the commentary which follows is to facilitate such an approach.

* For them it will certainly be part of the revelation.

† I cannot forbear to quote once again the admirable form in which Professor Hodgson formulates the question that must be asked in this connexion: 'What must the truth be, and have been, if it appeared like that to men who thought and wrote as they did?' Cf. e.g. *For Faith and Freedom*, I, pp. 87–8.

Mark 1^{1-13}

The Prologue

1[1–13] *The Reader Learns the Secret About Jesus Before the Story of the Ministry Begins*

At first sight these verses look like a brief, and rather artless, account of a number of incidents which took place over several months and had no essential connexion with each other. In fact, the narration is anything but artless, and the incidents, from the Evangelist's point of view, formed a fully coherent unity. The passage stands apart from the rest of the Gospel and is really a sort of curtain-raiser, in which the reader is made aware of the true theological situation; so that when the curtain goes up at the beginning of v. 14, he – unlike most of the actors – knows who the principal character is and can follow the full meaning of the action.

As the Introduction has shown, St Mark's Gospel is written from a very definite standpoint. St Mark accepted the general truth of the Jewish eschatological hope and he wrote about Jesus, not from any biographical or psychological interest, but because he believed that in his life the Jewish hope had found fulfilment. He and his fellow Christians saw in the earthly life of Jesus the beginnings of God's final intervention in history, the first, but decisive, stage in the overthrow of the powers of evil and the establishment of God's sovran rule (see Introduction, pp. 33–4). That was clearly ground for the utmost rejoicing, and the early Church called it 'the good news about Jesus Christ', or as it is translated in R.S.V. 'the gospel of Jesus Christ'.*

But St Mark realized that his readers might ask, as people ask in the Gospel, about the authority and credentials of Jesus. On what grounds did he and his followers see in his life the eschatological intervention of God? To a considerable extent the answer lay in the events themselves, if properly understood – and the aim of the Gospel is to describe those events in such a way that they *can* be properly understood. But St Mark believed that Jesus during the ministry deliberately prevented events from speaking for themselves

* The Greek word translated 'gospel' (*euangelion*) means basically 'good news'. In v. 1 'the good news of Jesus Christ' means, not the good news preached *by* Jesus Christ, but the good news *about* Jesus Christ.

(see pp. 31–2), and certainly the criminal's death at the end did not suggest the agent of God. It was all the more important, therefore, to put the reader in possession of certain circumstances, unknown to most of the characters in the actual drama, which established the identity and authority of Jesus beyond any doubt.

It will thus be seen that St Mark is doing in his prologue something very similar to what St Matthew and St Luke were doing in their stories of supernatural birth and infancy, and what St John was doing in his preliminary teaching (John 1^{1-18}), that is, demonstrating that Jesus was in fact the eternal word of God become flesh.

1^{1-11} JESUS' IDENTITY AND CREDENTIALS

1 *The beginning of the gospel of Jesus Christ, the Son of God.*[a]
2 *As it is written in Isaiah the Prophet,*[b]

> *'Behold, I send my messenger before thy face,*
> *who shall prepare thy way;*
> 3 *the voice of one crying in the wilderness:*
> *Prepare the way of the Lord,*
> *make his paths straight –'*

4 *John the baptizer appeared*[c] *in the wilderness, preaching a baptism of*
repentance for the forgiveness of sins. 5 *And there went out to him all the*
country of Judea, and all the people of Jerusalem; and they were baptized by
him in the river Jordan, confessing their sins. 6 *Now John was clothed with*
camel's hair, and had a leather girdle around his waist, and ate locusts and
wild honey. 7 *And he preached, saying, 'After me comes he who is mightier*
than I, the thong of whose sandals I am not worthy to stoop down and untie.
8 *I have baptized you with water; but he will baptize you with the Holy*
Spirit.'

9 *In those days Jesus came from Nazareth of Galilee and was baptized by*
John in the Jordan. 10 *And when he came up out of the water, immediately*
he saw the heavens opened and the Spirit descending upon him like a dove;
11 *and a voice came from heaven, 'Thou art my beloved Son;*[d] *with thee I am*
well pleased.'

a Other ancient authorities omit *the Son of God*

b Other ancient authorities read *in the prophets*
c Other ancient authorities read *John was baptizing*
d Or *my Son, my* (or *the*) *Beloved*

The first eight verses might seem to be devoted entirely to John the Baptist, but in fact they have much to say about the credentials of Jesus. For they treat John almost exclusively in his capacity *as the forerunner of the Mighty One – or Messiah*, though as a matter of fact he was a considerable person in his own right and St Mark knew a good deal more about him (cf. e.g. 2^{18} and 11^{32}).

In verses 2 and 3 passages are quoted from the Old Testament which show that the Messiah would be preceded by a forerunner, and then the subsequent account of John is almost exclusively directed to showing that he was that prophesied forerunner. Thus the point of mentioning that he lived and worked 'in the wilderness' is that he thereby fulfilled the prophecy; St Mark has no interest in locating the wilderness or helping his readers to do so; it is simply the wilderness of the prophecy.* The whole population came out to be baptized by him; that is hardly to be taken literally – the point is that nothing less than a national repentance would constitute the expected messianic preparation. Even in v. 6 the point is not simply historical. It was widely believed, on the basis of Malachi 4^{5-6}, that the prophesied forerunner would prove to be Elijah returned to earth, and so it is highly significant that the account of John's clothes is an almost exact echo of the account of Elijah's clothing in 2 Kings 1^{8}. One historical fact about John which did not immediately tie up with the prophecies was yet too prominent to be omitted, namely the fact that he baptized. Yet even this is brought into conformity with the prophecies, for it is presented as something he 'proclaimed' (v. 4), and the prophecies had spoken of a 'messenger' or 'proclaimer', 'the voice of one who *cries*'. It is also noteworthy that when John is heard explaining his baptism, the only point he really makes about it is that it is no more than a *preparatory* rite, not to be compared with the baptism of the coming 'mightier one'. That, and the explicit prophecy of the immediate coming of the mightier one, exhaust the teaching of

* That need not make it doubtful whether John did in fact live in a wilderness; the point is simply that Mark's interest in the matter was theological and not historical or geographical.

John as reported by St Mark, though in fact John had his own message of social righteousness to proclaim and St Mark almost certainly knew of it. As a result, by the end of v. 8 the reader has the overwhelming impression that the herald of the Messiah has come and so the stage is fully set for the entry of the Messiah himself. Whoever next appears at that place and time must surely be the Messiah. St Mark continues: *In those days* (a solemn biblical phrase) *Jesus came from Nazareth of Galilee*. The conclusion, as the French say, 'imposes itself.'

But in the following verses (9–13) it receives striking confirmation, not now indirectly through the fulfilment of prophecy, but directly through the action of God and His Spirit.* To understand this confirmation fully it is necessary to know something of Jewish beliefs and expectations at the time; but before they are described, one further point must be made. Just as St Mark showed no interest in John the Baptist except as the forerunner of the Messiah, in vv. 9–11 he shows no interest in the events he is describing except as proving the truth he wants to convey. He makes no attempt, for example, to say what effect these events had on Jesus himself; did they, for example, constitute a 'call' or a sudden revelation about himself, or only a confirmation of views he had already formed about himself?† On the basis of St Mark's account it is impossible to be sure and even idle to speculate.

Contemporary Jewish Beliefs

The Jews felt themselves to be in rather a trough. They looked back with yearning to the days of the prophets, for in their own day God seemed in some ways very remote. The Holy Spirit had not been sent since the days of the prophets and the voice of God which had spoken directly to the prophets was no longer heard direct – even the holiest rabbis were allowed to hear only the echo of it, the 'daughter of the voice' (*bath qol*) as it was called. In the old days, it was believed, God had been in the habit of piercing through the heavens to come to men's assistance (cf. Pss. 18⁹, 144⁵, 2 Sam. 22¹⁰),

* It is noteworthy that in vv. 9–13 human agents and agency almost totally disappear.

† It is quite possible that St Mark had not even formulated the question. If he did ask himself about the original purpose of these events, he may well have thought they were for the benefit of such later Christians as himself and his fellow believers. See carefully John 12²⁸⁻³⁰, and cf. John 11⁴².

but now, despite entreaties (Isa. 64[1]),* that seemed a thing of the past; the sky had become a fixed barrier between heaven and earth and seemed likely to remain so, as far as the ordinary course of history was concerned. If the Jews were not without hope, that was because, as we have seen, they looked for a decisive deliverance by the hand of God himself; the heavens would once again be rent asunder and the voice and Spirit of God would descend to earth. One or two passages may be quoted in illustration of such expectations – e.g. *Test. Levi* 18 (a document dating probably from 109–108 B.C.):

Then shall the Lord raise up a new priest
And to him all the words of the Lord shall be revealed.
The heavens shall be opened
And from the temple of glory shall come upon him sanctification
With the Father's voice as from Abraham to Isaac.
And the glory of the most High shall be uttered over him
And the spirit of understanding shall rest upon him.

Or again, *Test. Judah* 24[2f]. (same date):

And the heavens shall be opened unto him
To pour out the Spirit (even) the blessing of the Holy Father.

The one on whose head these blessings were to be poured would be the Messiah (whether called by that precise name or not), the one who would judge and save and pass on the divine gifts to men. One example must suffice (*Test. Levi* 18):

And he shall execute a righteous judgement upon the earth for a multitude of days . . .
He shall give the majesty of the Lord to his sons in truth for evermore . . .
And he shall open the gates of paradise.

The reader should consult this and similar passages in full in R. H. Charles, *The Apocrypha and Pseudepigrapha of the Old Testament*, vol. II. In the light of them and the widespread expectations they betoken, St Mark's account of the baptism practically speaks for itself.†

* 'O that thou wouldest *rend the heavens* and come down.'

† After the above was written, my attention was drawn to *The Testament of the Twelve Patriarchs* by M. de Jonge, in which it is argued that the *Testaments*

1

In another sense, as we have seen, the beginning is at 1^{14}. Some MSS. omit the words *the Son of God*, and it is hard to decide whether they are original; but the question is not of great moment, since St Mark certainly believed that Jesus *was* the Son of God and that belief underlies the whole Gospel.

2–3

in Isaiah the Prophet: In fact verses 2 and 3 are a composite prophecy taken from Mal. 3^{1} and Isa. 40^{3}. The mistake may have arisen because the Malachi quotation was added later, or possibly St Mark took the texts, already combined, from a testimony-book, i.e. a collection of passages from the Old Testament put together by the early Church as throwing light on the life and work of Christ.*

In the Old Testament it was God himself for whom the forerunner was to prepare, and certain small changes have been introduced into the texts to make the quotations refer to Christ. This should not be taken as a sign of dishonesty or intention to deceive. Neither Christians nor Jews approached the Old Testament along the lines of modern historical or critical study; both agreed that such passages as these referred to God's eschatological intervention, and if in the event, as Christians believed, God had chosen to intervene in the person of his Messiah, then it was right to rephrase the prophecy so as to put its precise application beyond doubt. It was their way of doing what we should perhaps do by means of an exegetical note.

4ff.

There is no need to attempt here the full account of John that St Mark does not attempt. Suffice it to say that he was certainly a historical character, famous for his powerful moral teaching – see Matt. $3^{1ff.}$, Luke 1^{5-80}, $3^{1ff.}$, and the Jewish historian Josephus (*Antiquities*, XVIII, 5, 2). Despite Josephus, it is probably true that his life and teaching were controlled by expectations of the imminent coming of the kingdom of God (cf. Matt. 3^{2}). What he promised was that, if men would truly repent of their sins, his cleansing of their bodies in water might be an effective

* For the existence of such books in very early times see e.g. C. H. Dodd, *According to the Scriptures*.

are a *Christian* work of the second century. It is too soon to say whether this thesis will win approval generally, but even if it does, the main lines of the interpretation suggested above will not be affected; the passages quoted from the Old Testament and the known teaching of the rabbis are enough by themselves to show how the incident is likely to have been understood.

sign of the cleansing of their souls from guilt, so that they could become members of the New Israel, cleansed and ready for the coming judgement. Where the Christian tradition may perhaps have exaggerated was in suggesting – St Mark does not actually say it – that already at this early stage John identified Jesus as the coming one he was expecting. The Church may also have sharpened somewhat the contrast John drew between the messianic baptism and his own. Perhaps in fact he merely faced people with the choice: 'Either my water baptism now for forgiveness, or, very soon, the Messiah's fire-baptism' – i.e. the painful prospect of (condemning) judgement.

4
repentance: See on v. 15 below.

6
wild honey: i.e. honey from wild bees, though some think a plant product is meant.

10
saw: St Mark, unlike St Matthew and St Luke, represents these things as seen only by Jesus, and no doubt he thought that the voice in v. 11 was heard only by Jesus. But this did not for him imply any lack of reality or objectivity; God was fully capable of making himself visible and audible to one, while remaining invisible and inaudible to others (cf. Acts 22[9]). The significance St Mark saw in the fact was probably as explaining how Jesus could have been proclaimed Son by God himself and yet not recognized as such by men during the subsequent ministry; it is part of his theory of the 'messianic secret'. What significance he saw in the dovelike form (or possibly mode of descent) of the Spirit cannot now be discovered; it no doubt rests on some dove symbolism current in late Judaism but no longer known to us.

11
The words of the voice raise such important questions for the Christian understanding of Christ that they demand a more extended treatment.

Whatever the correct translation may be,* the general meaning is clear; the voice declares Jesus to be the messianic Son of God.

* There is a further possibility in addition to those noted in the text, viz: 'Thou art my *only* Son.' The correct translation is either that or: 'Thou art my Son the Beloved.' If the last is right, the word *agapētŏs* (beloved) is equivalent in this context to *ĕklĕktŏs* ('chosen' or 'elect'). 'The Elect One' is known from contemporary Jewish literature to have been a common title for the Messiah. See S. Mowinckel, *He That Cometh*, and J. Armitage Robinson, *Ephesians*, pp. 229ff.

But the actual words used are reminiscent of a number of Old Testament passages (e.g. Gen. 22^{2}, Isa. 62^{4}, and especially Ps. 2^{7} and Isa. 42^{1} and 44^{2}) and important conclusions have been drawn from these resemblances. In particular:

(*a*) In such passages as Ps. 2^{7} the pronouncement: *Thou art my Son* is an adoption formula; that is, it declares that a certain person (usually a newly crowned king) will from that day onward be treated by God as if he were his own child. Are we then to understand that Christ, not having been the Son of God before, was constituted such by these words? This suggestion is often coupled with another. As part of his coronation, a king was anointed with oil; it is sometimes suggested that St Mark understood v. 10 as the anointing of Jesus with the Holy Spirit in virtue of which he became the King-Messiah.* The adoption formula would then come with special appropriateness in v. 11.

(*b*) In certain passages of (second) Isaiah (42^{1-4}, 49^{1-6}, 50^{4-9}, 52^{13}–53^{12}) there is reference to a servant of God (perhaps Israel as a whole) who fulfils a divinely given, redemptive mission through suffering. In Isa. 42^{1} and 44^{2} God's election of this servant-figure is described in words similar to those spoken here, particularly as the Greek word for 'servant' (*pais*) can also mean 'son', and the gift of the Spirit is part of the servant's equipment for his work. From this it is argued that the voice is doing more than declare Jesus Messiah, it is revealing that he is a Messiah who will fulfil his messianic function through suffering and humiliation after the pattern of the 'suffering servant' of Isaiah.

It would be rash to deny dogmatically that any such ideas were in St Mark's mind, but we must beware of over-ingenuity so far as the 'suffering servant' is concerned. The similarity between our passage and the two texts from Isaiah, though considerable, amounts to nothing like exact quotation; and the Messiah is connected with the gift of the Spirit in very many passages which have no connexion with the servant: cf. for example, the passages quoted above from *Tests. Levi* and *Judah*, and Isa. 11^{2} and 61^{1}. It is true that in the servant passages of Isaiah the idea of election and good pleasure is expressed in terms not unlike those in Mark, but so it is in many other passages in the Old Testament, and, as we have seen, 'The Elect One' was a recognized messianic title, quite apart from the servant. Suggestion (*a*) is perhaps more plausible, though even that may read into the passage more than St Mark intended to say. He may simply have understood the voice as confirming to his readers

* Cf. Acts 10^{38} which, referring to the baptism of Jesus, says: 'God *anointed* Him *with the Holy Ghost* and with power.' Cf. too Isa. 61^{1}; in the Old Testament anointing was often followed by Spirit-possession – cf. e.g. 1 Sam. $10^{1, 6, 10}$.

what would already have been clear to them from v. 10 – that Jesus was God's messianic agent.* (See also on 10^{45} below.)

my Son: On the rather general, but highly significant, sense in which St Mark thought of Jesus as Son of God, see Introduction, pp. 47–8. It may well be that in the material on which he was here drawing, the phrase bore a more distinctively messianic sense.

1^{12-13} THE BATTLE WITH THE DEVIL JOINED

[12]*The Spirit immediately drove him out into the wilderness.*[13] *And he was in the wilderness for forty days, tempted by Satan; and he was with the wild beasts; and the angels ministered to him.*

We now learn that not only was Jesus endowed with messianic Spirit, he had been led by it into a trial of strength with the prince of evil. St Mark tells the story so baldly that it is not altogether clear exactly how he understood it, though once again it was clearly nothing to do with the inner experience of Jesus.† The background lies rather in the current belief that the Messiah was the divine agent for the overthrow of Satan and all his powers, and that therefore a tremendous battle, or trial of strength, between him and Satan would form an integral element in the last days. The Greek word *peirazein* is much wider than the English word *tempt* and can include 'testing' or 'trying' of any sort. Probably here it includes moral temptation, but only as part of the wider 'trial of strength' the Messiah was expected to have with the Devil. In this passage the great eschatological battle is joined. The details are meant to suggest that Jesus was victorious (see below) but this stage of the battle,

* Cf. what was said above on p. 58 and notice that St Mark does not attempt to say whether the heavenly words conveyed anything new to Jesus, and, if so, what.

† St Mark could no doubt presuppose more detailed knowledge of the story in his original readers, though it is not to be assumed that the version they knew was identical with the version known to us from Matthew and Luke. That version seems to come from a quite different strand of tradition, and, with its emphasis on *moral* temptation, may well mislead us if we try to use it as the key to the understanding of the Marcan narrative.

though decisive, was not the final one; the struggle would continue in the various activities of Jesus during his ministry, and indeed in the lives and sufferings of the early Christians as well. At least part of the point of telling the story here was to help the reader to see the true character of Jesus' subsequent ministry – and of the life of the early Church – as the carrying on, and completing, of a decisive battle with the powers of evil successfully begun before ever the ministry opened. (See further on p. 121. That this battle had been joined is another truth known to the reader but not to the actors in the Gospel drama.)

ꙮ

12–13

Cf. V. T.: 'We do not know what ideas the first Christians read into the narrative, but it is probable that, while the language is pictorial and imaginative, the ideas are religious and theological.' Certain things, however, are fairly clear. The wilderness was traditionally the haunt of evil spirits, and Satan is the chief of the evil powers opposed to the will of God and the establishment of his kingdom. (See Introduction, p. 34). It should be noted that the 'trial' is represented as lasting for the whole forty days and that there is no reference to fasting or hunger; on the contrary, the 'ministry' of the angels, which is represented as continuous, probably consisted in keeping Jesus supplied with food, just as angels fed Elijah in 1 Kings 19.

13

the wild beasts: They may be mentioned to emphasize the loneliness and awfulness of the desert (cf. e.g. Isa. 34^{11} for how the presence of 'doleful creatures' was felt to heighten the desolation of the wilderness). More probably they are thought of as subject and friendly to Our Lord, and the passage should be understood against the background of the common Jewish idea that the beasts are subject to the righteous man and do him no harm (cf. the story of Adam, and also Job 5^{22} and *Test. Benj.* 5^{2}), and also that when Messiah comes, all animals will once again be tame and live in harmony (cf. e.g. Isa. $11^{6ff.}$, Hos. 2^{18}). In Ps. 91^{11-13} dominion over the wild beasts is coupled with the promise of service by angels, and St Mark probably means that by his victory over Satan Jesus has reversed Adam's defeat and begun the process of restoring paradise. Thus the whole passage is illuminated by this remarkable quotation from the *Test. Naph.* 8^{4}: 'If you do good, my children, both men and angels shall bless you, and the Devil shall flee from you and the wild beasts shall fear you and the Lord shall love you.'

Mark 1^{14}–8^{26}

The Galilean Ministry

1[14–15] THE MINISTRY BEGINS

[14]Now after John was arrested, Jesus came into Galilee, preaching the gospel of God, [15]and saying, 'The time is fulfilled, and the kingdom of God is at hand; repent, and believe in the gospel.'

The messianic herald has appeared, the Messiah himself has been designated and has entered secretly on the first stage of his final battle with the powers of evil. It remains only for him to declare himself publicly and to rally men round him as sharers in the kingdom and in the remaining stages of his battle with evil. All that is the subject of the Gospel proper, which accordingly begins with Jesus publicly declaring himself (vv. 14–15). But he could not do that till the work of the forerunner had been completed, and so it is significant that v. 14 begins with a notice of the conclusion of John's work. John was 'handed over', i.e. to imprisonment or death; Mark reserves the details till Chapter 6, and he could in any case assume that his original readers knew them. The point for the moment is that the forerunner's work was finished* and the hour had come for the principal's work to begin.

What form did that work take? St Mark does not answer that question, as a modern writer might, by giving a list of activities, calling disciples, teaching, healing, praying, and the like. Instead he depicts a typical day in the ministry of Jesus, which contains examples of these activities and is intended as a sample, or microcosm, of the whole (vv. 21–31).†

But first in vv. 14–15 Jesus publicly proclaims himself, and these verses are extremely important because they seem to be intended by

* And finished just at the appropriate moment by the providential action of God; for the Greek word *paradidōmi*, used of John's 'handing over', seems always in Mark to imply that the hand of God was in a special sense behind what was done – see on p. 249.

† It is not a matter of great importance whether the various events described occurred in the course of a single day as a matter of historical fact, or whether, as is more probable, St Mark has put them together to form an 'ideal' day.

St Mark as a sort of manifesto which sums up the substance and essential meaning of the whole public ministry. 'Jesus came into Galilee proclaiming the good news from God' – in the light of Isa. 40^9, 52^7, 61^1, etc., everyone knew what that meant, the good news that the time of waiting was over and God's sovran rule had arrived. The reader knows the grounds on which this proclamation is based, though Jesus does not include them in his public pronouncement – indeed it will be noticed that he says nothing about any personal messianic agent, still less does he identify himself as that person. In view of the programmatic character of these verses, this is significant, and we are here introduced to a fact of the utmost importance about Mark's Gospel.

According to St Mark, although the public ministry of Jesus was quite unmistakably the inbreaking of the kingdom of God, *Jesus did not seek public recognition as the messianic bringer of the kingdom; on the contrary he silenced such recognition when it was forthcoming and took careful steps to hide his identity*. For this 'messianic secret' see Introduction, pp. 31–2, and meanwhile notice that, while Jesus' hearers are not told or challenged at all about his identity, they *are* openly challenged to decision in respect of the kingdom. The precise nature of the decision demanded will be made clear as the Gospel proceeds; here it is stated summarily in words taken, like the other words in these two verses, from the Christian terminology of St Mark's own day. It may seem strange that the Evangelist should have Jesus solemnly proclaim his ministry in the technical terminology of later Christianity, but that, despite the opinion of some scholars, appears to be what St Mark has done. In explanation it may be pointed out that what St Mark is here doing is to *précis* in his own words the substance of the many discourses with which Jesus must have opened his ministry. By using the terminology of the later Christian mission he no doubt seeks to show that the 'Gospel of God' preached in that mission, and the response of repentance and faith demanded to it, were in essence identical with the proclamation and demand of Jesus himself.

❧

14
arrested: This conveys the sense of the Greek word in this passage, but the word itself is a general one ('hand over') which had many overtones

for St Mark. See above and cf. 9^{31}, etc.; the word is used in Isa. $53^{6 \text{ and } 12}$ (LXX).

the gospel of God: This could mean 'the good news about God', but more probably here it means 'the good news *from* God', i.e. the news of his intention to bring in his kingdom immediately.* The phrase was widely used in the early Church (cf. 1 Thess. $2^{2, 8-9}$, Rom. 1^{1}, 15^{16}, 2 Cor. 11^{7}) to describe the Christian message of salvation; and if it be asked how Jesus could have been thought to have preached that when he makes no reference to himself, the answer will be that 'to the Evangelist, Jesus, in preaching the gospel of God, or the gospel of the kingdom of God, must ultimately be referring to himself' (*H. & I.*, p. 107).

15

The time is fulfilled: The idea is that God had from the beginning determined the length of time that must elapse before the coming of his kingdom, and that time is now up. Such beliefs were common in apocalyptic – see e.g. Dan. $12^{4 \text{ and } 9}$ and cf. Ezek. 7^{12}, Gal. 4^{4}, Eph. 1^{10}, and for closely related ideas Mark $13^{20, 33}$.

the kingdom of God: For this vitally important phrase see p. 44.

is at hand: This is the meaning most scholars assign to the Greek word (*ēngikĕn*), though Professor Dodd and others translate it 'has arrived', 'is here'. R.S.V. is to be preferred, though the difference is not very great, since in any case only a comparatively short interval is thought of as intervening between Jesus' proclamation and the arrival of the kingdom. More significant is the question how far, and in what sense, Jesus believed the kingdom actually to have arrived during his earthly life. St Mark's view on that will emerge as the commentary proceeds. Here at any rate he seems to envisage its coming as being in the immediate future.

repent: The Greek word (*mĕtanŏein*) means literally 'to change one's mind', but as it is used in the New Testament, it comes very near to the Old Testament word *shubh* ('to turn back', cf. e.g. Joel 2^{12-13}), implying a coming to one's senses, a deliberate turning away from one's sinful past towards God, with the corollary of a change in conduct. Cf. A. Richardson (*A Theological Word Book of the Bible*, p. 192), 'in its New Testament usage it implies much more than a mere "change of mind"; it involves a whole reorientation of the personality, a "conversion".'

* Some MSS. read: *the gospel of the Kingdom of God.*

believe in the gospel: Over-literal – rather 'believe the gospel'. It is impossible to be sure whether St Mark here understood *the gospel* to mean simply 'the good news' (so R. and V. T.) or whether, as is perhaps more probable in view of his usage elsewhere, he understood it in its full Christian sense and pictured Jesus as using the later Christian terminology (see above p. 68). Certainly *repent and believe in the gospel* is exactly how the later Christian preachers summarized what men must do to be saved.

1^{16-20} THE CALLING OF FOUR DISCIPLES

16 *And passing along by the Sea of Galilee, he saw Simon and Andrew
the brother of Simon casting a net in the sea; for they were fishermen.* 17 *And
Jesus said to them, 'Follow me and I will make you become fishers of men.'*
18 *And immediately they left their nets and followed him.* 19 *And going on a
little farther, he saw James the son of Zeb'edee and John his brother, who
were in their boat mending the nets.* 20 *And immediately he called them; and
they left their father Zeb'edee in the boat with the hired servants, and
followed him.*

Before we come to the specimen day of the ministry we are given the story of the calling of four disciples.

The passage will not be properly understood unless it is recognized as a typical pericope (see Introduction, p. 28 and n.) originally without any note of time, or indeed of place, for the words *by the Sea of Galilee* were added by St Mark.* The placing of it here at the beginning of the ministry is thus entirely St Mark's doing but his reasons for it are not altogether clear. It may have been simply that these disciples play a considerable part in the sequel and so have to be introduced very early; or perhaps the Church had a tradition according to which the Messiah, after his baptism, chose disciples who should be able to bear witness to his subsequent ministry (cf. Acts 1^{21-22}, 10^{37}).

Originally the point of the story was a religious one concerning the nature of Christ's call and the Christian's response; that is still its

* So almost all commentators conclude from the awkward way they fit into the context in the original Greek.

primary point in Mark, and it entirely controls the form and content of the narrative. Thus we are given no purely biographical information about why Jesus chose these particular men or what previous knowledge they had of him, though clearly without some such knowledge their dramatic action would have been inexplicable and irresponsible, and they would not even have known what was meant by becoming *fishers of men*. But from St Mark's point of view, the absence of these details only serves to bring out more clearly the moral of the story. The call of God in Christ comes with a divine power which does not need to wait upon accidental human circumstances; it can create the response it demands. And that response must be one of unconditional obedience, even to the point of sacrificing the means of livelihood and the closest natural ties, as many of St Mark's contemporaries must have known from experience (cf. $10^{28ff.}$ and Matt. 10^{37-38} // Luke 14^{26-27}). The call is always to 'go after' Jesus in the path of discipleship (cf. 3^{13}, 8^{34}, 10^{52}) and in this particular case the special vocation to which the converts were called was that of assisting Jesus in 'catching' men, i.e. drawing them out of the waters of this world into the net of the eschatological life of the age to come. We are to see that that was – and is – part of the vocation of all converts, even if all are not called, as these four were, to devote themselves exclusively and 'professionally' to it.

❧

16
passing along by the Sea of Galilee: The construction in the Greek (*paragein para*) is unusual, and commentators generally are agreed that the reference to the Sea of Galilee is an addition made by St Mark – no doubt a deduction from the contents of the story. The Sea of Galilee – see map (p. 14) – was about twelve miles long and about six across at its widest point.

Simon and Andrew: St Mark assumes that his readers will know who these men were. See Introduction, pp. 35–6.

17
Follow me: The language may suggest that in which a rabbi summoned new disciples to his school, but the Gospel means far more by 'following Jesus' than is implied in that sort of relationship. The present story shows that it may often mean a total renunciation of one's past

relationship and way of life, and later stories will bring out further aspects of what is involved.

will make you become fishers of men: In Our Lord's time 'catching' men was already widely used as a metaphor, both by Jews and Gentiles (cf. e.g. Hab. $1^{15 \text{ and } 17}$, Prov. 6^{26}, and, for a Greek example, Diogenes Laertius II 67, *Rhein. Mus. N.F*, 35, 413); but it is doubtful if this would have prepared the two disciples for its use here, for the metaphor seems always to have been applied to *harmful* activities, especially, in the Old Testament, haling men off to divine retribution – cf. Jer. 16^{16}, Amos 4^{2}, Ezek. $19^{4\text{f.}}$ To the modern reader, looking back, the phrase seems readily intelligible in the present context, and perhaps the two brothers, if they knew something of Jesus beforehand, could already have understood it, as meaning to win further converts to his movement. But 'the call is in the first instance to discipleship rather than to apostolate', and the words make much more obvious sense in the light of later Christian practice and usage (cf. e.g. Matt. $13^{47\text{ff.}}$ and John $21^{3\text{ff.}}$ and the metaphor of the 'Ark' of the Church); so, despite V. T., we cannot rule out the possibility that the saying owes at least its formulation to the early Church.

18

If the details are pressed as biographically accurate, we are bound to suppose that the two men had had previous contact with Jesus (see above and cf. John $1^{35\text{-}42}$*). In order to understand the significance the early Church found in the verse, we must realize that the word translated *followed* was the term they generally used for acceptance of Jesus' call and attachment to his person. We are thus meant to see in the conversion of the Prince of Apostles what such 'following' must always be like. Jesus' demands brook no delay (*immediately*); the response must be decisive and must include willingness to give up one's means of livelihood and make a clean break with one's past; the best commentary is Luke $9^{57\text{-}62}$ (and cf. Mark $10^{28\text{ff.}}$); also the Evangelist no doubt had the story of Elisha's call in mind (1 Kings $19^{19\text{-}21}$). To many of Mark's original readers all this will have had very immediate relevance.

19

going on a little farther: This linking phrase may well be due to St Mark, who wanted to record the call of the three pre-eminent apostles (cf.

* Though cf. R., p. 14: 'In an oriental setting the Marcan account is credible as it stands: men will sometimes in India today with equal abruptness leave home and occupation to become disciples of a wandering religious teacher or *guru*.'

5^{37}, 9^{2}, 14^{33}) before that of any others, and it does not necessarily follow that the two incidents occurred at the same time. Indeed some scholars, impressed by the similarity of the two stories, have regarded them as variant accounts of a single episode. Such a view is certainly not inescapable, though for the possibility of such a thing, see on 6^{35}–7^{37} and 8^{1-26}.

20
The previous story shows how 'following' Jesus may involve the severance of economic ties; this one shows that it may involve the severance of personal and family ties (cf. Luke 14^{26} // Matt. 10^{37}). Does the reference to *the hired servants* serve to defend the apostles against the charge of completely abandoning their aged father, or does it add to the pathos – he is now left entirely at the mercy of 'hirelings'? The Greek word (*misthōtŏs*) is frequently used in a bad sense (cf. John 10^{12-13}) – can it be that the contrast here is between the apostles, who answer Jesus' call, and the 'hirelings', who are held back by mercenary considerations?

1^{21-34} *A Specimen Day in Capernaum*

The day opens, after an unspecified interval, in Capernaum, a flourishing little frontier town and customs post on the north-west shore of the Sea of Galilee (probably the modern Tell Hum – see map, p. 14). According to St Mark's account this was very much the centre of Jesus' ministry.

1^{21-28} JESUS' AUTHORITY

21 *And they went into Caper'na-um, and immediately on the sabbath he*
entered the synagogue and taught. 22 *And they were astonished at his teaching,*
for he taught them as one who had authority, and not as the scribes. 23 *And*
immediately there was in their synagogue a man with an unclean spirit;
24 *and he cried out, 'What have you to do with us, Jesus of Nazareth? Have*
you come to destroy us? I know who you are, the Holy One of God.' 25 *But*

Jesus rebuked him, saying, 'Be silent, and come out of him!' 26*And the*
unclean spirit, convulsing him and crying with a loud voice, came out of him.
27*And they were all amazed, so that they questioned among themselves,*
saying, 'What is this? A new teaching! With authority he commands even
the unclean spirits, and they obey him.' 28*And at once his fame spread*
everywhere throughout all the surrounding region of Galilee.

The first picture is of Jesus teaching, which is interesting as suggesting that St Mark was well aware how vital a part teaching played in the ministry. If so, why does he devote so little of his Gospel to the contents of the teaching? No doubt he could assume that his original readers were already familiar with it, but that hardly serves to account for the great disparity in this respect between him and the other synoptists. We must remember that the different Evangelists were moved to write by very different motives (see Introduction, p. 49n.) and it was not a paramount aim with St Mark, as it was with St Matthew, and also with St Luke to some extent, to preserve the teaching of Jesus in systematic and memorable form.* It is thus typical that in vv. 22–23 he makes no attempt to tell us *what* Jesus taught; what interests him is the manner and effect of the teaching. It was marked by an authority which astonished the hearers and differentiated it sharply from the teaching of the scribes, to which they were accustomed. The point of the contrast is generally taken to lie in the fact that the teaching of the scribes was almost wholly derivative and consisted in repeating the opinions of their predecessors; but it is by no means certain that that is true of scribal teaching in the time of Christ. An alternative explanation is that properly ordained rabbis with full rabbinic authority seldom penetrated to Galilee and the

* If the reader seeks a further explanation of this difference of aim he should note that early Christians seem to have varied somewhat in their attitude to the teaching of Jesus. St Matthew, for example, clearly regarded obedience to Christ's new law (*observe all that I have commanded you*, Matt. 28[20]) as of the very essence of Christianity. St Paul, on the other hand, very seldom refers to Christ's earthly teaching, even when discussing questions of practical conduct; he tends rather to seek the 'mind of Christ' through meditation on the Old Testament and direct communion with Christ in the spirit. This difference should not be exaggerated, but perhaps St Mark was nearer St Paul in this matter; certainly such teaching as he does reproduce is almost wholly concerned with Jesus' person and work and not with questions of conduct.

Galileans were therefore amazed to hear one who had, or spoke as though he had, such authority.*

But even if that was what the story meant in its pre-Marcan form, St Mark will not have had anything so specific in mind. He knew – and, in the light of the prologue, the reader also knows – that Jesus in fact spoke with all the divine authority of God's Son. Such authority could not escape notice, and St Mark would have us see that when Jesus began his public ministry, his hearers, although they did not penetrate to the true character of this authority, could not help being made aware of its presence and contrasting it with even the highest authority they knew among human teachers.

And this authority was not confined to the teaching of Jesus; it was manifested also in his actions, and particularly in his dealings with the powers of evil, of which we shall hear so much as the Gospel proceeds. Here a typical example is given (vv. 23–26); Jesus simply utters a word of command and such is its authority that the unclean spirit must obey, however unwillingly.

But now a new element is added, for the powers of evil not only recognize the fact of Jesus' authority; with their supernatural insight they penetrate to the true explanation of it – they recognize that Jesus is the Messiah and that he has come to destroy them and set up God's kingdom (v. 24).† (Notice the plural '*us*'; he speaks for his fellow spirits as well. Some MSS. even read 'we know . . .'.) The truth we learned in the prologue is thus strikingly confirmed from a supernatural source. But the evil spirit does not speak simply to give information. It was widely believed at the time that if you knew a person's true identity and could utter his name, you could gain a magic power over him, and this the spirit tries to do with Jesus. Jesus needs no counter-magic; it is nothing less than the power of God which works in him and a mere word from him will suffice. It must be pointed out, however, that the words used in v. 25 for *rebuked* (*ĕpĕtimēsĕn*) and for *be silent* (*phimōthēti*, lit.; 'be muzzled') are both known to have been used in the ancient world as formulas of exorcism, which perhaps suggests that at an earlier stage this incident was

* See Professor D. Daube's important article in *J. T. S.*, XXXIX, pp. 45–59, and cf. *H. S. G. T.*, pp. 79ff.

† The middle sentence in this verse should probably be punctuated as a statement, not as in R.S.V. See below.

interpreted simply as an exorcism, albeit of a particularly striking kind. That presumably is how the crowd understands it; they are amazed and impressed by the authority of Jesus, both in his teaching* and in his encounter with the unclean spirit, but they are not led to recognize anything more than a very high degree of that spiritual power with which they were familiar in other divine or spirit-filled men (see Introduction, p. 47). And it was presumably as such that Jesus became so renowned in 'the whole Galilean region'.†

We are thus shown how even the mightiest works of Jesus, though they were capable of revealing his true identity and arousing faith in him as Messiah, could also veil his identity from those who had not eyes to see; for they were not, so to say, *inescapably* messianic, but capable of a lesser, non-messianic interpretation. In principle there is nothing impossible in that, though it must be admitted that in this particular case, as in a number of others in Mark, it is not without its difficulties. Did the crowd not hear what the spirit said? And if they did, why did they not at least canvass the possibility of its being right? St Mark would probably have answered in terms of a supernatural darkening of their minds – see further pp. 31–2.

One further point calls for comment, as it will arise in connexion with a number of subsequent passages. What are we to make of a story in which an unclean spirit parleys with Jesus in human speech and a crowd gives expression to its reactions in one common formula? The latter trait is clearly artificial and reminds us of the part played by the chorus in Greek tragedy. It was quite a common habit among writers at the time to attribute to a group words expressive of the feelings which its individual members might have been expected to have. The modern equivalent would be a paragraph describing the sort of impact Jesus' various activities seemed to have on those who witnessed them. In any case we are dealing with a generalization, and what the words express in the last resort is the inadequate response that sinful humanity can make in its own strength to the coming and the saving activity of the Son of God.‡

* The words 'with authority' in v. 27 should probably be taken with the words 'new teaching' – i.e. 'a new and authoritative teaching'.

† This seems to be the meaning of the phrase in v. 28.

‡ That, of course, does not preclude the possibility that individuals may have uttered the words reported in Mark or something like them.

The point about the evil spirit raises deeper issues. According to a widely accepted suggestion the case was one of what we should call hysteria, and the words attributed in the Gospel to the spirit were in fact spoken by the sufferer himself in a hysterical fit. It should be realized, however, that if this suggestion is adopted the words lose the authority they had for St Mark as issuing from a being of supernatural insight.* We here touch on a wider question raised by certain fundamental differences in outlook between St Mark and most of his modern readers, which cannot adequately be discussed in a short commentary; see pp. 51–2.

21

No attempt is made to relate this story to the previous ones; clearly at least a night must have intervened, for the apostles would not have been fishing (v. 16) or mending nets (v. 19) on a *sabbath* (v. 21) which was the Jewish day of rest (Saturday) on which only certain very limited and absolutely essential kinds of activity might be carried on. For the very detailed rules governing sabbath observance at this time see a Bible dictionary and cf. on 2^{23}ff., 3^{1}ff.

he entered the synagogue and taught: If we say that the synagogue corresponded roughly to the English parish church, we shall not give a wholly wrong impression; at any rate every town or village of any size possessed at least one synagogue, in which services were held on all sabbaths and also on certain week-days. All sacrificial rites were reserved to the temple in Jerusalem, so the synagogue services were not wholly unlike Anglican Morning and Evening Prayer; they consisted of various praises, blessings, and other prayers, together with readings from the Old Testament which were subsequently expounded by a preacher; this is the 'teaching' referred to here.

In one important respect, however, the parallel with the modern Church breaks down; there was no ordained ministry in our sense of the term connected with the synagogue. There were elders responsible for the administration of the synagogue and its discipline, among them one or more 'rulers of the synagogue', who arranged for the services

* It is interesting in this connexion that in the ancient world a clear distinction was drawn in such cases between the person possessed and the spirit which possessed him – for example Lucian, *Philopseudes*, XVI: 'the sick person himself is silent; it is the demon who answers, whether in Greek or some barbarian tongue.'

and might lead the worship, and a paid official who was a sort of cross between a verger and a village schoolmaster and might fulfil a number of other duties as well. But it was perfectly competent for any male Israelite who was qualified to do so to deliver the 'sermon', and it would appear that Jesus was often invited by synagogue rulers to do this. Indeed for him – as later for his disciples (cf. Acts $13^{15\text{ff.}}$, 9^{20}) – such invitations afforded one of the chief opportunities for spreading the gospel.

22
authority: On this, see pp. 74–5. If the explanation put forward by Daube and others is correct, the question is raised whether Jesus was trained and formally ordained as a rabbi. We do not know exactly what becoming a rabbi entailed at this period, and in any case the evidence about Jesus is not sufficient to enable us to answer the question with certainty; but the case for thinking he was an official rabbi is stronger than is often supposed – cf., for example, Mark 9^{5}, 10^{51}, 11^{21}, 14^{45}, and see R. Bultmann, *Jesus and the Word*, pp. 57ff., in addition to the discussions referred to above.

the scribes: In the time of Jesus these were men devoted to the study of the Law and to drawing out its implications in terms of the detail of daily life, their accumulated teaching being known as 'the tradition' (see further on 7^{3}). If not of independent means, they had to ply a trade as well as performing their scribal duties. Though they were laymen* they were highly esteemed in the community (being called 'Doctors of the Law' and addressed as 'Rabbi') and were well represented in the Sanhedrin. Most of them belonged to the party of the Pharisees, though some may have been Sadducees (see on 12^{18}). They mostly worked in Jerusalem, gathering round them circles of disciples, to whom they imparted the Law and the tradition by a method of education which was almost entirely oral and involved the learning by heart, and exact repetition, of innumerable maxims and memorable sayings (see Introduction, pp. 50–1, and cf. on 7^{1-23}). Also see previous note; it will be obvious how exactly, in certain respects, Jesus' ministry fitted into the pattern of scribal activity. A comparison between him and the scribes, such as is here described, would have been very natural.

23
an unclean spirit: i.e. possession by the spirit made the man *unclean* –

* The fact that they seem to have been 'ordained' by the imposition of hands should not lead to any confusion of their status with that of the priestly families connected with the Temple.

either in the sense of ceremonially impure, or in the more general sense of being unfitted for worship and fellowship with God. However, the word translated *unclean* (*acathartos*) sometimes meant little more than 'vicious', and the phrase may be used by Mark to mean simply 'an evil spirit'.

24

cried out: In the Greek a strong word indicating deep emotion. For this note of stridency in the ministry, and its meaning, see Introduction, p. 45.

What have you to do with us? In classical Greek this would mean 'What have we in common?' Here, under the influence of Hebrew usage, it probably means 'Why are you interfering with us?' cf. e.g. 1 Kings 17^{18}.

of Nazareth: In Greek a single word (*Nazarēnĕ*) the meaning of which is very uncertain. On balance the R.S.V. translation is probably the right one, though among other possibilities are that it is connected with the Hebrew word for 'shoot' or 'branch', or that it means 'consecrated', 'holy', in which case it is picked up by *Holy One of God* at the end of the verse. For a full discussion see G. F. Moore in *The Beginnings of Christianity*, vol. 1, p. 426ff. The question is of course linked with that of the locality of Nazareth, the existence of which is not attested outside the New Testament.

Have you come to destroy us? Perhaps better translated as an assertion – the spirits, with their supernatural insight, could not fail to recognize that the hour of their destruction had arrived. For the expectation of the destruction of evil powers in the messianic age, cf. 1 *Enoch* 69^{27}, Luke 10^{18}, Rev. 20^{10}.

the Holy One of God: Presumably used in a messianic sense, though there is no evidence that the term was so used by the Jews. Possibly a later Christian term (based on the association of Ps. 16^{10} with the resurrection – see Acts 2^{27}) is here attributed to the demon.

25

On the associations of the terms used here see pp. 75–6.

27

A typical conclusion to a healing pericope, emphasizing the reality and remarkable character of what had been done by describing the stupefying effect it had on the bystanders.

amazed: like the different Greek word used in v. 22 (*astonished*) this implies profound astonishment. Since the Jews were not unfamiliar with exorcisms, such a reaction may seem strange, but St Mark's point is that Jesus' exorcisms were not like any others.

1^{29-31} PETER'S MOTHER-IN-LAW

29*And immediately he*[a] *left the synagogue, and entered the house of Simon*
and Andrew, with James and John. 30*Now Simon's mother-in-law lay*
sick with a fever, and immediately they told him of her. 31*And he came*
and took her by the hand and lifted her up, and the fever left her; and she
served them.

a Other ancient authorities read *they*

In the last incident we saw how the messianic power of Jesus could deal with a case of demonic possession. We now learn that it can also deal with other forms of sickness. Luke seems to have thought of the fever here as a personal force, or at any rate semi-personal – it could be 'rebuked' (Luke 4^{39}). St Mark does not explicitly say that, but he may well have shared the feeling, for the Jews tended to think of all illness as due to personal forces (cf. e.g. Luke 13^{11-16} and Matt. 12^{22}), which explains why so many of the healing stories in the Gospels read like accounts of exorcisms (see p. 204). Since these forces were hostile to God, the establishing of God's kingdom clearly involved their overthrow as part of the Messiah's work – cf. e.g. Isa. 35^{4-6} and Rev. 21^{4}.* In the last incident the power of Jesus worked through a word; here there is an action – he *took her by the hand and lifted her up* – but no word is reported.

* This aspect of the Messiah's work, although it is occasionally referred to by the rabbis, is not at all prominent in pre-Christian prophecies about the Messiah. This may be because it was not foreseen that he would have an extended earthly ministry such as Jesus actually had. His activity was thought of as concentrated in one decisive battle against the Prince of Evil which was expected to include the defeat of the inferior tormentors of mankind (see the discussion in *H.S.G.T.*, p. 59).

29

If we accept the reading '*they* left', we get a very awkward sentence; why are James and John not included in the 'they'? By way of explanation it has been suggested* that St Mark got the story direct from Peter in the form: '*we* went out and came into *our* house together with James and John'.† This section would then be a more or less direct eyewitness account, and it is certainly in favour of the suggestion that the story is told quite straightforwardly, as a reminiscence might be, with very little attempt to underline the moral. But against it must be set:

(i) That the reading in the text is more likely to be correct.

(ii) That the names Andrew, James, and John may be a later gloss; they are not mentioned at this point by either Matthew or Luke, and some commentators take this to mean that they did not occur in the original text of Mark as Matthew and Luke knew it.

(iii) The question why, if St Mark did get the story direct from Peter in the first person plural, he should have been so exceedingly clumsy in translating it into narrative form.

It seems more likely, therefore, that the story reached St Mark, like the rest of his material, as part of the general oral tradition of the Church.

31

Once again the story gives the general impression of a cure performed effortlessly without the need for any magic or special technique. But just as in the last incident the words used were current terms in contemporary exorcism, so here the action is that recorded in the case of various healings by rabbis in the Talmudic literature. The phrase 'lift up' (*ĕgeirein*) seems indeed to have been the conventional Talmudic expression meaning to 'cure' or 'heal'; and the phrase *the fever left her* is likewise known from contemporary narratives of healings.

she served them: i.e. presumably at table. The words show both the completeness of the cure (cf. Introduction, p. 24) and also its miraculous speed; St Jerome comments: 'The human constitution is such that after fever our bodies are rather tired, but when the Lord bestows health, restoration is immediate and complete.'

* e.g. by Zahn and, following him, C. H. Turner (see *A New Commentary on Holy Scripture*, Pt III, pp. 48–9 and 55).

† cf. 1^{16}, a passage where the same sort of thing is held to have happened.

I 32–34 THE POWER OF JESUS MORE WIDELY EXTENDED

32 *That evening, at sundown, they brought to him all who were sick or possessed with demons.* 33 *And the whole city was gathered together about the door.* 34 *And he healed many who were sick with various diseases, and cast out many demons; and he would not permit the demons to speak, because they knew him.*

The specimen day ends with the performance of a large number of exorcisms and healings. These are not described individually but their very number (*all* v. 32 and *many* v. 34) and variety (*various diseases* v. 34) serve to show that the two cases just described in detail were not freaks or fortunate coincidences, but the manifestations of a power which can deal with 'all those who are in a bad way' (the literal translation in v. 32), no matter what the various ills from which they may be suffering. A power so great and universally effective as this can be no other than the eschatological power of God; and it accords with this that it is exercised in strict conformity with God's will as expressed in the Old Testament Law (see below in v. 32).

❦

32
The sabbath ended in the *evening, at sundown*, and the note of time is duplicated (contrast Matthew // and Luke //) to emphasize that Jesus did not exercise his power until the sabbath was quite over and it was lawful to 'bring' (lit. 'carry') the sufferers through the street.

32–34
Here as in v. 5 we have hyperbole ('*all*', '*the whole city*') and once again the intention is symbolic, to convey the universal scope and efficacy of the Messiah's activity. St Mark will have intended no distinction between '*all*' in v. 32 and '*many*' in v. 34, especially as the word for 'many' in Hebrew and Aramaic did not have the exclusive sense ('a large number but not all') it bears in English.

34
and he would not permit the demons to speak: By refusing to let the demons

say who he was, Jesus deliberately makes it harder for people to deduce his identity from his works. Why? (See on this subject Introduction, pp. 31–2). Some MSS. read 'because they knew that he was the Messiah'; though not the original reading, that is certainly a correct interpretation of St Mark's meaning. Once again the reader has his own belief confirmed by the supernatural insight of the evil powers.

1^{35-39} JESUS – NOT RIGHTLY UNDERSTOOD – EXTENDS HIS MINISTRY TO OTHER PLACES

35 *And in the morning, a great while before day, he rose and went out to a*
lonely place, and there he prayed. 36 *And Simon and those who were with*
him followed him, 37 *and they found him and said to him, 'Every one is*
searching for you.' 38 *And he said to them, 'Let us go on to the next towns, that*
I may preach there also; for that is why I came out.' 39 *And he went*
throughout all Galilee, preaching in their synagogues and casting out
demons.

Just as the power of Jesus was not confined to particular cases or types of case, so it is not confined to any particular place; we now learn how it was extended to all parts of Galilee, where Jesus undertook an itinerant ministry (v. 39).

It is not easy to be quite sure what further significance St Mark saw in the incident which marks the transition; but he has been careful to relate it exactly in time and place to what has gone before, and this is so contrary to his usual custom that it must have been deliberate; we are meant to take the incident closely with what precedes – as a sort of appendage to the specimen day and as offering an important comment on it.

The most probable interpretation is as follows:

Early on the morning after his experience with the crowds Jesus seeks a quiet place to be alone and perhaps to pray. The reference to his prayer may be meant simply to remind us that he, and the power he wields, are entirely dependent on, and subordinate to, the will of God. But both the other occasions in the Gospel when Jesus prays are times of great stress, and it may be that this too is seen as a point of crisis and stress; for the only results of the ministry so far have been excitement and amazement on the part of the crowds and the thronging of invalids in the evening at the door of Peter's house – neither of them results in accordance with Our Lord's purpose. Peter and his companions do not help, for instead of leaving Jesus in peace, they track him down (the Greek word *katadiōkein* usually implies '*hostile* following', 'persecuting') to give him what they regard as the good news that everyone is looking for him. But to be 'searched for' (Greek 'sought') in this way as a wonder-worker is not the 'following' Jesus has been sent into the world to attract, so he decides to go elsewhere in order to proclaim the inbreaking of the kingdom both by word and deed. The true significance of all the words and mighty works of Jesus is that they 'proclaim' (literal meaning of the Greek in v. 38) and usher in the kingdom. Any response to them, however favourable, which does not recognize that as the essential truth about them is unacceptable, even if it comes from professed followers such as *Simon and those who were with him* – a noteworthy phrase by which they are pointedly denied the title 'disciples'. Theirs is not the attitude of true disciples; they come simply as representatives of the crowd, wholly identified with its worldly attitude and interests.*

35
a great while before day: prayer in the early morning was a pious habit among the Jews (cf. e.g Pss. 5^3, 88^{13}, 119^{147}). It is just possible however that the reference to prayer here is a later addition; Luke // (4^{42}) omits it, and since it is specially characteristic of him to include references to Jesus at prayer, some commentators take his silence to mean that the statement was not included in the version of Mark known to him.

37
They presumably expect Jesus to return to Capernaum. The Greek word for *is searching* (*zētousin*) is used in nine other places in Mark and always

* Possibly at an earlier stage in its transmission the story was also seen as containing a lesson for the itinerant preachers of the primitive Church, who might well be tempted to stay for a disproportionate length of time in places where their preaching met with obvious outward success and so brought them friends and comfort. In fact it was their duty constantly to push on to new places (cf. e.g. *Didache*, XI, 4–5) and here the lesson is reinforced by the example of the Lord himself.

in a derogatory sense; it refers either to actual persecution or to seeking Jesus in a wrong and unacceptable way (cf. especially 3^{32} and 16^{6}).

38

towns: Greek *kōmŏpŏleis* – strictly small towns with only the status of villages, but here generally of the small market towns in the neighbourhood.

I came out: Possibly just referring back to v. 35 but more probably as Luke thought (Luke 4^{43}) meaning 'I came forth from heaven to earth', 'I was sent into the world'.

1^{40-45} EVEN LEPROSY YIELDS TO THE POWER OF JESUS

[40]*And a leper came to him beseeching him, and kneeling said to him, 'If*
you will, you can make me clean.' [41]*Moved with pity, he stretched out his*
hand and touched him, and said to him, 'I will; be clean.' [42]*And immediately*
the leprosy left him, and he was made clean. [43]*And he sternly charged him,*
and sent him away at once, [44]*and said to him, 'See that you say nothing to*
any one; but go, show yourself to the priest, and offer for your cleansing what
Moses commanded, for a proof to the people.'[a] [45]*But he went out and began to*
talk freely about it, and to spread the news, so that Jesus[b] *could no longer*
openly enter a town, but was out in the country; and people came to him
from every quarter.

a Greek *to them*
b Greek *he*

This story clearly circulated at one time as an isolated unit of tradition without any note of time or place (see Introduction, pp.27–8). Presumably, therefore, St Mark's motive for placing it here was theological, though it is not easy to say precisely what it was, unless the incident is intended as a sort of final appendix to the specimen day, showing that Christ's power was able to deal even with leprosy – a claim which would certainly have seemed something of a climax to the contemporary reader. For leprosy, besides being a loathsome and disfiguring disease, involved ritual uncleanness and complete segregation from the community and religious life of Israel. The Law could do nothing for the leper; it could only protect the rest of the community against him. Moreover it is probably significant that according to the rabbis, the healing of leprosy was 'as difficult as the raising of the dead'. What, therefore, the Old Testament religion – the Law – could not do was done readily by Jesus, and Lightfoot (*G. M. M.*, p. 26) suggests that Rom. 8^3 is the best commentary on this passage; and cf. Matt. 11^5 // Luke 7^{22}, for the view that the cleansing of leprosy was an expected sign of the Messiah's arrival.

But even if it is thus clear that the general meaning of the story is to emphasize the surpassing nature of the salvation now accessible to men, the text, when studied in detail, presents several problems, some of them concealed in the English translation.

(i) It is uncertain whether the words *and kneeling* (v. 40) are original; but probably they are, and, if so, stress is laid on the emotional urgency of the leper's approach. Lightfoot notes, *à propos* of this and other touches, that 'this story has more emotional tone than any other in the four Gospels' (*G. M. M.*, p. 25 – see next note).

(ii) For *Moved with pity* (v. 41) we should almost certainly read, with many MSS., 'moved with anger'. With this goes the fact that in v. 43 the R.S.V. translation is too weak. The word translated *sternly charged* implies indignant displeasure, or at least a wave of great emotion; and the word translated *sent away* really means 'drove out' (it is often used in connexion with demons, and cf. 1^{12}).

(iii) The last words of v. 44 mean literally: 'for a testimony to them'. A testimony *to whom* about *what*?

(iv) In v. 45 R.S.V. translation assumes that the first half of the verse refers to the healed leper. The Greek, however, could equally well mean: 'And he [i.e. Jesus] went out and preached [the gospel] constantly and spread abroad the word [of God] so that he could no longer . . .' In some ways this would be the more natural interpretation of the Greek.

A great deal of discussion has not so far produced any generally agreed solution of these difficulties. Perhaps the most likely solution is that the story in its present form arose out of a conflation at some stage of two accounts of the incident told from rather different points of view. According to one account Jesus was moved to pity by the leper's appeal, healed him by a touch and a word, and bound him to secrecy, as in so many other healing stories in the Gospel. According to the other account, Jesus' reaction was one of hot indignation against the leprous spirit which had produced the agonized urgency of the man's appeal. In this state of extreme emotion he 'drove out' the spirit and bade the man carry out the prescribed procedure for having himself declared clean and readmitted to the community. In the present conflate form of the story Jesus' strong emotion and his action, originally directed towards the leprous spirit, have come to be applied to the man, and the command to silence has been rather awkwardly combined with the instruction: *go, show yourself to the priest* (v. 44).

However that may be, St Mark's understanding of the story as he gives it is likely to have been:

(*a*) That the anger of Jesus arose from his opposition to the combined forces of disease, death, sin, and Satan.

(*b*) That Jesus wished, as usual, to conceal his identity.

(*c*) That the command to carry out the requirements of the Law showed Jesus as fully obedient to this Law (see note on v. 32 above) – rather an important matter in view of what was immediately to follow. This may in fact account, partly at least, for Mark's placing of the story at this precise point.

(*d*) That the leper, through his action in having himself officially declared clean (v. 44b), would bear witness to all and sundry that there was a power among them capable of healing leprosy, a task, as we have seen, reputed to be as difficult as raising the dead.

❧

40
There is nothing in the story itself to show when or where it happened.

41
touched him: To touch a leper would have seemed at the time an unthinkable action; even if it did not actually violate the Law, it brought ceremonial defilement, quite apart from the loathsome appearance of leprosy. Montefiore writes (I, 39): 'Here we begin to catch a new note in the ministry of Jesus: his intense compassion for the outcast, the sufferer, who, by his sin, or by his suffering, which was too often regarded as the result of sin, had put himself outside respectable Jewish society, who found himself rejected and despised by man and believed

himself rejected and despised by God. Here was a new and lofty note, a new and exquisite manifestation of the very pity and love which the prophets had demanded.'

44
For the procedure involved see Lev. 14.

45
No doubt a Marcan addition to the traditional story; on balance St Mark may be taken to have referred the first half of the verse to the healed leper.

For the second half of the verse see on 1^{1-11}, p. 57.

2^{1}–3^{6} *Jesus Meets Opposition*

In the opening chapter we were first told who Jesus really was and then shown how some typical words and actions of his ministry pre-supposed and revealed this identity, although, for various reasons, including deliberate self-concealment on the part of Jesus, people at the time did not penetrate the secret. Now a further question arises. The ministry of Jesus was wholly helpful and healing (cf. Acts 10^{38}); even if men did not fully penetrate its secret, how came they to respond to it – as the original readers knew that in the end they did – with hostility, hatred, and persecution? This was one of the cardinal questions about the ministry of Jesus that faced the early Church.

St Mark begins his answer to it in this section of his Gospel (2^{1}–3^{6}), which consists of five stories of conflict between Jesus and the Jewish authorities. Once again the arrangement is according to subject-matter rather than historical sequence; there is no reason to think these five incidents in fact occurred one after another all at the same point in the ministry. They are selected and described here because:

(i) They show that opposition to Jesus came not from the ordinary Jewish people, but from authorities who had religious vested interests to maintain; and

(ii) they make clear the true character and grounds of the opposition, showing that it arose entirely from misunderstanding and shortcoming on the part of the authorities, and not at all from any fault on the part of Jesus.

'It is possible, perhaps probable, that these five stories formed a collection before they reached their present position in this Gospel; in certain respects they contrast sharply with 1^{14-45} and 3^{7-19a}, the passages on each side of them. Thus there is no command to, or desire for, secrecy, on the part of Jesus; rather the reverse. There is no reference to the casting out of demons, or to the prohibition of their confession of the Messiahship of Jesus. On the contrary, we find a constant if indirect emphasis by Jesus himself on his office and its purpose ($2^{10, 17, 28}$), and the shadow of the final Passion is already present (2^{19-20}, 3^{6})' (*H. & I.*, p. 110). In any case it is clear that St Mark envisaged a sharp break between 1^{45} and 2^{1} (see below on 2^{1}) and regarded 2^{1} as introducing a new element in his Gospel.

2^{1-12} HEALING AND FORGIVENESS

2 *And when he returned to Cap-er'na-um after some days, it was reported*
that he was at home. 2 *And many were gathered together, so that there was*
no longer room for them, not even about the door; and he was preaching the
word to them. 3 *And they came, bringing to him a paralytic carried by four*
men. 4 *And when they could not get near him because of the crowd, they*
removed the roof above him; and when they had made an opening, they let
down the pallet on which the paralytic lay. 5 *And when Jesus saw their faith,*
he said to the paralytic, 'My son, your sins are forgiven.' 6 *Now some of the*
scribes were sitting there, questioning in their hearts, 7 *'Why does this man*
speak thus? It is blasphemy! Who can forgive sins but God alone?' 8 *And*
immediately Jesus, perceiving in his spirit that they thus questioned within
themselves, said to them, 'Why do you question thus in your hearts?
9 *Which is easier, to say to the paralytic, "Your sins are forgiven," or to say*
"Rise, take up your pallet and walk"? 10 *But that you may know that the*
Son of man has authority on earth to forgive sins' – he said to the paralytic –
11 *'I say to you, rise, take up your pallet and go home.'* 12 *And he rose, and*

immediately took up the pallet and went out before them all; so that they were all amazed and glorified God, saying, 'We never saw anything like this!'

The first of the five stories concerns the healing of a paralytic, but the real point of the narrative lies in the words (v. 10): '*the Son of man has authority on earth to forgive sins*'. The reader, knowing that the power of Jesus is messianic and having seen it drive out demons and deal with illness of every sort, is not surprised to learn that it can also forgive* the sin and guilt from which, according to most Jewish thinking, the illness and demon-possession arose.

But the Jewish authorities had not read the signs of the times and they were deeply shocked by such a claim. The forgiving of sins, they say, is the prerogative of God alone and for anyone else to claim it is blasphemy. They are certainly right on the first point, and would be right on the second point too in the case of any ordinary person such as they took Jesus to be ('*this man*' – *houtŏs* in v. 7 should really be translated 'this person'; it implies contempt). But it is just in taking Jesus for an ordinary person that their error lies. They fail to recognize that he is the messianic agent of God and that with his coming the kingdom of God is breaking in. That being so, the power that works in Jesus is, of course, the power of God himself, and there is no blasphemy in his claim that it forgives sins.

However, there is no obvious means of checking a claim to forgive sin – no one can see whether or not it has justified itself in practice; and to that extent the suspicion of the scribes is natural. But Jesus in the story does not leave them even that excuse, for:

(i) he offers to 'prove' his power by exercising it in a 'more difficult' matter, i.e. a case where its supernatural effects can be visibly tested (vv. 9 and 11); and

(ii) he says openly that he is the Son of man and that it is as such that he exercises the divine power of forgiveness on earth (v. 10).

The evidential healing is a triumphant success (v. 12) and if, in the face of all that, St Mark implies, the scribes continue with their opposition, they are utterly without excuse. In fact they do continue, and it is

* Or at any rate declare authoritatively that God has forgiven it. The original readers, as Christians, would have been familiar with forgiveness through Christ in their own experience.

of such stuff, St Mark would have us conclude, that the final charges against Jesus were composed.

'But though this is plainly the meaning of the incident from the standpoint of the Evangelist,* as it is its spiritual meaning for us to-day, there are great difficulties about it if it is taken as a record of history precisely as it stands' (R., p. 24).

In its present form the story clearly contains artificial elements. The scribes do not voice their feelings; Jesus is represented as discerning them by supernatural insight, but how was St Mark able to formulate them so precisely? Clearly they are in fact *representative* Jewish reactions to the Christian claim that sin could be forgiven by, and in the name of, Jesus.

More important, the behaviour of Jesus himself raises questions; are we to suppose that, but for the scribes and their criticism, he would not have healed the paralytic? The suggestion that the healing was performed not for the sake of the sufferer, but purely for its evidential value, conflicts with what we learn of Jesus' attitude elsewhere, especially the refusal of just such 'signs' as this at $8^{11\text{ff.}}$.

Similarly with the title *Son of man*, Jesus is not elsewhere in the Gospel represented as openly claiming this status and the right to act in virtue of it – indeed, apart from one dubious exception in Luke ($7^{36\text{ff.}}$), he is not elsewhere represented as claiming the power of forgiving sins by his own *fiat*. Constantly he urges men to repent in order that *God* may forgive them, or, more specifically, he demands that their repentance shall take the form of forgiving their brothers in order that God may forgive them. And if the story implies† that Jesus shared the current belief that illness is caused by, and proportionate to, the sufferer's sin, this would appear to conflict with such passages as Luke 13^{1-5} and John $9^{2\text{f.}}$. Finally it should be noticed that in v. 12 the scribes are not mentioned and no hint is given whether they were convinced by Jesus' demonstration; what is described seems more like the normal reaction to a simple healing (cf. e.g. 1^{27}).

The explanation of these facts given by most commentators is that the story originally consisted only of vv. 1–5a and 11–12 (or perhaps 1–5 and 11b–12), which give a perfectly coherent and straightforward account of the healing of a paralytic (and the forgiveness of his sins),

* And also, no doubt, that of the Church before him.

† It is by no means obviously clear that it does, though this is often assumed.

the vivid detail in vv. 3–4 strongly suggesting an actual incident. As it was discovered that the claim to forgiveness of sins through Jesus caused so much offence to the Jews, the middle verses got added to the story to show that the claim was not blasphemous because of Jesus' messianic status and eschatological significance. It is impossible now to discover the origin of these verses or the details of the process by which they came to be added,* but the passage provides an excellent example of how a story might be moulded and developed during the stage of oral tradition in the interests of instruction and apologetics.

1

after some days: There is clearly a pronounced break between this verse and 1^{45}. There Jesus, having left Capernaum, was unable to enter cities openly; now he is back in Capernaum once more.

2

preaching the word: A well-known expression in the early Church for preaching the good news, the gospel (see on 1^{14} and cf. Acts 11^{19}, $4^{29, 31}$, 8^{25}, 15^{36}). Once again the content of Jesus' word is not more closely specified.

4

No doubt they got on to the the roof by the outside staircase such as Palestinian houses often had. It is just possible that the Greek words translated *removed the roof* are a mistranslation of an Aramaic phrase which really meant 'they brought him up to the roof'. If so, the picturesque detail about making an opening may be an addition inspired by the false rendering of the Aramaic original. More probably the reference is to making a hole in the wattle and daub of which a Palestinian roof would have been built. Mark's expression (lit. 'unroofed the roof') suggests that *he* was thinking rather of the tiled roof customary at Rome.

pallet: The correct rendering of the original; it was the poor man's bed and could fairly easily be carried, which helps to explain v. 12a.

5

On *faith* see pp. 158 and 244, and notice it is the friends' faith as well as the man's own that Jesus takes into account.

* Possibly the early Church was in the habit of justifying its claim to absolve sin by reference to the power it claimed to have to work miracles, and that had some effect on the story.

son: A term of endearment. *Your sins* . . . Jesus' words need not be any more than an authoritative declaration that the man's sins had been forgiven *by God* (cf. 2 Sam. 12^{13}) and perhaps that was their meaning in the original form of the story. In view of v. 10 St Mark clearly gave them a fuller meaning; he was perhaps influenced by the sense in which he and his fellow Christians experienced forgiveness 'through', 'in the name of', Jesus Christ. The distinction is, in any case, a fine one, for prophetic words and actions were often thought to bring about what they proclaimed.*

7
It is sometimes thought that, according to the scribes, God himself could not, and does not, forgive sin from free grace, but requires every sin to be either expiated by sacrifice or paid for by good works. This is a serious misunderstanding, as is the notion that they held that a sinner could not be forgiven by God until he had achieved merit by works of the Law.† Their sole ground of opposition to Jesus here was his claiming for himself what they rightly regarded as the sole prerogative of God.

9
easier: For the rather artificial sense in which this seems to be used here see above; Jesus took sin so seriously that it is perhaps rather surprising to find him describing its forgiveness as 'easier' than healing. Perhaps this is a further indication that these verses are a later addition to the story. Some scholars indeed have taken him to be assuming that healing is the easier, but then it is difficult to follow the logic of the passage.

10
Son of man: For the meaning of this phrase to Mark and the early Christians see Introduction, pp. 46–7, where it is explained that the words were a literal translation of an Aramaic original which could mean simply 'man' (cf. the Irish 'mother's son' in the expression 'every mother's son of them'). It has accordingly been suggested that in the original Aramaic here Jesus was making no special claim for himself but was simply teaching that man on earth (as well as God in heaven) can forgive sins; cf. Matthew 9^{8} (*such authority to men*) and note that a similar interpretation is possible at Mark 2^{28}. If it is followed in both passages, Jesus in Mark avoids using the phrase 'Son of man' in its technical 'messianic' sense until after his recognition by his disciples at Caesarea Philippi ($8^{27ff.}$) and we thus get a coherent development.

* There is a useful detached note on the matter in V.T., pp. 200–1.

† Cf. I. Abrahams, *Studies in Pharisaism and the Gospels*, I, Chapters XIX and XX.

This suggestion is linguistically possible, but:

(i) Mark certainly understood the phrase here in its full messianic sense.

(ii) He, therefore, did not share the modern theory that Jesus only used the expression messianically after Caesarea Philippi.

(iii) The doctrine that men as such have the right to forgive sins would have been an odd one for Jesus to teach, and is without parallel in Jewish or subsequent Christian teaching.*

on earth: The scribes, we have seen, were fully persuaded of God's ability and willingness to forgive, but for them forgiveness must await the future judgement. It was distinctive of Christianity that it proclaimed the possibility of forgiveness as a present reality here 'on earth'.

he said to the paralytic: As the story stands, these words are a sort of stage direction, presumably represented in fact by some gesture. But they are undoubtedly awkward and some see this as the point of junction between the additional material and the original story.

12
The man's action and the reaction of the onlookers demonstrate the reality and completeness of the cure; there are some close parallels in contemporary pagan stories of healing, e.g. Lucian, *Philopseudes* 11: 'Midas himself, taking up the bed on which he had been lying, went off into the country.'

2^{13-17} JESUS' RELATIONS WITH THE OUTCAST

13*He went out again beside the sea; and all the crowd gathered about him,*
and he taught them. 14*And as he passed on, he saw Levi the son of Alphaeus*
sitting at the tax office, and he said to him, 'Follow me.' And he rose and
followed him.
15*And as he sat at table in his house, many tax collectors and sinners were*
sitting with Jesus and his disciples; for there were many who followed him.
16*And the scribes of*[a] *the Pharisees, when they saw that he was eating with*
sinners and tax collectors, said to his disciples, 'Why does he eat[b] *with tax*

* Moreover it is hard to see how Jesus' working of a miracle would demonstrate such a *general* human power of forgiveness.

collectors and sinners?' [17]*And when Jesus heard it, he said to them, 'Those who are well have no need of a physician, but those who are sick; I came not to call the righteous, but sinners.'*

a Other ancient authorities read *and*
b Other ancient authorities add *and drink*

This section consists of two short narratives, combined (perhaps by St Mark himself) because both are concerned with the same subject, Jesus' friendly relations with moral and religious outcasts. The first story tells, in terms very reminiscent of the calling of the four (1^{16-20}),* of the calling of Levi. Again there is no reference to Levi's motives, or to his having had any previous acquaintance with Jesus; the emphasis falls on the power of Jesus' call, which, being the word of God, constrains men to obey it.

But this time the man called was a customs official and, as such, not regarded by the Jewish religious authorities as fit company for anyone who took seriously the will and demands of God (see below). So it was very remarkable to them that Jesus should go out of his way to include such a man in his circle, and when in the second narrative he sat at table with a number of similar people, their surprise could no longer be contained; for in the ancient world table-fellowship was regarded as a sign and pledge of real intimacy.

The true character of the scribes' reaction should be noticed. Their motive for avoiding close contact with such as Levi was twofold:

(i) To eat in their homes might entail the consumption of food on which tithes had not been paid or which had been improperly killed, prepared, or served. It would probably involve also personal defilement through contact with garments, dishes, or furniture that were unclean.

(ii) In the second place, association with such people might lead one to adopt their manner of life.

It is easy to criticize such an attitude on the grounds that it is excessively concerned with morally insignificant details. But the scribes could point, not without justification, to the Old Testament, where it was revealed:

* 'The same vicinity, the sea-shore, Levi engaged at his professional work, the sudden leaving, and the entertainment in his house' (J. Weiss).

(*a*) that God demands unconditional obedience to his commands, and

(*b*) that those commands include tithing, ritual cleanliness, and the rest.

Who then were they to disregard as 'morally insignificant' what God expressly demanded? They might welcome back repentant sinners, and even take steps to bring sinners to repentance,* but they felt, not altogether illogically, that those steps could never be such as to involve them themselves in contravention of God's expressly declared will. How then could one who claimed to be the very agent of God's will keep company which he must have known was constantly involving him in the contravention of that will?

The question is addressed to the disciples; the reply, which comes direct from Jesus, takes the form of a well-known proverb about a doctor and his patients. Its bearing in the present context seems to be: it would be wrong for a doctor to keep company exclusively with healthy people, for then he could not do his job, which is to bring health to the sick. Likewise the Messiah ought not to keep exclusively righteous company, for his work is to 'invite' sinners, i.e. to see that they get into the (Messianic) Banquet, a common metaphor for the kingdom of God; this he could not do unless he consorted with them.

Mark does not record the scribes' response,† which is a pity, because Jesus' reply as given by Mark, thought-provoking and profound as it is, does not really answer their question. What it does is to show why it was God's will that Jesus should consort with sinners, but it does not deal with the discrepancy between the will of God for Jesus and his general command, expressed in the Old Testament, that the righteous should *not* consort with people who were liable to be a source of impurity. Did Jesus intend to supersede the Old Testament

* Though even their strongest defenders are prepared to admit that they did not always do quite as much in the latter direction as they might have done; cf. e.g. Abrahams, *Studies in Pharisaism and the Gospels*, I, 58: 'There was in the Pharisaism of all ages a real anxiety to make the return of the sinner easy, though it was inclined to leave the initiative to the sinner, except that it always maintained God's readiness to take the first step.' Montefiore goes further and admits that there was something really new and original in Our Lord's attitude: 'He did not avoid sinners but sought them out.'

† No doubt, in the light of such passages as 3^6, he thought it was one of wilful refusal to understand and accept.

at this point or did he imply that on this matter the Old Testament did not express the real will of God? (In the latter case cf. 10^5 and context, where he says this explicitly about another matter.)

It has been customary to accept one or other of these interpretations and to regard Jesus as here introducing a new moral principle into human behaviour. Thus Harnack regarded the words as 'one of the greatest landmarks' in the history of morality and religion, and the Jewish scholar Montefiore wrote: '*He did not avoid sinners, but sought them out.* They were still children of God. This was a new and sublime contribution to the development of religion and morality. When tenderly nurtured women work in the streets of London, and seek to rescue the degraded victims of deception or cruelty, they are truly following in the footsteps of their Master' (I, 55; the italics are his).

But in so far as these views treat Jesus simply as a purveyor of new moral principles, however sublime, they do not do full justice to Mark's point. For St Mark, Jesus' exceptional conduct at this point rests not on some new general principle, but *on his unique status as Messiah.* A divine figure who had power to remit sin need not fear the contagion of human sinfulness. And in any case his 'coming' (v. 17) introduced a completely new situation which set a question-mark against the whole Old Testament dispensation. If Jesus' disciples are justified in following his example in this matter,* that is simply because they live in the new situation he has introduced and partake of his messianic power. It was this that the scribes failed to see; once again their basic error in Mark's eyes was failure to recognize the true – messianic – identity of him with whom they were dealing.†

* In Mark's day this was still questioned in some Christian circles.

† Cf. J. M. Robinson, *The Problem of History in Mark*, p. 46. 'The illustration of the doctor is not left as a general principle but rather is focused on the (messianic) coming.' Perhaps the point can be clarified by extending the medical metaphor a little. If a person is suffering from a dangerous infectious disease, the *general* rule is that other people ought to avoid contact. But when the doctor 'comes' to deal with the situation it is right for him to consort with the patient; indeed he must, in order to do the job for which he 'came'. The same is true of the nurses he sends, who share to some extent in his status and in his knack of keeping immune from infection. But the doctor and, to a lesser extent, the nurses are exceptional people, and *no doubt is cast on the wisdom of the general rule.* This analogy must not be overpressed, but if the doctor is

This story, like the last, is not without its difficulties; some of these are discussed in the notes below, but the most important arises in connexion with the second half of v. 17. In the first half of the verse the reference to '*those who are well*', while not vital to the sense, is fully understandable as pointing the contrast between sick and healthy; but when the metaphor is explained in 17b we are told outright that Jesus did not come to call people who are righteous. Why not? Because they did not need calling? Or did Jesus use the word *righteous* ironically, meaning 'self-righteous', righteous in the external sense of the Pharisees? The latter is unlikely, but even if it were right, why should they remain outside the scope of his call? We are told by many commentators that we should not raise such questions; as in 17a, the words serve simply to point the contrast, and were not meant to be pressed, any more than similar expressions in e.g. Luke 15^{7}.

It may be so, but it is at least a plausible suggestion that the words are in fact a comment of the early Church referred back to the life of Jesus; the early Christians were all very conscious of themselves as saved sinners, and saved, most of them, not from among the ranks of the scribes and Pharisees, but from among the lower, 'sinful' ranks of Jewish society (cf. e.g. 1 Cor. 1^{26-28}). In retrospect it was indeed true that the saving call of Jesus had been to sinners and not to the *righteous* in the community.

And if this half verse *is* secondary, that, taken with the difficulties discussed below, gives some support to the view of those who hold that v. 17a was orally preserved in the Church without a context, and that Mark – or the Church before him – provided 15, 16, and 17b out of the known habits of Jesus as a – not completely suitable – context for it.*

ꕤ

* Even if these verses are secondary, the impression they convey is certainly accurate. On all the evidence, if one thing is more certain than another about Jesus, it is that he was the friend of tax gatherers and sinners and frequently in their company.

---

taken to represent Jesus and the nurses the followers of Jesus, it may help to illuminate the difference, at least in emphasis, between Mark and the modern scholars referred to above. Of course Mark hoped that in time all men would become followers of Jesus – nurses, in terms of the analogy, who share the doctor's immunity.

13
again: The Greek word is here probably just resumptive – 'on another occasion' 'some time later'; Mark makes no attempt to link this section chronologically to the preceding one. The content of the teaching is again unspecified.

14
Levi: Not one of the twelve, and some have wondered why Mark, who records only five 'callings' in all, should include the call of one who was not an apostle. James, one of the twelve, was 'the son of Alphaeus', and so presumably Levi's brother, though of that again Mark makes no mention. Matthew (9^9) identifies Levi with Matthew (one of the twelve) presumably on the ground that he too was a tax collector (Matt. 10^3) and some early copyists of Mark identified him with James (as being son of Alphaeus) and altered Levi to James in this verse. Mark gives no hint of making either identification; possibly the original readers knew who Levi was and why Mark singled out his call for description.

Whoever he was, he will have been a customs officer in the service of Herod Antipas and so not quite a tax collector in the ordinary sense (see below); but no doubt the Jewish authorities would have seen little difference.

15
If this story once circulated independently of the preceding one, the meaning will originally have been that Jesus was the host in *his* house. Probably, however, Mark understood that the meal was in Levi's house and he was the host.

sat at table . . . sitting: Strictly, 'reclining' – the posture the ancients often adopted at feasts.

tax collectors: The traditional English translation, 'publicans', is from the Latin *publicani*, but that word referred in fact to the contractors who farmed out the public taxes under the empire. The people referred to in the Gospels were the very subordinate officials who actually collected the taxes and dues. Such people had a bad reputation everywhere at the time for their dishonesty and petty extortion (cf. the pagan writer Lucian, who in *Nekyom* 11 couples them with 'adulterers and panders, flatterers and sycophants'). In Jewish eyes they had the additional faults of serving heathen masters and mixing with (unclean) non-Jews of all sorts; it was virtually impossible for such people to keep the Law strictly after the manner of the Pharisees.

By *sinners* Mark probably means exactly what he says. But there is the difficulty that 'sinner' is too broad a word to designate a class such as seems to be envisaged here and in v. 16 (lit. '*the* sinners'). It has been suggested therefore that it may be Mark's way of referring to 'the people of the land', those Jews who had not the opportunity or inclination to study the Law and carry it out in detail as the Pharisees did. The Pharisees always shunned the company of such people – cf. John 7^{49}. If, however, these verses are secondary, the word 'sinners' may well have been used in its general sense to prepare for the accusation of the scribes in v. 16.

for there were many who followed him: Lit. 'they were many and they followed him': an awkward parenthesis, but quite in Mark's style; it probably refers to the disciples and the meaning is: 'for there were [now] many [disciples] who followed Jesus'. The four of Chapter 1^{16-20} have now grown into a sizeable number of disciples.

16

the scribes of the Pharisees gives rise to a number of difficulties. The phrase itself is an odd one presumably meaning 'scribes belonging to the Pharisaic party'. How came they to be in Galilee in such numbers? And what is more, how came they to be present at a meal in a sinner's house so that they could 'see' Jesus partaking of it?* These questions may perhaps best be answered (see above) if the scene is an ideal one, a formulation in terms of a single incident of a general charge brought by the Pharisees against the followers of Jesus.

The name *Pharisee*, which seems to date from about 120 B.C., is generally taken to mean 'those who are separated', i.e. from defilement and irreligion, and those who took no pains to avoid them. The Pharisees were probably the successors of the *hasidim* who in the second century B.C. resisted attempts on the part of many Jews to come to terms with pagan culture. They were not in any sense a priestly caste, though they seem to have banded together in fraternities for the purpose of keeping the Law more strictly and promoting their interpretation of the Old Testament, which was incorporated in a series of oral traditions regarded by the Pharisees as no less binding than the Old Testament Law itself. Many of them were men of the highest principles and integrity, and they frequently championed the cause of the ordinary people and those in need of protection against oppression (see Josephus, *Antiquities*, XIII, 10, 6 and XVIII, 1, 3 and, for a vivid account of the Pharisees, E. Bevan, *Jerusalem under the High Priests*; also *Beginnings of Christianity*, I.

* It is of course possible to take 'see' in the general sense of 'getting to know' and to assume that the question was asked later. But that is hardly St Mark's understanding of the matter.

2^{18-22} A CONFLICT OVER FASTING

[18]*Now John's disciples and the Pharisees were fasting; and people came
and said to him, 'Why do John's disciples and the disciples of the Pharisees
fast, but your disciples do not fast?'* [19]*And Jesus said to them, 'Can the
wedding guests fast while the bridegroom is with them? As long as they have
the bridegroom with them, they cannot fast.* [20]*The days will come, when the
bridegroom is taken away from them, and then they will fast in that day.*
[21]*No one sews a piece of unshrunk cloth on an old garment; if he does, the
patch tears away from it, the new from the old, and a worse tear is made.*
[22]*And no one puts new wine into old wineskins; if he does, the wine will
burst the skins, and the wine is lost, and so are the skins; but new wine is for
fresh skins.'*[a]

a Other ancient authorities omit *but new wine is for fresh skins*

The third conflict story, like the previous one, comprises two pericopae which have been combined on account of their common subject-matter. This time the question arises because pious Jews were observing a fast and the disciples of Jesus did not join them, as they (and their Master) might have been expected to do if they were really concerned for the kingdom of God.

The reply of Jesus takes the form of an analogy, or short parable. Wedding guests do not fast during the wedding celebrations. For a wedding is essentially a time for rejoicing, and during the festivities the guests, according to Jewish custom, are exempted from certain religious duties precisely for that reason. Likewise, Jesus means, his coming, and the news he brings of the kingdom of God, are the supreme occasion for rejoicing (cf. p. 55). Fasting may have been suitable as a means of preparing oneself for the kingdom and hastening its coming, but now that it is actually dawning, fasting and mourning are as out of place as they would be at a wedding. Once again the issue turns not on the abstract desirability of some principle or practice, but on the identity of Jesus, and the eschatological character of his coming; it is *this* the questioners have failed to discern.

However, Jesus will only be with his disciples continuously when the kingdom has come in its fullness (cf. 9^1), and they will have occasion enough for mourning in the period of waiting, after his withdrawal. But even then theirs will be a new and eschatological fasting, quite different in character and motives from that which was appropriate before the new age dawned. For the fact is that the state of affairs he has inaugurated is quite different from what went before, and the conduct appropriate to it is as incompatible with the practices of Judaism as a new patch with an old garment or new wine with old wineskins.

It must have been along some such lines that St Mark understood the passage, but it has often been noticed that the reference to Christians fasting in v. 20 seems to break the logic of the argument, which is that Jesus has introduced a new situation to which fasting and mourning are wholly inappropriate (cf. e.g. Matt. 8^{11}, $22^{2\text{ff.}}$, 25^{10}; the kingdom of God is often likened to a feast). It has also been noticed that whereas v. 19 presents a straightforward picture (fasting and wedding celebrations *are* incompatible), the addition in v. 20 spoils the verisimilitude (the bridegroom is not normally *taken away* from the guests, and when he does go, it is no special cause for mourning and fasting). What we have in fact in v. 20 is a thinly veiled allegory of the death of Jesus and the subsequent condition of the Christian Church. That in itself, as V. T. points out, does not necessarily impugn the authenticity of the words;* but in this case, even if the marriage analogy was so widely used by the Jews with reference to the kingdom of God that bridegroom = Messiah would have been immediately understood (see below), it seems doubtful if Jesus' opponents would have known at that stage in the ministry what he meant by the 'taking away' of the Messiah. Moreover, if Jesus spoke these words, he was presumably interesting himself in the detailed practice of the Church after his death, and that, so far as we can tell, would have been very uncharacteristic of him. Accordingly, most commentators regard v. 20 as an addition by the Church (before Mark's time) designed to justify the resumption of the habit of regular fasting which Jesus and his immediate circle had abandoned. Some of these commentators reject 19b also, as being a reformulation of 19a designed to lead on to v. 20.

* A. Jülicher in his great book on the parables, *Die Gleichnisreden Jesu*, went practically so far as to say that the original parables contained no allegory at all. Though that is an exaggeration, there is enough truth in it for the presence of allegory to put us on our guard about a parable (see below on Chapter 4).

For the reasons for thinking that vv. 20 and 21 were originally independent of vv. 18–20 and had a somewhat different reference, see notes below.

ꙮ

18
It is generally agreed by commentators for a number of reasons that both references to the Pharisees were added when the incident came to be treated as one of the conflicts between Jesus and the Jewish authorities. The introductory sentence may simply be a deduction from the story itself; in any case no connexion is established with what went before in either time or place.

19
wedding guests: Probably the correct translation, though the phrase might mean 'groomsmen', young men who attended the bridegroom rather as the bridesmaids attended the bride.

the bridegroom: In v. 20, as we have seen, this almost certainly stands allegorically for Jesus himself. Does it do the same in v. 19a, if 19b and 20 be regarded as secondary? J. Jeremias* has argued strongly that it does, and many commentators agree with him. In the Old Testament, marriage is several times used as a figure for the true relationship between God and his people; and the eschatological act by which God will finally secure that relationship is sometimes described in terms of marrying, or restoring a broken marriage; cf. especially Hos. 2^{16-20}, Isa. 54^{5-6} and 62^{4-5}. There is also evidence that, in the light of such passages, rabbis sometimes used the metaphor of a wedding in connexion with the coming of Messiah; and certainly the early Christians used the marriage relationship to describe the relation between Christ and the Church (cf. Eph. 5^{22-33}, Rev. 19^{7}ff., 21^{9}, 2 Cor. 11^{2}). So it may be that by choosing this particular illustration Jesus intended to allude to himself, at least covertly, as the Messiah. Yet the evidence for the bridegroom = Messiah equation is not quite strong enough for us to suppose that Jesus could simply speak of a bridegroom and expect his audience to understand it messianically without any word of explanation. And we cannot rule out the possibility that the original saying contained no reference to a bridegroom; it would have been more natural perhaps to say: 'can the wedding guests fast while the celebrations are still on?' and that wording might have been changed to the present wording in order to facilitate the transition to vv. 19b and 20.

* In his book *Jesus als Weltvollender*, pp. 21–5; see also V. Taylor, *The Names of Jesus*, pp. 87ff.

So it is safest to take the words as a general reference to a wedding as an occasion of joy, at which, as at the coming of the kingdom, mourning and fasting would be utterly out of place.

20–21
The general bearing of these verses in the position here assigned to them has already been suggested; cf. R., p. 32: 'It had proved impossible for the Christian Church – or, at least, for the Gentile-Christian Church – to express its religious life through the ancient forms of Judaism. . . . The new wine had burst the old wine-skins; the new patch had destroyed the old garment.' But as they stand, the words appear to be at least as much concerned with the preservation of the old as with the welfare of the new. Moreover, if Jesus had spoken them in this context he would have been displaying a very radical attitude towards the practices of Judaism, whereas he seems in fact to have been distinctly conservative with regard to them (cf. e.g. 7^{8}ff., Matt. 5^{17}ff. // Luke 16^{17}). So the further comment of R. seems justified: 'The sayings in themselves are little parables about the relation between old and new. We do not know – and it is idle to guess – in what context they were originally spoken.'*

Wine-skins grew brittle in time and fresh grape juice, as it fermented, would easily burst them. How exactly a new patch tears a garment is not quite so obvious; presumably by shrinking and pulling the surrounding threads.† But Luke (5^{36}) thought the idea was that to get the new patch it would be necessary to cut it out of a new garment and so ruin that!

* It should, however, be noted that Professor Jeremias, in the passage referred to above, argues for the unity of the whole section as a single utterance of Jesus, who often gave his sayings a threefold form. He thinks that just as the figure of the bridegroom stands for the Messiah, the garment stands for the Universe which Jesus has come not to patch up but to re-create completely, and the wine stands, as often, for a banquet – the final Messianic Banquet which is utterly beyond, and incompatible with, even the highest in this 'old' worldly order. This should be considered in the light of what was said on p. 102 n.

† The Greek word translated 'new' meant strictly 'untreated', 'unbleached', 'unshrunken', though it was sometimes used, in reference to cloth, simply to mean 'new'. However, it is said that even a patch of new (but already treated) cloth is so strong that it pulls the surrounding threads and makes a worse hole.

2^{23-28} JESUS AND THE BREAKING OF THE LAW

[23]*One sabbath he was going through the grainfields; and as they made*
their way his disciples began to pluck ears of grain. [24]*And the Pharisees said*
to him, 'Look, why are they doing what is not lawful on the sabbath?' [25] *And*
he said to them, 'Have you never read what David did, when he was in
need and was hungry, he and those who were with him: [26]*how he entered*
the house of God, when Abi'athar was high priest, and ate the bread of the
Presence, which it is not lawful for any but the priests to eat, and also gave
it to those who were with him?' [27]*And he said to them, 'The sabbath was*
made for man, not man for the sabbath; [28]*so the Son of man is lord even*
of the sabbath.'

Like the previous stories in the conflict section, this one is told without any precise statement of time or place, and like them it seems to consist of two (or possibly three) originally independent units bound together by unity of subject – this time failure to keep the regulations governing the observance of the sabbath.

One sabbath the disciples of Jesus as they passed through some cornfields began to pluck the ripe grain and eat it. In normal circumstances the Law allowed the hungry traveller to help himself in this way (Deut. 23^{25}) but to do it on the sabbath was tantamount, in the eyes of the scribes, to reaping; and reaping was one of the thirty-nine key activities traditionally forbidden on the sabbath (cf. Exod. 34^{21}). So a complaint was lodged with Jesus.

This time his reply took the form of an argument deduced from the Old Testament very much in the manner of the rabbis themselves. King David, despite his lapses, was regarded as the very model of piety; yet even he, when pressed by hunger and hardship, had frequently transgressed the Law, for both himself and his followers, thus demonstrating that in exceptional cases the Law might rightly be regarded as subordinate to human needs. The Law was for man's good, and if the good of man was really furthered by violating it, then a lower law was broken in order to keep a higher. (In the case of David, and presumably in that of the disciples of Jesus, the higher law was that of men's necessary bodily needs.) The rabbis themselves,

Jesus reminds them, recognized this principle, for were they not in the habit of telling the people: 'The sabbath is delivered unto you and you are not delivered to the sabbath'?*

So far this conflict has differed from the previous ones in that here the argument is a general one about the right way of understanding the Law, and does not turn upon the special, eschatological status of Jesus. The dispute up to this point might have occurred between any two rabbis, and no doubt many of the more liberal rabbis of the time would very largely have agreed with Jesus. But in the last verse Jesus claims – or Mark claims for him, it is not clear which – that it is in virtue of his eschatological status as Son of man that he is 'Lord of the sabbath' and so can dispense his disciples. This statement brings the section formally into line with the previous conflict stories, and no doubt it was on the basis of it that the early (gentile) Christians felt justified in ceasing to observe the sabbath and observing Sunday ('the Lord's day', e.g. Rev. 1^{10}) instead.

There is, however, the difficulty that v. 28 does not really seem to fit with the rest of the section. According to it the disciples of Jesus are justified simply because they *are* disciples of Jesus, and he has a special status; according to the earlier verses, it is *special need* which justifies such breaches of the Law, and it justifies them whenever anyone is in need, quite apart from any connexion with Jesus and his coming (David was not a disciple of Jesus). Moreover v. 28 does not in strict logic follow from v. 27; if the sabbath is subordinate to the needs of *men in general*, as v. 27 says, why should it need the eschatological Son of man to be Lord of the sabbath? Probably, therefore, with the majority of commentators, we should regard v. 28 as a Christian comment – probably added before Mark's time – 'expressing the conviction that Jesus is Lord of all that belongs to man, including the Sabbath' (V. T.);† v. 27 would then go quite naturally with what precedes, serving to make explicit the principle implied in the action of David. However, the introductory words *And he said*

* This appears to have been a rabbinical commonplace; it is ascribed in different contexts to two different rabbis. Presumably the words of Jesus in v. 27 are meant as a variant of it.

† Certainly Jesus does not elsewhere claim in so many words to abrogate the Law in virtue of his messianic status. Such a claim would be quite incompatible with his secrecy about his Messiahship, but the messianic secret, as we have seen (p. 89), is conspicuously absent from the conflicts section 2^{1}–3^{6}.

to them show that it was originally an independent saying,* and the fact that it is omitted by Matthew // and Luke // and also by some important MSS. of Mark has led some commentators to think that it was inserted later as a well-known saying relevant to Our Lord's argument.

❧

24
It is idle to ask what *the Pharisees* were doing in the middle of a cornfield on a sabbath day; the process of oral tradition has formalized the stories, hence the considerable element of truth in the comment: 'Scribes or Pharisees appear and disappear just as the compiler requires them. They are part of the stage-property and scenery, like "the house" and "the mountain"' (cf. Bundy, p. 183).

25
Have you never read ... ? 'This use of the counter question with an appeal to the scriptures is characteristic of rabbinical arguments' (V. T.) cf. $12^{10, 26}$. The argument here rests on a similarity between the action of the disciples and an action of David; both broke a commandment of the Law (though not the same commandment) and both did it under the compulsion of hunger (though this is not explicitly stated in the case of the disciples). The similarity is admittedly not very close, and some commentators have sought a closer connexion; Jesus as Messiah was son of David, and so David and his men corresponded to Jesus and his disciples.† But R. and V. T. agree – rightly – that it is over-subtle to find such a veiled messianic claim here.‡

25–26
A close comparison of these verses with 1 Sam. $21^{1ff.}$ will reveal several discrepancies in detail. In so far as these are not simply due to the condensing of the original narrative, they probably arise from its being quoted from memory; or possibly there were still current variant

* This phrase is used in Mark's Gospel to link together independent sayings; cf. 4^{11-13}, 7^{8}, 9^{1}.

† Matthew and Luke, as we have seen, omit v. 27 and pass straight from the story of David to the saying about the Son of man being Lord of the sabbath; it is quite possible therefore that they *did* see a messianic connexion.

‡ David's breach of the Law was so flagrant that it was notorious and had been much discussed by the rabbis, which may help to explain why it came to mind here when it was not conspicuously *à propos*. It was quite in the manner of the rabbis to use an argument of this kind, especially as, according to the *Midrash* on 1 Sam. 21, David's action was also performed on a sabbath.

traditions of the event besides that in 1 Sam. 21. It seems over-subtle to see doctrinal motives behind these changes – e.g. the belief that David's action prefigured the eucharistic giving of bread by the Messiah (Riesenfeld). Most notable among the differences, but to be explained like the others, is that 1 Samuel gives Ahimelech, and not his son Abiathar, as high priest at the time of the incident. For *the bread of the Presence* see Exod. 25^{30} and Lev. 24^{5-9}, with commentaries.

27–28

In v. 28, as in 2^{10}, it has been suggested that Son of man is a mistranslation of an Aramaic original meaning simply 'man'. This would certainly mend the logic of the argument, but it would be a very remarkable statement that 'man is Lord of the sabbath', and if the Aramaic is mistranslated in v. 28 why not in v. 27? See also notes on 2^{10}. Conversely Professor T. W. Manson has suggested that originally 'Son of man' stood in both vv. 27 and 28. But the view suggested above (p. 106) seems preferable.

3^{1-6} A FURTHER DISPUTE ABOUT THE SABBATH

3 *Again he entered the synagogue, and a man was there who had a*
withered hand. 2*And they watched him, to see whether he would heal him*
on the sabbath, so that they might accuse him. 3*And he said to the man who*
had the withered hand, 'Come here.' 4*And he said to them, 'Is it lawful on*
the sabbath to do good or to do harm, to save life or to kill?' But they
were silent. 5*And he looked around at them with anger, grieved at their*
hardness of heart, and said to the man, 'Stretch out your hand.' He stretched
it out, and his hand was restored. 6*The Pharisees went out, and immediately*
held counsel with the Hero'di-ans against him, how to destroy him.

In this fifth conflict story, the last of the series, it is taken for granted by everyone that Jesus has the power to perform miracles of healing; the one question is whether he will exercise his power on the sabbath and so give ground for an official accusation, for healing was technically work and, as such, an infringement of God's sabbath law. Jesus unhesitatingly performs the miracle, but the words in which he defends his action (v. 4) raise certain problems of interpretation. Is Jesus implicitly contrasting his own act of healing – which is 'doing good' and 'saving life' – with the hostile activity of his opponents who are trying to 'do harm' to him and to 'kill' him (cf. v. 6)? If so, the sense is: 'If *I* am working on the sabbath, it is at least in the interest of life and health – you who accuse me are yourselves working on the sabbath, working against me, working for death and destruction.' This interpretation is in some ways attractive, but it involves reading a good deal into the text of v. 4; and if it is correct, the argument is purely *ad hominem* and Jesus offers no real justification for his breach of the sabbath law.

So it is perhaps preferable to take the words as expressing a general principle: 'On the sabbath day should one not rather do good than evil, rather save a life than kill it?' To heal is regarded as an instance of doing good, and not to heal is equivalent to doing evil, for if the life is not saved, it is killed. The difficulty about this is that the man with the withered hand was in no danger of death; there was no question of saving or destroying life; if there had been, the rabbis themselves would have been completely at one with Jesus, for they were quite clear that the sabbath law might and must be broken in cases of danger to life. But Jesus seems to extend this principle so as to make it justify healing work of all kinds – and indeed all other kinds of benevolent work – on the sabbath. If that was his meaning, the effect would have been to supersede the sabbath law entirely, for the prohibition on sabbath work would become simply a prohibition of evil and life-destroying activity on the sabbath, and that is forbidden on any day.

However, in the light of $2^{23\text{ff.}}$ and of the sayings quoted in Matt. 12^{11-12}, Luke $13^{15\text{f.}}$ and 14^{5}, it seems more probable that what Jesus in fact defended was an *occasional* breach of the sabbath law in the face of some special need, just as the rabbis themselves were prepared to do at any rate the minimum of work required to save a sheep or an ox that had got into difficulties on the sabbath. But in what way did the man with the withered hand constitute such a special need? Could he not perfectly well have waited till the morrow? It has been suggested that in this, and similar cases, Jesus felt a need for haste because of his belief that he was engaged in God's final battle against the forces of evil and 'the king's business required haste'; '. . . the work of the kingdom of God in the mind of Jesus . . . is a warfare against the power of Satan. Every healing is a blow struck against the supreme enemy of the kingdom of God. . . . Evil works seven days a week. And the warfare against Satan must go on on the Sabbath as well as on the other six days'. (*S. J.*, p. 190; see the whole of Manson's Additional Note: *Jesus and the Sabbath Laws.*) If this is right, it will be seen that once again the real issue is the failure of Jesus' opponents to realize that his coming has inaugurated a new situation so urgent and unprecedented that the laws applicable in the 'old age' are no longer always binding.

Verse 6 is clearly meant as a conclusion not only to this story, but to the whole series of conflicts. Even so, St Mark can hardly have intended to say that the authorities seriously began to work for Jesus' death almost at the beginning of his ministry, simply on the grounds of these five disputes. 'Jesus has said or done nothing which, in Jewish justice, would result in a plot to destroy him. In the series he appears perhaps as a nonconformist and non-sectarian but he is still Jewish' (Bundy, p. 181). The point is rather that these conflicts are typical of the grounds on which eventually the religious and secular authorities combined to destroy Jesus. We have seen that throughout these conflicts their opposition rested on a fundamental misunderstanding – an inability, or refusal, to see that Jesus was God's eschatological agent and that his sovereign freedom with regard to law and custom sprang from that fact. Mark wants to make clear that it was precisely this which underlay *all* their opposition to Jesus and their ultimate attempt to destroy him; and no doubt that is why in v. 5 this *hardness of heart* on their part is so much emphasized as being a source of anger and grief to Jesus.

ꙮ

1

again: The sense is: 'On another occasion when he went to the synagogue . . .' *Again* is not meant to refer back to 1^{21} but to suggest that Jesus regularly went to the synagogue – and so could not be accused of wantonly disobeying Jewish law and custom.

3

come here: The Greek means literally: 'Arise into the midst' – a terse way of saying: 'Stand up and come where everyone can see you.'

4

but they were silent – because they had nothing to say; when the principles on which Jesus acts are clearly stated they are seen to be so self-evidently right that no rational opposition is any longer possible. Of course men can still oppose Jesus, but that is because, in their sin, they refuse to recognize the truth.

5

It is just such refusal which is meant by the phrase *hardness of heart*. To the ancients the *heart* (*cardia*) was the seat of understanding, and although the other Greek word (*pōrōsis*) originally meant *hardness*, its meaning in the New Testament is 'obtuseness' or 'intellectual blindness'. See on Rom. 11^{25} and the note by J. A. Robinson, *St Paul's Epistle to the Ephesians*, pp. 264–74. See also the note on parables below, pp. 127–8 and 136 and n.

In the eyes of the early Christians, such blindness was a punishment by God for the sin into which men were led by the supernatural forces of evil (see fully on 8^{17}). Our Lord's attempts to cure such blindness were all part of his struggle against the forces of evil, which explains the strong emotions here aroused in him.

6

the Herodians (cf. 12^{13}): It is not certain who these were. The usual view is that they were friends and political supporters of Herod Antipas, rather than a religious sect, and that they joined forces with the Pharisees against Jesus because of the danger of political unrest inherent in his movement: cf., however, B. W. Bacon, *The Gospel of Mark*, pp. 74ff., who thinks the term is an anachronism here and refers to the religious group which gathered round Agrippa I in St Mark's own day.

3^{7-12} SOME TYPICAL INCIDENTS IN GALILEE

^{7}*Jesus withdrew with his disciples to the sea, and a great multitude from*
Galilee followed; also from Judea ^{8}*and Jerusalem and Idume'a and from*
beyond the Jordan and from about Tyre and Sidon a great multitude, hearing
all that he did, came to him. ^{9}*And he told his disciples to have a boat ready*
for him because of the crowd, lest they should crush him; ^{10}*for he had healed*
many, so that all who had diseases pressed upon him to touch him. ^{11}*And*
whenever the unclean spirits beheld him, they fell down before him and cried
out, 'You are the Son of God.' ^{12}*And he strictly ordered them not to make*
him known.

3^{7-12}

It is generally agreed, mainly on grounds of language and style, that this section is what is called a 'generalizing summary'; that is to say it did not reach St Mark as a simple unit of tradition (pericope) but was freely composed by him on the basis of general information he possessed, and the general picture of the Lord's ministry he had formed. It is very largely by the use of such 'generalizing summaries' that St Mark was able to weave the separate units of tradition together into a connected account.

The question then arises why St Mark composed this particular summary for this particular point in the Gospel. The clue lies partly in realizing that this section and the next (13–19a) were meant to form a unity. Together they provide a foil to the dark picture of mounting misunderstanding and hostility by which they are surrounded (2^{1}–3^{6} and $3^{19b-end}$). (St Mark is fond of insertions between two halves of a single story, time being thus given for the initial action to develop; cf. 5^{21-24} and 5^{35-43} separated by 5^{25-34}, 6^{7-13} separated from 6^{30-32} by 6^{14-29}, and 14^{1-2} separated from 14^{10-11} by 14^{3-9}.) As for the content of the present insertion, Lightfoot writes (*G. M. M.*, p. 39): 'After withdrawing from the synagogue in Chapter 3, He first meets a great multitude of enthusiastic followers on the shore of the lake, and proceeds to make a selection from them, with whom He withdraws to the high ground; and we then read of the appointment of the twelve, and a list is given of their names. We may see here, if we choose, the foundation of the new Israel, Israel after the flesh having proved itself unworthy.' In particular vv. 7–12 show that, though the leaders of Israel could not understand them, the deeds of Jesus spoke so loudly that ordinary, unprejudiced folk, and unclean spirits possessed of supernatural insight, could not mistake them; it was only the prejudice of the scribes and Pharisees that led them to reject Jesus. So St Mark hammers home his answer to those who doubted whether Jesus could have been the Messiah, seeing that the religious leaders had not recognized him.

And the point is strengthened by the fact that those who followed Jesus were not some isolated section of the community; we have not only 'the whole country of Judea' gathering as they did around John the forerunner, but crowds from every part of the Holy Land inhabited by Jews. The idea is clear – and for St Mark it is theologically very significant. All Israel gathers to Jesus and there he creates the new community which was expected in the last time, and appoints its leaders. And the horrified cries of the unclean spirits explain why he can do this – he is the Son of God come into the world to destroy them and their power and set up the reign of God; what the sin of the Jewish leaders hides from them the evil spirits dare not conceal from themselves, for in proclaiming the real name and identity of Jesus lies their only hope of avoiding destruction by him (see below). If the supernatural powers take Jesus so seriously, we see by contrast what the denial of the earthly rulers is worth.

❧

7

withdrew: Why? Some have said as a means of escape from danger, others 'because He wished for the present to avoid further controversy with opponents, and yet to be readily accessible to the people' (R., p. 37). Probably all such attempts to discover Jesus' motives on the basis of St Mark's report are idle; St Mark did not intend to provide such information about the Lord's motives. The word itself is a quite general one and if it had any special significance for St Mark, it was probably that suggested above; Jesus withdrew from the old Israel, the synagogue, and turned to the creation of the new Israel.

R.S.V. assumes a distinction between the Galilean multitude which *followed* and the multitude from farther afield who *came to him*. The MSS., however, give a number of different readings and we should probably prefer one which makes no such distinction.

A glance at the map will confirm the statement made above that the districts named cover the whole of the Jewish-inhabited Holy Land. Samaria is excluded as not Jewish and likewise the cities of the Decapolis which were mainly Gentile in character. Jerusalem, the holy city, is mentioned separately from the rest of Judea. Idumea (the Old Testament Edom) had been conquered under John Hyrcanus *c.* 128 B.C. and its inhabitants forcibly circumcised, so it now counted as Jewish territory. *Beyond the Jordan* refers to Perea between the Arnon and the Jabbok, while Tyre and Sidon, though not strictly Jewish territory, had large Jewish populations and were always closely connected with Galilee.

9ff.

There is perhaps a hint that, although the crowd, unlike the authorities, *followed* Jesus, its following was largely directed to what it could get out of him, and it was quite prepared to *crush* him in the process. For it would rather appear that simply to touch him was to receive healing without any specific action on his part. Luke // (6^{19}) expressly says this – cf. also Mark 5^{28} etc.

10

diseases: Literally, 'scourges'; some commentators see in the word a reflection of the idea that diseases were 'scourges' in the sense of punishments for sin. But that is perhaps over-subtle.

11

cried out: Perhaps rather 'shouted' or 'screamed' (*krăzo*); their words are closely paralleled in various incantations of witchcraft which have survived, so, although their action is a recognition of the superior power of Jesus, the intention was no doubt to overcome it by naming his name and revealing his identity (see Introduction, p. 45). It may have been to counter any such attempt that Jesus silences them, but it would seem from the wording that St Mark understood the command in terms of Jesus' purpose of self-concealment (see Introduction, pp. 31–2).

On *Son of God* see Introduction, p. 47.

3^{13-19a} THE APPOINTMENT OF THE TWELVE

13 *And he went up into the hills, and called to him those whom he desired;*
and they came to him. 14 *And he appointed twelve,*[a] *to be with him, and to*
be sent out to preach, 15 *and have authority to cast out demons:* 16 *Simon*
whom he surnamed Peter; 17 *James the son of Zeb'edee and John the brother*
of James, whom he surnamed Bo-aner'ges, that is, sons of thunder; 18 *Andrew*
and Philip, and Bartholomew, and Matthew, and Thomas, and James the
Son of Alphaeus, and Thaddaeus, and Simon the Cananaean, 19 *and Judas*
Iscariot, who betrayed him.

a Other ancient authorities add *whom also he named apostles*

Jesus now climbs a mountain – the traditional setting for a solemn divine act – and chooses, from all Israel gathered together, the foundation members of the eschatological community; as we saw on 1^{16}ff. his word is with power, and those who are chosen obey the summons without more ado. They are the new Israel, and since the old Israel, as God originally formed it, was a twelve-fold body, the new Israel is conceived in the same way (cf. Matt. 19^{28} // Luke 22^{30}) and is accordingly provided with twelve leaders, whose appointment is also described here. An older generation of scholars were inclined to think such symbolism 'childish' and to explain the story as an invention of the early Church. More recent scholars are inclined to take biblical theology more seriously and, impressed by the extent of Our Lord's involvement in the thought-forms of his day, are less ready to pass an adverse judgement on this story. If we accept the story at its face value, we shall have to say that in the event these twelve did not, as a body, provide the effective leadership of the Church after the Lord's death. Some of them, Peter especially, became recognized leaders of the primitive community, but others of them appear to have played little part, and the leadership quickly passed to men like Paul and James the Lord's brother, who did not belong to the twelve. So, by St Mark's time, although the memory of the appointment of the twelve survived, very little was known about them or their functions, and even their names in some cases were no longer clearly preserved in the tradition (see notes below). It has been pointed out that the very fact that the twelve did not, as a body, have a very important role in the life of the early Church makes it the less likely that the early Church invented this story of their appointment.

❧

13

the hills: Although the Greek is literally 'the mountain', many commentators favour this translation as making a smoother transition and not raising the question 'what mountain?' (There is an Aramaic word, *tura*, which can mean either 'mountain' or 'open country' in contrast to inhabited places: M. Black, *An Aramaic Approach to the Gospels and Acts*, p. 96.) Probably, however, we should translate literally. For Mark the point of including the detail is *theological*; it emphasizes the solemn, divine character of what was done, and helps to point the connexion with the foundation of the old Israel (cf. commentary on Matt. 5^{1}).

called . . . came to him: The best commentary on this is in 1^{18} and ^{20}; the word used for 'call' is a variant of that used in 1^{20} and is used elsewhere of a divine call (cf. e.g. Acts 2^{39}, 13^{2}). Moreover the Greek stresses that the initiative lay entirely with Jesus, just as of old it lay entirely with

God when he 'called' Moses and Israel to him on Mount Sinai. The response of those called entirely fits in with this; again the word used is the same as that used in 1[20] and seems to have been almost a technical term for unreserved discipleship – cf. John 12[19] and Jude[7].

14–15

The idea seems to be that the twelve are singled out from the larger number of disciples just called; cf. Luke 6[13]. As we have seen, the twelve did not in fact become the leaders of the Church, and Mark can, therefore, give only a very general account of the purpose of their appointment. This section, like the last, appears to be a 'generalizing summary' and what Mark has done is to deduce the purpose of their appointment from what they did in fact do during the remainder of Jesus' ministry (cf. e.g. 6[7-13]).*

The Greek is difficult and the MSS. have a number of variants; but the general sense is unaffected, and is very fairly conveyed by R.S.V., which rightly rejects the extra words introduced from Luke 6[13].

16

From now on in this Gospel the original name Simon (= Hebrew, *Symeon*) is discarded (except at 14[37]) in favour of Peter (Greek for 'rock' or 'stone', translating the original Aramaic form *kephas* for which see John 1[42], 1 Cor. 1[12], 3[22], Gal. 1[18] etc.). The Evangelist does not tell us the reason for which the new name was chosen (rock-like character, status as the rock on which the Church was founded, etc.) and the commentator does well to preserve a like silence. About the precise circumstances in which the new name was given there were variant traditions in the Church – cf. Matt. 16[18] and John 1[42]; it is presumably on the basis of one of these that St Mark has introduced the information here into his generalizing summary.

17

Boanerges is not the natural Hebrew for 'sons of thunder'; possibly the word represents an obscure Hebrew or Aramaic form with that meaning, or perhaps the original was already corrupt by Mark's day and 'sons of thunder' was the best he could make of it. If his translation is correct, the word either refers to their character ('sons of thunder' in Hebrew would mean 'persons of a thundery kind') or, if Rendel Harris is right in saying that 'sons of thunder' is closely connected with the cult of twins, the name may have been given because James and John

* For an interesting, though perhaps over-subtle, discussion of the phrase *to be with him* see J. M. Robinson, *The Problem of History in Mark*, pp. 79–80.

were twins. In some MSS. the name refers to all the twelve, the connexion being, presumably, that they were called in pairs just as they were sent out in pairs. The whole matter is very obscure and has not yet been satisfactorily cleared up.

18
In Matthew and Luke, Andrew is listed in the natural place, next to his brother Peter; the Marcan order is presumably designed to give priority to the principal disciples (cf. 5^{37}, 9^{2}, 14^{33}). Bartholomew is simply a patronymic, 'son of Talmai' (? = Ptolemy). Presumably, he had another name but St Mark did not know it; and later identification with Nathanael rests on conjecture.

Matthew: If St Mark had identified him with Levi, the tax collector, (so Matt. 10^{3}) he would surely have said so.

Thomas appears to mean 'twin' (so once again we have the pairing motif) and presumably was used as a surname or even a nickname; a later tradition thought his first name was Judas.

Thaddaeus: With this name the uncertainties in the list reach a climax. Luke omits it both in Luke 6^{16} and Acts 1^{13} and has Judas the son of James instead. In Mark the MSS. vary between Thaddaeus and Lebbaeus, and the same is true of the // passage in Matthew (10^{3}). The probability is that Lebbaeus is the original reading in Matthew and Thaddaeus here in Mark, and we thus have a different name in each of the three Gospels. See concluding note below.

Simon the Cananaean: The adjective has nothing to do with Cana or Canaan but derives from a Hebrew word meaning an adherent of the party later known as the Zealots (so Luke 6^{15}, *Simon who was called the Zealot*). Though the Zealot party in the strict sense arose later, there were already at this time many who advocated the same warlike, nationalistic, and anti-Roman policy. Unless the word here simply refers to Simon's strong religious zeal, he presumably came from this nationalistic group.

19
Judas Iscariot: the meaning of the latter word is very obscure. The least unlikely suggestion is that it means 'from (the village of) Kerioth', but 'it is a very plausible conjecture that the word was already unintelligible to the Evangelist' (Dalman), who does not explain it for that reason.

It will be seen that the lists of the twelve give rise to considerable problems and uncertainties, especially as John (14^{22}) agrees with Luke in recognizing a second Judas distinct from the traitor and also includes in the Lord's most intimate circle a certain Nathanael (John 1 44ff., 21 2) not mentioned, at any rate by that name, in any of the Synoptic Gospels. These difficulties have led some scholars to conclude that the whole story of the appointment of twelve apostles is a later Christian invention, connected with what they believe to be the post-resurrection idea that the Christians were the new Israel. But if so, it is hard to understand why the early Christians included a traitor in the list, and the explanation of the uncertainties offered above seems generally preferable.

3 19b–35 JESUS REJECTED BY HIS OWN PEOPLE

Then he went home; 20*and the crowd came together again, so that they*
could not even eat. 21*And when his friends heard it, they went out to seize*
him, for they said, 'He is beside himself.' 22*And the scribes who came down*
from Jerusalem said, 'He is possessed by Be-el'-zebul, and by the prince of
demons he casts out the demons.' 23*And he called them to him, and said to*
them in parables, 'How can Satan cast out Satan? 24*If a kingdom is divided*
against itself, that kingdom cannot stand. 25*And if a house is divided against*
itself, that house will not be able to stand. 26*And if Satan has risen up against*
himself and is divided, he cannot stand, but is coming to an end. 27*But no one*
can enter a strong man's house and plunder his goods, unless he first binds
the strong man; then indeed he may plunder his house.

28*'Truly, I say to you, all sins will be forgiven the sons of men, and*
whatever blasphemies they utter; 29*but whoever blasphemes against the*
Holy Spirit never has forgiveness, but is guilty of an eternal sin' – 30*for they*
had said, 'He has an unclean spirit.'

31*And his mother and his brothers came; and standing outside they sent to*
him and called him. 32*And a crowd was sitting about him; and they said to*
him, 'Your mother and your brothers[a] *are outside, asking for you.'* 33*And he*
replied, 'Who are my mother and my brothers?' 34*And looking around on*
those who sat about him, he said, 'Here are my mother and my brothers!
35*Whoever does the will of God is my brother, and sister, and mother.'*

a Other early authorities add *and your sisters*

This long section is one to which the Evangelist attached high significance and it has a great deal of light to throw on the meaning of the Gospel story as a whole. The first verse re-emphasizes what has been shown in the previous passage (vv. 7–19a) – that ordinary, unprejudiced folk, recognizing (we may assume) the goodness and God-given character of Jesus' power, flocked to avail themselves of it. In the rest of the section we are shown by contrast how those who might have been expected to share this attitude to the full, Jesus' own family and the religious leaders of the people, not only failed to recognize the true source and character* of his actions, but insisted on attributing them to evil sources. His family thought he was *beside himself* (v. 21, i.e. under the power of demons), while 'the scribes from Jerusalem' (i.e. the fully official representatives of the Jewish religion) alleged that he was possessed by Satan and that it was by Satanic power that his supernatural works were performed. Mark's readers knew it was just such attitudes which finally brought Jesus to his death, so it is all the more significant that they are here analysed and shown to be due to sin, and sin of the most grievous kind. So far as Jesus' family are concerned, they are sharply contrasted in v. 35 with 'those who do the will of God', while the attitude of the scribes is expressly described as *the* sin which never has forgiveness (v. 29). We are thus shown very early in the Gospel how, when the Son of God 'came unto his own, his own' – both family and nation – 'received him not'; this is a theme which will recur in the Gospel (cf. e.g. 6^{1-6}), but already it is made clear not merely how groundless,† but how positively sinful, their rejection of him was.

At this point no motive is suggested for such sin; to some extent it remained a mystery to the early Church. How *could* the wholly beneficent activities of Jesus have given rise to such charges? Sometimes, we have seen, it was suggested that those who made them were under diabolic influence or even had their eyes blinded by God himself. St Mark deals with this fully in the next chapter, but meanwhile he drops a hint when he says (v. 23) that Jesus' reply to his critics was *in parables*. He thus paves the way for the collection of parables in Chapter 4 and for his theory that the result, if not the purpose, of this indirect, allusive way of teaching on the part of Jesus

* It will be observed that this is *now* (contrast 2^{1}–3^{6}) the explicit subject of controversy.

† That has already been brought out in 1^{32}, 1^{44}, and $2^{23\text{ff.}}$, for example.

was to make it possible for those who heard to misunderstand and reject what he said. These preliminary 'parables' also accustom us to the fact that Jesus' parables are not usually concerned with timeless truths about heaven and earth but with Jesus' eschatological battle on behalf of the kingdom.

The 'parables' themselves comprise three sayings of Jesus (vv. 24–26, 27, and 28–30) which appear to have been originally independent of one another, but were early connected in the tradition (see below). All three presuppose, as the accusation itself had done, that the activity of Jesus was so remarkable as to argue *some* supernatural power; the only question is whether it was God's or the devil's. But Jesus points out that the results of his activity are exactly the opposite of those the devil usually tries to achieve; the devil tries to *produce* madness, disease, and falsehood, not to remove them; if then the activity of Jesus were due to the devil, we should have the absurd situation that the Satanic realm was pursuing two directly conflicting policies at the same time. It would in fact be at civil war with itself, and civil war, as we all know, means the destruction of the realm in which it occurs. In fact, if Satan were responsible for the activity of Jesus, as the scribes allege, he would be setting one of his subjects against the work of the others. Clearly he would not be such a fool, and, if he were, there ought to be signs of the break-up of his kingdom. This is taken as sufficient refutation of the charge that Jesus' activities are Satanic in inspiration.

The second 'parable' goes on to make a further point; it is based on the proverbial saying that you cannot rob a strong man unless you have first overpowered him and tied him up. The ruler of the demons is strong, yet Jesus is clearly robbing him, as in his exorcisms and healings he releases those who have become his vassals and chattels. The inference is clear; Satan must have been assailed and 'bound' by one even stronger than himself. And in the light of Isaiah $49^{24f.}$ (? and 53^{12}) there could be no doubt who this 'stronger' one (cf. 1^{7}) was – the Messiah, armed with God's own power.*

* *The strong one* is an expression with a long history behind it, cf. Isa. 49^{25}, 53^{12}, Rev. 6^{15}, 19^{18}, 10^{1}, 18^{21}, 18^{8}, 1 Cor. 10^{22}, etc. On the basis of the first of those passages it appears to have been used to describe the expected eschatological deliverer (here by implication, and in Luke 11^{22} and Mark 1^{7}) and some scholars think it may have been a very primitive messianic title for Jesus.

Are we meant to go further and distinguish, in the activity of Jesus, between the initial binding of Satan and the subsequent process of spoliation which it made possible? If so, the initial binding is no doubt to be found in the 'Temptation' (1^{12-13}) when Jesus fought with the devil and decisively defeated him in the power of the Spirit given him in his baptism. That, as we saw, was a presupposition rather than strictly a part of the Gospel. So St Mark's view would then have been that the exorcisms and other activities of Jesus, which form the central part of the Gospel, were a second stage in the Messiah's great battle against the powers of evil – the following up, as it were, and exploiting of the initial victory won before the opening of the Gospel proper. (For a very cogent presentation of this view see J. M. Robinson, *The Problem of History in Mark*, p. 30ff.) Some commentators feel that it is over-subtle, but certainly the present passage and the baptism-temptation story contain two of the very few Marcan allusions to the Spirit, and both also contain allusions to Jesus as 'the mighty one'. In any case it is clear from this passage that St Mark interprets the various activities of Jesus as so many episodes in the encounter between the Spirit of God working in Jesus and the hostile powers.

The third 'parable', which is in fact a straightforward pronouncement by Jesus, should be read against the background of the teaching of the rabbis, who are often reported as declaring certain sins so heinous that those who commit them 'have no part in the world to come'.* It is difficult to be sure just how seriously they intended the phrase, and it may well be that 'such sayings are to be viewed as a warning against a too great trust in God's mercy rather than as a fixed limitation of the divine grace . . . the emphasis falls not on the punishment and its duration, but on the heinousness of the sin' (B., pp. 73–4). In the light of this rabbinic practice, we can understand what the Gospel is here teaching: 'Whatever the *rabbis* may think about the relative heinousness of sins, from the true, Christian standpoint the one absolutely heinous sin is blasphemy against the Holy Spirit.' And the context, particularly v. 30, makes quite clear what St Mark understood by such blasphemy. In the exorcisms of Jesus, and indeed in his whole ministry, as Mark's prologue made

* Cf. e.g. *Mishnah Sanh.* x, 1: 'These are those who have no part in the future world; he who says, "There is no resurrection from the dead"; he who says "The Law is not from God", and the heretics.'

clear, the Spirit – that is the power – of God himself was at work winning for men their ultimate salvation. If the people who so desperately needed that saving work refused to recognize it for what it was, and rejected it as of diabolic origin, then indeed they were 'biting the hand that fed them' and cutting themselves off from the possibility of salvation. And if it be asked whether honest doubt or disbelief is therefore a crime, it must be replied that any such attitude lies quite outside the purview of the Gospel at this point. The opponents of Jesus agreed that his work was supernatural, and to the early Church it seemed that failure to respond to such patently *benevolent* supernatural activity must be due to conscious and deliberate opposition to God. 'Blasphemy against the Holy Spirit . . . is the extremest form of opposition to God. He who blasphemes against the Holy Spirit has identified himself so completely with the kingdom of evil that for him evil is good, ugliness beauty, and falsehood truth; and so the workings of the Holy Spirit appear to him as madness' (*S. J.*, p. 110). To the mind of the first century, formed by the rabbis, it would not necessarily have seemed incompatible with the goodness of God that those who adopted such an attitude neither could nor would ever be redeemed or forgiven. It is probably a mistake to try to show that the words *never* and *eternal* in v. 29 are too strong for the original they represent, but in regard to the saying as a whole the reader should bear in mind the uncertainty voiced above about similar sayings of the rabbis.

When now we take up again the story of Jesus' family we are in a position to understand the full poignancy of it. By coming in a body to restrain him, they showed unmistakably how far they were from recognizing that his ministry was the work of God himself. But that recognition is the acid test, and those who fail it *are outside* (v. 32) the body of the Church, the sphere of salvation, however closely they may be related to the Lord on the natural level. Natural relationship in itself avails nothing, and what applies to 'his own people' in the family sense applies equally to 'his own people' in the national sense; if they reject him, it will avail them nothing that they are his brethren, the chosen people of God by natural descent (cf. 6^{1-6} and e.g. Matt. 3^{9} and 8^{11-12}). By contrast it becomes clear who are within the sphere of salvation – those who do *the will of God* (v. 35) and take Jesus' ministry seriously, 'gathering round him' in faith and discipleship. Through thus following him they might find themselves breaking even the closest earthly ties (see 10^{28-30}), but in the Church they would find close personal fellowship not only with their fellow disciples but with Jesus himself; it never ceased to impress the early Church that their Lord was prepared to call them his brethren – cf. Heb. $2^{11f.}$ and Matt. 25^{40}. In Jesus' conception of it, the kingdom of God 'was to be constituted by a number of people whose spirit of mutual service and fellowship would make it a social body with the ethical quality and value of a family group. The early Church grew naturally out of this conception. The reign of God was not in Jesus' mind an abstract concept or a theological necessity, but a personal fellowship with men and women who would do the will of God' (B., p. 75).

❧

19b–20

This seems to be an editorial link. By *home* Mark probably means some house (in Capernaum?) which Jesus used as the headquarters of his Galilean ministry;* *again* might refer back either to 2^{1} or to $3^{7f.}$ but probably the reference is quite general – 'on another occasion'.

21

his friends: The original Greek is not very precise; the colloquial expression 'his people' perhaps comes nearest to it, since it refers first and foremost to the members of his family. It has been denied that this verse has any connexion with vv. 31–35, but whatever may have been the case in his source, St Mark surely saw this verse and 31ff. as two parts of a single story, with vv. 22–30 as an interlude, inserted in his usual manner (see p. 112) to give events time to develop.

He is beside himself: Since the Jews regarded madness as due to demon possession, this was equivalent to saying that he was under demonic compulsion; see the instructive parallel John 10^{20-21} and also cf. John 7^{20} and 8^{48} and ^{52}.

22

scribes from Jerusalem would represent the official Jewish reaction to Jesus more fully and authoritatively than any others. It is all the more significant that the controversy with them deals openly with the nature and source of Jesus' authority and power, whereas previous controversies had been chiefly concerned with questions of religious practice.

* The original could also mean 'he went indoors'.

The question is here fairly posed: What will Israel do with its Messiah? Through its official representatives it at once describes his work as Satanic, for so St Mark probably took the remark about *Beelzebul*, regarding *Beelzebul* as an alternative name for Satan, although it is not so used elsewhere. In 2 Kings 1² there is a reference to a Philistine god of this name, but it is difficult to know what St Mark understood the word to mean, particularly as the MSS. and versions have a number of different spellings of it. Probably it was thought to mean 'lord of the house' or 'dwelling'; if so v. 27 and Matt. 10²⁵ have added point. V. T. takes the scribes' words to contain two distinct charges, and thinks *Beelzebul* was the name of an evil spirit distinct from *Satan*. But this seems unlikely; cf. Matt. 12²⁴ // Luke 11¹⁵.

23–26

For the argument, see p. 120. Barrett (*H.S.G.T.*, p. 61) paraphrases thus: 'I am accused of using demonic powers for the expulsion of demons. But this would involve the complete break-up of the demonic world, in accordance with usual human experience of seditious activity. Now it is clear that the empire of Satan still holds out (this assumption is necessary to the argument), therefore I do not cast out demons by Beelzebul, but in some other way.'

23

For the meaning of *parable*, see pp. 125ff.

25

house can in Aramaic be used in a broad sense for a political domain.

28–29

The detailed exegesis of these verses is difficult, particularly as Q (Matt. 12³¹⁻² // Luke 12¹⁰) contained a different version of the saying which contrasted speech against the Son of man, which *is* forgivable, with speech against the Holy Spirit, which is *not* forgivable. Most scholars incline to prefer the Marcan form as being the more original, though some deduce from the reference to *the sons of men* (v. 28) a still earlier form in which blasphemy or railing against men (for *sons of men* = 'men', see pp. 47 and 93) was contrasted with blasphemy against the Holy Spirit. If so, it is easy to see how the Q form of the saying might have arisen, especially if in some recensions *son of man* (meaning originally 'another human being') was in the singular. It is even just possible that Jesus used *son of man* with reference to himself, but not in a messianic sense (so R., pp. 44–5).

28

Truly: Literally *amen*, a Hebrew word (= 'so be it') normally used to *conclude* a prayer or wish (cf. e.g. Jer. 11^5). Its use at the beginning of a sentence, to add emphasis and solemnity to what follows, is confined to the Gospels and may well have been a characteristic way of speaking peculiar to Our Lord.

blasphemies: This is not simply a matter of bad language. The word *blaspheme* meant in Greek to slander men or to show irreverence towards the gods, and in the Bible it is used of 'defiant hostility to God, His name, or word, in speech which defies His power and majesty' (V. T.).

29
never: Some MSS. read simply 'has no forgiveness', but even if they are right, the sense is little altered in view of the rest of the verse.

guilty of an eternal sin: A strange phrase which presumably describes the act of sin as a permanent barrier raised by the soul between itself and God; cf. R., p. 45: 'It is clear that our Lord declared that to blaspheme the Holy Spirit by ascribing to Satan what was manifestly a work of God was to be guilty of essential wickedness: it was to be in a state of mind which, so long as it lasted, was essentially unforgivable, and might easily become permanent.' Black, however (p. 102), suggests that an Aramaic phrase lies behind the Greek here meaning 'is liable to an eternal judgement'.

31
his brothers: For the *brothers* of Jesus see on 6^3.

4^{1-34} *Parables*

This is one of the few sections of any length in the Gospel devoted to the *teaching* of Jesus; although St Mark often pictures Our Lord as teaching (e.g. 1^{21}, 2^{13}, 6^2, and 6^6), only here and at $13^{2\text{ff.}}$ (and perhaps in 7^{1-23}) does he make any attempt to give a sustained account of the *content* of the teaching. It might be expected, therefore, that in these three chapters he would be at pains to provide a balanced sample of the various kinds of teaching Our Lord was in the habit of giving; but although in the present section he has used a dramatist's licence and collected together sayings which were not originally uttered on a single occasion, his aim in making this selection was evidently not that of providing a representative cross-section of Our Lord's teaching. For it will be noticed that all the teaching given consists either of parables or of teaching about parables. St Mark's aim was not even to provide a typical set of parables, for all the parables given here, and the sayings about them, are connected in one way or another with the question of the nature and purpose of parables themselves.

To the modern reader this may seem a very straightforward question; for we are accustomed to think of parables as simple and vivid stories used to illustrate Our Lord's teaching and make it easier to understand and remember. But whatever we may think, that was certainly not St Mark's view; he thought the parables were intended to wrap up Our Lord's teaching and make it obscure, and so prevent it from having its full impact on those who were not meant to be enlightened and saved by it.

Where does the truth in fact lie? The word 'parable' is simply the English form of a quite common Greek word (*parabŏlē*) which in ordinary Greek usage meant the putting of one thing alongside another by way of comparison or illustration. Aristotle, for example, defines the word as meaning 'comparison' or 'analogy'. (*Rhet.* II, XX, 2–4). But in the Greek Bible the meaning of the word is affected by the meaning of the Hebrew word *māshāl* (Aramaic: *m^ethel*) which it was used to translate; and as *māshāl* has a number of uses, so, in *biblical* Greek, does the word 'parable'.

It often means a brief sentence of popular wisdom, an ethical maxim, or just a proverb in general, e.g. 1 Sam. 24^{14}, Ezek. 16^{44}, 18^{2}; it will be noticed that though such sayings sometimes involve a comparison (e.g. Prov. 10^{26}) they are often just terse epigrams – what we should call 'aphorisms' rather than 'parables'. (Cf. in the New Testament Luke 4^{23} or Mark 7^{15}.) The word also has other meanings in the Old Testament – it is used, for example, of the 'oracles' or 'discourse' of Balaam in Num. 23^{7} etc., but curiously enough, the passages in the Old Testament which we should naturally call parables (e.g. 2 Sam. 12^{1-14}, $14^{1ff.}$, Isa. 5^{1-7}) are not normally described by the word *māshāl*; though two exceptions, Ezek. 17^{3-10} and Ezek. 24^{3-5} are enough to show that the word *māshāl* could refer to them.

Thus, when we are told that Our Lord made great use of the *māshāl* in his teaching, we have to ask which of the many forms of speech covered by the word is being referred to. The answer seems to be that Our Lord used more than one form of the *māshāl*. At one end of the scale we have the current proverb in Luke 4^{23}, to which Our Lord himself applies the word 'parable' (cf. Mark 7^{17}); while in Luke $14^{7ff.}$ the word is applied to advice on the conduct of ordinary life, much as it is in the book of Proverbs. Then at the other end of the scale are full-blown stories, like that of the Prodigal Son, which we tend to think of as the parables *par excellence*. Can we then tell for what purpose he used any, or all, of these types of *māshāl*, and in particular is there any evidence that the *māshāl* was ever used to *veil* or *obscure* the truth?

A further point about the Old Testament use of *māshāl* is worth noticing. In the Old Testament the word is sometimes used in connexion with the word *hidah** which literally means a 'riddle' and came to denote speech which is indirect, as opposed to speech which is plain, open, and straightforward. In the later books of the Old Testament there are no riddles in the literal sense, so where, as at Prov. 1^{6}, the word *hidah* occurs, it must refer to figurative sayings or pregnant aphorisms which call for reflection before they can be understood. The *hidah* and the *māshāl* clearly have affinity, since both depend on analogy for their force, and it may well be that the *māshāl* was sometimes used, not simply to illustrate and clarify teaching, but, like the *hidah*, to puzzle people and provoke them into reflection and consequent enlightenment; it might then be regarded as obscure, as some of Ezekiel's parables were (20^{49}), and its lesson might afterwards be expounded and driven home by an explanation – cf. e.g. Ezek. $24^{3ff.}$ It is obvious that when used in this thought-provoking way the *māshāl* would have different effects on different people; those who could and would undertake the necessary reflection would be illuminated, while those who would not, or could not, would gain no insight from the *māshāl* even though they understood the literal meaning of the words.

Attention is also sometimes drawn to the frequent complaint of the Old Testament prophets that the word of God, which was meant to bring life and salvation, was so misunderstood and rejected because of people's sin and ignorance, that it became in fact an instrument of judgement and condemnation (cf. e.g. Isa. 28^{13}, Jer.

* e.g. Ezek. 17^{2}, Hab. 2^{6}, Ps. 78^{2}, Ecclus $39^{2,3}$.

23^{29}). Such misunderstanding of the prophetic message became so much a commonplace that when Isaiah was called to proclaim God's word, his commission from God took the form of an ironical command to *say to this people:* 'Hear and hear, but do not understand; see and see, but do not perceive. Make the heart of this people fat, and their ears heavy, and shut their eyes; lest they see with their eyes, and hear with their ears and understand with their hearts and turn and be healed' (Isa. 6^{9-10}).

Yet when the force of all this has been admitted, it remains doubtful whether it amounts to evidence that the *māshāl* was ever used as a deliberate means of obscuring, rather than revealing, the truth.* And there is one strong piece of evidence to the contrary. Parables were constantly used by the rabbis at and after the time of Our Lord, and the very numerous examples of their parables which have been preserved make it clear that they used them for the sole purpose of clarifying and driving home their teaching. When we observe the very close similarity of many of these rabbinic parables to Our Lord's – both in form and subject-matter – it seems natural to suppose that he used parables in the same sort of way, and with the same purpose, as the rabbis. That is to say, his general purpose in using parables was to make the truth as fully understood as possible; he may well have used parables, as the rabbis did, to provoke reflection and so bring his hearers to a recognition of the truth. But that is something very different from attempting to conceal the truth.

It is perfectly true that *to us* the bearing of one or two of the rabbinic parables is obscure, but that is mainly because they have been transmitted to us without their original context which would have made their application clear, or because the saying was a current one whose bearing was generally understood at the time of utterance, though it is no longer known to us. From this an important point emerges; although a *māshāl* in Our Lord's time was not *intended* to be obscure, its meaning was essentially bound up with its original context and the circumstances of its utterance, and so it would become enigmatic as

* The use of the word *māshāl* in Ezekiel makes it clear that the obscure *māshāl* was the exception rather than the rule: and even where a *māshāl* was used to provoke reflection, that was because such reflection was held necessary for the *uncovering of the truth*; the aim was still solely the positive one of conveying, and not hiding, the truth.

soon as those circumstances were forgotten. But as we have seen (pp. 25–6 and 28), in the oral tradition of the early Church, the sayings of Our Lord were commonly preserved without their original context, and as a result the precise bearing of them, and particularly of the parables, very soon became a matter of uncertainty and conjecture. Moreover, as time went on, the conditions which had originally given rise to the parables frequently changed, and the Church, being naturally unwilling to discard the known words of the Lord, found new applications for them which made sense in the changed circumstances. So by the time a parable reached the Evangelists its original bearing might have been entirely lost* or it might have attracted to itself one or more later applications and meanings. It was thus natural that parables should come to be thought of as rather enigmatic and mysterious utterances.

Another factor which operated strongly in the same direction was the tendency to treat the parables as allegories; this has become so established a practice in the Church that it is difficult for the modern reader to emancipate himself from it, though it is essential to do so if the truth about parables is to be appreciated. The essence of an allegory is that it must be interpreted point by point, feature by feature; as far as possible every single item in an allegory must represent something else.† An allegory in fact is a sort of description in code, and when we come across one, the question we have to keep asking is: 'What does that person or that article or that event in the story *stand for*?' It is in this way, for example, that St Mark interprets

* Examples of 'parables' whose original context, and therefore meaning, had become completely obscure by the time of the Evangelists are the sayings about throwing pearls before swine (Matt. 7^{6}) and the saying about the eagles in Matt. 24^{28} // Luke 17^{37}.

† Provided that each item stands for something 'it is not essential that the allegorical presentations should conform to any laws of probability or possibility. Many of the pictures of the allegorists, wherein eagles can plant vines, beasts be winged, and stars become bulls, seem properly to belong to that dream-world in which they are not infrequently stated to have had their origin. Even when the symbols are drawn from the world of everyday events, unnatural features will often obtrude themselves and rob the picture of its surface realism.... We notice again a contrast between allegory and parable or similitude: the figures in the latter are always precisely what they profess to be, stones are stones and burdens are burdens.' (B. T. D. Smith, *The Parables of the Synoptic Gospels*, pp. 21–2.)

the parable of the sower – the seed *stands for* the word, those sown on the pathway *stand for* a certain class of people, and so on with all the other items in the parable. And it seems to be St Mark's view that the reason why the hearers could not understand the parable was because they could not discover these equivalents – they could not find the key, as it were, to the code.

But our evidence suggests that in fact the *māshāl* was seldom, if ever, of this allegorical sort; it was a quite different type of saying, with a different purpose. The typical parable consisted of a story, which might be either true or imaginary, but in either case was completely life-like and self-consistent. The persons and events did not stand, item by item, for anything else, but the story was meant to be heard out to the end, when it would be found that *as a whole* it had something to teach. It might exemplify the right sort of conduct in a memorable and appealing way (e.g. the parable of the Good Samaritan),* but very often the lesson would depend on an argument by analogy. For example, in Luke 17^{7-10} Jesus is saying in effect: 'Do you find it hard to understand that men can claim no merit for obedience to God's will? Well, think of the relation between a slave and his master; you can see that there is no question of claiming a reward there – can you not see that a like principle holds between God and his creatures?' It will be noticed that there is no question of allegory here; the slave does not *stand for* the Christian nor the owner for God; and certainly the preparing of the meal is not meant to represent any element in the Christian's relationship to God! We are simply meant to consider the little story as a whole, and to reflect on its central feature until it brings home to us the hitherto unrecognized truth about our relationship with God. Many of the parables are basically arguments from analogy, like that one; and it is also typical in having only a single point to make. The German scholar A. Jülicher† was broadly right in his claim that this limitation to a single point is one of the chief distinguishing features of the parable as opposed to the allegory;‡

* Which is not an allegory. The Good Samaritan is not Jesus or St Paul or anyone else; he is just a good Samaritan.

† Over fifty years ago he published what is still in some ways the classic book on parables, *Die Gleichnisreden Jesu*; rather strangely, it was never translated into English.

‡ The allegory is normally a *literary* form and so can afford to be more complicated.

and he went on to argue that if a parable in its present form has several lessons, that is *prima facie* evidence that it has been allegorized in the course of transmission.* For there can be little doubt that the process of allegorization started early;† most scholars are agreed, for example, that the allegorizing explanation of the sower parable ascribed to Jesus in Mark 4^{14-20} is in fact an allegorization by the early Church (see below) and other examples will be found in the story of the unwilling guests (Matt. $22^{1ff.}$) or the explanation of the parable of the tares in Matt. 13^{36-43}.

If then the Church was not altogether correctly informed about the *character* of parables, was it right about the purpose for which Jesus originally used them? (Mark 4^{10-12}.) Once the contexts had been lost and the parables had come to be thought of as allegories which had originally been uttered without any clue being provided to their interpretation, they would indeed come to seem enigmas whose application could not possibly have been appreciated by the original hearers without explanation by Jesus or direct illumination from God himself. Why then, it would be asked, had Jesus chosen to teach in this enigmatic way? There was one answer which had the advantage of throwing a flood of light on what had happened subsequently.

Despite Jesus' gracious words of truth, he had been misunderstood, and his claim to Messiahship repudiated by those who heard him. How could the Son of God have met with such treatment unless he had himself willed it? Unless he had declared his meaning and status only in an obscure way which would be unintelligible to the great mass of Jews, not destined for faith and salvation? On this view, Christ's use of parables was one of his ways of preserving his messianic secret, and it also helped to explain how he – and his Father – not only

* It can only be *prima facie* evidence, for we cannot of course rule out the possibility that the Lord himself may have composed allegories on occasion. P. Fiebig, arguing against Jülicher, claims that some of the extant rabbinic parables are really allegories, but it is doubtful if that claim can be substantiated. Cf. e.g. B. T. D. Smith, pp. 23ff. Jülicher would seem to be right in his general contention that the parable is a form quite distinct from the allegory.

† The motives for this are obvious, and innocent, enough. Allegorical exegesis was highly regarded at the time both by Jews and Greeks, as a means of extracting meaning from obscure or apparently unedifying texts. And the Christians would naturally be anxious to squeeze all the edification and enlightenment they possibly could from the words of their divine Master.

foreknew, but brought about, the Jews' failure to understand, and the rejection and crucifixion to which it in turn eventually led. Such an interpretation of events would gain strength from the Old Testament passages discussed above, which saw the word of God as often an instrument for blinding and condemning; indeed it may partly have rested on a saying of Our Lord himself which in its original form did not refer specifically to parables, but ironically likened his mission as a whole and its results to that of the prophet Isaiah (see below).

Starting from there, we can get* a general picture of how 4^{1-34} was built up. St Mark, or someone before him, first collected the three allied parables in vv. 3–9, 26–29, and 30–32; but there was attached to the sower parable (vv. 3–9) the explanation of it, introduced by a question and marked by a change of scene (vv. 10 and 13–20). It would appear that v. 33 belongs to the same stage as the explanation. Next to be added was the other answer to the question in v. 10 (viz. vv. 11–12 and 34), and it may well be that the two other parables (about the lamp and about hearing) were added at the same time (vv. 21–25). Finally, St Mark must have provided vv. 1–2 (which, on linguistic evidence, are clearly his composition) to provide a setting for the public teaching. The importance of this analysis is that it prepares us to recognize that the material in these verses is not all from the same stage of tradition and may not therefore be all informed with the same view about the purpose and interpretation of parables.

But before we discuss the various points one by one we must first ask about the section as a whole: why St Mark collected just this material for inclusion at this particular point in his Gospel. As far as the five parables are concerned, Lightfoot writes:† 'The reason for their insertion at this point is probably not far to seek. The preceding two chapters have been full of controversy, and there has been little to relieve the darkness of the gathering storm. And yet the gospel opened with the proclamation of the arrival (in some sense) of the kingdom of God. In these parables a supreme confidence is expressed in the certain triumph of good, and of that kingdom, which we may say is tacitly identified with the cause and work of Jesus, and of his followers.

* On the basis very largely of linguistic evidence.

† *H. & I.*, pp. 112–13. See also the rather fuller statement in *G. M. M.*, pp. 39–40.

Just as in Chapter 13, the only other extensive section of teaching in this Gospel, the purpose of the *private* instruction to the four disciples is to implant the conviction that the suffering which lies ahead is to find its explanation and denouement in the coming of the Son of man, identified silently with the person of the speaker, so in Chapter 4 those who listen to Jesus, himself now outside the synagogue, are assured of the silent but irresistible forces at work upon their side, as certain and unfailing as the work of nature, yet at the same time not to be perceived by all (4^{10-12}).'

If the parables thus reveal the *ultimate ineffectiveness* of the opposition to Christ, the rest of the material in the section (vv. 10–20 and 33–34) reveals the deep theological issues and forces which lie behind that opposition. In order really to accept Jesus you need to understand him, not merely at the superficial level (referred to as 'seeing but not perceiving', 'hearing but not understanding', v. 12) but also at a profound, existential, level at which understanding him and his mission involves understanding your own need for repentance and forgiveness (v. 12). Such understanding is not easily attained; what prevents it is not so much stupidity as sin, that hardness of heart (compound of inattentiveness and positive sinful resistance) which prevented the older Israelites from 'hearing' the word of God (see above). The interpretation of the sower parable is devoted to an explanation of these two levels; the superficial level is exemplified by those who 'hear' the word and then fall away (vv. 15–18), the deeper level, which the explaining of parables is designed to produce, is exemplified by those who bring forth fruit (v. 20). It is noteworthy that it is Satan (v. 15) working through persecution (v. 17) and the lure of this world (v. 19) who prevents transition from the first level of understanding to the second, while the second is given by God (v. 11, see notes) working through Jesus' parables and his direct explanations to his disciples. Thus the words of Jesus, no less than his other activities, are part of the warfare he wages on God's behalf against Satan and his power over men. 'When Jesus gives understanding to those "who have eyes but do not see and ears but do not hear" (8^{18}, cf. $4^{9, 12, 23f.}$) he is engaged in the same activity as when he gives sight to the blind (8^{22-26}; 10^{46-52}) and hearing to the deaf (7^{32-37}; 9^{14-29}).' (J. M. Robinson, *The Problem of History in Mark*, p. 77, on which the last paragraph is largely based.)

4^{1-9}

4 *Again he began to teach beside the sea. And a very large crowd gathered*
about him, so that he got into a boat and sat in it on the sea; and the whole
crowd was beside the sea on the land. 2*And he taught them many things in*
parables, and in his teaching he said to them: 3*'Listen! A sower went out to*
sow. 4*And as he sowed, some seed fell along the path, and the birds came and*
devoured it. 5*Other seed fell on rocky ground, where it had not much soil,*
and immediately it sprang up, since it had no depth of soil; 6*and when the*
sun rose it was scorched, and since it had no root it withered away. 7*Other*
seed fell among thorns and the thorns grew up and choked it, and it yielded
no grain. 8*And other seeds fell into good soil and brought forth grain,*
growing up and increasing and yielding thirtyfold and sixtyfold and a
hundredfold.' 9*And he said, 'He who has ears to hear, let him hear.'*

1–2
V. T. says aptly: 'The passage is editorial, but the picture of a very great crowd, so large that Jesus is compelled to teach from a boat, may well be based on good tradition.' *Again* is simply resumptive; there is no real attempt to link up with 3^9 or any other passage.

3
Listen! Cf. Deut. 6^4 etc.; this word adds solemnity and intensity of tone; it is not in Matt. and Luke // and no doubt St Mark saw it (and vv. 9 and 23) as emphasizing that the words of Jesus were the word of God bringing true understanding to the receptive hearer (see above).

3ff.
There are good grounds for thinking that the parable goes back to an Aramaic original. In order to understand it fully one needs to remember that in Palestine sowing precedes ploughing. That means that the sower here is not particularly careless – he sows intentionally on the path which will subsequently be ploughed up.

4
along the path: This was probably the original meaning, though the Aramaic phrase, which is presumed to be behind the Greek, could also mean 'beside the path'.

5
rocky ground: Not ground strewn with rocks, but a limestone base

thinly covered with soil such as is frequently found in Galilee. Often the limestone barely shows above the surface until the plough-share jars against it, so it is not surprising that some of the grain should fall on such land, and there is no suggestion of bad farming.

8
Originally the wording may have been: 'yielding one lot thirtyfold, another lot sixtyfold, and another lot a hundredfold'. In any case there seems to be a touch of extravagance in the suggestion of such an enormous yield – no doubt designed to drive home the point of the parable.

As the present placing of the parable is due to St Mark and the original context is lost, it is not easy to be sure what the parable originally taught. There have been many conjectures in modern times, most of them assuming that, since the kingdom of God is so central to the teaching of Jesus, the parable referred to that; the meaning will then have been either that the harvest of God's age-old activity has ripened and the kingdom has come despite the unresponsiveness to God's word in the Old Testament period; or, more probably, that despite the opposition and lack of response with which Jesus was meeting, his speech and actions would yet produce an unspeakably rich harvest – the establishing of the kingdom of God. However, we cannot be dogmatic about the reference to the kingdom; it is just possible that the original intention was simply to give encouragement to the disciples in face of the many disappointments and set-backs their sowing of the seed was bound to meet, or even that it was to bring home to the hearers the great responsibility that lay upon them. For St Mark's understanding of the parable see below.

4^10–12

10*And when he was alone, those who were about him with the twelve asked him concerning the parables.* 11*And he said to them, 'To you has been given the secret of the kingdom of God, but for those outside everything is in parables;* 12*so that they may indeed see but not perceive, and may indeed hear but not understand; lest they should turn again, and be forgiven.'*

The meaning of these verses as they stand is clear enough, provided we bear in mind the early Christian conviction (based on an earlier

Jewish belief) that the varied response of different people to Christ was due to the deliberate decree of God, who had willed that some should believe and be saved but others should not.* Jesus is asked why he teaches in parables. His answer is that it is a form of teaching which enables him to produce and preserve this divinely willed division among his hearers. For, being enigmatic, it conceals the truth from those who are not meant to have it, while to those who are, Jesus can easily give explanations (such as that in vv. 13–20) which will transform the mysterious words of the parable into vehicles of saving insight.

However, the verses can hardly be accepted as they stand, for that would necessitate Jesus being alone with the disciples, which is quite in conflict with the situation described in vv. 1–3 and still presupposed later in the chapter (e.g. vv. 33–36). In fact there are difficulties in the way of accepting this account of parables at all.

(i) 'Had Jesus not wished outsiders to understand certain teachings, the most obvious method would have been not to have dealt with those particular topics in public discourse.

(ii) 'Furthermore, the explanation advanced totally misrepresents Jesus' attitude towards the common people. In contrast with other teachers, he appealed to the publicans and sinners, went to the multitudes with his message and thanked God that it was understood even by "the babes"' (B., p. 78).

(iii) Such a view of parables conflicts with v. 13 and v. 33 of this same chapter, both of which seem, in their different ways, to imply that the parables were meant to be intelligible to any who made the effort to understand them.

(iv) And finally the words demand an understanding of parables as *enigmatic* utterances which we have already seen to be highly questionable.

So, 'It is plain that we have to do with a theological explanation

* For a full working out of this see St Paul in Rom. 9–11. The following words of Loisy are well worth pondering: 'The language of the Old, and even of the New, Testament does not as a rule distinguish, in the matter of God's providential decrees, between what is directly willed and what is merely permitted. From the "absolute" point of view of semitic theology, all that God foreknows and regulates in advance is regarded as equally willed: it all appears "necessary". The Biblical writers, however, do not adopt this idea as a philosophical dogma, the logical consequence of which would of course be the denial of human freedom. They do not regard Israel as being in some unique sense the victim of fate, or consider the sin of Israel as though it were not to be set down to the account of Israel's evil will; the blindness and reprobation of Israel, foretold centuries beforehand, happen as though by a kind of divine necessity, which yet does not destroy her responsibility.'

which the early Church created' (B., p. 78), which helps to explain the rather curious terms by which the two contrasted groups are designated – *those who were about Him with the twelve* and *those outside* (vv. 10 and 11). From the standpoint of the early Church, it was not only the twelve to whom the mystery of the kingdom was revealed, but all those who with them gathered round Christ in his Church; by contrast, those Jews who remained 'outside' the Church showed thereby that they were among those whom God had not destined for salvation and from whom therefore Jesus had deliberately veiled the truth.

It remains a question, however, whether the passage is a pure invention by the early Church; several touches in it suggest an Aramaic source and a Palestinian origin. It could well be that at some stage in his ministry, perhaps after some fruitless endeavour such as that reflected in Matt. 11^20-24 // Luke 10^13-15, Jesus thanked God for having made the truth clear to a little band of faithful followers, while at the same time he ruefully recognized that, as far as those outside the little circle were concerned, the truth about him remained completely obscure. In that case cf. a close parallel in Matt. 11^25-26 // Luke 10^21. His experience thus entirely confirmed and fulfilled that of the prophet Isaiah. If that was how this passage originated, the words would originally have meant: 'Apart from my few disciples no one understands the first thing about me and my work – but then, what else could be expected seeing what the prophets experienced and foretold?' The words 'everything is obscure (to those outside)' could well have been translated into Greek 'everything is *en parabolais*' (literally 'in parables') and this translation may have misled St Mark into thinking that the saying was concerned with parables in the usual sense of the word, and so including it in the context. Such a suggestion could be no more than a conjecture, though it is an attractive one. (See further Jeremias, *P.J.*, pp. 11ff.)

10

The change of scene is of the utmost significance to St Mark. For as he understood the matter, it was only in private, and to a select circle, that Jesus gave the explanation needed to transform the enigmatic words of the parable into vehicles of revelation. It is important to notice who constitute this inner group. Some scholars have suggested that Our Lord's habit was to utter a dark saying and then to wait, ready to explain it further to any who, by coming to ask questions, showed that they had taken seriously what had already been said. But this is a modern approach, and hardly agrees with St Mark's view, which is much more in line with the Old Testament ideas of predestination and the remnant. The circle to whom the explanations are given is a determinate number, *his own disciples* (v. 34) predestined to be 'given' the mystery of the kingdom of God. Loisy writes: 'The parables are not intended to effect a selection among the hearers – the selection is thought of as already made; Jesus confines his explanation of the parables entirely to disciples and nothing gives ground for thinking that others could have obtained the same favour. The explanation is given to the disciples not as a reward for their questions but because, quite independently, they have a right to the knowledge of the truth.'

11

the secret: mystērion, a word used in St Paul's Epistles for something that God long kept secret but has now made known to certain selected people (e.g. Col. 1^{26}). The word was also widely used in the Hellenistic religions of the day; in many of these such emphasis was laid on hidden esoteric knowledge which was known only to the devotees and must not be divulged to those outside, that they are actually known as 'mystery religions'. The present passage would be bound to suggest this analogy to Gentile readers and its language and thought may well have been influenced by Hellenistic religious ideas. 'Christianity too, was a "Mystery" Religion, disclosing to men a great Secret of God, a saving "mystery" which in its completeness was revealed only to the initiated.' (R., p. 52.) *The secret of the Kingdom of God* means the 'mystery' that in and through the ministry of Jesus the kingdom of God is breaking into history.

has been given: The passive form implies God as the agent; this was a Hebrew way of speaking designed to avoid having to use the sacred name.

everything is in parables: See p. 137; the Aramaic behind this may only have meant: 'everything is obscure.' If so, the words *so that* at the beginning of v. 12 may *originally* have meant: 'this must be in order that God's word through Isaiah (6^{9-10}) may not be falsified.' Likewise the *original* intention of the final words of v. 12 may have been to express a hope that the unresponsiveness of the outsiders might yet be overcome (cf. *T. J.*, p. 79); but that was not St Mark's understanding.

4[13–20]

[13]*And he said to them, 'Do you not understand this parable? How then*
will you understand all the parables? [14]*The sower sows the word.* [15]*And*
these are the ones along the path, where the word is sown; when they hear,
Satan immediately comes and takes away the word which is sown in them.
[16]*And these in like manner are the ones sown upon rocky ground, who,*
when they hear the word, immediately receive it with joy; [17]*and they have*
no root in themselves, but endure for a while; then, when tribulation or
persecution arises on account of the word, immediately they fall away.[a]
[18]*And others are the ones sown among thorns; they are those who hear the*
word, [19]*but the cares of the world, and the delight in riches, and the desire*
for other things, enter in and choke the word, and it proves unfruitful.
[20]*But those that were sown upon the good soil are the ones who hear the*
word and accept it and bear fruit, thirtyfold and sixtyfold and a hundredfold.'

a Or *stumble*

13
The probability is that v. 10 originally ran: they asked him about the parable, i.e. they asked the meaning of the sower parable,* and that v. 13 followed immediately giving the answer.

In rebuking the disciples for not understanding the parable Our Lord takes for granted that it was intelligible enough; there is no suggestion here of the unintelligibility of parables.

14–20
The parable is interpreted on the assumption that it was an allegory (see pp. 129–30). The doubts which that raises about the originality of the interpretation are more than confirmed by linguistic considerations.† What is more, a long period is assumed in which the genuineness of Christian faith would be tested, and religious persecutions would have arisen (v. 17) to test it, so we can have little doubt that the interpretation is an early Christian creation, 'a sermon on the parable as text' (Dodd). It is a moving sermon, though not altogether consistent. The seed is

* St Mark has substituted the plural (*parables*) in order to turn the question into a general one about parables and so pave the way for vv. 11–12; the introductory words of v. 11 strongly suggest that vv. 11–12 were a separate saying unconnected with v. 10, which was originally part of the section vv. 13–20.

† For details see Jeremias, *P.J.*, pp. 61f.

the word; yet the crop is composed of various classes of people. There seem in fact to be two lines of interpretation combined here; one thinks of a divine word sown *in* men to bring forth fruit, the other, which thinks of men as themselves seeds sown by God, resembles the following passage from 2 Esdras (8^{41}): 'As the farmer sows much seed upon the ground and plants many trees but in the season not all that are planted take root, even so not all that are sown in this world shall be saved.' (Cf. also Isa. 61^{3}, etc.) Professor Dodd sees in this confusion yet another sign of the secondary character of the interpretation; as he says 'we may suppose that the Teller of the parable knew exactly what He meant by it' (*Parables*, p. 14).

In the interpretation the parable has lost its original *eschatological* bearing; it becomes simply a warning and encouragement to Christians in conditions of persecution and worldly temptation. There is no suggestion that Christ is the sower. Any faithful Christian preacher is a sower. He will find much of his work wasted. Some of his hearers will never grasp the truth effectively at all, others will be discouraged by difficulties or beguiled by prosperity. Yet the preacher may be sure that in the end there will be abundant results from his labours.

14, etc.
the word: It is typical of the later period when this interpretation was composed that 'the word' should be used absolutely as a technical term for the gospel (cf. Gal. 6^{6}, Col. 4^{3}, 1 Pet. 2^{8}, etc.).

4^{21-25}

[21]*And he said to them, 'Is a lamp brought in to be put under a bushel, or under a bed, and not on a stand?* [22]*For there is nothing hid, except to be made manifest; nor is anything secret, except to come to light.* [23]*If any man has ears to hear, let him hear.'*

[24]*And he said to them, 'Take heed what you hear; the measure you give will be the measure you get, and still more will be given you.* [25]*For to him who has will more be given; and from him who has not, even what he has will be taken away.'*

21–25
This section comprises five, or possibly six, separate sayings of Jesus so combined as to form a pair of related parables (vv. 21–22 and vv. 24–25),

linked by a solemn warning (v. 23). Matthew and Luke reproduce all the sayings in different contexts,* so they presumably circulated without any indication of their original context, and each evangelist had to provide his own context, thereby, of course, assigning his own meaning to the sayings.

In the light of the Evangelist's general habits, the basis of the Marcan combination is easily seen; v. 22 was attached to v. 21 by similarity of subject-matter and similarly v. 25 to v. 24 by the common theme of what will be *given*; the two resultant 'parables' were then connected as a pair on the basis of the catchword *measure*. (In v. 21 the word translated *bushel* really means a two-gallon *measure*.) The whole complex was placed by St Mark in its present context because he thought the reference was to the temporary concealment of the kingdom by parabolic teaching and the like. It is unlikely that this was the original reference, at any rate in the case of all the sayings included, but the original context and meaning cannot now be recovered.

21–23

St Mark clearly takes this to mean that the concealment aimed at in the parables is not the *ultimate* purpose of Jesus' ministry. Beyond that it is not altogether clear how he applied the saying. He may have:

(*a*) taken it to refer to the contrast between Jesus' concealing of his meaning from the crowds through the parables and his full revelation of it to the initiated through such explanations as that in vv. 14–20. Or

(*b*) he may have understood by it that though the mystery of the kingdom was meant to be concealed during Our Lord's lifetime, it was meant to be disclosed and widely proclaimed after the resurrection. In that case (cf. 9^{9}), the emphasis would be on the responsibility of the disciples, whose duty it now was 'to preach the gospel to all nations'. In view of the solemn warning in v. 23 this is the most likely explanation. However, the meaning might be eschatological: although the ministry of Jesus may at that stage have seemed insignificant and ineffective, God would not have sent him unless he had intended to achieve through him the introduction of his kingdom in its full and manifest form. On this view the saying should be coupled with the parables in 4^{26-32}.

24–25

These two verses are even more obscure than the preceding ones, from which they were probably quite separate in the tradition.†

* Luke also reproduces them *en bloc* in his parallel to the present section – Luke 8^{16}ff.

† That is strongly suggested by the introductory formula.

24
The connexion between the two halves of the verse is obscure. Perhaps the second half was a current proverb and St Mark took it to mean here: 'your attention to the teaching will be the measure of the profit you will receive from it' (Swete). This seems rather forced, however, and the connexion of the proverb with judgement in Q (Matt. 7^2 // Luke 6^{38}) is far more likely to be original.

25
This too was very likely a current proverb based on the conditions of oriental society, in which the rich man, being powerful, constantly receives presents, whereas the poor and uninfluential are consistently fleeced. The structure of the Greek in the Marcan form of the saying suggests an Aramaic original, but in what sense the proverb was originally applied to Christianity is obscure. St Mark presumably took it to mean that anyone who possesses spiritual insight will have it enlarged (? by considering the parables); anyone who does not possess it will only be led (? by the parables) into worse ignorance and bewilderment.

4^{26-29}

[26]*And he said, 'The kingdom of God is as if a man should scatter seed upon the ground,* [27]*and should sleep and rise night and day, and the seed should sprout and grow, he knows not how.* [28]*The earth produces of itself, first the blade, then the ear, then the full grain in the ear.* [29]*But when the grain is ripe, at once he puts in the sickle, because the harvest has come.'*

This is the one parable which is peculiar to Mark. In default of a context it is extremely difficult to interpret and many interpretations have been offered in modern times.

We can safely dismiss those which put the emphasis on v. 28b and take the point to have been the *gradualness* of the coming of the kingdom. All we know of the teaching of Jesus and of the Jewish eschatology in which it was cradled make it extremely unlikely that he taught such a doctrine; and in I *Clement* XXIII, 3 and 4 (*c.* A.D. 96) a very similarly worded parable is used to show that the kingdom will *not* be long delayed.

In our parable the emphasis in fact falls on the inactivity of the farmer after the sowing. The Greek stresses (see below) how his life follows its normal ordered round while the seed grows to maturity without his taking anxious thought (the real point of *he knows not how*) or any active steps (*the earth produces of itself* – that is very emphatic in the Greek). The lesson, as understood by most commentators, is that the disciples must model themselves on the farmer. Just as he leaves it to the earth or, if we prefer it, to God* to produce the harvest, so they must have faith in God to bring about his universal rule. In that case the parable was an answer to a mood either of impatience or of discouragement. Perhaps originally it answered impatient remarks from over-zealous disciples and expressed Jesus' conviction that it would be God's act and not human activity like that of the Zealots which would bring about the kingdom. St Mark, however, sees it as an answer to discouragement. Although Jesus' ministry had met with hindrances and produced no spectacular results, the seed was being sown and the disciples need not be consumed with anxiety; God, who produces the harvest, would also produce the kingdom. The identification of the seed-sowing with Jesus' activity may well be a piece of allegorization suggested to St Mark by his interpretation of the Sower parable; but no doubt he and his contemporaries applied the parable to their own evangelistic activities as well.

More recently Professor Jeremias has suggested a rather different line of interpretation in order to do better justice to the contrast suggested in v. 29; after a period of inactivity suddenly a moment arrives for intense activity – the corn is ripe and the sickle is thrust in. On this view it is God, rather than the disciples, who in a general way resembles the sower. For a long while 'He lets things run their course, passes them by, and ignores them. But when his hour has come, when the eschatological term is complete, then his wondrous act brings in the kingdom. What a reward for patience!'† (*P. J.*, pp. 91–2).

The last ten words of v. 29 are a quotation from Joel 3[13]; there, as often in the Bible, harvest is a symbol for the end of the world, particularly in its aspect as judgement, but it is questionable whether the idea of judgement was very prominent in this parable, at any rate in its original form.

* Cf. R., p. 57: 'The modern idea of a "law of Nature" conceived as working itself out by a kind of inner necessity *apart from God* is of course foreign to the thought of Jesus.'

† A reason can then be given for the careful 'build up' in 28b – it is designed to keep up the listeners' expectation and point the contrast when it comes.

26–27

scatter is, in the Greek, in the aorist *sleep*, and *rise* in the present, which emphasizes the unbroken, untroubled way the latter activities go on after the sowing has taken place.

4^{30-32}

[30]*And he said, 'With what can we compare the kingdom of God, or what*
parable shall we use for it? [31] *It is like a grain of mustard seed, which, when*
sown upon the ground, is the smallest of all the seeds on earth; [32]*yet when*
it is sown it grows up and becomes the greatest of all shrubs, and puts forth
large branches, so that the birds of the air can make nests in its shade.'

An alternative version of this parable appears to have been preserved in the tradition. (Cf. Matt. 13^{31-32} // Luke 13^{18-19}.) In Mark's version the chief point is the contrast between the *smallness* of the seed and the size of what comes from it.

The unspectacular and outwardly insignificant ministry of Jesus may not look the sort of thing that can usher in the kingdom of God, but then, the parable says, the example of the mustard seed should prevent us from judging the significance of results by the size of the beginnings.

Here again the Evangelist no doubt applied the lesson to the evangelistic activities of the early Church as well as to the ministry of Jesus himself; the insignificant beginnings of Christian missions must not daunt the missionary's faith.

Jeremias stresses that, in order to get the full flavour of this type of parable, we must lay aside our modern concern with the intervening process by which the seed is transmuted into the grown bush, and concentrate, as the oriental does, on the contrast between two wholly different situations (*P. J.*, pp. 90–1).

30

The introductory formula has close parallels in rabbinic parables and no doubt this whole section rests on an Aramaic original (See Black, *An Aramaic Approach to the Gospels and Acts*, p. 123.)

31

It is like: This suggests a direct comparison; strictly the idea is 'It is the case with ... as with ...' See above on the nature of parables and cf.

further Jeremias, *P. J.*, pp. 78–9. Thus there need be no suggestion of the kingdom *growing*.

the smallest of all the seeds: The mustard seed is not in fact the smallest seed, though proverbially regarded as such in Palestine.

32
the greatest of all shrubs: By the Lake of Gennesaret it attains a height of about eight or ten feet.

the birds of the air, etc.: Just possibly, in the light of such passages as Dan. $4^{10ff.}$ and ^{21}, Ezek. $17^{22ff.}$, St Mark interpreted these words allegorically as implying that the preaching of the gospel would bring all nations within the scope of the kingdom.

4^{33-34}

33 *With many such parables he spoke the word to them, as they were able to*
hear it; 34 *he did not speak to them without a parable, but privately to his*
own disciples he explained everything.

For these verses, see p. 132. Most commentators detect some inconsistency between them and think that v. 33 reflects the original purpose of the use of parables, while v. 34 reflects St Mark's understanding of them as designed to veil the truth from those outside. (See, however, V. T.)

4^{35}–5^{43} *Three Acts of Divine Power*

4^{35-41} THE STILLING OF THE STORM

35 *On that day, when evening had come, he said to them, 'Let us go across*
to the other side.' 36 *And leaving the crowd, they took him with them, just as*
he was, in the boat. And other boats were with him. 37 *And a great storm of wind*
arose, and the waves beat into the boat, so that the boat was already filling.
38 *But he was in the stern, asleep on the cushion; and they woke him and said*
to him, 'Teacher, do you not care if we perish?' 39 *And he awoke and rebuked*
the wind, and said to the sea, 'Peace! Be still!' And the wind ceased, and

there was a great calm. 40 *He said to them, 'Why are you afraid? Have you*
no faith?' 41 *And they were filled with awe, and said to one another, 'Who*
then is this, that even wind and sea obey him?'

This story must have been used again and again in the early Church for purposes of instruction and edification. In that way it attained its present form, which clearly reflects the religious significance and practical encouragement the early Christians found in it.* In order to appreciate how they understood it, it is necessary to have in mind, as they will have done, ideas and passages from the Old Testament.

According to a myth which was widespread in antiquity, and was shared at one time by the Jews, the original act of creation involved God in a desperate, but finally victorious, contest with the forces of chaos and evil, which were identified with, or at any rate located in, the waters of the sea. As a consequence:

(*a*) ability to control the sea and subdue tempests was regarded as one of the characteristic signs of *divine* power; cf. Pss. 89^{8-9}, 93^{3-4}, 106^{8-9} and Isa. $51^{9b, 10}$.

(*b*) the image of a storm, or of great waters, was frequently used as a metaphor for the evil forces active in the world, and particularly for the tribulations of the righteous, from which only the power of God could save them; cf. Pss. $69^{1, 2, 14-15}$, 18^{16}, etc.

(*c*) the complete confidence in God the religious man ought always to display can be expressed by saying that even in the most terrible storm he will not doubt God's power and determination to save him; cf. Isa. 43^{2}, Pss. 46^{1-3}, 65^{5}, and on the whole matter see carefully Ps. 107^{23-32}.

Two other points from the Old Testament should be noticed. The ability to sleep peacefully and untroubled is a sign of perfect trust in the sustaining and protective power of God; cf. Prov. 3^{23-24}, Pss. 4^{8} and 3^{5}, also Job 11^{18-19} and Lev. 26^{6}. But there were sometimes moments of national or personal disaster when it hardly seemed possible to have such trust, when it almost seemed as if God had lost interest in his people, and had ceased to watch over them. At such times they would speak of God as being 'asleep'† and they did not hesitate to

* See further Appendix B, p. 458.

† We may be reminded how the English peasants, in their terrible sufferings under Stephen and Matilda, complained that 'Christ and his saints are asleep'.

call upon him to 'wake up' and busy himself to help them; cf. Ps. 44^{23-24} 'Awake, why sleepest thou, O Lord', also Pss. 35^{23}, 59^{4}, and Isa. 51^{9a}.

Against this background, our story can be readily understood. Jesus and his disciples put out in a boat at night. Although sudden violent storms were liable to blow up on the lake (as they still do), Jesus 'laid him down and slept in peace', for he had complete faith in the divine power to 'make him dwell in safety'. By contrast the disciples showed themselves, as on other occasions, to be men of little faith. When a storm arose which threatened to fill the ship, they became terrified, and were so far from sharing Jesus' untroubled faith that they mistook it for careless indifference and woke him with a rebuke. Once awake, he performed the characteristically divine act (stilling the waves with a word of rebuke),* and the disciples were now filled with a different kind of fear and awe, realizing that they were in the presence of one who disposed of power nothing less than divine.

Their dawning realization is expressed in the form of a question and the early Christian congregations would have had a ready answer. They will have seen in the story evidence that Jesus was, if not actually God, undoubtedly the eschatological agent of God, entrusted with the plenitude of divine power for the protecting and saving of his Church. And there was the further point that, just as in Old Testament times God sometimes seemed indifferent to the sufferings of his righteous servants, so at times it might almost seem as if Christ was asleep while the Ark of his Church was being buffeted by waves of persecution and suffering; but from this story they could learn that he was in fact by no means indifferent – in response to their prayer, even if it was not accompanied by perfect faith, he would arise and deal with the forces arrayed against them, no matter how powerful those forces might seem to be; for was he not armed with the power of God himself?

In cases like this, where a story has been many times told and retold in such a way as to bring out its practical lesson, the details are often lacking which would enable us to reconstruct exactly what happened.†

* Cf. Ps. 104^{6-7} 'At thy rebuke the waters shall flee'.

† For example, experienced seamen, such as the fishermen disciples, would presumably have taken all normal steps dictated by good seamanship to keep the boat afloat in a storm; cf. Jonah 1^{5}.

So, without needing to be excessively sceptical about the historical basis of the story, we may agree with R. that: 'the precise historical basis, whatever it may have been, is now irrecoverable' (p. 60).

36
just as he was: i.e. presumably, without going ashore. Possibly these words were added in order to fit this story, originally independent, on to the preceding scene where Jesus was already in a boat (4^1). Without the addition the Greek would read more naturally and would imply that Jesus went on board the boat at this point.*
other boats were with him: These boats are rather mysterious, for they do not figure in the sequel, yet nothing is said to account for their disappearance. Could they be meant to emphasize how the story 'fulfils' Ps. $107^{23\text{ff.}}$? In that passage it was those who *went down to the sea in ships* (plural and the same Greek word as here) who *saw the deeds of the Lord, his wondrous works in the deep.*

38
Jesus sleeps on the high afterdeck, away from the splashing of the waves, resting his head on the wooden or leather seat normally used by the rower or helmsman. (This, rather than 'cushion', is the meaning of *prŏskĕphalaiŏn*; note the definite article.) These details are sometimes taken as proving direct eyewitness testimony, but it is difficult to know how else it would have been possible to sleep in such a vessel; cf. Vergil, *Aeneid* IV, 554.

39
rebuked the wind, and said to the sea, 'Peace! Be still!': The wording recalls the Old Testament, cf. Ps. 104^7. The word translated 'Be still' means literally 'Be muzzled' and is the same as that used at 1^{25}. See the note there, which suggests that the word may have been in use among contemporary wonder-workers as a means of binding hostile powers and making them powerless to harm. If so, its use here reflects a stage in the development of the story at which the storm was seen as the work of demonic powers, and Jesus' silencing of them as all part of his eschatological struggle against God's enemies.

40
Another reading gives 'Have you not yet faith?', and this may be right; those who had had such opportunities of getting to know Jesus ought by now to have realized that, while he was with them, there was

* Lohmeyer points out that the sort of little boat envisaged in 4^1 would be a different type of craft from the sea-going vessel of this story.

no need to fear that the powers of evil would prevail against them. Whichever is the right reading, that is no doubt the lesson the early Christians will have drawn from the story; seeing the Church and themselves, with all their experiences of Christ's grace and power, exemplified in the boat and its passengers, they no doubt took to themselves the rebuke as well as the encouragement provided by the story. For the same reason, they probably interpreted the 'faith' demanded as faith in Christ, whatever the original meaning may have been.

5^{1–20} AN EXCEPTIONALLY POWERFUL DEMON OVERCOME

5 They came to the other side of the sea, to the country of the Ger'asenes.[a]
2And when he had come out of the boat, there met him out of the tombs a man
with an unclean spirit, 3who lived among the tombs; and no one could bind
him any more, even with a chain; 4for he had often been bound with fetters
and chains, but the chains he wrenched apart, and the fetters he broke in
pieces; and no one had the strength to subdue him. 5Night and day among the
tombs and on the mountains he was always crying out, and bruising himself
with stones. 6And when he saw Jesus from afar, he ran and worshipped him,
7and crying out with a loud voice, he said, 'What have you to do with me,
Jesus, Son of the Most High God? I adjure you by God, do not torment me.'
8For he had said to him, 'Come out of the man, you unclean spirit!' 9And
Jesus[b] *asked him, 'What is your name?' He replied, 'My name is Legion;*
for we are many.' 10And he begged him eagerly not to send them out of the
country. 11Now a great herd of swine was feeding there on the hillside; 12and
they begged him, 'Send us to the swine, let us enter them.' 13So he gave them
leave. And the unclean spirits came out, and entered the swine; and the herd,
numbering about two thousand, rushed down the steep bank into the sea, and
were drowned in the sea.

14The herdsmen fled, and told it in the city and in the country. And people
came to see what it was that had happened. 15And they came to see Jesus, and
saw the demoniac sitting there, clothed and in his right mind, the man who
had had the legion; and they were afraid. 16And those who had seen it told
what had happened to the demoniac and to the swine. 17And they began to beg
Jesus[c] *to depart from their neighbourhood. 18And as he was getting into the*

boat, the man who had been possessed with demons begged him that he might be with him. [19]*But he refused, and said to him, 'Go home to your friends, and tell them how much the Lord has done for you, and how he has had mercy on you.'* [20]*And he went away and began to proclaim in the Decap'olis how much Jesus had done for him; and all men marvelled.*

a Other ancient authorities read *Gergesenes*, some *Gadarenes*
b Greek *he*
c Greek *him*

The primary point of this story, especially in the earlier form in which it appears to have ended at v. 15, was to stress the overwhelming power available to Jesus in his contest with the demonic powers, no doubt with the idea of provoking the same sort of question as that with which the previous story ended: 'Who can this be that such immense divine power is at his disposal?'

Accordingly, the immensity of Jesus' power is stressed in various ways; the case-history of the possessed man is given in unusual detail, as showing that no natural power was effective against the supernatural forces which had him in their grip (vv. 3–5). In vv. 6–13 the vast number and power of these forces is emphasized; yet they are shown freely admitting that they have met their match in Jesus. He is able to deal with them simply by means of a word of command, and the rest of the story shows how complete was the cure thus effected. And there is independent testimony to this; the man's fellow countrymen who knew from experience that no earthly power could succeed with him were so impressed at the success of Jesus' treatment of him that they became afraid of the supernatural power it argued, to the extent, if we include vv. 16–17, of asking Jesus to leave their country.*

It will thus be seen that the main point of the story is almost entirely independent of the presence and destruction of the swine, a feature which is confined to two verses (vv. 12–13), and there are in fact some grounds for thinking that this element in the story is a later addition (see notes below). However, original or not, the Evangelist will have seen great significance in it. To begin with, the manifest evidence that

* That, rather than the fear of losing more pigs, is the motive presupposed in v. 17!

the evil force had entered the swine was, according to the popular ideas of the time, clear confirmation that it really had been cast out of the man; the reality of the miracle is thus confirmed. It was widely believed at the time that when spirits were exorcized, they often vented their spite by some piece of mischief clearly visible to the onlookers, such as upsetting a statue (Philostratus, *Apollonius of Tyana*, IV, 20), or jugs of water (Josephus, *Antiquities*, VIII, 48). If in this case enormous and multiple mischief was caused, then clearly the evil power had been equally vast and multiple; yet it had been no match for Jesus. The divine immensity of his power receives further confirmation.

Are we also to see significance in the fact that the incident occurs in a preponderantly Gentile area, and that it was swine – to the Jews completely unclean and unfit for food – into which the spirits were driven? Some commentators feel that these considerations are essential to the complete understanding of the story, at any rate in its present form. This is the first time in the Gospel that Jesus has been in Gentile territory, so it is the more noteworthy that his holy presence routs and banishes uncleanness. In effect the land is cleansed by his coming, and the way prepared for its Christianizing, a task which, at the end of this story, Jesus explicitly lays upon the man previously possessed by the demons (vv. 18–20). The story may thus have been intended to explain how this predominantly Gentile area early became a home for Christianity, and will also perhaps have provided support for the Gentile mission of the early Church. Lightfoot indeed ventured an interpretation of the whole section 4^{35}–5^{20} along these lines, though he did so, as he himself put it, 'with great reserve and a keen sense of the dangers inherent in this form of exposition'. Though too long to be quoted here, it is very stimulating and deserves to be consulted (*H. & I.*, pp. 89–90). As Lightfoot himself points out, this mission aspect is not made very emphatic, or even very clear, in the story itself and much will depend on the detailed discussion of vv. 18–20, for which see notes below.

Should we also perhaps find in the story a 'fulfilment' of Ps. 68^{6}, which, in Mark's Greek psalter, will have run: 'God maketh the solitary to dwell in a house (cf. v. 19a) leading forth mightily them that are bound (v. 4) and also them that behave rebelliously and that dwell in tombs' (vv. 2–3)? Certainly there seems to be a sense that the man, who was quite unfit for any society, is restored by the power of Jesus to that family and community life which is proper to man.

If the reader feels that it must be fanciful to suggest so many lines of interpretation for a single story, he should remember what was said in the Introduction about the process by which these stories came to their present form. This particular story has clearly passed through a number of stages, and if, at each stage, further significance was found in it, it is quite natural that in its final form it should yield more than one interpretation.

In answer to the question: What actually happened? the suggestion has often been made that the cure of a hysteria sufferer was accompanied by a paroxysm which frightened the swine and so led to a stampede. This was naturally interpreted by the onlookers in terms of contemporary beliefs about demon possession. Such a view is quite plausible, but in view of what has been said about the history and character of the story, it is perhaps safer to agree with J. M. Creed that 'it is not profitable to attempt rationalizing versions as to what may have occurred.'

With regard to St Mark's placing of this story, he may well have seen great significance in its juxtaposition with 4^{35-41}. We have already seen that in the Old Testament it was a signal mark of God's power to be able to 'rule the raging of the sea'. It was likewise a sign of his power that he could at will subdue the tumultuous activities of Israel's enemies which are often likened to the wild raging of the sea. Thus in Ps. 65^{7} we read of God *Who dost still the roaring of the seas, the roaring of their waves, the tumult of the peoples*. 'So,' St Mark would seem to be saying, 'if Jesus displayed the ability to do both these things, is it not plain that his power is divine? Have we not, in these two incidents taken together, the fulfilment of Ps. 65?' For a full discussion of this see Hoskyns and Davey, *The Riddle of the New Testament* (1936 ed.), pp. 86ff.*

* In the Greek version of the Old Testament which St Mark seems normally to have used, the reference to 'the madness of the peoples' is missing, but we read instead 'The nations (or the Gentiles) shall be troubled'. The passage goes on (Ps. 65^{8}) *so that those who dwell at earth's farthest bounds are afraid at thy signs*. Since our incident occurred in Gentile territory and those who were *afraid* (v. 15) and 'troubled' (v. 17) by Jesus' sign were Gentiles, it looks as if the story was seen as fulfilling the words of the Psalm both in the Hebrew and the Greek forms.

1

Gerasenes: This is probably what Mark wrote, the other names being guesses by copyists who knew that Gerasa is over thirty miles to the south-east of the Sea of Galilee (see map), and so does not fit the story. *Gadara* is about six miles from the sea, while *Gergesa* cannot certainly be identified, and *Gergesenes* may be simply a conjecture of Origen based on Gen. 10^{16}. Modern archaeologists have located the ruins of a small town called Kersa or Kursa, on the east coast of the Sea, and this may be the place Origen was thinking of, though it has no 'cliffs overhanging the Lake' such as he describes. No doubt St Mark took over the name from tradition, but he plainly thought of the city as close to the Sea (v. 14), which hardly suggests that he was familiar with Palestinian geography (see Introduction, p. 40).

2–3

Tombs were thought to be a favourite haunt of demons, and we know from the rabbis that those who spent the night among them were regarded with suspicion. Cf. also Ps. 68^{6} (as quoted above from the Greek version) and also Isa. 65^{1-4}, a passage which may not have been without its influence on the whole story. (Note especially 65^{4}.)

5

Moffatt, probably rightly, has 'shrieked' and 'gashed himself'.

6–7

worshipped: Literally 'went down on his knees to'. In so doing the spirit recognized the superiority of Jesus, yet he made one effort to appease him and render him powerless by the use of his name; see on 1^{24}, and note that here a Gentile demon uses a typically Gentile way of referring to Israel's God! Cf. Dan. 3^{26} and 4^{2}.

Foiled in this attempt he begins to sue for terms (v. 7b), thereby tacitly admitting defeat. The notion of an exorcist torturing a demon he has expelled was a common one, but Matthew (8^{29}) is probably right in seeing here a reference to the punishment God was expected to inflict on Satan and his demons at the end of the world – cf. e.g. Rev. 20^{10}. The demon realizes that with the coming of Jesus the eschatological event has begun, and begs Jesus to spare him the corresponding punishment.

9

Jesus in his turn seeks power over his opponent by discovering his name, and such is his authority that his question is answered at once.*

* This seems preferable to Wellhausen's interpretation according to which the demon refuses to give his name, but gives his number instead!

Jeremias, however, has another suggestion (*Jesus' Promise to the Nations*, p. 30, n. 5). At some stage the tradition must have existed in Aramaic, and in Aramaic the word translated *Legion* could also mean *soldier*. Jeremias thinks that it originally meant *soldier* here, and he paraphrases the demon's reply: 'My name is "soldier", since we (the demons) are a great host, (and resemble one another as soldiers do).' Such a reply would amount to a refusal on the part of the demon to disclose his identity, but then 'owing to the fact that the translator rendered the Aramaic word by the Greek *Legion* the mistaken idea arose that the demoniac was possessed by a whole "regiment of demons".' Once this idea arose it was a short step to the expansion of the story by the material in vv. 12–13, especially if, as many scholars believe, we have in those two verses a 'popular' story of a Jewish exorcism in a heathen land which existed independently and has simply been attached to Jesus. In that case 'the original continuation of v. 11 was v. 14, and the herd of swine was only mentioned because the swineherds witnessed the expulsion of the demon'.

Whatever may be thought of this rather radical way of dealing with the story, it certainly explains the curious alternation between singular and plural in describing what possessed the demoniac, the plural being confined to v. 10 and vv. 12–13.

10

out of the country: This verse betrays the essentially popular character of much of the gospel material. According to popular beliefs demons often asked favours in return for leaving a demoniac, and, since they were specially associated with a particular building or locality, they were loath to be removed – cf. Luke 11^{24} for the same circle of ideas and Bultmann, p. 239 and n. 2, for other parallels.

13

about two thousand: A detail peculiar to Mark. It seems a fantastically large number, and curiously enough does not correspond with the demon's name, for a Roman legion was normally 6,000 strong. Jeremias suggests that what was in mind was the military unit known as a *tĕlŏs* ('battalion') which consisted of 2,048 men.

Are we to assume that the spirits perished with the swine? That appears to have been St Luke's understanding of the incident, and it may have been St Mark's as well; certainly we must assume so if the story signifies the banishing from the land of what is unclean.

15

A typical conclusion to a healing pericope (see Introduction, p. 24); it has been suggested, therefore, that at one stage the story ended at this point and that vv. 16–17 and 18–20 were added later, the former in order to make a connexion with what follows, where Jesus is on the other side of the Lake, the latter to point the moral of the incident as the beginning of Gentile Christianity.

18–20

The vocabulary and style of these verses are Marcan; the contents have given rise to much discussion. Some commentators take Jesus' words in v. 19 as tantamount to a command to secrecy ('keep it within the family circle'), which is disobeyed by the man in v. 20; cf. 1^{43-45} and 7^{36} for very similiar situations.*

Against this is the fact that the Greek unmistakably has *and* (*kai*), not *but* (*dĕ*) at the beginning of v. 20. It would seem, therefore, that whether or not we accept the interpretation of Lightfoot quoted above, the man's action in v. 20 is represented as an obedient fulfilment of Jesus' command in v. 19. We then need some explanation of Jesus' refusal to allow the man to join his company (v. 18, for *be with him* cf. 3^{14}). The most natural one seems to be that he wanted to reserve him for a Gentile mission as distinct from the apostles' proclamation to the Jews in Galilee and Judea. In favour of this are the facts that the word for *proclaim* in v. 20 is the one normally used in the New Testament for preaching the gospel (*kēryssein* – though cf. 1^{45} and 7^{36}) and that *your friends* (*tous sous*, v. 19) implies a wider circle than just the man's family.

20

Decapolis: The word means '(a league of) ten cities', and refers to a group of cities lying for the most part east of the Jordan (see map), and enjoying since the time of Pompey a certain amount of independence. The population was mixed, but predominantly Gentile, as is shown by the presence of swine and herdsmen; Jews were forbidden even to keep swine.

5^{21-43} THE HEALING OF THE WOMAN WITH A HAEMORRHAGE AND THE RAISING OF THE DEAD CHILD

21 *And when Jesus had crossed again in the boat to the other side, a great*
crowd gathered about him; and he was beside the sea. 22 *Then came one of the*

* On this view Jesus' motive for his refusal in v. 18 is that he does not want to have with him in Palestine anyone who might divulge his status.

rulers of the synagogue, Ja'irus by name; and seeing him, he fell at his feet, 23 and besought him, saying, 'My little daughter is at the point of death. Come and lay your hands on her, so that she may be made well, and live.' 24 And he went with him.

And a great crowd followed him and thronged about him. 25 And there was a woman who had had a flow of blood for twelve years, 26 and who had suffered much under many physicians, and had spent all that she had, and was no better but rather grew worse. 27 She had heard the reports about Jesus, and came up behind him in the crowd and touched his garment. 28 For she said, 'If I touch even his garments, I shall be made well.' 29 And immediately the haemorrhage ceased; and she felt in her body that she was healed of her disease. 30 And Jesus, perceiving in himself that power had gone forth from him, immediately turned about in the crowd, and said, 'Who touched my garments?' 31 And his disciples said to him, 'You see the crowd pressing around you, and yet you say, "Who touched me?"' 32 And he looked around to see who had done it. 33 But the woman, knowing what had been done to her, came in fear and trembling and fell down before him, and told him the whole truth. 34 And he said to her, 'Daughter, your faith has made you well; go in peace, and be healed of your disease.'

35 While he was still speaking, there came from the ruler's house some who said, 'Your daughter is dead. Why trouble the Teacher any further?' 36 But ignoring[a] *what they said, Jesus said to the ruler of the synagogue, 'Do not fear, only believe.' 37 And he allowed no one to follow him except Peter and James and John the brother of James. 38 When they came to the house of the ruler of the synagogue, he saw a tumult, and people weeping and wailing loudly. 39 And when he had entered, he said to them, 'Why do you make a tumult and weep? The child is not dead but sleeping.' 40 And they laughed at him. But he put them all outside, and took the child's father and mother and those who were with him, and went in where the child was. 41 Taking her by the hand he said to her, 'Tal'itha cu'mi'; which means, 'Little girl, I say to you, arise.' 42 And immediately the girl got up and walked; for she was twelve years old. And immediately they were overcome with amazement. 43 And he strictly charged them that no one should know this, and told them to give her something to eat.*

a Or *overhearing*. Other ancient authorities read *hearing*

What we have here is without precise parallel in the Gospel – an incident broken into by another incident which takes place in the middle of it. It may well be that the incidents actually occurred in this way, though in view of the fact that St Mark is fond of insertions between the two halves of a single story (see p. 112),* and that the style of 5^{25-34} is distinctly different in the original Greek from that of the rest of the passage, it is perhaps more probable that the arrangement is due to St Mark, who inserted the incident of the woman with the haemorrhage to give time for the situation in the main incident to develop. In any case, St Mark no doubt regarded the section as a single story which, with the stories of the storm and the Gerasene demoniac, makes up one of the groups of three of which he is so fond.

After a formal connecting link with what has gone before, probably, in part at least, of his own composition (v. 21), the Evangelist tells of a Jewish notable who fell at Jesus' feet in front of a large crowd and begged for his help. This would indeed be a remarkable thing, and Mark's first readers would know what conclusions to draw. The Jewish authorities might affect to think Jesus an impostor, but there were those among them who, when trouble forced them to face realities, could not help admitting his power and even begging for its exercise, with a public display of humility which showed that they really recognized its character and source. In Mark, as opposed to Matthew (9^{18}), the man does not say that his daughter is already dead but that she is *in extremis,* as we say; the meaning is that the child is beyond the help of any *earthly* power, so the man's request witnesses to his belief that there is in Jesus a *supernatural* power, and one which must be derived from God, since it makes for 'healing and life' (v. 23). But there is no thought at this point in the story of raising one who is actually dead. Jesus accedes to the man's request and goes with him towards his house, closely followed by the crowd. This provides the setting for the 'inserted' episode.

A woman with a (? continuous uterine) haemorrhage, who, like the notable's daughter, had exhausted all *earthly* possibilities of healing (v. 26), had been led to believe that Jesus possessed a supernatural power of healing, which resided in him almost as a physical fluid, and could be tapped by touch, even the touching of his clothes, without Jesus himself being aware of what was happening. Beliefs of this kind

* The cases cited there are admittedly only partial parallels. Nowhere else in the Gospel does an insertion divide up what are so obviously the interdependent halves of a single story.

were common in antiquity in connexion with great and holy men; it was said of Abraham, for example,* that the very *sight* of him brought healing to the sick, and see Acts 5^{15} and 19^{11-12} for similar beliefs about the apostles. And our passage is not the only one in the Gospels to suggest that the miracles of Jesus were sometimes interpreted in this way by his contemporaries and early followers (cf. e.g. Luke 6^{19} and 5^{17} and Mark 3^{10} and 6^{56}, and see further C. K. Barrett, *H.S.G.T.*, pp. 75–6). Indeed, up to a point, this story supports such a view, for it goes on to relate that the woman's expectation was fulfilled as she hoped. Power *did* pass through Jesus' clothes to heal her (v. 29). But if the story had ended there it might have been seriously misleading, especially to people with a Hellenistic background. The Hellenistic world was well acquainted with such stories and with the kind of power (*dynamis*) they seemed to imply. Thus Ramsay writes that the word (*dynamis*) 'was one of the most common and characteristic terms in the language of pagan devotion. "Power" was what the devotees respected and worshipped', though they frequently conceived it as a more or less impersonal energy, largely outside the control of the person through whom it manifested itself.

But the rest of the story sets things in a different light. To begin with, Jesus is in fact in full control of the power he wields; 'immediately' it is tapped he is aware of it (v. 30) and is conscious of having been touched, by reason of a supernatural insight which completely baffles the natural intelligence of his disciples (v. 31). What is more, his question and his look have the power to make the woman come forward and confess (this seems to be the implication in v. 33). It is only when *in fear and trembling* she has personally confronted Jesus (v. 33), that her action is approved and her cure confirmed. Her action gains the approval of Jesus because what she had in fact relied on for release from her plague was the one thing that men are *meant* to rely on for release from *all* their 'plagues', namely 'the things concerning Jesus' (v. 27, see notes), that is, the life and work of Jesus recognized as the saving power of God active in the world. To rely on it in that way is 'faith', and through 'faith' men can have 'salvation' or 'wholeness' from all their sins, and the evils which result from them, known to the Jews as 'plagues' (see on 3^{10}). It is therefore no accident that the Greek of v. 34 is ambiguous and can

* By R. Huna (about A.D. 350) see S.-B., I, p. 521.

equally well be translated: 'Your faith *has brought you salvation.* Go in peace and be whole of your plague.' What happened to the woman is thus an example of 'salvation by faith', and helps to explain what that phrase means; but it does that only when thus interpreted, as the words of Jesus interpret it in the story. Then it can become a model for those who want to enter into relationship with Jesus and win from him the affectionate address 'Son' or 'Daughter' (v. 34).

This interpretation of the woman's deed in terms of faith provides the point of return to the main story. The father's original request had shown his faith in Jesus, but it was faith in his power to heal the sick; now the news of his daughter's death poses the question of faith in Jesus' power to raise the dead. The words of the messengers show that they have no such faith; seeing that the child is actually dead, there can be no point in 'troubling the Teacher further' (v. 35). Even *his* power, it is implied, cannot be expected to deal with death. We may be reminded of the attitude of Martha and Mary, the sisters of Lazarus, in the eleventh chapter of John. If Jesus had been there before their brother died, they are convinced that something could have been done (vv. 21 and 32), but now that Lazarus is actually dead, they have no hope (or only the vaguest hope, v. 22) that even the power of Jesus can be of any avail. Their hopeless attitude finds expression in weeping for the dead, and likewise in our story those who share the faithless attitude of the messengers fall to (ritual) lamentation for the child (v. 38b). In the same sort of way, as we know from Paul's Epistles, some of the early Christians believed in Christ's power to save those who survived till his final coming, but they 'were sorry as men without hope' (I Thess. 4^{13}) for those who had already died before his coming. St Paul repudiates such grief and the lack of faith it betokened, and Jesus' attitude is the same, both here and in John. He 'ignores' the words of the messengers (v. 36): in John the weeping moves him to angry emotion; here it moves him to rebuke (v. 39) and finally to expel the mourners (v. 40). By contrast with such faithlessness, the father (like Martha in John 11^{26}) is urged to have faith (v. 36). Jesus is the agent of God himself and so death is by no means outside his control.* For those who rely on him, it is only a

* In the light of the rabbinic evidence, it is not possible to say how far Jews of Jesus' time would have regarded the raising of the dead as a sure sign of the power of God or of his Messiah, but the following saying, often repeated in

sleep from which he can and will awaken them (v. 39, *The child is not dead but sleeping*). In the case of most Christians, such awakening will not come in the course of this world's existence; it is, as St John shows, something which involves the glory of God himself (John 11[40]) and, as such, is appropriate to the world to come. But, 'in order that the disciples may believe' (John 11[15]), Jesus here brings one such awakening forward into history, though it is to be witnessed only by a small group of believing people who would rightly understand and proclaim its significance (vv. 37 and 40). The shattering impact made upon them (v. 42b) witnesses that they have beheld nothing less than an epiphany. (Cf. the transfiguration.)

❦

22
one of the rulers of the synagogue: More idiomatically, simply: 'a synagogue-ruler'. The title was applied to the supervisor of the worship of a synagogue, but it was also used more generally of the prominent members of a synagogue congregation.

Jairus by name: These words were probably not in the original text; they may possibly have been introduced into it from Luke 8[41]. Cf. Introduction, p. 28.

23
be made well, and live: According to early Christian usage, the Greek words here could also mean: 'that she may be saved and attain (eternal) life'. This is the more significant because in vv. 41 and 42 the words translated '*arise*' and '*got up*' are the normal Greek words for resurrection. Such facts support the interpretation of the story offered above.

26
Popular stories of this sort in the ancient world often included deprecation of the medical profession. Contrast Luke 8[43].

27
the reports about Jesus: Literally 'the things concerning Jesus', a vaguer phrase which could also mean, to a Christian reader, the religious truth about Jesus and his work (cf. Luke 22[37] and 24[19] and [27]). Possibly there is a deliberate ambiguity; see above.

---

various forms, is interesting: 'Three keys are in God's hand, which are not entrusted to the hand of any other, however fully authorized by God, namely, the key to the rain, the key to motherhood, and the key to giving new life to the dead.' S.-B., I, p. 523.

30
that power had gone forth from him: R.V. translates more accurately: 'that the power proceeding from him [i.e. his messianic power of healing] had gone forth'.

31
The common sense of what they say only serves to emphasize the wonder of Jesus' ability to distinguish the healing-touching from any ordinary touch.

35
Teacher = 'Rabbi', as in 4^{38}.

36
ignoring: Certainly the right reading and very probably the right translation.

37
'The three form an inner ring in the apostolic band.' They are the ones chosen to be present at the transfiguration (9^{2}) and in Gethsemane (14^{33}); cf. also 13^{3}.

38–39
The reference may be to the professional mourners it was customary to employ on such occasions.

39
The child is not dead but sleeping: It has often been suggested that this was originally meant literally; the family had been over-hasty and mistaken in coming to the conclusion that the child was dead. But how should Jesus have known that before he 'went in where the child was' (v. 40)? In any case there can be no doubt at all that St Mark and his contemporaries saw the incident as a raising from the dead and interpreted it along such lines as those suggested earlier; and, having regard to the history of the material, it is hazardous to attempt a re-construction of what originally happened on the basis of a single phrase. Those interested should consult the very balanced and careful discussion in V.T. R. writes: 'Assuming the narrative to have a historical basis, it is plainly impossible now to determine, except on *a priori* grounds, what the original facts may have been' (p. 70).

sleeping: The use of 'sleep' as a *euphemism* for death was common enough among the ancients, but the Christian usage was quite different from that. The Christians described the dead as 'sleeping' (e.g. Matt. 27^{52}, 1 Cor. 11^{30}, 15^{6}, 1 Thess. 4^{13-15}), because they believed that they would one day be awakened, just as people who are asleep are awakened, For a parallel use among the Jews compare the rabbinic statement:* 'God said to Jacob "Thou shalt sleep, but thou shalt not die".' The word normally used by the early Christians in this connexion was *koimasthai* (whence our cemetery, literally 'a sleeping place'), but for the verb (*katheudein*) used here, cf. Eph. 5^{14} and 1 Thess. 5^{10}.

40
they laughed at him or 'laughed him to scorn'. Richardson (*The Miracle Stories of the Gospels*, p. 74) thinks there is a reference to the way the world often laughs at the Christians' hope of resurrection.

41ff.
The actual narrative of the miracle has many traits typical of such stories in the ancient world, e.g. the gesture ('taking her by the hand', v. 41), the vivid description of the results (v. 42, cf. v. 29), the powerful effect produced on the witnesses (v. 42), and such proofs of the reality and effectiveness of the miracle as the fact that the girl got up and walked and also that she needed food (v. 43) – ghosts do not eat solid food! Cf. Luke 24^{41-43}. We know of parallels to all these; we also know that ancient wonder-workers often used formulas in a foreign tongue, and Origen tells us that such words lose their power if translated into another language. Some such motive may have lain behind the preservation of the original Aramaic words in v. 41. When Greek-speaking Christians attempted to work wonders after the example of their Lord (cf. e.g. Acts 8^{6-13}, $9^{36ff.}$, $20^{7ff.}$, 1 Cor. $12^{10 \text{ and } 28}$) they may well have felt it important to preserve the wonder-working words in their original – and to them foreign – form (cf. 7^{34}). Matthew and Luke omit the Aramaic.

42
The words used to describe the amazement are unusually strong; what had been witnessed was remarkable even in the life of Jesus (see above).

43
The command here is odd, as being so obviously impossible of fulfilment. Most commentators think this is a case where St Mark has rather artificially intruded his theory of the messianic secret (see Introduction, p. 32). He may also have been influenced by the feeling that a sight which was too sacred for all and sundry to see ought not too lightly to be described to all and sundry.

* S:-P., 1, p. 523

6^{1-6a} JESUS AGAIN REJECTED BY HIS OWN PEOPLE DESPITE THE SIGNS OF DIVINE POWER

6 *He went away from there and came to his own country; and his disciples*
followed him. [2]*And on the sabbath he began to teach in the synagogue; and*
many who heard him were astonished, saying 'Where did this man get all
this? What is the wisdom given to him? What mighty works are wrought
by his hands! [3]*Is not this the carpenter, the son of Mary and brother of*
James and Joses and Judas and Simon, and are not his sisters here with us?'
And they took offence[a] *at him.* [4]*And Jesus said to them, 'A prophet is not*
without honour, except in his own country, and among his own kin, and in
his own house.' [5]*And he could do no mighty work there, except that he*
laid his hands upon a few sick people and healed them. [6]*And he marvelled*
because of their unbelief.

a Or *stumbled*

This apparently trivial episode of the rejection of Jesus by his fellow-townsmen undoubtedly possessed profound significance for the Evangelist. To understand that, we must remember how puzzled the early Church was by the refusal of the Lord's own people to believe the gospel, when the Gentiles were accepting it in ever-increasing numbers; and the problem was the more acute because it exposed the Church to the objection: 'How can you claim that Jesus is the Jewish Messiah, the fulfilment of the Jewish religion, when the Jews themselves flatly deny it?'

Naturally the matter was much pondered; and, following a hint in Isaiah (8^{14-15}), the early Christians came to believe that the Jewish attitude was all part of the mysterious providence of God, who had foretold it when he said that the precious cornerstone which he intended to lay in Sion (Isa. 28^{16}) would prove a stumbling-block and a snare for the Jews (Isa. 8^{14}) – something that would stop their progress along the right road and drive them into error and sin. (For this combination and interpretation of the two passages from Isaiah, see Rom. 9^{32-33} and 1 Pet. $2^{6ff.}$; the whole of Rom. 9–11 is concerned with this problem.) After the crucifixion what 'offended' the Jews about Jesus was the accursed manner of his death (cf. Deut. 21^{22-23}

and 1 Cor. 1^{23}). But it was they, after all, who had brought about his death, so already, in the days of his flesh, they must have found some ground of offence in him. In a sense the whole of Mark's Gospel is concerned with that offence, and with showing that it had no basis except in men's blindness and sin. That has already been shown in the case of the controversies of 2^{1}–3^{6} and in 3^{20-35}, where, if the authorities from Jerusalem and Jesus' own relatives allowed themselves to be offended at him, it was only because they put on his activities blasphemous interpretations ($3^{21 \text{ and } 22}$) quite at variance with the evidence (3^{7-12}). Now, as Jesus' ministry in Galilee draws to a close, his own people, the inhabitants of his own home place, are called upon to decide upon his claims; and they too take offence at him (v. 3, the same, almost technical, word in the Greek as is used at Rom. 9^{33}, 1 Pet. 2^{8}, and 1 Cor. 1^{23} – see notes below).

Both the context and form of the story are designed to bring out the true character of this rejection; Jesus has just given three signal indications of his true status (4^{35}–5^{43}). The Nazarenes cannot deny the reality of these mighty works or of the supernatural wisdom which informs his preaching; nor can they withhold their wondering admiration (v. 2). They are even led to ask the right questions about the origin and the meaning of such power and wisdom (v. 2). But then, between vv. 2 and 3, there is an abrupt change; the questions do not receive their true answer and the wonder does not pass over into faith, and all because the Nazarenes remind themselves that Jesus has been a tradesman in their town, whose family and early career are well known to them. But why should that prevent his being the Messiah? Just as the later Jews could not believe that one who had been crucified could be Messiah, so the Nazarenes could not believe it of one who was an ordinary artisan from among them. If he came from a humble family in their midst, he could not come from God (cf. John 6^{41-42}); such was their misconception, and it arose from obstinately clinging to the traditional expectations of a wholly glorious and supernatural Messiah when the facts pointed in a completely different direction.*

* And although, as St Mark will elsewhere seek to show, the scriptures themselves, if properly understood, did not support the traditional expectations.

On the moral aspect of the Nazarenes' attitude Montefiore has a very just observation: 'They are half inclined to marvel and believe, but this very half-

So St Mark exposes the character and worthlessness of this rejection of Jesus; and he does it so carefully because he sees it as typical of the Lord's rejection by his people at large; what happens at the end of the whole ministry will be the same in essence as what happens here at the close of the Galilean ministry. That final repudiation of the divine words and works will be as unjustified as this. So 'this apparently trivial story of rejection, followed by the evangelizing activity of the twelve, reminds us once more of what will be the final issue, and how from it will develop the world-wide mission of the Church' (*H. & I.*, p. 113). The tragedy was that by their refusal to believe, the Lord's very own people made impossible the great things he longed to do for them (v. 5a); small wonder the Christians were perplexed by a thing so surprising and terrible – the Lord himself had 'marvelled' at such unbelief (v. 6). Yet perhaps after all they ought not to have been so surprised for, as Jesus himself had reminded them, other messengers of God had had similar experiences – so often indeed that it had become proverbial that 'a prophet does not lack honour except in his own country'.

1

The connecting formula is vague and no doubt purely conventional.

his own country: Rather 'his native town'. The Greek word (*patris*) could mean either, and was therefore very suitable for use here. The reaction of his native town to Jesus was a symbol and foreshadowing of how his *patris* in the wider sense would react.

3

carpenter: The Greek word (*tĕktōn*), like the Hebrew *charasch*, means a worker in stone, wood, or metal, and the precise reference has to be gathered in each case from the context. The Church fathers are very divided as to the meaning here; perhaps Jesus was the village builder, in which case he will have included a certain amount of carpentry among his skills.

---

belief makes them the more irritated and incredulous. His teaching seems very wise; but yet how could this man, whose family they knew so well – just ordinary people – say such wise things? He was no rabbi by profession. It is impossible. This seems true to human nature. They do not *want* to believe. If Jesus *was* a veritable prophet, it would be annoying. "We are as good as he, but we could not teach as he does, and we could not do the wonders he is said to have done. Therefore, after all, his teaching is *not* wise and he did not do the wonders!"' (I, 118–19.)

the carpenter, the son of Mary: Strangely, the R.S.V. margin does not mention the well-attested variant 'the son of the carpenter and of Mary'. Both readings have strong arguments in their favour and there is no general agreement which is original. If it is the reading given in R.S.V. and the words go back to a Jewish source, it would be significant that Jesus is described solely with reference to his mother, without mention of his father. This would be an unheard-of thing among the Jews* who always described a man by reference to his father, and it could only be intended as an insult (cf. Judges 11^{1}). But we cannot be sure that St Mark appreciated such niceties of Jewish usage, and J. M. Robinson suggests that St Mark omitted the father in order to underline that *God* is the father of Jesus – just as he is the father of the disciples when once they have joined Jesus. See *The Problem of History in Mark*, p. 81 and note 1, which refers also to Mark $3^{31ff.}$ and 10^{29-30}.

brother of James, etc.: 'The theory of the perpetual virginity of our Lord's Mother had not yet arisen when this Gospel was written. Later ecclesiastical tradition argued that the Lord's "brothers" were either His reputed half-brothers, children of Joseph by a former marriage (so Epiphanius and Origen), or else His cousins (so Jerome and others). Tertullian and Helvidius among ancient writers defended the more natural interpretation' (R., p. 75).

they took offence (*ĕskandalizŏntŏ*)*:* The noun (*skandalŏn*) means something which trips a person up or snares a person or animal into a trap. Hence the verb comes to mean either to trip up or to entice astray. The important thing to notice here is that by St Mark's time Christians were applying it almost as a *technical term* to those who, when confronted by Christ, found something in him which prevented them from going on to full Christian faith and discipleship.

4

In one form or another this proverb was widely current in the ancient world. It is ascribed to Jesus himself in slightly different forms – cf. John 4^{44}, Matt. 13^{57}, and *The Sayings of Jesus from Oxyrhynchus*, p. 40.† Whatever the precise form he used, the meaning is clear: strange and terrible though it is that God's people should reject God's final agent of salvation, it is only the extreme example of something which has happened often enough in human experience. Early Christian missionaries whose own faith was sorely tested by consistent Jewish denial

* The sons of Zeruiah (1 Sam. 26^{6}, 2 Sam. 23^{18}, etc.) are only an apparent exception to this statement; see the relevant commentaries.

† ed. H. G. White, 1920; cf. M. R. James, *The Apocryphal New Testament*, p. 27.

of Jesus' claims, must have valued the saying, and indeed the whole story, very highly. It is possible that the last two clauses of the proverb as given here were added by the Evangelist to make the saying fit the context more exactly.

5
he could do no mighty work there: The limitation of Jesus' power is boldly stated; and Matt. (13^{58}) has softened the statement. But it is a mistake to interpret St Mark's phrase psychologically, as meaning that Jesus worked his cures by suggestion and so was powerless, like a modern psychiatrist, when a patient had no confidence in him. (See further J. M. Robinson, *The Problem of History in Mark*, p. 75 and n. 1.) St Mark's perspective is, as always, theological.

6^{6b-13} THE SENDING OUT OF THE TWELVE

And he went about among the villages teaching.
7 *And he called to him the twelve, and began to send them out two by two,*
and gave them authority over the unclean spirits. 8 *He charged them to take*
nothing for their journey except a staff; no bread, no bag, no money in their
belts; 9 *but to wear sandals and not put on two tunics.* 10 *And he said to them,*
'Where you enter a house, stay there until you leave the place. 11 *And if any*
place will not receive you and they refuse to hear you, when you leave,
shake off the dust that is on your feet for a testimony against them.' 12 *So they*
went out and preached that men should repent. 13 *And they cast out many*
demons, and anointed with oil many that were sick and healed them.

This section is in some ways curiously obscure. No doubt Mark understood the incident as the foundation event on which all subsequent Christian missionary activity was based. The twelve were appointed in Chapter 3 *to be with* Jesus (3^{14}) and also *to be sent out to preach and have authority to cast out demons.* They have now spent their period of preparation with Jesus, hearing his words (4^{1-34}) and witnessing his mighty works (4^{35}–6^{6}), and the time has come for them to take an active part in the ministry, both by words and works.

We should thus have expected this to be a decisive stage in the development of the Gospel, but, as Wellhausen points out, it is not.

Wellhausen may have exaggerated in saying that the disciples remain as passive after this incident as they were before, but it is certainly true that though they appear fairly frequently hereafter, it is always in a strictly subordinate position; so far from becoming responsible and independent emissaries of the gospel, they seem usually to misunderstand its character and implications (see C. K. Barrett, *H.S.G.T.*, pp. 127–8). We may say, in fact, that this incident, which might have been expected to be so important, plays no vital part in the structure and development of the Gospel. And in line with that is the extremely sketchy way in which the story is told. Why did Jesus send the twelve at precisely this point, and what did he do while they were away? Where were the disciples sent and what were they told to say? St Mark does not even say explicitly that they were told to *say* anything at all (vv. 7–8, though cf. vv. 11–12), nor does he offer any explanation of the very specific instructions they are given.

One explanation of all these facts is that the incident is unhistorical, but that is doubtful.* More probably the explanation lies in a lack of tradition about, or interest in, the incident in the Church in which St Mark was writing. St Mark probably knew of a general tradition that the disciples were sent out on a missionary tour and he may have had one or two sayings of Jesus which seemed to derive from some such occasion (e.g. vv. 8–9 and 11). On the basis of these he composed the present account,† but he did not assign a central position, or any deep significance, to it any more than the tradition of his Church had done. The instructions belong essentially to Palestine and presuppose the conditions to be found there. In the missionary circumstances of St Mark's time and place they have lost a great deal of their relevance, and even their practicability; St Paul, for example, could never have carried through his immense missionary journeys had he remained faithful to the letter of these commandments. So in St Mark's Church it was only to a very limited extent that these instructions had any practical importance as 'marching orders' for contemporary missionaries. But in and around Palestine it was

* 'The fact that, quite apart from Mark, Matthew, and Luke, each had a mission charge in his private source makes a mission by the disciples one of the best-attested facts in the Gospels.' (G. B. Caird).

† The vocabulary and style in any case suggest that the narrative framework is of St Mark's own composition – see V.T., pp. 302ff.

different; there the conditions of missionary work changed little* and Jesus' instructions remained fully practicable. Consequently the tradition of them was treasured more carefully, and Matthew and Luke were able to reproduce them from their common source in a form much fuller than Mark's (cf. Matt. 9^{35}–10^{42} and Luke 9^{1-6} and 10^{1-16}). From their accounts we can learn that what the disciples were bidden to proclaim was the coming of the kingdom and that it was considered so imminent that if the news of it was to spread in time, the missionaries must travel light and not waste efforts over unreceptive audiences. That information helps to make sense of some elements in the instructions which in Mark's account stand unexplained.

7

gave them authority over the unclean spirits: Since the power which Jesus wielded was the eschatological power of God, working to bring the world into subjection to God's rule, the Christians believed that the same power could, and did, manifest itself in their lives in so far as they had been subjected to God's rule. See, from among numerous examples, Acts 3^{1-10}, 9^{37-42}, 20^{7-12}, 1 Cor. $12^{9-10, 27-30}$. This passage will have been valued as showing how the process began and how the power was intended to be exercised in the service of the spreading of the kingdom. Cf. what Josephus says of the Essenes: 'They carry nothing with them on a journey except arms as a protection against brigands. In every city there is one of the order expressly appointed to attend strangers, who provides them with clothing and other necessaries.' (*Jewish War*, II, 125.)

8

except a staff: Matthew and Luke forbid even this; and likewise in v. 9, where Mark allows 'sandals', Q (Matt. 10^{10} // Luke 10^{4}) forbids 'shoes' of any sort. 'These modifications, if they are not accidental, are probably due to the fact that in the Roman version of the tradition the circumstances of later missionaries were in view' (R., p. 77). For them, as explained above, a staff and sandals will have been quite indispensable; indeed sandals, so far from being a concession, would have been a hardship, an uncomfortable alternative to walking shoes.

* We have independent evidence of that from a work known as the *Didache*, which most scholars believe to have been compiled about the middle of the second century. It is instructive to compare what is said in Chapters 11ff. of that work with what is said about the sending out of the disciples in the Gospels.

no bag: Probably a begging bag rather than a provision bag; the twelve were not to beg.

no money in their belts: Literally 'not a copper for their girdle'. Ancient custom was to keep small change in the girdle, and the disciples were not to carry even small change.

and not put on two tunics: Literally, 'and do not put on two tunics'; the sudden change to direct speech suggests the combination of two sources at this point. The Q version forbids even the *possession* of such garments. *Tunic* (*chitōn*) is the inner garment worn next to the skin.

10
The introductory formula is evidence that what follows formed an independent item in St Mark's material. As for the command itself, 'forsaking the humbler hospitality of the first host for more luxurious quarters is a practice unworthy of the true Evangelist' (B. W. Bacon). Frequent change of lodging was a habit deprecated by the rabbis.

11
shake off the dust, etc.: Strict Jews performed the same symbolic action when they re-entered Palestine after journeying abroad; the idea was to avoid contaminating God's holy land and people even with the dust of profane places. The disciples, when they performed the action, would thus be dissociating themselves completely from the places which rejected them and proclaiming them to be, to all intents and purposes, heathen, destined for the fate reserved for the rest of the heathens. Such a solemn action would indeed be a testimony calculated to make the unbelievers think again,* but in the circumstances of the original event the idea may rather have been of a testimony *to God* indicating to him the appropriate fate for such people in the judgement that was so soon expected.

12
preached that men should repent: No doubt they spoke of the coming of the kingdom, which made repentance so urgent a matter (cf. 1^{15}). But Lightfoot may well have been right in thinking that the content of their 'preaching' is deliberately distinguished from the full Christian gospel to which the word 'preach' normally refers. 'If so,' he writes 'the meaning is that at $6^{7ff.}$ the twelve, like John the Baptist, are only able to preach a mission of repentance in connexion with the coming person or event; not until the period after the Passion, when the death of Jesus has taken place and their eyes have been opened and

* The Greek may mean 'a testimony *to*' or '*for* them'.

their understandings finally enlightened, will that same preaching become a message of salvation' (*H. & I.*, p. 106, n. 2).

13

anointed with oil: The oil is not thought of simply as healing in virtue of its natural medicinal powers; anointing is regarded, like touching or laying on of hands, as a vehicle of miraculous power. The fact that healing by unction was practised by the early Church (James $5^{14\text{f.}}$) is no ground for denying that the disciples, or even Jesus himself, may have practised it.

6^{14-29} THE DEATH OF JOHN THE BAPTIST

14*King Herod heard of it; for Jesus'*[a] *name had become known. Some*[b] *said,*
'John the baptizer has been raised from the dead; that is why these powers
are at work in him.' 15*But others said, 'It is Eli'jah.' And others said, 'It is a*
prophet, like one of the prophets of old.' 16*But when Herod heard of it he*
said, 'John, whom I beheaded, has been raised.'
17*For Herod had sent and seized John, and bound him in prison for the*
sake of Hero'di-as, his brother Philip's wife; because he had married her.
18*For John said to Herod, 'It is not lawful for you to have your brother's wife.'*
19*And Hero'di-as had a grudge against him, and wanted to kill him. But she*
could not, 20*for Herod feared John, knowing that he was a righteous and holy*
man, and kept him safe. When he heard him, he was much perplexed; and
yet he heard him gladly. 21*But an opportunity came when Herod on his*
birthday gave a banquet for his courtiers and officers and the leading men of
Galilee. 22*For when Hero'di-as' daughter came in and danced, she pleased*
Herod and his guests; and the king said to the girl, 'Ask me for whatever you
wish, and I will grant it.' 23*And he vowed to her, 'Whatever you ask me,*
I will give you, even half of my kingdom.' 24*And she went out, and said to*
her mother, 'What shall I ask?' And she said, 'The head of John the
baptizer.' 25*And she came in immediately with haste to the king, and asked*
saying, 'I want you to give me at once the head of John the Baptist on a
platter.' 26*And the king was exceedingly sorry; but because of his oaths and*
his guests he did not want to break his word to her. 27*And immediately the*
king sent a soldier of the guard and gave orders to bring his head. He went

and beheaded him in the prison, [28]*and brought his head on a platter, and gave it to the girl: and the girl gave it to her mother.* [29]*When his disciples heard of it, they came and took his body, and laid it in a tomb.*

a Greek *his*
b Other ancient authorities read *he*

To fill in the gap between the sending out of the twelve (vv. 6b–13) and their return (vv. 30–34)* St Mark tells the story of the beheading of John the Baptist by Herod (vv. 17–29). By way of introducing it, he describes briefly the impression made by Jesus on various different people, including Herod. The little section in which he does so (vv. 14–16) is again his own composition, though no doubt it rests in part on popular tradition. For St Mark the various guesses that were being made about Jesus' identity have a twofold significance. The very fact that they were being made shows that Jesus' contemporaries could not help seeing in him someone supernatural and divinely inspired; while the fact that, stupendous though they were, they were not stupendous enough, serves to emphasize the unique status that in fact belonged to Jesus.

We are thus introduced to the story of John's execution (vv. 17–29), a narrative which 'stands apart from other narratives in Mark as being the only one which is not in some sense or other a story about Jesus' (V. T., p. 310). An independent account of the same events is preserved by Josephus (*Antiquities*, XVIII, 5, 1–2), who ascribes Herod's action to political motives and says that when, later, his repudiation of his first wife in favour of Herodias involved him in war with the Nabataean Arabs, 'some of the Jews thought that the destruction of his army came from God, and that very justly, as a punishment for what he did against John who was called the Baptist'. A great deal of discussion has taken place about the relationship, and relative trustworthiness, of our two accounts. Details of this will be found in the larger commentaries; for our purposes, it will suffice to quote the conclusion of R. (p. 82): 'Both [accounts] are no doubt *bona fide* and independent: it is a mistake to try to harmonize the two. Josephus' version will give the facts as they presented themselves to

* For this practice of making an insertion between the two halves of a single story, see p. 112.

a historian who wrote sixty years later, and who was concerned to trace the political causes of a war. The story in Mark will be an account, written with a certain amount of literary freedom, of what was being darkly whispered in the bazaars or market-places of Palestine at the time.' This hits off admirably the character of Mark's account; it is essentially a popular report, frequently inaccurate, and with something of the character of the fairy tale.* In such an account it is idle to inquire too minutely into questions of historicity, though see notes below.

On the basis of the Synoptic Gospels (see especially Luke 3^{1}), it is usually assumed that John was executed in A.D. 29–30. On the other hand Herod's defeat by the Arabians, referred to in Josephus, took place not long before the death of Tiberius in March A.D. 37. The cause of the Arabian war was Herod's repudiation of his first (Arabian) wife for Herodias, so, if the dates are to be reconciled, the Arabians must have waited a very long time before taking their revenge, and the Jews must have attributed Herod's defeat to an event which had taken place six or seven years earlier. As we know nothing of the attendant circumstances, neither of these possibilities can be ruled out.

As we have seen, the story is not strictly about Jesus, but for St Mark, John the Baptist was Elijah, sent to earth again as the forerunner of the Messiah; it may well be for that reason that the story of his death is told so fully. The fate of the forerunner is a presage of the fate of the successor. (See further on $9^{11\text{ff.}}$.)

❧

14
King Herod heard of it: There is nothing in the Greek corresponding to *it*. What Herod is supposed to have heard was either a general report of Jesus' activities, like the one we have been given in the previous chapters, or the opinions about him reported in the following verses.

This Herod was a son of Herod the Great, born in about 20 B.C. He ruled the tetrarchy of Galilee and Perea (see map) from 4 B.C. till A.D. 39, when his ambition to be king led to his banishment by the

* Such themes as the banquet and the dance, the request and the sworn promise, are constantly recurring motifs in literature of a similar kind; moreover in its present form the narrative appears to have been influenced by the story of Elijah's dealing with Ahab and Jezebel (1 Kings 18ff. – for Mark, John was Elijah. See on $9^{11\text{ff.}}$) and possibly the story of Esther (cf. especially Esther 5^{3}).

Emperor Caligula. Strictly, therefore, St Mark's description of him as *king* is inaccurate, and Matthew and Luke correctly substitute 'tetrarch'. But St Mark's usage may well reflect local custom (cf. Matt. 14^{9}).

The identification of Jesus as John the Baptist risen from the dead suggests that Jesus' activities did not begin, or did not become famous, till after John's death. But cf. Matt. $11^{2\text{ff.}}$, Luke $7^{18\text{ff.}}$, and John 4^{1-2}.

15
It is Elijah: So many Jewish hopes centred on the reappearance of Elijah that it is not possible to say exactly what this view of Jesus amounted to. But certainly all these hopes associated Elijah's appearance closely with the coming of God's kingdom. (See further on $9^{11\text{ff.}}$.)
one of the prophets of old: There is nothing in the Greek corresponding to the words *of old*, but they correctly bring out the meaning. The Jews believed that the direct contact with God enjoyed by the prophets had long since ceased; the assurance, originality, and authoritative tone of Jesus (see on 1^{21-28}) may have suggested its fresh, and possibly final, emergence. (For the extent to which Jesus was regarded, and perhaps regarded himself, as a prophet, see C. H. Dodd, 'Jesus as Teacher and Prophet', (*Mysterium Christi*, ed. Bell and Deissmann, pp. 53ff.), and J. Knox, *The Death of Christ*, pp. 115ff.

16
The rather awkward reintroduction of Herod has led some commentators to think that originally the tradition behind Mark dealt only with Herod's reaction to Jesus and that Mark has introduced the other reactions from 8^{28}. It is quite feasible that the section was built up in this way.

17–18
In fact it was Herod's half-brother in Rome, also called Herod, to whom Herodias had been married. Philip was another half-brother who was tetrarch of Iturea and Trachonitis, and married Herodias' daughter, Salome.

John's objection was presumably based on Lev. 18^{16} and 20^{21};* in view of Deut. $25^{5\text{f.}}$ the relationship could hardly have been regarded as incestuous.

19
Cf. 1 Kings 21 for Jezebel's similar attitude to Elijah.

* In certain circumstances Jewish law allowed a husband to divorce his wife, but there is no evidence that Herodias' husband had availed himself of this provision. Roman law allowed a wife to divorce her husband, and Herodias, not being of Jewish blood, may just possibly have acted under this provision; we simply do not know.

20
The latter part of the verse reads awkwardly in the Greek, which contains nothing corresponding to *yet*. Some commentators think we should accept an alternative reading which is quite well attested, and might be translated: 'he kept him safe and when once he had heard him, heard him often and heard him gladly'.

21
Josephus says that John was executed at Machaerus, a frontier fortress near the Dead Sea. There was a palace as well as a prison at Machaerus; the court, if Mark's account is historical, must have been resident there at the time of Herod's birthday feast, though the Gospel taken by itself would more naturally suggest the Galilaean capital, Tiberias, as the scene of the banquet.

22
when Herodias' daughter came in: This translates one reading, but there are two others with at least equal claim to acceptance. One of them is usually translated 'when the daughter of Herodias herself came in', which is as awkward in the Greek as it is in English. It can also be translated 'when her daughter Herodias ...', though this involves making *her* refer back to v. 19 and involves Mark in saying that Herodias' daughter was called after her mother when in fact her name was Salome. The third, and probably best-attested reading, gives 'his daughter Herodias'; if this is right, either Herod had a natural daughter of this name and 'mother' is used loosely in v. 24 or else the illicit union between Herod and Herodias was of longer standing than the story seems to presuppose.

and danced: Experts in such matters say that only those who are ignorant of Oriental customs and have never seen an Oriental solo dance could regard it as credible that a king's daughter should demean herself in this way in front of a half-intoxicated crowd of men.*

22–23
As a tetrarch under the aegis of Rome, Herod had no 'kingdom' to dispose of, but popular stories of this kind take no account of such constitutional niceties. The king's words recall Esther $5^{3f.}$. The offer of half one's possessions is a familiar expression in stories of this kind, but in view of the fact that v. 22 also recalls Esther 2^{9} it is generally assumed that this story has been influenced by the Book of Esther.

* If so, we have another indication that the story cannot be taken *au pied de la lettre*, though what we know of the Herods and their families may make us cautious about putting anything beyond them on moral grounds.

27
immediately: Everything happens in quick succession (cf. v. 25), as at the end of a fairy tale. The story appears to envisage that the execution took place and the head was brought while the girl waited.

a soldier of the guard: spĕkoulatōr (the Latin *speculator*); originally a 'scout' and then in Hellenistic Greek a royal attendant who served as a messenger and, when necessary, as executioner.

29
his body: Literally 'his corpse' – cf. 15^{45} where the same word is used of Jesus. Perhaps the parallel (and contrast) are intentional; at the vital point the Passion of the forerunner does not anticipate that of the Messiah. The subsequent fate of the head became a fruitful source of legend.

6^{30-52} THE RETURN OF THE DISCIPLES AND TWO NATURE MIRACLES

30 *The apostles returned to Jesus, and told him all that they had done and*
taught. 31 *And he said to them, 'Come away by yourselves to a lonely place*
and rest a while.' For many were coming and going, and they had no leisure
even to eat. 32 *And they went away in the boat to a lonely place by themselves.*
33 *Now many saw them going, and knew them, and they ran there on foot*
from all the towns, and got there ahead of them. 34 *As he landed he saw a*
great throng, and he had compassion on them, because they were like sheep
without a shepherd; and he began to teach them many things. 35 *And when*
it grew late, his disciples came to him and said, 'This is a lonely place, and
the hour is now late; 36 *send them away, to go into the country and villages*
round about and buy themselves something to eat.' 37 *But he answered them,*
'You give them something to eat.' And they said to him, 'Shall we go and
buy two hundred denarii[a] *worth of bread, and give it to them to eat?'* 38 *And*
he said to them 'How many loaves have you? Go and see.' And when they
had found out, they said, 'Five, and two fish.' 39 *Then he commanded them*
all to sit down by companies upon the green grass. 40 *So they sat down in*
groups, by hundreds and by fifties. 41 *And taking the five loaves and the two*
fish he looked up to heaven, and blessed, and broke the loaves, and gave them
to the disciples to set before the people; and he divided the two fish among

them all. 42*And they all ate and were satisfied.* 43*And they took up twelve*
baskets full of broken pieces and of the fish. 44*And those who ate the loaves*
were five thousand men.

45*Immediately he made his disciples get into the boat and go before him to*
the other side, to Beth-sa'ida, while he dismissed the crowd. 46*And after he*
had taken leave of them, he went into the hills to pray. 47*And when evening*
came, the boat was out on the sea, and he was alone on the land. 48*And he saw*
that they were distressed in rowing, for the wind was against them. And
about the fourth watch of the night he came to them, walking on the sea. He
meant to pass by them, 49*but when they saw him walking on the sea they*
thought it was a ghost, and cried out; 50*for they all saw him, and were*
terrified. But immediately he spoke to them and said, 'Take heart, it is I;
have no fear.' 51*And he got into the boat with them and the wind ceased.*
And they were utterly astounded, 52*for they did not understand about the*
loaves, but their hearts were hardened.

a The denarius was worth about a shilling

We come now to two remarkable nature miracles, the feeding of the 5,000 (vv. 30–44) and the walking on the sea (vv. 45–52). They will be treated together, because St Mark has deliberately (and artificially) combined them, and clearly intended them to be interpreted in connexion with each other (see notes below, and note the reference back to the first miracle in the course of the second, 6^{52}).

Although the feeding is such a spectacular miracle, the account does not conclude with the usual expressions of amazement on the part of the bystanders, which suggests that it was not primarily in its aspect of 'wonder' that St Mark understood the miracle. It may also suggest that, at the time of its performance, the significance of the miracle was not understood, either by the disciples or the multitude (see also v. 52). Of course, they could not help realizing that something very remarkable had been done, but it was only after their eyes had been opened at Caesarea Philippi ($8^{27ff.}$), or even perhaps after the resurrection and the gift of the Spirit, that the disciples realized the truly momentous character of what had occurred. To members of the early Church, with these later events behind them, and with their experience of the Christian Eucharist, the meaning of the miracle appeared obvious, so obvious that to them the apostles' original lack of understanding seemed indeed wilful and sinful blindness (v. 52).

The essence of the miracle consisted in providing abundant food (more exactly loaves) in the wilderness; but this was precisely what God had done in the course of rescuing his people from Egypt by that great act of salvation which was the basic foundation of Israel's history, and the central theme of its Law. (See e.g. Exod. 16, especially vv. 12b, 15b, 32b, etc., and Num. 11 – noting in both cases the emphasis on abundance. Passages such as Neh. 9^{15} or Ps. $78^{17ff.}$ show how lively the remembrance of these events remained. John suggests (6^{14}) that Jesus' action immediately put the people in mind of them; no doubt Mark thought it ought to have done so.) Moreover, the great prophet Elisha had performed a miracle which, though on a smaller scale, was strikingly like this one; through his servant he had distributed twenty barley loaves and a little fresh grain among one hundred men so that 'they all ate and had some left' (2 Kings 4^{42-44}). Thus Jesus' action was the 'fulfilment of the Law and the prophets'. It witnessed, though in a veiled fashion, to Jesus' Messiahship; he was the one sent by God to usher in the ultimate salvation to which Law and prophets had pointed forward.*

But if so, his actions must have a forward, as well as a backward, reference; they must have some vital connexion with the ultimate state of blessedness they are to be instrumental in introducing. So far as this particular action is concerned, the nature of the connexion is suggested by the fact that the Jews commonly pictured the state of the blessed under the image of the 'Messianic Banquet', at which the Messiah presided as host to his elect.† In St Mark's account of the feeding, the actions of Jesus are precisely those of a host entertaining guests (see detailed notes below). Here perhaps we come near the original significance of the incident; it may have been intended by Jesus as an anticipation, more or less sacramental in character, of the Messianic Banquet, designed to communicate his conviction that he was the one men would soon see presiding over the Messianic Banquet, and also perhaps to consecrate those who shared the food

* See also Ps. 132^{15} – noticing that it is part of a prophecy of what God will do in the days of David's great successor, *my anointed* (v. 17b).

† The most pertinent example of this in Jewish writing is 1 *Enoch* 62^{14}, though the idea goes back to such passages as Isa. $55^{1ff.}$, $65^{13f.}$, and Isa. 25^{6-8}. For evidence that it was an image familiar and acceptable to Jesus, cf. Matt. 8^{11}, 22^{1-4}, and 25^{1-13}.

as partakers in the coming messianic feast, and to give them a guarantee that they who had shared his table in the time of his obscurity would also share it in the time of his glory. (For an explanation somewhat along those lines see A. Schweitzer, *The Mystery of the Kingdom of God* (E. T., 1950), pp. 103ff., and *The Quest of the Historical Jesus* (E. T., 1922), pp. 374–8.)

One further point any early Christian reader would have been bound to notice: the actions of Jesus as described by Mark are exactly the same as his actions at the Last Supper (cf. 14^{22} and 1 Cor. 11^{23-24}). Indeed to the early Christians the whole story would have been strongly reminiscent of their eucharistic worship, at which they too sat in orderly fashion while deacons brought round to them loaves blessed and broken by the celebrant. The story was interpreted as an anticipation of the Last Supper and the Eucharist. Often, no doubt, it will have been narrated when the little communities met to celebrate the Lord's Supper; how moving it must then have been,* speaking, as it did, of one who would not let his followers perish in the 'desert' of this world but who could be relied on, not only for the necessities of this life, but for a supply of bread which is the pledge of (and the means of sustaining) survival into the kingdom of God. This last line of interpretation is, of course, fully and explicitly carried out by St John (Chapter 6); that fact, and the way he explicitly links the feeding with the gift of manna in the wilderness (vv. 31ff. and 49f.), may be held to justify the assumption that interpretation was already leading that way in St Mark's time, and so make plausible the fairly full exposition that has been derived from St Mark's few hints.

Numerous attempts have been made in modern times to rationalize the story,† but, in view of the nature of the material, such rationalizations can be little more than unsupported guesses. Many commentators think well of Wellhausen's suggestion that the numbers may have been exaggerated, and also of Schweitzer's suggestion (see references above) that, as the meal was of a sacramental character, each person received only a small fragment of bread. In that case,

*cf. *H & I.*, pp. 55–6.

† For example along the lines that the disciples in fact just shared their rations with a group of people, or set an example in doing so, which was followed by others until everyone got something to eat.

the words 'and were satisfied' (v. 42) and the suggestion of the miraculous multiplication of bread were not original but simply 'a materialization of the original tradition when the true nature of the event (as an "eschatological sacrament") had not unnaturally become obscure' (V. T., p. 321).

The transition to the next incident, whether due to St Mark or not, is plainly artificial. It is surprising enough to be told that Jesus 'immediately' (v. 45) made his disciples embark and sent away the crowd, for by now it would have been well on into the night, seeing that it had already 'grown late' (v. 35) before the feeding. But when we read in v. 47 that the disciples were already well out on the Lake by the time *evening came*, we realize that it is futile to try to fit these chronological indications into a single coherent whole. The same is true of the geographical statements. The words *to the other side* in v. 45 normally imply an east–west or west–east journey across the Lake, and will hardly fit a voyage from a place within walking distance of Capernaum (v. 33) to Bethsaida, which is at the north of the Lake. (See map and notes below.) 'It is possible that the Evangelist himself had no clear picture of the locality in mind; to him, as to his readers, the various places he mentions may have been little more than names in the tradition' (R., p. 89). In fact, the purpose of these verses seems to have been to set a scene in which the disciples were *out on the sea*, while Jesus *was alone on the land* (v. 47.)

For the essence of the incident which follows is that the disciples are alone in a boat, without Jesus, and see him walking on the water. Their reaction is one of extreme alarm, and their first thought is of a ghost (vv. 49–50); even when they realize who it is, their response is wild astonishment (v. 51). All this ought not to have been so, for the feeding should have shown them, if nothing else had (v. 52), that in Jesus they were dealing with the eschatological power of God and the fulfilment of the Old Testament, and this walking on the water should only have provided joyful confirmation of that truth; for the Old Testament frequently spoke of God's mastery over the sea and described it in terms of the power to walk on, or through, the waves (cf. e.g. Job 9^{8}, Ps. 77^{19}, Isa. 43^{16}, and see p. 146).

There seems to have been an original version of the story in which that was the whole point. But one who has complete mastery over the waves also has power to rescue from them, and at some stage, additions (? taken from another story) were made to the original story to make it convey this further truth; the action of Jesus thus now becomes an act of rescue,* but the secondary character of this interpretation is shown by the fact that the disciples were not really in any plight from which they *needed* rescuing (see note on v. 48) and also perhaps by the absence of any word or act of Jesus which specifically effected the rescue (contrast 4^{39} and see notes on it).

But St Mark's contemporaries, of course, knew and accepted the story in the present form. To recapture its significance for them it is necessary to remember the rich symbolical meaning they attached to the sea and its raging. In the light of what was said about that on pp. 146–7, the reader will appreciate the aptness of R.'s comment (p. 88): 'To the Roman Church, thus bereft of its leaders and confronted by a hostile government, it must have indeed appeared that *the wind was contrary* and progress difficult and slow: faint hearts may even have begun to wonder whether the Lord Himself had not abandoned them to their fate, or to doubt the reality of Christ. They are to learn from this story that they are *not* forsaken, that the Lord watches over them unseen (vv. 47b and 48), and that He Himself – no phantom, but the Living One, Master of winds and waves – will surely come quickly for their salvation, even though it be in *the fourth watch of the night*.'

Both stories thus bring into relief the disciples' lack of understanding, something which was of the greatest significance to the Evangelist. On the one hand, it helped to explain how the Son of God could have remained so largely unrecognized in the days of his flesh (see Introduction, pp. 31–2); on the other hand, given the truly remarkable works which Jesus did, it was so inexplicable that it could only be due, St Mark felt, to the 'hardening' providence of God (see above, p. 111). Verse 52 is thus very deliberately framed as the conclusion to the whole section. Incidentally, it serves to show that, according to the Marcan theory, there is more in miracles than their outward appearance; they are, to use the fourth Evangelist's word, 'signs' of the power of God. According to Mark the miracles 'like the parables, are understandable and ought to be understood, and yet are misunderstood; they are signs with a potency either for revelation or for

* Whereas originally it was seen simply as a manifestation of his true being and status, comparable perhaps to the transfiguration.

hardening the heart. Even the disciples are in grave danger of completely misapprehending their meaning' (*H.S.G.T.*, p. 89).

ꕥ

30–33

These verses may contain scraps of tradition, but in the main they seem to be a composition by the Evangelist, designed to link the feeding with what has gone before. The disciples have been away from Jesus, but they are present at the feeding, so they must be brought back, and they and Jesus must be transported to a *lonely place*, since for St Mark it is of the essence of the miracle that it took place in a 'desert place'. (The word translated *lonely* in vv. 31, 32, and 35 is *ĕrēmŏs*, which literally means 'desert' and was the word used in the Greek Old Testament for 'the wilderness'.) The crowd too are present at the feeding, so Jesus and the disciples are followed. We are told nothing about the *content* of the disciples' report (v. 30) or about the locality of the desert place; such things do not interest St Mark. In fact, as B. says, the details, the crowd pressing on Jesus, the boat in which he seeks rest and yet his inability to escape, are little more than stage scenery, already familiar to us from 3^{7-9}, and helping to fix in our minds the background of popular support and acclaim against which the ministry was carried on. B.'s further comment is worth quoting: 'If this be so, we need not bother about the questions which have perplexed many exegetes, whether or not people on foot could get around the northern shore of the lake and arrive on the other side before the boat. For those to whom this seems an arbitrary treatment, however, it might be pointed out that there is nothing in the text which says that the boat in which Jesus and His disciples set out went to the eastern shore. If the boat headed a few miles north or south, it would have been possible for the crowd to keep it in view and even to be waiting on the shore when the boat came to land' (p. 112).

36

the country: Or perhaps 'the hamlets' (Gr. *hoi agroi*).

37

This verse is instructive for St Mark's understanding of the story; for clearly the disciples find Jesus' command baffling, but St Mark can hardly have thought they were meant to do so. The Jews in the wilderness, who had seen so many proofs of God's power, ought to have trusted him to provide food (Ps. 78^{18-20}); Elisha's servant ought to have trusted his master's power. In the same way, the disciples, having seen so many signs that the power of God was with Jesus, ought to have trusted that power and foreseen that it would provide food for them to give to the people in the desert. Certainly their reply is reminiscent of 2 Kings 4^{43} and of Moses' faithless questions in Num. $11^{13, 21-22}$.

denarii: Worth perhaps rather more than R.S.V. suggests – about two shillings each.

38
two fish: Alan Richardson writes: 'The introduction of the symbol of the fishes along with that of the loaves is not entirely explicable by us; but we know that the symbol of fish was widely used as a "sign" amongst the earliest Christian communities. Since the original Galilaean disciples numbered several fishermen in their company, and since the fishing industry of the district was so important, it was appropriate that fish, along with bread, should have been one of the "common things" by which the Lord chose to make Himself known to those who had eyes to see. Bread and fish appear frequently in early Christian frescoes in the catacombs as a symbol of the Eucharist.' (*The Miracle Stories of the Gospels*, pp. 95–6; cf. W. Lowrie, *Christian Art and Archaeology*, pp. 223ff.)

Is there some connexion with Num. 11^{22}?

39
upon the green grass: i.e. on the bare ground, without the spreading of any cloth. It would be a mistake to see in these words evidence of eye-witness recollection; and it is *probably* over-subtle to interpret them symbolically as meaning that the miracle took place at the time of green grass, i.e. spring time, which was the time of the Passover meal; though cf. John 6^4. B. aptly comments: 'Even if the detail be authentic, it could not be argued that a year had elapsed since the episode of the plucking of the ripe grain recounted in $2^{23ff.}$, for the Marcan arrangement is not chronological. Both episodes may have occurred at practically the same time, or at a considerable interval' (see Introduction, pp. 28–9).

41
The verbal similarities between this verse and 14^{22} are as close in the Greek as they are in the English; for their significance see above.

That Jesus' action was that of a host entertaining guests is shown by the following quotation from B. (p. 114): 'As Billerbeck has shown in his commentary from the rabbinic writings, the approved ritual for beginning a meal when guests were present was for the host, or the most distinguished person present, to take bread, to pronounce the blessing over it, break it, give portions to the guests present, and to begin the meal by eating a portion of it.' Where numbers were large, the distribution might be undertaken by companions, or servants, of the host.

he looked up to heaven: Some commentators regard this simply as a normal gesture of prayer (cf. e.g. Job 22^26 and Luke 18^13); others, holding that it would not normally form a part of this particular ritual, attach special significance to it as the miraculous medium through which the multiplication of loaves was effected (cf. M. Dibelius, *F. T. G.*, p. 90). It is the basis of the rubric in the Missal directing the priest to raise his eyes before the act of consecration.

43
This serves to make vivid the reality and extent of the miracle (cf. 1^31, 2^12, 5^42, etc.). It also points to the Old Testament connexion (see especially 2 Kings 4^43, 44 – the twice-repeated 'have some left'). On this and the next verse see further on chapter 8.

45–46
There seems no obvious reason why the disciples should not have been present at the dismissal of the crowd; v. 46 provides an alternative motive for Jesus' separation from the disciples, which has nothing to do with the crowd. All this suggests a twofold attempt to explain how Jesus and the disciples came to be separated, perhaps connected with the twofold origin of the section as a whole (see above).

Bethsaida (see map): Rebuilt by Philip as Bethsaida-Julias; the attempt to solve the geographical difficulties by positing another, and otherwise unknown, Bethsaida on the shore of the Lake is now generally abandoned.

48
about the fourth watch of the night: Between 3 a.m. and 6 a.m. St Mark adopts the Roman reckoning; the Jews had only three night watches.

He meant to pass by them: These words have never been really satisfactorily explained. It is tempting to follow the suggestion of Lohmeyer that they belong to the original version of the story and are to be interpreted in the light of such passages as Exod. 33^18ff. and 1 Kings 19^11ff. (where the same Greek word *parerchĕsthai* is used); in that case Jesus' intention was 'to make his glory (as Son of God) pass by the disciples' in an epiphany like that in Exodus and Kings. Cf. the transfiguration. But such a suggestion can be no more than a tentative conjecture and the obvious parallel, Luke 24^28, hardly supports it. However they are to be explained, the words do not suggest that the story was originally one of rescue.

50
Take heart, it is I; have no fear: Perhaps better punctuated as follows: *Take heart; it is I, have no fear.* The second half of the sentence probably belonged to the original story; while the first two words were perhaps part of the interpretative additions. In the presence of Jesus men should never be afraid of any danger they may be in, still less of Jesus himself; the only proper attitude is one of faith, love, and obedience. The Greek words translated *it is I* mean literally *I am.*

6^{53-56} HEALINGS IN GENNESARET

[53]*And when they had crossed over, they came to land at Gennes'aret, and*
moored to the shore. [54] *And when they got out of the boat, immediately the*
people recognized him, [55]*and ran about the whole neighbourhood and began*
to bring sick people on their pallets to any place where they heard he was.
[56]*And wherever he came, in villages, cities, or country, they laid the sick*
in the market places, and besought him that they might touch even the fringe
of his garment; and as many as touched it were made well.

A generalized description of healing and of popular enthusiasm (cf. 1^{32-34} and 3^{7-12}). The vocabulary shows that it is a composition by the Evangelist, and it is uncertain whether he had any basis for it other than stories he has already told in more detailed form elsewhere in the Gospel (cf. e.g. 2^{1-12} and 5^{25-34}). Most commentators think not (though cf. V. T., pp. 331–2, and see detailed notes below) and, if they are right, St Mark is simply saying that Jesus continued to work further in the way already described. That he should say it in this particular way is instructive with regard to the manner and circumstances in which the Gospels were composed. Dibelius writes:* 'these collective notes . . . are generalizations, where what is instanced in detail in single stories is now said of a number of cases without any detail . . . the collector, whose material consisted only of isolated examples, possesses hardly any other means of expanding these individual instances into a representation of the whole. No objective

* *F. T. G.*, p. 224.

pictures of the life of Jesus [as a whole] were in existence.' (See Introduction, pp. 27 and 36.) By putting the summary here St Mark has made the enthusiasm of the crowds serve as a foil to the attitude of the Jewish leaders to whom renewed attention is drawn in the next section.

ꕥ

53
Gennesaret: A fertile plain about three miles long and a mile wide, to the south of Capernaum, thickly populated. In v. 45 the disciples set out for Bethsaida, and their arrival in a totally different locality (see map) is often put down to adverse winds or a change of plan. But St Mark says nothing of this, and, in any case, a journey from near Capernaum to Gennesaret could scarcely be called 'crossing' the Lake (v. 53). The fact is that we are really dealing here with a quite separate section, and, for the reasons given above, it is a mistake to try to build St Mark's geographical notices into a single, coherent scheme. On the other hand, St Mark could have had no motive for introducing Gennesaret unless he had found it in some source, so he probably had a general notice of a ministry in Gennesaret to serve as the basis for his generalizing summary.

56
For the impression this would make on a Hellenistic reader see on $5^{25\text{ff.}}$ above. Jesus here does not react to the 'touching' as he did there, and, on the face of it, the verse might suggest the 'animistic' belief that miraculous powers could reside in an object and produce effects without any exercise of personal will taking place. No doubt, however, as Schniewind suggests, St Mark will have assumed that those who touched Jesus, or those who brought them (cf. *besought him*, and see on 2^{5}) were in fact expressing a fully personal faith-response to Jesus' person and ministry.

fringe: Probably a reference to the blue fringe or tassel every male Jew was required to have on the corners of his robe (see Num. $15^{38\text{f.}}$ and Deut. 22^{12}). If so, and the tradition is good, it is a further indication of Jesus' loyalty to the religion of the Law.

7 1–23

A SECOND COLLECTION OF THE TEACHING OF JESUS

7 Now when the Pharisees gathered together to him, with some of the scribes,
who had come from Jerusalem, 2they saw that some of the disciples ate with
hands defiled, that is, unwashed. 3(For the Pharisees, and all the Jews, do not
eat unless they wash their hands,[a] observing the tradition of the elders; 4and
when they come from the market place, they do not eat unless they purify[b]
themselves; and there are many other traditions which they observe, the
washing of cups and pots and vessels of bronze.[c]) 5And the Pharisees and the
scribes asked him, 'Why do your disciples not live[d] according to the tradition
of the elders, but eat with hands defiled?' 6And he said to them, 'Well did
Isaiah prophesy of you hypocrites, as it is written,

'This people honours me with their lips,
but their heart is far from me;
7in vain do they worship me,
teaching as doctrines the precepts of men.

8You leave the commandment of God, and hold fast the tradition of men.'
9And he said to them, 'You have a fine way of rejecting the commandment
of God, in order to keep your tradition! 10For Moses said, "Honour your
father and your mother"; and, "He who speaks evil of father or mother,
let him surely die"; 11but you say, "If a man tells his father or his mother,
What you would have gained from me is Corban" (that is, given to God)[e] –
12then you no longer permit him to do anything for his father or mother,
13thus making void the word of God through your tradition which you hand
on. And many such things you do.'
14And he called the people to him again, and said to them, 'Hear me, all of
you, and understand: 15there is nothing outside a man which by going into
him can defile him; but the things which come out of a man are what defile
him.'[f] 17And when he had entered the house, and left the people, his disciples
asked him about the parable. 18And he said to them, 'Then are you also
without understanding? Do you not see that whatever goes into a man from
outside cannot defile him, 19since it enters, not his heart but his stomach, and
so passes on?'[g] (Thus he declared all foods clean.) 20And he said, 'What
comes out of a man is what defiles a man. 21For from within, out of the heart
of a man, come evil thoughts, fornication, theft, murder, adultery, 22coveting,

wickedness, deceit, licentiousness, envy, slander, pride, foolishness. [23]*All these evil things come from within, and they defile a man.'*

a One Greek word is of uncertain meaning and is not translated
b Other authorities read *baptize*
c Other authorities add *and beds*
d Greek *walk*
e Or *an offering*
f Other ancient authorities add verse 16, *if any man has ears to hear, let him hear*
g Or *is evacuated*

The Evangelist makes no attempt to locate this section either in space or in time. His reasons for placing it at this point in the Gospel seem to have been two.

1. The preceding passage was taken up with the true power and glory of Jesus (6^{30-52}) and with the success of his ministry (6^{31-34} and $^{54-56}$); but the Evangelist will never leave us for long without a reminder that this ministry, though God was behind it and the people welcomed it, was to be brought to an ignominious end by the pride and blindness of men, particularly of the Jewish authorities.*

2. This section, with its message of emancipation from Jewish particularism, is a fitting prelude to the account which follows of Jesus' ministry on Gentile soil ($7^{24ff.}$).

The section itself is composite (see below) and has no single, easily definable theme, though much of it deals with the question of defilement, real and imaginary, and all of it is connected, in one way or another, with Jesus' reaction to contemporary Judaism. It begins with a question put to Jesus by leaders of Jewish thought, who are said to have come from Jerusalem, a trait (see on 3^{22}) which indicates their more or less official status and so hints at the serious consequences the ensuing debate might ultimately have.

The question itself is quite specific: why do some of Jesus' disciples eat without washing (in the sense of ritually cleansing†) their hands?

* Cf. how Chapter 1 was followed by 2^{1}–3^{6}, culminating in the plotting against Jesus in 3^{6}; and how Chapters 4–5 were followed by Jesus' rejection at Nazareth, 6^{1-6}, and the sombre and prophetic story of the death of John the Baptist, 6^{14-29}.

† It hardly needs to be said that throughout this section the 'cleanliness' referred to is ritual cleanliness and has no reference to hygiene.

But this soon becomes a peg for the wider question why the disciples do not conform their lives as a whole to the demands of the Pharisees' code, of which handwashing is only one item. To the earliest Jewish Christians, this must indeed have been a live question. They believed, as all Jews believed, that the written Law, found in the Pentateuch, was absolutely binding. But over the years an oral code had grown up alongside the written Law; essentially it was designed to ensure the full observance of the written Law by prescribing for its detailed application, settling disputed points of interpretation, reconciling apparent inconsistencies, and the like. This oral tradition was the work of learned experts known as rabbis, or scribes, who publicly debated, and pronounced on, the various points at issue, until, by the time of Jesus, there had grown up a formidable body of probable or undisputed oral Law; it is this which is here described (v. 5) as *the tradition of the elders* (see detailed notes below and cf. on 1^{22}).*

The conservative among the Jewish leaders (the Sadducaic party) would have nothing to do with this oral tradition, but the increasingly powerful and popular Pharisaic party (with whom in fact the future of Judaism lay) regarded it as of at least equal importance with the written Law itself. Where was Christianity to take its stand in this matter?

The reply of Jesus is in two parts (vv. 6–8 and 9–13) and it is quite clear that he comes down against the oral tradition. But both sections of his reply raise problems. The first part consists in applying to the upholders of the oral tradition a prophecy from Isaiah (29^{13}) which is interpreted (v. 8) as meaning that the Pharisees follow their oral tradition *at the expense* of the written Law, even (cf. *hypocrites*, v. 6) with the express purpose of having an excuse to disobey it. From our point of view, there are two problems here.

First of all, this interpretation of Isaiah depends on the use of the Greek version (see below), and it is hardly likely that Jesus, teaching in Palestine, quoted Isaiah in Greek.

Secondly, the Pharisees claimed that the purpose of the oral tradition was not the evasion of the written Law but on the contrary its

* The first formulation of the code *in writing*, the *Mishnah*, dates from the latter part of the second century, which means, since the tradition was continually developing, that the *Mishnah* can be used only with great caution as evidence for the dictates of the oral tradition in the time of Jesus (see below).

more complete and exact performance. Were they wrong about this? To show that they were, St Mark appends a section (vv. 9–13) containing a concrete example of how the oral tradition set aside one of the most clear and unmistakable obligations under the written Law, that of children towards their parents. The difficulty here is to know precisely what custom in contemporary Judaism is being alluded to. The Law made it unmistakably clear that children had a solemn duty to support their parents, but apparently some Jews were evading the duty by taking a solemn oath that the resources available for the purpose would be devoted to the temple, or, at any rate, would not be used for their parents' support. They then argued that to allow their parents to have any of the money would be a violation of their solemn oath and, as such, a violation of the Law itself; and, according to this passage, some of the scribes upheld that view.

The practice was clearly a disgraceful evasion of the demands of the Law, and indeed of common decency; but it must be added at once that according to the *Mishnah* the rabbis themselves said so very emphatically. The passage in the *Mishnah* dealing with the subject is unfortunately a little obscure, but, according to the best authorities, it means that if a vow prevented a man from supporting his parents, it was right for him to break his vow. It is possible, of course, that the rabbis of Jesus' day took a different line (cf. above p. 189 note), but in view of the overwhelming importance the Jews have always attached to filial piety, it may be taken as certain that at no period did the rabbis actively connive at, still less invent, a system for the evasion of duty to parents. If, in Jesus' day, rabbis took the view that a son who had made a solemn vow could not break it, even in favour of needy parents, that was presumably because they regarded the teaching of the written Law about the inviolability of oaths as being absolutely paramount – and indeed the statements of the Law on that subject are exceptionally strong* (see Deut. 23^{21-23}, Num. 30^{2}, etc). We may well feel that this reveals an insensitiveness to moral priorities which fully justifies the attack made in this passage, but the question is strictly one about the relation of two provisions in the written Law and not about the subjection of the written Law to an oral tradition.

It is an attractive suggestion of R. that: 'The case need not have

* We can hardly suppose that the rabbis approved the *taking* of such vows; but once they were taken, they may well have felt bound to uphold them.

been purely hypothetical; there may have been some contemporary *cause célèbre* of this description, which formed a subject of current talk in the bazaars of Galilee' (p. 95).

There is now a clearly marked break in the section; Jesus summons a new audience (v. 14) and offers them, in epigrammatic form, what St Mark presumably regarded as a comment on the preceding discussion. In fact, however, it is only very loosely related to the Pharisees' question* or to Jesus' two replies to it. The comment itself is a very radical one, quite in the prophetic tradition, and, as interpreted in vv. 18–19, would cut the ground from under a very large part of the written Law. For it assumes that the only kind of cleanliness that matters for religion is *moral* cleanliness, whereas large tracts of the Old Testament Law presuppose that there is also a purely ritual cleanliness and that its maintenance is of vital importance in the eyes of God. Thus, Jesus' statement, if consistently followed out, would emancipate men from obedience to large areas of the written Law, and it comes oddly from one who has just been attacking the Pharisees for not taking the written Law seriously enough. For that reason, and also because the controversies which arose among the early Christians suggest that they had no clear pronouncement from Jesus on this matter, some commentators have doubted the authenticity of v. 15 and seen in it an invention of the 'liberalizing' party in the early Church. More plausible and widely accepted is the view expressed in the following quotation: 'I suggest . . . that the saying of verse 15 is basically authentic, but that the original utterance was less sweeping and categorical than it here appears. . . . So far as we can see from the Gospels, Jesus' criticisms of Judaism were occasional and specific rather than general. If He spoke about man's acceptableness with God as resting upon the state of his heart rather than upon what he ate, it is likely that the saying was in connexion with some specific issue and was probably *ad hoc*, and not so detached and sweeping as we have it here. His handling of the law of the sabbath furnishes probably the safest analogy. He never abrogated the sabbath nor its laws. But He did ignore and reject the laws against sabbath work on occasions when human needs were at stake. In line with this, it

* There was no suggestion in Judaism that the uncleanness of unwashed hands might impart itself to the food being eaten and so defile the inner man.

would probably be too much to maintain that, in the saying in 7^{15}, Jesus abrogated the food codes of Leviticus and declared that one could eat swine or camel with freedom. But He may very well have declared, in connexion with some specific case that arose, that a good man who was engaged in doing a good deed did not become evil in God's sight through the food which he ate, that men were defiled rather by what came from their hearts . . . The scribal insistence on the food laws was simply because they were commanded in the scriptures. Jesus had a much freer attitude towards the scriptural commands. His attitude was more intuitive and untrammelled' (B., pp. 126–7). Was this because he was Messiah? Did he as the bringer of the new age feel free to abrogate the Law in a way that was quite illegitimate for the Pharisees, so long as they remained under the old dispensation? St Mark may have thought something of the kind, but he gives no hint of it in this passage, and the wording does not suggest that any such idea was present in his sources.

In the remainder of the section the saying of v. 15 is represented as a 'parable' (v. 17) in the Marcan sense of an obscure utterance which can only be interpreted by those who have the key to it (see notes on Chapter 4). Accordingly the disciples retire privately with Jesus (v. 17, cf. $4^{10 \text{ and } 34}$) and receive the key to the first part of the saying in vv. 18–19, and to the second part in vv. 20–23. The catalogue of sins in vv. 21–22 has close affinities with the Pauline epistles and suggests the influence of the Hellenistic world, where such lists were a common feature, though they were not unknown among the Jews. Accordingly vv. 20–23 are usually regarded as an early Christian interpretation of v. 15. That brings us to the character of the section as a whole.

It is generally agreed that in its present form it is a composition of the Evangelist, though we cannot tell how much of the material may already have been combined for catechetical purposes before it reached him. Nor is it easy to decide what, if anything, he himself contributed by way of setting; some scholars, for example, assign vv. 1–5 to him (as an introduction to vv. 6–8 and the rest of the section), others regard vv. 1–8 as an already existing pronouncement-story. Some regard vv. 19b and 20–23 as St Mark's own interpretations, others think he found them already embedded in the tradition (see further the notes below). The whole question is of some importance, because, as already hinted, some of the arguments which in their present context are somewhat problematical, might have made a perfectly valid point in another context. It is possible, for example, to imagine contexts in which the *Corban* saying would have constituted an overwhelming indictment of some aspects of Pharisaism. And see the passage from B. quoted above.

❧

1
scribes: See on 1[22].

2–4
These verses have given rise to a voluminous discussion which can only be lightly sketched here. The Jewish authority for the customs in question is the *Talmud* – a written recension of the oral tradition considerably later than the *Mishnah*.* According to the Jewish experts in such matters, the evidence of the *Talmud* is that in the time of Jesus ritual washing of hands before meals was obligatory only on the priests. An occasional 'pietist' might try to live, so far as outward purity was concerned, as if he were a priest, but the ordinary layman – including the Pharisee and the scribe – was not concerned with such questions of religious defilement unless he was about to enter the temple and make a sacrifice. Accordingly, the story as it stands can hardly be historical.

Christian scholars have replied that this is precisely the sort of case in which the lateness of the Jewish sources seriously detracts from their value as evidence for the time of Jesus. It is agreed by everyone that about A.D. 100, or a little later, ritual washing did begin to become obligatory on all; such a change will not have been completely sudden, so may it not be that there was already a strong move in this direction in the time of Jesus? If so, it would certainly have found its chief supporters among scribes and Pharisees, and they might well have expected a religious leader such as Jesus to exact the highest standards from his followers. If that suggestion can be accepted, it may preserve the historicity of the story itself, though it cannot save St Mark's generalizing aside that *the Pharisees, and all the Jews* practised such ritual washing, for the Talmudic evidence makes clear that, as a group, they did not.

The reference to the washing of various vessels is too vague for detailed comment,† while the first part of v. 4 raises a problem of

* The *Mishnah* was compiled by Rabbi Judah ha-Nasi, (*c.* A.D. 135–220). The 'Palestinian *Talmud*' dates from *c.* A.D. 450, and the much larger, Babylonian, *Talmud* from *c.* A.D. 500.

† Those interested can consult Schürer, *History of the Jewish People*, E. T. II, 106ff.

translation. It is usually translated as in R.S.V. and in that case, in the words of the Jewish authority, A. Büchler: 'All efforts to prove this a custom even of the strictest Jews must fail.' But there are no words in the Greek corresponding to *when they come* or *themselves* and it is just possible that what we are meant to supply is 'what they buy' and 'it'. However, in view of the possibility mentioned above that vv. 1–5 are St Mark's own composition, we cannot rule out another suggestion of Büchler's. He has discovered some evidence that Jews of the Diaspora who were constantly surrounded by Gentile 'impurity' may have had quite strict rules about handwashing earlier than the Jews of Palestine; in that case, St Mark may have assumed that customs common among the Jews known to him were also current in Palestine. (See Introduction, p. 40, for the bearing of this on St Mark's identity and see Montefiore, I, pp. 130ff., for a very full discussion of the whole passage.) It may be worth pointing out that these questions, for all their undoubted importance, do not vitally affect the logic of the section as a whole. The subject of vv. 1–13 is the propriety or impropriety of obeying the Jewish oral tradition; Jesus' teaching on this subject is not affected if St Mark in his comments, or even in his setting of the scene, is not altogether accurate about some of the details of the tradition.

3

wash their hands: The Greek word not translated in the R.S.V. is *pygmē*, literally: 'with the fist'; as the R.S.V. note says, the meaning here is quite uncertain. The alternatives in some MSS. (e.g. *pykna* = 'often') are simply the guesses of later scribes who could not understand the original any better than we can.

the elders (vv. 3 and 5): Greek, *prĕsbytĕrōn*, literally 'older men' or 'men of fairly advanced years', a word used by the Greeks in many senses, mostly honorific, among them 'ancestors' or 'forefathers'; that may be the meaning here and the phrase would then mean: 'the ancient tradition of our race'. But probably the reference here is more specific, to the 'honoured Jewish teachers of the Law whose judgements were handed down and were considered binding by the scribes and Pharisees' (V. T.).

6–8

Well did Isaiah, etc.: The meaning is brought out in Moffatt's translation: *Yes, it was about you hypocrites indeed that Isaiah prophesied.* The quotation is from Isa. 29^{13}, and, with some modifications, follows the LXX version. As can be seen by looking at the R.S.V. version of the Isaiah passage which is based on the Hebrew, the Hebrew text differed a good deal, and it is just the part where the Greek text deviates from the Hebrew that affords the point of the quotation here – the 'doctrines they teach are but human precepts' (v. 7, Moffatt). So in its Hebrew form the passage would hardly be relevant here, *pace* V. T. It may well have been one of the texts used by Greek-speaking Christians in their polemic against the Jews (cf. Col. 2^{20}ff. and Titus 1^{14}), and perhaps that was how St Mark came to hear of it and insert it here. But even if the quotation is St Mark's, v. 8 may well contain a word of Jesus. The style and attitude are entirely his (cf. Matt. 23^{23}); though, as suggested above, the words would be more devastating in a context proving that the Pharisees actually disregarded the written Law in the interests of their oral tradition, but vv. 1–5 give no hint of that.

9–13

To provide evidence for this word of Jesus, St Mark appends a section which seems to have been derived from a different source and context (cf. how it has kept its introductory formula *And he said to them*, which is not necessary in the Marcan context). The general drift of Jesus' criticism is clear enough, but it is difficult to be sure of its precise bearing without knowing more than we do at present about the practice criticized. *Corban* is a transliteration of a Hebrew word meaning 'an offering', 'a gift devoted to God'. If the literal sense of the word is the key to the meaning here, as St Mark perhaps suggests by translating it into Greek (v. 11), what is envisaged is a man's evading his obligation to his parents by vowing to give the temple treasury (either actually or by legal fiction) the earnings that might otherwise have been available for their support. It is even possible that if a man informed his parents with a solemn vow that anything they might have hoped to get from him was henceforth *for them* as though it had been dedicated to the temple, that was held to prevent the parents touching it, although the son retained it none the less. (So S.-B. – who quote from Jewish sources a case with some affinities.) But the word *Corban* was also used without stress on its literal meaning simply as a formula for a particularly binding oath or vow. So probably what Jesus had in mind was a man who, using the solemn *Corban* oath, swore (perhaps in a fit of passion) that he would not support his parents. If the rabbis upheld the inviolability of even such a monstrous oath, we can see what a handle was given for the evasion of the plainest and most fundamental duties. Strictly, of course, this is not a case of setting aside the written Law in favour of the oral tradition, for the duty of keeping oaths was as much part of the written Law as the duty to parents. When religion is conceived simply as literal obedience to a legal code there is no means of distinguishing between the lesser and the 'weightier matters of the law'; thus Jesus' words are really an indictment of the whole idea of purely legal religion. Cf. B., pp. 124–5: 'The issue involved was plainly one of the conflict of two laws, both of them biblical. Jesus seems to have felt that in such a case of conflict it was obvious that the abstract law of the validity of oaths should give way before the law commanding respect and care for parents. The ruling that the former should be observed He deemed as simply human tradition. It was not from God. The scribes, of course, in reply could have cited Deut. 23^{21}. But there are other instances which we shall encounter wherein Jesus appears to have been indifferent even to the text of scripture where it ran counter to His conception of God's will. And this imperative prophetic consciousness of God's will was formulated in terms which gave the right of way, in cases of conflict, to human needs and interests.'

10
The quotations are from Exod. 20^{12} (Deut. 5^{16}) and Exod. 21^{17} – the double quotation underlines the overwhelming importance the written Law attached to this duty.

14
In Mark a crowd is always waiting in the wings, as it were, to be summoned on to the stage when needed (see on 2^{24}).

19
The words in brackets are a paraphrase rather than a translation, literally: 'cleansing all meats'. If the R.S.V. interpretation is right (as it probably is) the words are a note by St Mark or even a marginal comment by an early reader, which has slipped into the text. (On the question how correctly it interprets Jesus' original intention see above.) It is just possible, however, that a change has crept in at some point and that in the original Aramaic the meaning was something like: 'all the food being cast out and purged away' (cf. Black, *An Aramaic Approach to the Gospels and Acts*, p. 159).

21
evil thoughts: 'Designs of evil' (Moffatt), 'not merely evil thoughts, but evil devisings which issue in degraded acts and vices now mentioned' (V. T.).

21–22
R.S.V. does not make clear that down to *wickedness* the words are all plurals in the Greek, implying '*acts* of fornication...'

envy: Literally 'the evil eye'; in a Jewish context 'envy' would probably be the correct translation, but if the list is of Gentile provenance, a reference to the malevolent glance which casts a spell cannot be ruled out.

$7^{24}–8^{26}$ *Jesus' 'Gentile Mission'*

The wording at the beginning of v. 24 suggests that the Evangelist wanted to mark a considerable break between vv. 23 and 24,* presumably because at this point Jesus' active ministry in Galilee comes to an end, although he later 'passes through' it incognito (9^{30}).† Some scholars have made much of this, and have pictured an extended missionary tour on Gentile soil undertaken by Jesus either because he was forced to flee before the hostility of Herod (cf. Luke $13^{31ff.}$) or because of the failure, as he saw it, of his ministry in Galilee. It is probably true that in the next section of the Gospel, where Jesus is represented as continually in Gentile territory, St Mark sought to depict a 'Gentile ministry', as part of his endeavour to meet the needs of Gentile readers and show that the interest and saving power of Jesus were not confined to Jews. He has already shown his interest in this theme in the story of the Gerasene demoniac (5^{1-20}) and has prepared the way for the present section in the strikingly universalistic teaching of 7^{1-23}.

Nevertheless, as V. T. writes (p. 633), the limitations imposed on this attempt by the tradition are apparent: 'No preaching or teaching to Gentiles is recorded because the tradition had no knowledge of it, and, although the disciples suddenly reappear in 8^{1-21}, in the region of Tyre Jesus is alone. No mission to Gentiles is recorded; only intimations of such a ministry. The section is a defeated attempt to represent what would have been welcomed if the tradition could have supplied the evidence. St Mark truly divined the universalism implicit in the teaching of Jesus, but he could find little that suggested that His mission had extended beyond Israel, and it is to his credit as an

* Notice that he uses *dĕ* instead of *kai*, which is his usual word at the beginning of a paragraph. This is elsewhere a sign of a definite break in the Gospel – see *H. & I.*, p. 62n., and cf. C. H. Turner in the *J. T. S.*, XXVII, p. 152.

† And in 8^{10-13} is possibly 'represented as passing through the western region of Jordan'.

Evangelist that he does not force the tradition to yield more than it will bear.'* As for attempted historical reconstructions of the tour and its motives, Mark offers no help;† such evidence as there is, is derived from Matthew and Luke, and suggestions based upon it must be pronounced highly speculative.

7^{24-30} A GENTILE COMES TO JESUS

24 *And from there he arose and went away to the region of Tyre and Sidon.*[a]
And he entered a house, and would not have any one know it; yet he could
not be hid. 25 *But immediately a woman, whose little daughter was possessed*
by an unclean spirit, heard of him, and came and fell down at his feet.
26 *Now the woman was a Greek, a Syrophoeni'cian by birth. And she begged*
him to cast the demon out of her daughter. 27 *And he said to her, 'Let the*
children first be fed, for it is not right to take the children's bread and throw
it to the dogs.' 28 *But she answered him, 'Yes, Lord; yet even the dogs under*
the table eat the children's crumbs.' 29 *And he said to her, 'For this saying you*
may go your way; the demon has left your daughter.' 30 *And she went home*
and found the child lying in bed, and the demon gone.

a Other ancient authorities omit *and Sidon*

This is a miracle story; for there can be no doubt that in St Mark's view vv. 29–30 implied an act of long-distance healing on the part of Jesus. However, the emphasis lies not on the healing itself, but on the dialogue which precedes it. A mother comes and pleads with Jesus to free her daughter from a demon; she addresses him as '*Lord*' (v. 28) and shows all the signs of faith and reverence we have met in similar cases before (cf. e.g. 1^{40} and $5^{22f.}$). But in this case there is a vital difference; Jesus is in a region where a good many of the people are Gentiles (7^{24}) and the woman herself is Jewish neither by descent nor

* See further the detailed note on v. 24. Jeremias goes so far as to say 'an analysis of the section [i.e. 7^{24}–8^{26}] leads to the result that the only concrete material which the evangelist possessed for this supposed Gentile activity on the part of Jesus consisted of the story of the Syrophoenician woman' (*Jesus' Promise to the Nations*, p. 33).

† Lightfoot rightly remarks that the Marcan arrangement in this section is 'especially obscure'.

by religious conviction (v. 26: see notes below). How will this affect Jesus' response? – that question is the real subject of the pericope. The answer may seem surprising to the modern reader. Jesus explains that he is not at liberty to feed dogs, i.e. Gentiles, because the food at his disposal is for the children, i.e. the Jews.

Whatever other implications it may have, this brings our miracle into line with the general understanding of miracles in the Gospel (see on 3^{20-30}). The power of Jesus is not a general, but a particular spiritual power,* and one that is associated with the Jewish race. For it is the power of the Messiah, the agent of *Israel's* God for the establishment of *His* kingdom and, in the first instance at any rate, the salvation of *His* people.

But at first sight, the second part of the story might seem to contradict all this, for Jesus does in fact grant the woman an exercise of his power unprecedented in Mark; he performs an act of healing at a distance. Once again, however, the dialogue is all-important. The woman does not contest Jesus' first reply; she accepts the analogy and its implications, only pointing out that when the children are fed, the dogs also get some small benefit incidentally. She thus recognizes the divinely ordained division between God's people and the Gentiles. Moreover, by the very fact of her persistence, she reveals her conviction that it is from Jesus, the Jewish Messiah, that salvation is to be obtained. Cf. Matt. 15^{28}, where her attitude is described as one of 'great faith'. It is only in the light of all this that Jesus grants her request, and even then the impression remains that his action is very much an exception.

Naturally such a story has presented Christian commentators with something of a puzzle. For a discussion of the general question of Jesus' attitude to the Gentiles see now J. Jeremias, *Jesus' Promise to the Nations*. Briefly, the fact seems to be that Jesus accepted a fairly sharp distinction between Jew and Gentile as part of God's plan, and regarded his commission, and that of his disciples, as being limited to Israel. But he seems to have shared the old Jewish hope that when – through his work as *Jewish* Messiah – the final salvation arrived, large numbers of Gentiles would be called to share in it. (Cf. such passages as Isa. 19^{19-25}, 60, $66^{19f.}$, Mic. $4^{1f.}$, Zech. $8^{20ff.}$, and see Jeremias pp. 56ff.)

* See, for example, what was said about faith on p. 158.

Their call, however, would belong essentially to the last days, and meanwhile, if he extended his beneficent activities to a non-Jew, it must be on the understanding that such an extension was exceptional and did not call in question the distinction between Jew and Gentile or their relative places in the order of salvation. After his use of the word 'dog' – to this day the supreme insult in the East – little room for doubt in the matter could remain.

In the rather changed perspective after the resurrection one party in the Church came to hold that God wanted Gentiles called to a share in salvation then and there. This story of Christ at least showed that there was nothing in principle wrong in extending his saving power to non-Jews before the end came, so these Christians made out of it an argument in their favour, modifying it somewhat in the process (see notes, especially on v. 27a). But the story could also be made the basis for a *denial* that Gentiles were meant to be admitted to the Church before the end came, and in the version of it quoted by St Matthew that seems to be the lesson it is meant to teach (cf. Matt. 15^{21-28}).

24
Sidon: Should be omitted with R.S.V.

the region of Tyre: Despite much that has been written, this was Gentile territory only in a very limited sense. 'The territory of Tyre stretched over the whole of the northern district of upper Galilee as far as the basin of Lake Huleh (see map), while that of Sidon extended as far as the territory of Damascus. The region lying between Galilee and Caesarea Philippi had once been part of the region of Israel and in the time of Jesus it was still mainly inhabited by descendants of the northern Israelite tribes. It would have been to these outposts of Israelite population and Jewish religion that the mind of Jesus first turned when he extended his activity so far to the north; even here we find no real, not to say final, crossing of the boundary of the Jewish population.'*

26
a Greek: hĕllēnis; to Mark's readers this word will have had religious, rather than racial, connotations – 'a pagan', 'a Gentile'. Her nationality is first referred to in the next word, which means a Phoenician from Syria, as opposed to a Phoenician from Libya, a *Liby*phoenician or Carthaginian.

* Jeremias, op. cit., p. 36.

27
Let the children first be fed: The implication of these words seems to be that once the children *have* been fed, others might expect to be fed in the same way. They could even be read as enjoining a Gentile mission.

As we have seen, such a view belongs to the early Church rather than to Jesus himself, and in the opinion of most commentators, therefore, the words are a later addition, designed to mitigate the apparent severity of Jesus' attitude. They are absent from St Matthew's version and seem to reflect St Paul's repeated statement 'to the Jew first and then to the Greek' (Rom. 1^{16}, etc.) and also the custom of the missionaries in Acts, who do not *turn to the Gentiles* until salvation has first been offered to the Jews (cf. e.g. Acts 13^{46} and 18^{6}); if they were original here, the woman's retort would lack a good deal of its point.

the dogs: In the Greek the diminutive form *kynariŏn* is used, and this may be another attempt to soften the offensiveness of Jesus' words. But it is uncertain whether the diminutive had any mitigating force in contemporary Greek, and, so far as Jesus' original words are concerned, Hebrew and Aramaic have no corresponding form; he will have said 'dogs', not 'puppies', still less, as has been suggested, 'doggies'!

7^{31-37} THE CURE OF THE DEAF MUTE

31 *Then he returned from the region of Tyre, and went through Sidon to*
the Sea of Galilee, through the region of the Decap'olis. 32 *And they brought*
to him a man who was deaf and had an impediment in his speech; and they
besought him to lay his hand upon him. 33 *And taking him aside from the*
multitude privately, he put his fingers into his ears, and he spat and touched
his tongue; 34 *and looking up to heaven, he sighed, and said to him, 'Eph'-*
phatha,' that is, 'Be opened.' 35 *And his ears were opened, and his tongue was*
released, and he spoke plainly. 36 *And he charged them to tell no one; but the*
more he charged them, the more zealously they proclaimed it. 37 *And they*
were astonished beyond measure, saying, 'He has done all things well; he
even makes the deaf hear and the dumb speak.'

This miracle story was originally an independent pericope. St Mark has related it to its present context by means of an introductory sentence, which is not without difficulty (see notes), but which appears to locate it in the predominantly Gentile district of Decapolis (for which see on 5^{20}). In its original form, the story probably consisted only of vv. 32–36 and told of a cure which Jesus effected by the use of a number of current wonder-working techniques (see notes on vv. 33–34). Verse 36 has been added in the interests of the doctrine of the 'messianic secret' (see Introduction, pp. 31–2), while v. 37, though very possibly derived from the pre-Marcan tradition, was originally 'rather the conclusion of a number of stories than the acclamation of the people to Jesus who is just passing by' (Dibelius).

A point to notice is the relation of the story to certain Old Testament passages and particularly to Isa. 35^{5-6}.* The last sentence of v. 37 seems a clear allusion to that passage and it has even been suggested that the comment *He has done all things well* means 'How exactly he fulfils the prophecies!' The story has been affected by the Isaiah passage in another, and more subtle, way. The phrase in v. 32 *had an impediment in his speech* represents the exceedingly rare Greek adjective *mŏgilalŏs*, which means literally 'speaking with difficulty' or 'hardly able to speak'. St Mark almost certainly derived the word from the only other place where it occurs in the Greek Bible, Isa. 35^{6}, where it translates a Hebrew word meaning 'dumb'. Then, seeing the incident as the fulfilment of the prophecy, and influenced by the literal meaning of the Greek word, he took the miracle to consist in making the man speak *plainly* (v. 35). No doubt the original story told of a deaf-mute who, before the miracle, could not speak at all (cf. *dumb* v. 37).

In St Mark's arrangement this story concludes the section which began with the feeding of the five thousand (6^{35}–7^{37}). The feeding of the *four* thousand, which comes next (8^{1-9}), is followed by a remarkably similar section (8^{10-26} – on which see below pp. 206f.); the story which occupies the corresponding place in that section is that of the healing of the blind man of Bethsaida (8^{22-26}). As the two stories are both peculiar to St Mark and have many features in common (see pp. 216–17) it may well be that St Mark saw a certain symbolic

* See also Isa. 29^{18-23}, $32^{3ff.}$, Ezek. 24^{27}, Ps. 38^{14}, and Wisdom 10^{21}. Some commentators go further and see in the first words of the onlookers in v. 37 a reminiscence of Gen. 1^{31} and Ecclus 39^{16}; Christ's work is seen as 'the new creation'. But this surely borders on the fanciful.

appropriateness in placing them as he has done. Taken together, against the background of such passages as Isa. 35 (esp. v. 5) they bear clear testimony to Jesus' ministry as the messianic fulfilment of prophecy.* Hence perhaps the quite overwhelming amazement attributed to the onlookers in v. 37 (see notes).

31
Since there is no indication that St Mark is thinking of a prolonged tour, the route described is hard to explain; a glance at the map will confirm R.'s statement that it is 'as though a man should travel from Cornwall to London via Manchester'. Even if *Sidon* stands for the whole area round the town, the difficulty is only partly met, and many scholars accept Wellhausen's suggestion that Sidon is a misrendering of *Saidan*, a variant form of *Bethsaida*. But we should expect 'to' rather than 'through' Bethsaida, and it is probably better to accept the text as it stands and say, with R., that 'Mark was not thinking very clearly of the actual geography'; indeed, he and his readers were probably not familiar with it. (See Introduction, p. 40.)

The reference to Decapolis is also somewhat strange; it is usually translated as in R.S.V., but literally the words mean 'in the middle of the Decapolis district'. Whatever the exact sense, the point of this reference is probably not so much to suggest that the deaf-mute was a Gentile (contrast 7^{26}) as to provide a Gentile setting for the feeding in 8^{1}ff.

32
lay his hands upon him: i.e. heal him. The gesture so frequently accompanied the act of healing that it came to be used as a metaphor for it.

33
taking him aside from the multitude privately: On the original motive for such privacy see on 5^{43}; but St Mark may have interpreted it here with reference to the messianic secret.

33–34
The order and character of the gestures vary slightly in different MSS. and versions; in any case, all of them are known to have formed part of the healing technique of contemporary wonder-workers. Touching, and manipulation of the affected organ, are too obvious to need com-

* B. W. Bacon in his analysis of Mark goes so far as to designate the two stories (with ref. to Isa. 35^{5}) as 'The Ears of the Deaf Unstopped' and 'The Eyes of the Blind Opened'. For the belief that such miracles were to be expected of the Messiah see C. K. Barrett, *H. S. G. T.*, pp. 70f.

ment; the use of saliva is widely attested (cf. John 9^6 and the story of Vespasian healing by means of his saliva in Tacitus, *History*, IV, 81); so are the look towards heaven, which sought and obtained power, and the sigh, or groan (v. 34), which is recommended in several magical texts as a potent action. (Further details and references in the bigger commentaries* and in Dibelius, *F. T. G.*, pp. 83ff.) On the motives for preserving the operative word, *Ephphatha*, in the original tongue see on 5^{41} above. The vividness with which the act is described may well suggest that St Mark had seen patients treated in this way by Christian healers (cf. 1 Cor. 12^9 etc.) and it was perhaps for the guidance of such healers that the details were preserved in the tradition. For the general significance of the fact that Jesus used such techniques see Introduction, p. 49.

35
his tongue was released: Lit. 'the fetter on his tongue was loosed'. Does this way of speaking imply an understanding of the story according to which the man was 'bound' by demonic powers (a common idea in the ancient world)? Such an understanding would certainly be in line with St Mark's understanding of Jesus as battling with the powers of evil in order to release their prisoners (see on 4^{39} and p. 120). But it must be confessed that there is little else in the story to suggest such an understanding.

36
they proclaimed it: Greek *ĕkēryssŏn*, on which see notes to 1^{14}, 5^{18-20}, and 6^{12}. If, as there implied, the word refers in Mark, directly or indirectly, to the Messiahship of Jesus, 'here . . . we must suppose that the Evangelist wishes to draw attention to the messianic nature of the act of Jesus' (Lightfoot).

37
astonished beyond measure: As described in the Greek the emotion is so very strong that something more than one successful act of healing would have been required to provoke it. (See above.)

* Though in V. T. the upward look and the sigh are arbitrarily, and surely implausibly, dissociated from the similar actions of contemporary wonder-workers.

8:1–10 A SECOND ACCOUNT OF THE FEEDING OF THE MULTITUDE

*8 In those days, when again a great crowd had gathered, and they had
nothing to eat, he called his disciples to him, and said to them, 2‘I have
compassion on the crowd, because they have been with me now three days,
and have nothing to eat; 3and if I send them away hungry to their homes,
they will faint on the way; and some of them have come a long way.’ 4And
his disciples answered him, ‘How can one feed these men with bread here in
the desert?’ 5And he asked them, ‘How many loaves have you?’ They said,
‘Seven.’ 6And he commanded the crowd to sit down on the ground; and he
took the seven loaves, and having given thanks he broke them and gave them
to his disciples to set before the people; and they set them before the crowd.
7And they had a few small fish; and having blessed them, he commanded
that these also should be set before them. 8And they ate, and were satisfied;
and they took up the broken pieces left over, seven baskets full. 9And there
were about four thousand people. 10And he sent them away; and immediately
he got into the boat with his disciples and went to the district of Dalmanu'tha.[a]*

a Other ancient authorities read *Magadan* or *Magdala*

This story is so closely similar to the story of the feeding of the five thousand, in both content and significance, that most of the comments made on that story are applicable here too and need not be repeated.

Indeed the resemblances between the two stories are such as to demand some sort of explanation. There is of course no reason why Jesus should not have performed similar feeding miracles on two different occasions. But when we observe the constant, detailed, and often verbal agreements between the two stories,* we can hardly avoid at least the conclusion that the account of one of the two miracles has very much influenced the account of the other. But even this conclusion will not satisfy most commentators; for if the disciples

* Note, e.g., the desert in both cases 6^{35}, 8^{4}; the same question: *how many loaves have you?* 6^{38}, 8^{5}; the same command to recline 6^{39}, 8^{6}; the same words used of the loaves: ‘took’, ‘gave thanks’, ‘broke’, ‘gave’, ‘set before’; the statement; *and they (all) ate and were satisfied*’ 6^{42}, 8^{8}; the same gathering of the remains in baskets, and in each case the dismissal of the crowd, followed by a journey in a boat.

had already been through the experience described in $6^{33\text{ff.}}$, it is incredible that they should have been so dull and uncomprehending as is here suggested (v. 4). Accordingly it is now generally accepted that we are dealing with alternative, and somewhat divergent, accounts of a single incident. No doubt because of its eucharistic connexions, the story was highly valued in the early Church, and in the course of constant repetition it acquired two, or, for aught we know, more than two, forms.*

But once these two stories were recognized as 'doublets', it could hardly escape notice that the sections which follow them also bear close resemblances, as the following table will show:

A	B
1. Feeding of the 5,000 (6^{35-44})	1. Feeding of the 4,000 (8^{1-9})
2. Crossing of the Lake (6^{45-56})	2. Crossing of the Lake (8^{10})
3. Controversy with Pharisees (7^{1-23})	3. Controversy with Pharisees (8^{11-13})
4. The Children's Bread (7^{24-30})	4. The Leaven of the Pharisees (8^{14-21})
5. Healing (? at Bethsaida) (7^{31-37})	5. Healing at Bethsaida (8^{22-26})

Such close parallelism can hardly be accidental, and accordingly it is often maintained that the tradition at St Mark's disposal contained alternative accounts, not only of the feeding, but of the whole cycle of events to which it belonged. But on a closer analysis, such as has recently been carried out,† this hypothesis appears too simple to cover all the facts. Thus, for example, while B 1 and 2 do appear to be 'doublets' of A 1 and 2, we have already seen that 7^{1-23} is a Marcan construction and was not, at any rate in its present form, an independent unit in the tradition, forming a doublet of 8^{11-13}. Again,

* The version in John 6^{1-15} suggests a third form, with features of its own (e.g. Philip and the 'lad'). The value attached to the story in the early Church is evidenced by its being one of the few incidents recorded in all four Gospels, though only Matthew and Mark record it twice. Lightfoot points out that certain features, the huge crowd, the lateness of the hour, the desert place, and its location on the east side of the Lake, remain fairly constant. Another of his comments is worth repeating: 'The view is sometimes expressed that the Evangelist did not realize that he was dealing with duplicate material. It may be doubted whether the question would have put itself to him in that form' (*H. & I.*, p. 115).

† See V. T., n. C, pp. 628–32.

although A 5 and B 5 have unmistakable affinities (see notes on them), they are quite different stories and can hardly be alternative reports of the same incident. The most plausible explanation is that St Mark, having two accounts of the feeding, with certain appendages to each, has reproduced them side by side, at the same time making additions to both sides, phrased and arranged in such a way as to preserve the parallelism between the two cycles as far as possible. In 8^{14-21} he has drawn the two cycles together,* and that passage may help us with a further question.

No one could fail to recognize the similarity at any rate of A 1 and 2 to B 1 and 2, and even if St Mark took them to record different incidents, 'we cannot but ask', as R. says, 'why, in a Gospel so short as Mark's, which presents every appearance of being ... a selection of typical and specially significant anecdotes from the much larger number of stories about Our Lord which must have been current in Apostolic times ... two such *similar* stories should have been included.'† As far as the feeding stories are concerned, it was suggested at least as early as the fourth century‡ that St Mark may have intended the feeding of the five thousand to symbolize the giving of the Bread of Life to the Jews, and the feeding of the four thousand the giving of the Bread of Life to the Gentiles – the disciples need have no anxiety about Jesus' ability to supply the spiritual needs of the whole Gentile world. Professor Richardson sets out the evidence as follows: 'The scene of the Feeding of the Five Thousand suggests a Galilaean (i.e. Jewish) crowd; that of the Feeding of the Four Thousand suggests a crowd drawn from the neighbourhood of the Decapolis (cf. Mark 7^{31}) on the south-eastern side of the Sea of Galilee, i.e. a Gentile crowd. The Five Thousand receive the five loaves (possibly a reminiscence of the Five Books of the Law); the Four Thousand receive seven loaves (cf. the seventy nations into which the Gentile world was traditionally divided, the Septuagint, the Seven Deacons of Acts 6^{3}, and St Luke's Mission of the Seventy, Luke $10^{1\text{ff.}}$). At the former miracle twelve baskets are taken up, representing the Twelve Tribes

* For Jesus there explicitly refers to both in the course of a single dialogue.

† p. 86. R. is thinking specifically only of the feeding stories; but the point clearly applies also to A 2 and B 2, and to some extent to other items in the lists printed above.

‡ See Trench, *Notes on the Miracles*, No. 25 and final note.

of Israel (cf. Matt. 19^{28}); at the latter, seven baskets remain over (cf. the above references). In the earlier story the word used for "basket" is *kŏphinŏs* (Mark 6^{43}), apparently a distinctively Jewish type of basket (Rawlinson, *St Mark*, p. 87, says that the word occurs in Juvenal III, 14 and VI, 542 to denote a basket commonly used by the poorer class of Jews in Rome); in the second story the word for "basket" is *spyris* (Mark 8^{8}), an ordinary kind of basket, or fish-basket. That the distinction between the two words is not merely accidental is shown by its reappearance in Mark $8^{19f.}$. In view of this wealth of accumulative evidence it is impossible to doubt that St Mark intended his readers to understand the interpretation of the feeding miracles which has been suggested above.'* In view of the ancients' love of allusiveness and symbolism, there is probably something in this theory, though it is surely going much too far to say that 'it is impossible to doubt' such an intention on St Mark's part; when St Mark wanted to distinguish Jew and Gentile, he was capable of doing it quite plainly (cf. 7^{26}) and the fact that the suggested distinction is made here in so *very* roundabout a way has led some reputable commentators† to doubt whether St Mark intended to make it at all.

8^{14-21} suggests that St Mark may have included both stories because he attached a very special significance to the scenes they depicted, with their obviously supernatural character and their unmistakable Old Testament background (see on Chapter 6). Here, if anywhere, he seems to have felt, Christ was clearly revealed as the fulfiller of the old dispensation, the one who brings the full and final satisfaction of the needs of all. (Cf. the comments on $6^{30ff.}$ and notice how in both cases there is enough and to spare.) If men could be blind to it even here, then this was the place to study and reveal the causes and cure of such blindness. This suggestion (which does not exclude the other) has the merit of explaining the reduplication not only of the feeding stories themselves, but, as will be shown, of the cycles of events which follow them; it also explains the connexion of this whole section (6^{30}–8^{26}) with what follows in $8^{27ff.}$ (see notes there).

The presence of such doublets is worth pondering for the light it throws on the transmission of the tradition and the character that tradition inevitably gave to writings based upon it. The point is put,

* *The Miracle-Stories of the Gospels*, p. 98.

† See e.g. Lohmeyer, p. 153, note 6.

perhaps rather strongly, by B.: 'One is struck by the presence of exact figures for the various items. If one had this story only, one might insist that this citation of the exact number of loaves of bread and of the baskets full of fragments indicates the recollections of a participant in the event. But it is evident, from a comparison with those of the other story, that they have no actual value; they are due to the necessities of the storyteller's art, a factor which plainly must be allowed for in attempting to understand and evaluate these early stories. One notes also the dropping out of the introduction or setting which the episode has in 6^{32-34}' (p. 136).

6
'As before, the scene is so depicted as to reflect all the features of the Church [eucharistic] ritual' (B. W. Bacon).

7
a few small fish: Regarded by some critics as an addition, due to assimilation of the two accounts. There is no reference to 'fragments' of fish in the next verse, as there is in 6^{43}.

10
the district of Dalmanutha: This is probably what St Mark wrote, though no such place is known, and the MSS. and versions offer innumerable alternatives, some of them influenced by the parallel passage in Matt. (15^{39}) which has 'Magadan' or possibly 'Magdala'. No satisfactory solution of the problem has so far been propounded, and in view of Mark's imperfect acquaintance with the geography of Palestine, speculation is perhaps not very profitable.

8^{11-13} A SIGN REFUSED

11 *The Pharisees came and began to argue with him, seeking from him a*
sign from heaven, to test him. 12 *And he sighed deeply in his spirit, and*
said, 'Why does this generation seek a sign? Truly, I say to you, no sign
shall be given to this generation.' 13 *And he left them, and getting into the*
boat again he departed to the other side.

St Mark now diversifies his account with one of the controversy stories which he includes from time to time in order to remind us of the continuing official hostility which was the background to the whole ministry (cf. e.g. 7^{1-23} and 10^{1-12}). In this case, the setting, as opposed to the saying it enshrines, appears to be St Mark's construction, and he has been at pains (even at some sacrifice of historical verisimilitude – see notes below) to place the incident in a context which will bring out its meaning. The Pharisees ask for a sign, and the moment they choose for doing so is one when Jesus has just crowned a long series of mighty acts with a twice-repeated nature miracle of stupendous magnitude and – at any rate to anyone with a Jewish background – profound significance. No doubt by a '*sign from heaven*' (v. 11) the Pharisees meant some apocalyptic portent more compelling than any healing or exorcism, and perhaps from their point of view the request was not altogether unreasonable (see notes below). But to the Christians of St Mark's day the signs that Jesus had already wrought seemed so compelling that they could only regard any further request for a sign as due to deliberate refusal to be convinced, or to a blindness so complete that it must have been produced by God as a punishment for sin (see pp. 135f.). The Pharisees' attitude, they felt, exactly mirrored the attitude of the notorious 'generation' of the great deliverance under Moses, which had repeatedly 'tempted' God by demanding further proof of his power and goodwill even after he had performed innumerable 'signs' for them (cf., from among many similar passages, Ps. 95^{9-10}, Num. $14^{11, 22}$, and Deut. 1^{35}). St Mark's choice of words strongly suggests that this parallel was in his mind, and certainly it will have occasioned him no surprise that 'the perverseness of Moses' generation repeated itself in that to which the greater than Moses had come' (M'Neile, *Matthew*, p. 157). God's message and messengers had ever met with misunderstanding and opposition (cf. e.g. Matt. 5^{12} and $23^{29\text{ff.}}$, and Acts 7^{51-52}), so it was only to be expected that the generation to which the final messenger was sent should be a wicked generation indeed.*

* The word 'generation' is in fact normally a term of rebuke or condemnation in the New Testament, no doubt with allusion to such passages as Deut. 32^{5} and Ps. 95^{10}. Cf. e.g. Matt. 11^{16}, 12^{39}, 16^{4}, Luke 11^{29}, Acts 2^{40}, and Phil. 2^{15}. It should be remembered that for St Mark, and other New Testament writers, Jesus' generation was virtually the last generation there was to be (see on 9^{1}).

In the light of all this, and of what Mark has already said in Chapter 4 in connexion with the parables, it is easy to see how he understood the emphatic refusal in v. 12. The miracles of Jesus, he thinks, have a meaning no less than the parables, and to those who understand that meaning they are 'signs' enough. Those for whom 'the mystery of the kingdom' is intended ought to understand them, and will certainly be able to do so when their eyes have been opened. Complete blindness to their meaning is a sure mark of 'outsiders' (4^{11}) for whom the mystery is not intended and to whom therefore no further sign will be given. These three verses are thus parallel to 4^{10-12} while the following passage corresponds in the thought of the Evangelist to $4^{13\text{ff.}}$ and leads in to a whole section of the Gospel (8^{22}–10^{52}) dealing with the opening of eyes to the meaning of Jesus and his words and signs.

❧

11

As Wellhausen says: 'The sudden emergence of the Pharisees, while Jesus breaks his journey and lands, is very awkward' and he is probably right in regarding v. 13 as virtually a doublet of v. 10. The arrangement is in any case topical, and no chronological or geographical account of Jesus' movements can safely be based upon it.

seeking from him a sign from heaven: We know that according to contemporary Jewish belief a sign might reasonably be demanded in confirmation of a man's claim to authority, whether for his teaching or his person. Thus a scribe who gave rulings on the Law contrary to the majority opinion offered 'signs' to try to convince his colleagues.* In view of this, and of such Old Testament passages as Deut. 18^{20-22} and Isa. $7^{10\text{ff.}}$, we may perhaps agree with the Jewish scholar Montefiore that: 'From their point of view the Pharisees were justified in showing the utmost caution towards . . . a teacher who either violated, or taught by implication a violation of, the Law. A sign from their point of view was reasonable enough'† – especially if, as was suggested above (on

* For this and similar examples see S.-B., I, 641.

† Montef., I, p. 175.

So it was only natural that the powers of evil should move it to special wickedness, as part of their final struggle against God; 'tempting' Christ (v. 11) was an activity of Satan (1^{13} and cf. the temptation narratives in Matt. and Luke where Jesus is urged to give 'signs').

6^{30-52}) the preceding nature miracles were not originally as spectacularly compelling as St Mark's account might imply.

to test him (*peirazŏntes*)*:* This can of course be no more than St Mark's interpretation of their intention. The word in itself could mean simply 'testing' or 'examining'; but in the Bible it usually has a bad sense, and the idea here may be that if Jesus could be proved unable to give a sign, that would help to discredit him. In any case, as explained above, there is at least a sidelong glance at the common biblical notion that men's faithlessness leads them to put God to the test in the sense of discovering whether he really can do a certain thing. (Cf., in addition, the passages mentioned above, Exod. $17^{2, 7}$ and Acts 5^{9}.)

12

Truly . . . : This word (for which see note on 3^{28}), the form of the saying (in the original: '[May I die] if any sign is given'), and the deep sigh all emphasize the solemn finality of the refusal.

For St Mark *this generation* means simply the Pharisees regarded as typical of the Jews who rejected Jesus, but if, in the tradition before St Mark, the saying was an isolated logion or appeared in a different context (for evidence that it did cf. Matt. 12^{39} and 16^{4} and Luke 11^{29}), it may originally have been of wider application and have expressed Jesus' absolute refusal to compel belief by means of marvels performed simply for the purpose. 'A belief into which a man is bludgeoned by some ocular demonstration which leaves him no course but to submit has none of the moral quality of that faith which avails to the saving of the soul.'* B. even suggests (p. 139) that Jesus may not have felt sure of his ability to perform such *ad hoc* marvels. All this would be quite consistent with a conviction on Jesus' part that in his healings and exorcisms the power of the kingdom was at work for the overthrow of Satan, so that, *in the context of the ministry as a whole*, they were *signs* which authenticated his claims. (Cf. Luke 11^{20} and Matt. 12^{28} and 3^{22-27} above.)

8^{14-21} THE BLINDNESS OF THE DISCIPLES

[14]*Now they had forgotten to bring bread; and they had only one loaf with them in the boat.* [15]*And he cautioned them, saying, 'Take heed, beware*

* W. F. Howard, *Christianity according to St John*, p. 160.

of the leaven of the Pharisees and the leaven of Herod.'[a] 16*And they discussed*
it with one another, saying, 'We have no bread.' 17*And being aware of it,*
Jesus said to them, 'Why do you discuss the fact that you have no bread?
Do you not yet perceive or understand? Are your hearts hardened? 18*Having*
eyes do you not see, and having ears do you not hear? And do you not
remember? 19*When I broke the five loaves for the five thousand, how many*
baskets full of broken pieces did you take up?' They said to him, 'Twelve.
20*'And the seven for the four thousand, how many baskets full of broken*
pieces did you take up?' And they said to him, 'Seven.' 21*And he said to*
them, 'Do you not yet understand?'

a Other ancient authorities read *the Herodians*

A truly remarkable incident. The disciples are at sea, and although they have Jesus with them and have just witnessed his two stupendous miracles with bread, they become concerned over the fact that they have only a single loaf on board, thus revealing an almost incredible failure to register, let alone understand, Jesus' mighty acts. Their attitude in fact is very like that of the Pharisees, and it earns from Jesus the severest rebuke so far directed against the disciples for failure to understand (vv. 17–18, cf. 4^{13}, 7^{18}, etc.). It would almost seem as if the powers of evil had been allowed to blind *all* men to the truth about Jesus (see v. 18 and note on it). But, in contrast with the Pharisees, these are men to whom the mystery of the kingdom is given (4^{11}), so Jesus wrestles with their incomprehension, and, by patiently forcing the right questions upon their notice, begins the work of opening their eyes.

Opening their eyes to what? In the story itself no explicit answer is given. In the first place, no doubt, to Jesus' ability to save them, if need be, from physical starvation; but the use of solemn language borrowed from the Old Testament (v. 18) and the repeated emphasis on the inexhaustible adequacy of Jesus (vv. 19–21) suggest a much deeper significance than that. St Mark seems here to be feeling after the interpretation which was finally elaborated in John 6, a passage to be carefully compared with our present one. On this view, the feeding miracles, with their obvious reference to manna, reveal Jesus as the 'fulfilment' of the great saving event, the Exodus, which lay at the basis of the Old Testament; he is the greater than Moses, the one sent and empowered by God to meet *all* human needs of whatever sort.*

To see Jesus in that light one needs to be given supernatural insight, to have one's 'eyes' opened by the power of God working through Christ; even if the process of conversion is gradual, it is nevertheless always supernaturally induced. All this St Mark teaches, or at any rate strongly hints, by capping this incident with the incident of Jesus miraculously but gradually giving sight to a blind man, and that incident by the story of how he gradually opened the disciples' eyes to the truth about his person (see p. 218). It is thus essential that the present section should be studied in context. It describes a process which is not completed till 8^{27-30},† after having its meaning illuminated in 8^{22-26}. In fact 8^{11-30} is conceived as a single whole which sets out the wrong reponse and the right response to the ministry of Jesus and shows how men pass from the one to the other. The side-glance to the missionary situation of St Mark's own day hardly needs demonstrating. Jesus is not only the bread of life, he is light in the sense of understanding and illumination, a combination, once again, to be found more fully worked out by St John.

Such an interpretation presupposes that v. 15 is an isolated saying of Jesus which has somehow found its way into this context without becoming an integral part of it. For that see the notes, which also discuss alternative interpretations of the passage, based on the assumption that v. 15 is an original and integral part of it. The interpretation of v. 15 is not the only difficulty in the passage. If there was in fact only one feeding incident, the words of Jesus in vv. 19–20 cannot be original as they stand. Nor does it seem humanly possible that the disciples could have behaved with quite such stupidity had they observed such an impressive miracle immediately before. The passage is generally

* According to R. and others 'the hidden meaning in the miracles of feeding' to which the disciples' eyes had to be opened was 'the eucharistic signification ascribed to them in early Christian thought'. 'The mysterious feedings were meant to be a "sign" to those who had eyes to see, and the eucharistic mystery is a "sign" to the faithful still. There is no need for the Church to be anxious about a shortage of spiritual bread' (p. 106). This idea is no doubt present here, as it is in John 6, but it is only part of the wider truth to which the feedings pointed.

† And then only partially; cf. the references to further denials and failures of understanding on the part of the disciples at 14^{50}, etc.

agreed to be 'an especially difficult one', and it would seem that St Mark has here moulded his material in a symbolic interest to a greater degree than is his wont.

ꕥ

15

Probably this verse reached St Mark as an isolated saying which he incorporated here because the reference to bread in v. 14 provided as good a context for it as he could find. If such an insertion seems impossibly clumsy by modern standards, we have to remember the generally 'naïve and non-logical composition of Mark's narrative', (C. H. Turner) and also the fact that the device of the footnote, which could have helped a modern writer out of the difficulty, was unknown to ancient authors. Certainly this verse seems to break the connexion of the story, and whereas 'leaven' is here used figuratively, the reference in the following verse, as in v. 14, is clearly to actual bread.

Some commentators, however, regard the verse as an organic part of the story and explain the literal application in v. 16 of what was meant symbolically (v. 15) as an instance of misunderstanding of a type which occurs frequently in St John (cf. e.g. John 11^{11-14}). Thus it has been suggested that we should translate: 'They argued with one another that what he has just said to us (in v. 15) must mean that we have no bread', or Moffatt renders: "Leaven?" they argued to themselves, "we have no bread at all!" Both these translations, however, like that of R.S.V., rest on the acceptance of a reading in the Greek which includes *lĕgŏntăs* and has *ĕchŏmĕn* instead of *ĕchousin*, whereas, according to another, and perhaps more probable, reading, St Mark wrote: 'They discussed with one another the fact that (or the reason why) they had no bread.' If so, it is not easy to establish any real connexion between this verse and v. 15.

If v. 15 is an isolated saying, it is difficult to be sure what Jesus meant by his symbolical use of *leaven*; and the difficulty is increased by doubts whether Herod figured in the original form of the saying. In Matt. 16^{5}ff., where his place is taken by the Sadducees, the leaven is explained as the teaching of the Pharisees and Sadducees; in Luke 12^{1}, where Herod has disappeared without substitute, the leaven is 'hypocrisy'. By the Jews leaven tended to be thought of as a source of corruption and unholiness (cf. Gal. 5^{9} and 1 Cor. 5^{6-8}) and we know that the rabbis used it as a symbol for the evil tendencies or inclinations in man's nature. That is probably the meaning here; in the case of the Pharisees it would manifest itself in the false teaching and piety which made them enemies of Jesus (cf. vv. 11–13 above) and would make them equally hostile to his disciples.

17–18
The words of Jesus here and in the following verses imply that the miracles, like the parables, have a meaning which can, and ought to, be understood but is in fact misunderstood. The reasons for such misunderstanding are not just intellectual or psychological, they are also moral; for the words translated 'hardened hearts' refer not to unkindness, but to obtuseness, blindness-to-truth engendered by moral shortcomings. The miracles, like the words of the Old Testament prophets, were capable of revealing truth; but it was all part of God's will that if they were met with culpable failure to understand, they could veil the truth and at the same time reveal the true character of those who failed to perceive their meaning; that appears to be the significance of the Old Testament language (cf. Isa. $6^{9ff.}$, Jer. 5^{21} and Ezek. 12^{2}) in which v. 18 is couched (see also on 3^{5}).

8^{22-26} HEALING OF A BLIND MAN FROM BETHSAIDA

[22]*And they came to Beth-sa'ida. And some people brought to him a blind*
man, and begged him to touch him. [23]*And he took the blind man by the hand,*
and led him out of the village; and when he had spit on his eyes and laid his
hands upon him, he asked him, 'Do you see anything?' [24]*And he looked up*
and said, 'I see men; but they look like trees, walking.' [25]*Then again he laid*
his hands upon his eyes; and he looked intently and was restored, and saw
everything clearly. [26]*And he sent him away to his home, saying, 'Do not*
even enter the village.'

This story rounds off the second 'feeding cycle' (8^{1-26}) just as, we saw, the healing of the deaf-mute (7^{31-37}) rounded off the first (6^{35}–7^{37}; see p. 202). That, however, by no means exhausts the similarity between the two stories. The verbal parallels are numerous and striking, especially in the Greek (for the details see the two set out in parallel columns in V. T., pp. 368–9), and the stories share a number of characteristics which set them apart somewhat from most of the other healing miracles in the Gospels; e.g. both stories have an impersonal beginning: 'And they brought to him . . .', neither story ascribes the affliction to demon possession, and faith is not mentioned in connexion with either cure; in both, interest centres on the technique of the cure which in each case involves the use of spittle, and almost suggests the work of a human healer rather than a miracle in the strict sense.* What is more, as mentioned on 7^{33-34} (and see notes below) the incidents both have close parallels in Hellenistic healing stories.

These data are not easy to assess. Many commentators have regarded the two stories as duplicate accounts of the same incident (cf. the duplication of the feeding cycles in which the stories are embedded), but V. T., who insists on the pronounced *differences*, as well as similarities, between the stories, suggests that 'Mark, or a predecessor, deliberately uses the framework supplied by 7^{32-37} but fits into it a new story suitable to his didactic purpose.' However exactly the similarity is to be explained, St Mark no doubt felt it appropriate to end the two feeding cycles with closely related stories which between them suggested the fulfilment of Isaiah 35 (see on 7^{31-37}).

As for the pagan parallels, most scholars see them (though cf. V. T., p. 371, col. 2) as suggesting that the two stories 'were developed, if not originated, in the syncretistic atmosphere of the Hellenistic world' (B.). The two passages are among the very few in Mark not reproduced by either Matthew or Luke, and some have concluded that they were added to the text after the time when Matthew's and Luke's copies of it were made. Others, however, think that St Matthew and St Luke read them, but deliberately omitted them from a feeling that the use of physical means to effect cures was not consonant with the Lord's dignity.

The feature which distinguishes the present story, even from $7^{31\text{ff.}}$, is the way the cure is effected in two stages (vv. 23–24 and 25), and this may have been an additional reason for its omission by Matthew and Luke, if it was taken to imply that the first laying on of hands was not successful. V. T. believes that the inclusion of this trait 'strongly

* Dibelius (*F. T. G.*, p. 86) sees the reason for the preservation of the story in the tradition as being 'to give guidance to Christians gifted with healing powers' – see on $5^{41\text{ff.}}$ St Mark, of course, will have had no doubts about the supernatural and eschatological character of the incident – see below.

supports the historical character of the incident'; however that may be, it was surely the trait which led to St Mark's inclusion of the incident at this highly significant point in his Gospel, when the first long phase of the ministry (1^{16}–8^{26}) is just about to give place to the second (8^{27}–10^{52}). As shown in the Introduction (pp. 37–8) the second phase will be taken up with Jesus' attempt gradually to open the eyes of the disciples to the truth about himself (see also on 8^{14-21}); the opening section of it, which sets the tone of the whole, is 8^{27}–9^{1}, and Lightfoot* has demonstrated a remarkable parallelism between that section and the present one which immediately precedes it. (Cf. *H. & I.*, pp. 90–1, where the two passages are set out in parallel columns.) Jesus takes Peter (according to John 1^{44} also a man from Bethsaida) and his companions, whom we know from 8^{14-21} (see especially v. 18) to be 'blind', away from crowded places (cf. 8^{23a}) and there, in two stages (vv. 27–28 and 29), the truth about him is made plain, and then as soon as the disciples 'see' they receive a strict injunction to secrecy as does the man in the present story, according to the correct reading in v. 26 (for which see below).

This parallelism, which, as Lightfoot says, 'can hardly be fortuitous', is clearly highly significant. Having in the first section of his Gospel shown us consistently, and with increasing emphasis, the blindness of the disciples, St Mark makes his transition to the second main section by means of this story, and he thereby shows us how to interpret the story immediately following, and with it the whole section of the Gospel it introduces (9^{2}–10^{52}). We are not to think of a series of guesses by the disciples at the truth about Jesus, but of God through Christ opening their eyes (to the truth) as he does here in the case of the literally blind man, and as he will always do for those who sincerely ask to 'see' Jesus for what he really is (cf. John 20^{29b}); the latter point is brought out in the story of the healing of another blind man with which – and this is all part of his careful arrangement – St Mark closes the section here introduced (see on 10^{46-52}).

Thus, as Lightfoot says, it is hard to say whether the present passage is the conclusion of the first section of the Gospel (cf. how it looks back to 8^{14-21}, etc.) or the introduction to the second; the point is perhaps not of any great importance provided the position of the

* To some extent following Loisy.

section as a 'bridge' passage is duly noted and its significance as such fully grasped.

ꕥ

22
Bethsaida: See on 6^{45-46}. It was a large and prosperous town, which makes the reference to *the village* in vv. 23 and 26 rather puzzling. No doubt the explanation is that the story, with its references to *the village*, reached St Mark in a form which contained no specific geographical indications, and he introduced the mention of Bethsaida in order to bring Jesus to the destination announced in 6^{45}; he was no doubt unaware that it was too large to be referred to as a *village*. (For the implication as to his identity see Introduction, p. 40.) This explanation is preferable to positing, as some do, an otherwise unknown village called Bethsaida, or accepting the reading *Bethany*, which occurs in a number of MSS. but is generally agreed to be a correction by a scribe who realized the difficulty about the size of Bethsaida.

some people brought . . . begged: Literally 'they bring . . . beg'. Impersonal plurals of the kind so common in Mark: 'A man was brought to Jesus and he was asked . . .'

23
For the use of spittle in healing see on 7^{33-34}.

asked him: Note the parallel with Jesus 'asking' in v. 27. (See further there.)

24
looked up: Or possibly: 'began to recover his sight'. The man's words are given in the MSS. in various slightly different forms; R.S.V. rightly reproduces a form which is very awkward in the Greek, the awkwardness being due either to a mistranslation of an Aramaic original or, more probably, to the awkwardness of the idea being expressed – i.e. in effect, 'I can see things like walking trees.'

A fairly close Hellenistic parallel can be cited from an inscription recording a cure in the Temple of Asclepios at Epidaurus (Dittenberger: *Sylloge Inscr. Graec.*[3], iii, 1168). A certain Alcetas of Halice was cured of blindness by the god and 'the first things he saw were the trees in the Temple precincts'.

26
'*Do not even enter the village*': i.e. presumably, in order that no one may know what has happened. C. H. Turner, however (*J. T. S.*, XXVI, p. 18) has shown that we should accept a more difficult reading, which might be translated: 'Tell no one in the village.'

While the desire to *perform* the miracle in private (v. 23) might possibly be due to the motives discussed on 5^{43}, this command to secrecy after the cure has been completed would clearly have been impossible of fulfilment and must be editorial, reflecting the Evangelist's doctrine of the messianic secret (see Introduction, p. 32).

Mark 8^{27}-10^{52}

From Galilee to Jerusalem: The Character of Jesus' Messiahship Gradually Disclosed

$8^{27} – 9^{1}$ THE RECOGNITION OF THE TRUTH ABOUT JESUS AND ABOUT SUFFERING

*[27]And Jesus went on with his disciples, to the villages of Caesare'a
Philippi; and on the way he asked his disciples, 'Who do men say that I am?'
[28]And they told him, 'John the Baptist; and others say, Eli'jah; and others
one of the prophets.' [29]And he asked them, 'But who do you say that I am?'
Peter answered him, 'You are the Christ.' [30]And he charged them to tell no
one about him.*

*[31]And he began to teach them that the Son of man must suffer many things,
and be rejected by the elders and the chief priests and the scribes, and be killed,
and after three days rise again. [32]And he said this plainly. And Peter took
him, and began to rebuke him. [33]But turning and seeing his disciples, he
rebuked Peter, and said, 'Get behind me, Satan! For you are not on the side
of God, but of men.'*

*[34]And he called to him the multitude with his disciples, and said to them,
'If any man would come after me, let him deny himself and take up his cross
and follow me. [35]For whoever would save his life will lose it; and whoever
loses his life for my sake and the gospel's will save it. [36]For what does it
profit a man, to gain the whole world and forfeit his life? [37]For what can a
man give in return for his life? [38]For whoever is ashamed of me and of my
words in this adulterous and sinful generation, of him will the Son of man
also be ashamed, when he comes in the glory of his Father with the holy
angels.'*

9 *And he said to them, 'Truly, I say to you, there are some standing here
who will not taste death before they see the kingdom of God come with
power.'*

This passage can only be understood if full weight is given to its position at the opening of a new section of the Gospel. In the first section we have heard of a whole series of deeds and incidents in the life of Jesus which raise the question: Who then *is* this that he can do such things? (Cf. e.g. 4^{41}.) Indeed, according to St Mark, the career of

Jesus had raised the question so inescapably that even *men* (v. 27) – i.e. ordinary people, people who made no pretence of being disciples – had found themselves not only asking it, but forced to answer that Jesus must be some very great figure indeed, John the Baptist or one of the great prophets risen from the dead (v. 28). But even such guesses did not go far enough; for even the Baptist and the prophets did no more than pave the way for the one who would actually *bring* the salvation to which they pointed forward. And those who were admitted to the full truth about Jesus (*you* in v. 29 – which is to be understood here in the light of 4^{11}, etc.* and of the fact that they have witnessed things not revealed to other *men* – cf. e.g. 1^{29}, 5^{37}, 9^{2}) realized that his was the final role of fulfilment, of the *achievement* of salvation. The true, and specifically Christian, answer† to the question posed by Jesus is: '*You are* (nothing less than) *the Messiah*' (v. 29).

Since these words express the Christian understanding of Jesus, we might have expected that they would be met with an enthusiastic and unambiguous acknowledgement from Jesus himself, and in St Matthew's version of the story that is exactly what happens (Matt. 16^{17}); the opening of the second section of the Gospel would then provide a simple and authoritative answer to the question posed by the first section. In St Mark's version, however, the incident is much more complex: Jesus' immediate reaction to the disciples' confession is ambiguous; he swears them to silence about himself (v. 30). On the one hand this implies a tacit acceptance of their description of him, but on the other hand, it will be noticed that he studiously avoids taking the title *Messiah* on his own lips; and in the Greek, the word used for *charging* the disciples to tell no one normally means 'rebuke', suggesting a hint of censure and displeasure; there was apparently some sense in which he was not, and did not wish to be known as, Messiah. The sequel helps to make clear what that sense was. However exactly the term *Messiah* was understood at the time – and, as we have seen, different groups understood it in different ways – there was general agreement that the Messiah would accomplish his work by

* In the Greek the *you* is emphatic; the meaning is: '*You* who form the nucleus of the new Israel, you to whom has been given the mystery of the kingdom of God (cf. 4^{11}), you whom I have called and chosen, who have consorted with me, who do *you* say that I am?' (*G. M. M.*, p. 34).

† As such it is voiced by Peter, the founder apostle of the Church.

the possession and exercise of brute power in one form or another – power is none the less power for being directly supplied from heaven – he would be a glorious and manifestly victorious figure to whom defeat and suffering would be entirely foreign. The disciples' confession therefore presents Jesus with a dilemma. If he is to choose between Peter's description of him and the lesser descriptions, of *men*, he must accept the higher title, for he *is* the final Saviour to whom all previous religious leaders pointed. Yet in its normal sense he cannot accept the title; and since it is at least partly in that sense that his disciples apply the title to him, he must 'rebuke' them and forbid them to make their confession public.* He apparently prefers the title *Son of man* (see pp. 46–7) which probably at the time smacked less of military and political methods and purely worldly success. In any case, whatever title is to be used, he hastens to remove any false impressions by proclaiming unambiguously that his earthly future would be one of ignominy, defeat, and suffering (vv. 31–32a).

It is now the turn of the disciples to react with shocked and strongly-felt disapproval. Through their spokesman Peter, they in turn *rebuke* Jesus for such ideas (v. 32 – same Greek word as in v. 30) and attempt to dissuade him from them. If he really is Messiah, they imply, any thought of such a future must be wrong, cf. Matt. 16^{22}.† The blistering severity of Jesus' reply is evidence enough that what is at stake is a matter of quite central importance, and that in two ways.

In the first place, when Jesus said *must* in v. 31 he meant this. He used the word in a sense in which it was often used in contemporary apocalyptic literature, as showing that certain future events were part of the firmly decreed will of God. Thus, to persuade Jesus to shrink from those events was to tempt him to disobey the will of God, as Satan had done in the wilderness (v. 33; cf. 1^{13}, and still more the accounts of Christ's temptation in Matthew and Luke, where the temptation is basically the same as it is here: to try to accomplish the Messiah's work by spectacular means involving no suffering).

* Wrede sees the motivation differently: for him Jesus is now the Son of man moving towards suffering and the resurrection, so the confession of him as Messiah cannot and must not occur till after Easter.

† Where Goodspeed translates: 'God bless you, Master, that can never happen to you.' It is *just possible* that some such words also stood in the original text of Mark. See V. T., p. 379.

Secondly, we have to ask *why* the disciples were so vehemently opposed to the suggestion that Jesus must suffer. The very vehemence of their opposition is meant to suggest that it is more than a matter of the intellect, more than a simple failure to understand what Jesus meant; the disciples did not *want* Jesus to suffer. And that was because it goes against the grain to be the followers of a Messiah who suffers instead of producing spectacular victories by an effortless exercise of power; it brings no kudos, and offends the pride of the natural man. And judged by ordinary standards, there seems no point in the suffering and death of the Messiah. What is more, if it is the will of God that the Messiah should suffer, it might well be his will that the Messiah's disciples should suffer a similar fate; from that again the natural man shrinks. So by their reaction to Jesus' prophecy the disciples reveal even more clearly than before the truth about themselves, that their minds and wills are governed by the standards of this world, of the unredeemed, natural man – 'they think as men think' (v. 33, see notes for that translation).

What they have got to be taught, therefore, is that 'God thinks otherwise' – that his standards of judgement and ways of going about things are completely the reverse of those accepted in the world. And since this is something all men need to know, and there is no secrecy about it, the crowd is called in to share the lesson (v. 34a; see note on the necessity of suffering, p. 227). In the following verses (8^{34b}–9^{1}) this is enlarged on. The only way to attain 'life' – i.e. true life, the life of the age to come – is through trust in God and obedience to his will. But since that must involve suffering and death in this world, the only way to get life is by behaving in a way which seems to unredeemed man unintelligent and self-defeating: willingly accepting loss and injury in the cause of Christ and his gospel, and refusing to bend all one's energies, as other men do, to preserving, securing, and enriching one's life in this world. No one can pretend that this is easy; we are all afraid of pain and suffering, and 'ashamed' of seeming fools to our fellows. But let the Christian remember what is at stake – even the life of this world is worth more than everything else in existence – how much more the life of the age to come? (vv. 36–37). And let the disciple remember that this is the only way; this age is thoroughly contrary to the will of God (v. 38) and if anyone is ashamed of Christ in deference to its standards he can expect only one verdict when the day of reckoning comes (v. 38). And come it will very soon; and with it the establishment of God's kingdom with power and the end of suffering for the Christian; those who persevere will not have long to wait (9^{1}).

There can be no doubt that this section was constructed by St Mark out of separate items or tradition (see notes below) and that in constructing it his purpose was to bring out two, or rather perhaps three, important truths.

(*a*) That although the answer to the question posed in the first section of the Gospel may be, indeed *must* be, put in the form: 'Jesus is the Messiah', that is only the true answer if the title Messiah is understood in the sense of Jesus' favourite self-designation *Son of man* as implying the necessity of redemptive suffering and death.

(*b*) That the disciples' failure to understand Jesus' teaching on the subject of suffering is only another manifestation of the hardening of their hearts and of their domination by the power of Satan and the values of this world. This theme will recur in the sequel (e.g. $9^{34, 38}$, $10^{35\text{ff.}, 41}$).

(*c*) The story is not so much intended to describe faithfully what happened on the *first* occasion when Jesus was recognized as Messiah as to show what is essentially involved and demanded whenever such a recognition takes place. See Introduction, p. 38. In that connexion it is particularly important to keep in mind the immediately preceding story of the opening of the blind man's eyes. Just as then it was Jesus who gradually enabled the blind man to see, so here it is Jesus who by his repeated question (from the historical point of view surely rather artificial) and his teaching gradually reveals to the disciples the fact, nature, and implications of his Messiahship. To see Jesus for what he really is, and to know how to respond, is always a gift of God in Christ.

Note on the Necessity of Suffering

Neither here nor elsewhere in Mark is any theory offered as to *why* it should be God's will that the Messiah and his disciples should suffer, but in this connexion we need to remind ourselves of the eschatological mould in which the thought of the early Christians was cast (see pp. 43ff.). For them God's realm in heaven entirely conformed to

God's holiness, and stood in the sharpest contrast to this age or world ruled by forces of evil and governed by their evil values and designs. One day God would judge this world and bring this age to an end, transforming whatever in it was capable of being transformed, and transferring it to the conditions of his realm. But meanwhile, so long as this world lasted, anyone in it who represented God's realm and its values must look for misunderstanding and persecution from the evil powers and the human beings under their sway. 'The Old Testament itself says of the children of Israel "They mocked the messengers of God, and despised his words, and scoffed at his prophets" (2 Chron. 36^{16} – cf. Ps. 34^{19}). For later [Jewish] writers it was axiomatic that the people of God were basically opposed to whatever really emanates from God, and that therefore they had always persecuted God's true servants and ambassadors and always would' (E. Stauffer, *New Testament Theology*, p. 98). Such ideas would thus seem natural to Jesus and his early disciples; for evidence that they shared them, see such passages as Luke $11^{49\text{ff.}}$, Acts $7^{2\text{ff.}}$, etc.

The true servant of God would not be disconcerted by such suffering, but would realize that in some mysterious way it was a means by which the redemptive purpose of God for this world was carried out. Isa. 53 is the classic passage for this idea but it by no means stands alone – cf. such passages as 2 Macc. 7^{37-8}, 4 *Macc.* 6^{27} and 17^{22}, and the discussion in Appendix I of the book by Stauffer quoted above. In view of the remarkably few references to the Isaiah passage in the Gospels, it is probably better to think of a general background of ideas than of direct influence from that particular passage.

Against this background, the true character of the disciples' reaction to Jesus' prophecy of suffering can be recognized. What the disciples had to learn was that until the kingdom came *with power* (9^{1}), the law of suffering applied at least as fully to the Messiah and his followers as it had done to earlier representatives of God see (9^{13} and 6^{17-29} in this connexion).

❧

27
the villages of Caesarea Philippi: An obscure expression generally taken to mean the villages in the area around Caesarea Philippi.* For the

* Can the reference to *villages* have been influenced by the parallelism with the previous story? Cf. $8^{23,\,26}$ and see on 8^{22}.

town itself, formerly called Paneas, and rebuilt by Herod Philip, see map. Bethsaida was some twenty-five miles away, but no doubt the connexion with the preceding incident is artificial.

28

Cf. 6^{14-15}, which may well have influenced, or been influenced by, this verse. Cf. also Malachi $4^{5, 6}$ and Deut. $18^{15, 18}$.

If vv. 27–29 existed before St Mark's time as an independent unit of tradition, the unit will no doubt have contained further verses making plain the significance of the event. Since St Mark has omitted these in the process of building up his longer unit, we can no longer tell how the pre-Marcan Church understood the incident; e.g. they may have seen its significance as showing that the decisive confession of the Church had already been made in the lifetime of Jesus. See further, *F. T. G.*, p. 44; and J. Knox, *The Death of Christ*, pp. 79–80, for the view that in effect Jesus here, as always, repudiated messianic claims.

31

the elders and the chief priests could be simply a way of referring to the lay and clerical aristocracy in Jerusalem who, with *the scribes*, formed the Sanhedrin. But even if so, the question has naturally been raised whether so detailed a forecast is not a prophecy after the event, ascribed to Jesus by the early Christians. We have no means of deciding for certain, but if Jesus did foretell disaster for himself, it seems unlikely that it was in terms as precise as these; in particular, if he had several times referred to the resurrection as explicitly as is suggested here (and in 9^{31} and 10^{34}), the behaviour of the disciples after the crucifixion is almost impossible to explain.* On the other hand, if he did foresee disaster he must presumably also have looked forward to ultimate vindication in some form or other.

chief priests: Greek *archiereus*, elsewhere (e.g. $14^{47 \text{ and } 54}$) translated *high priest.* The plural is at first sight surprising, as there was only one high priest at any given time, but it occurs frequently in the New Testament and also in Josephus, and the usual explanation is that, in addition to the ruling high priest, deposed high priests and other male members of the most prominent priestly families were included. See, however, J. Jeremias, *Jerusalem zur Zeit Jesu*, II, B I, p. 3ff.

after three days: cf. 9^{31}, 10^{34}, and Matt. 27^{63}. Elsewhere in the New Testament we have 'on the third day'. It is often held that, at any rate in

* Furthermore, the earliest tradition thought of Jesus as *being raised* from the dead by God (cf. Rom. 4^{25}, 6^{4}, 8^{34}, I Pet. 1^{21}); the use of the active verb 'to rise' seems to reflect a later Christian usage, perhaps influenced by Hos. 6^{2} (LXX).

popular usage, the two phrases were synonymous, 'after three days' meaning 'when the third day had begun'. But this is difficult to reconcile with the evidence of such a passage as Matt. 12^{40}, and the fact seems to be that the tradition on the matter was influenced in rather different directions by two Old Testament passages, Hos. 6^{2} and Jonah 1^{17}. In the light of the Hosea passage it would seem that such a phrase could be used simply as a conventional expression meaning 'after a short while'. On the assumption that the words go back to Jesus himself, it has been suggested that it was in that conventional sense that he used them; clearly, however, that was not St Mark's understanding.

33

seeing his disciples: 'The reproof which follows is for their benefit as well as Peter's' (V. T.).

on the side of: The Greek here is one of those expressions too rich in meaning to be fully represented by any single translation. R.S.V. may well be right in hinting at a political metaphor, but the basic meaning of the verb (*phrŏnein*) is 'to be minded' and there is certainly the idea of sharing, or failing to share, another's point of view and intentions (see above).

34

take up his cross: The Romans required a condemned criminal to carry part of his own cross to the place of execution; hence the metaphor. As the words stand, they seem to presuppose that 'the Cross' is already a familiar idea; no doubt Jesus' audience would have been familiar with crucifixion as a Roman method of execution, but it was normally reserved for criminals condemned by due process of law and it remains very doubtful whether, before Jesus' own crucifixion, they could have caught the allusion here. Probably the present formulation of the saying is the work of the early Church.

35

and the gospel's: These words, omitted by Matthew and Luke, and by John at 12^{25}, again suggest that the present formulation of the saying dates from a time when Christians were being martyred 'for the sake of the gospel'.

38

of my words: A better reading gives *of my* [followers]; as we might say, 'of me and mine'.*

adulterous: probably a metaphor for *idolatrous;* cf. such Old Testament passages at Hos. 2^{2}, Isa. $1^{4,\,21}$, Ezek. 16^{32}ff., Jer. 3^{3}.

* In the light of the discussion by Prof. C. K. Barratt in *New Testament Essays*, pp. 132ff., I am by no means sure that the shorter reading is in fact preferable.

The verse as a whole has given rise to a great deal of discussion, because *prima facie* it appears to distinguish between Jesus and the Son of man as if they were two separate persons, and some scholars believe that that was its original connotation on the lips of Jesus. St Mark, however, will certainly not have understood the words in that sense; if the wording struck him as strange, he may well have explained it in terms of the messianic secret. Jesus is here speaking to the crowd (v. 34), so in St Mark's view it would have been natural for him to use a form of words which gave no inkling of his identity as Son of man.

The tradition sometimes inserted the title Son of man in contexts where Jesus had simply used the first person singular (cf. Mark 8^{27} with Matt. 16^{13}) and some scholars have thought that that is what has happened here, a more original form of the saying being preserved in Matt. 10^{32-33}.

9^{1}

Not unnaturally, this verse has been the object of a great deal of discussion.

C. H. Dodd (*Parables*, p. 53, n. 1) proposes a different translation: 'until they have seen that the kingdom of God has come with power', and comments: 'The bystanders are not promised that they shall see the kingdom of God *coming*, but that they shall come to see that the kingdom of God *has already come* [i.e. in the words and works of Jesus] at some point before they became aware of it.' So interpreted the saying fits admirably with Professor Dodd's theory of 'realized eschatology', but even those who accept the theory do not all find this particular piece of exegesis in support of it entirely convincing – cf. on this subject *Expository Times*, XLVIII, pp. 91–4 (J. Y. Campbell) and pp. 184ff. (J. M. Creed) – and it is generally agreed that we must translate in some such way as R.S.V.

The most natural interpretation then is that, though in a very real sense the kingdom of God has already drawn near in the words and deeds of Jesus, its manifestation in its full and final form lies still in the future, though according to this verse in the very near future; *the kingdom of God come with power* will then refer, as we should expect it to do in the light of contemporary Jewish expectations, to the time of the final judgement and the supersession of the whole present world-order by a completely new one – in fact to the whole complex which we now describe – very inadequately – as 'the end of the world' (cf. such passages as Mark 13^{24-27} and 1 Cor. 15^{24}ff.).

The difficulty that has been felt about this interpretation is that it makes our Lord foreshorten the perspective drastically and sets very definite bounds to the extent of his accurate foreknowledge in the days of his flesh. Nevertheless, especially in view of such a passage as Matt. 10^{23}, and of the expectations of the early Church (cf. e.g. 1 Cor. 7^{29} and ^{31}, 10^{11}, Rom. 13^{11}, etc.), the interpretation is to be accepted,* and numerous writers have shown that admission of such ignorance, and even error, on the part of our Lord is fully compatible with belief in the Incarnation. (See e.g. the discussion by Professor Dodd referred to on 13^{30}.)

Possibly St Mark may have included the saying here because he saw at least a partial fulfilment of it in the transfiguration; many later writers have done the same, but see p. 236 for evidence that it cannot have been the original reference of the saying.

Others have supposed the prophecy referred to the fall of Jerusalem, the gift of the Spirit, or the spread of Christianity to the Roman empire. But though 'all these are partial manifestations of the kingdom ... none of them describes what Jesus had in mind in 9^{1}. A visible manifestation of the Rule of God displayed in the life of an Elect Community is the most probable form of His expectation; but what this means cannot be described in detail because the hope was not fulfilled in the manner in which it presented itself to Him, although later it found expression in the life of the Church, as it still does in its life and its impact on human society' (V. T.).

For a full discussion of the problems involved, see now W. G. Kümmel, *Promise and Fulfilment*, where the point is emphasized that though Jesus apparently expected the end within some fifty or sixty years, he did not necessarily, as Schweitzer suggests, expect it before his own death; indeed this verse definitely suggests the contrary. The point is important, among other reasons, in connexion with the question whether Jesus concerned himself about the future behaviour and organization of his followers after his death.

9^{2-8} THE TRANSFIGURATION – THE TRUTH ABOUT JESUS CONFIRMED

2 *And after six days Jesus took with him Peter and James and John, and led*
them up a high mountain apart by themselves; and he was transfigured
before them, 3 *and his garments became glistening, intensely white, as no*
fuller on earth could bleach them. 4 *And there appeared to them Eli'jah with*

* St Matthew (16^{28}) interpreted it in this way.

Moses; and they were talking to Jesus. 5 *And Peter said to Jesus, 'Master,*[a]
it is well that we are here; let us make three booths, one for you and one for
Moses and one for Eli'jah.' 6 *For he did not know what to say, for they were*
exceedingly afraid. 7 *And a cloud overshadowed them, and a voice came out of*
the cloud, 'This is my beloved Son;[b] *listen to him.'* 8 *And suddenly looking*
around they no longer saw any one with them but Jesus only.

a Or *Rabbi*
b Or *my Son, my* (or *the*) *Beloved*

If full weight is given to the context in which the Evangelist has placed this story, there can be little doubt about its general significance for him. In the preceding section the disciples have formally declared that Jesus is the Messiah, and in return have received teaching about the way this Son of man–Messiah is to accomplish his work so unexpected as to cause bewilderment and grave doubts in their minds. But now

(*a*) the truth of their declaration is confirmed, for Jesus appears in a glory which can only be messianic (v. 3), and

(*b*) Jesus' teaching that he must suffer is shown to be fully in accordance with the will of God by a voice from God himself which designates him as the one whose teaching God wants all men to accept (v. 7).*

But if the general significance of the story is thus clear, there is considerable uncertainty and controversy about the meaning of some of the details. This is partly because of the extremely compressed form in which the incident is narrated and partly because various figures and elements in it (e.g. Elijah and Moses) will have had associations and overtones for the Evangelist and his first readers which we cannot now recover. Indeed, the possibility should not be ruled out that by the time the story reached the Evangelist, some of it was already obscure to him. For example, the opening statement (v. 2), *after six days*, is a precise note of time so unparalleled in St Mark's account of the ministry that he must have included it because it

* It is noteworthy that in St Mark's version of it 'the whole event, from first to last, takes place solely for the sake of the three disciples. "He was transfigured *before them*"; "there appeared *unto them* Elijah with Moses"; "there came a cloud overshadowing *them*"; "this is my only Son; hear *ye* him"; "and suddenly, looking round about, they saw no one any more, save Jesus only *with themselves*"' (Lightfoot *G. M. M.*, p. 44).

seemed to him specially significant, probably as binding this and the preceding episode together in a single complex, one part of which must be interpreted in the light of the other. But there is some evidence that this was traditionally the length of time required for preparation and self-purification before a close approach to God (cf. e.g. Exod. 24:16 and B. W. Bacon in *Harvard Theological Review*, 1915, pp. 94ff.; also W. A. Heidel, *American Journal of Phil.*, 45, 1924, pp. 218ff.) and in the original form of this story some such preparation may have been implied or even described. Also unexplained is the precise sense of *transfigured* (v. 2) (*mĕtĕmŏrphōthē*).* The literal meaning is 'to be transformed', or 'to change one's form', and in the light of v. 3, the idea seems to be that Jesus temporarily exchanged the normal human form that he bore during his earthly life for that glorious form he was believed to possess after his exaltation to heaven, and which believers also hoped to be clothed with after his second coming. Cf. carefully Phil. 3:21, 1 Cor. 15:43, 49, 51–53, and 2 Cor. 3:18 where the same Greek word is used, bearing in mind that at the time 'glory' was 'conceived as actual shining ethereal substance ... the sort of body generally supposed to belong to heavenly beings and indeed to be the vesture of God Himself' (G. H. Boobyer, *St Mark and the Transfiguration Story*, p. 23). The idea that in the final state the glorification of the form would extend to clothes was quite a common one at the time – cf. e.g. 1 *Enoch* 62:15–16, the elect will be 'clothed with garments of glory from the Lord of spirits, and their glory shall never fade away', 2 *Enoch* 22:8 'Take Enoch from his earthly garments and clothe him in garments of glory', Rev. 4:4, 7:9, 3:5, etc. (See Boobyer, pp. 67–9.)

It would therefore seem that what was vouchsafed to the three disciples was a glimpse of Jesus in that final state of Lordship and glory to which he would eventually be exalted. The reference to Elijah and Moses (v. 4) points in that direction, for it was widely believed by the Jews of Our Lord's time that various prominent figures of Old Testament history would appear at the end of this world and play a part in the events leading up to it, cf. e.g. Matt. 8:11 and Luke 13:28f. From the time of the writing of Malachi 4:5f. Elijah's is the name most frequently mentioned in this connexion, and it is perhaps for that

*No doubt to Mark's original readers it was already a familiar term, as the word *transfiguration* is to a modern English congregation.

reason that St Mark puts his name first;* in the case of Moses, explicit evidence for his inclusion in such expectations is late and not certainly trustworthy, but on many grounds it seems almost certain that he will have had a place in them.† In the last days false prophets were expected to appear, and so Moses and Elijah will have been seen as the two great representatives of the Law and Prophets who, by their presence with Jesus as he comes, testify to him as the true Christ. We have in fact an expression in concrete historical terms of the early Christian conviction that the Law and the Prophets testified to Christ. Cf. Matt. 5^{17}, Luke $24^{27, 44}$, $16^{29, 31}$. But then, lest there should be any danger of Christ's being misunderstood as simply one among the others – a further prophet of the old order – the voice in v. 7 clearly singles him out as the prophet of the last days whom Moses had foretold as superseding himself. (Cf. how Deut. $18^{15, 18-19}$ is clearly echoed here.) But Jesus is more than that – he is actually God's own Son – indeed his only Son, the one to whom alone now men should give ear. With his coming, the Law and the Prophets are fulfilled, the old covenant is superseded by the new. The voice which makes this pronouncement is described as coming *out of the cloud* which had overshadowed the scene, and for St Mark this will have meant that it was the voice of God himself; for, in the later Jewish writings, the cloud was *par excellence* the vehicle of God's *Shekinah*‡ and the medium in and through which he manifested himself. (This idea runs all through the Exodus story – cf. e.g. Exod. 16^{10}, Num. 14^{10}, and Exod. $19^{9, 16}$, $24^{15ff.}$, noting the close parallel with our passage in v. 18. Cf. also such passages as Ezek. $1^{4ff.}$.)

So much about the symbolism of the cloud seems clear enough, but there may well be more to it. In view of their beliefs about the past, it was natural for the Jews to include a cloud-manifestation of God in their expectations of the end, and for evidence that they did, see e.g. 2 Macc. 2^{8}. Moreover other supernatural beings besides God himself could use clouds to manifest themselves and to travel through

* Contrast St Matthew and St Luke who change to the more natural order, but note that, at the end of Malachi, Elijah and Moses are mentioned in close proximity in LXX *in that order*.

† See Boobyer, pp. 70ff.; many scholars see an allusion to Moses and Elijah in Rev. $11^{3ff.}$.

‡ The Hebrew word used to denote the 'presence' or 'dwelling' of God in any place, normally to the accompaniment of glorious outward manifestations.

the heavens – angels, for example, or the Messiah: Dan. 7^{13}, 4 Ezra 13^{3}, Rev. 10^{1}, 11^{12}, 1^{7}. The early Christians certainly thought that it was in this way that Christ would appear at his final coming (Luke 21^{27}, Mark 13^{26}, 14^{62}, Matt. 24^{30}, 26^{64}, Rev. 1^{7}, etc.) and even that it was in, or on, clouds that they themselves would be taken up to meet him and ascend with him to heaven (1 Thess. 4^{17}). All this suggests that what the three disciples were understood to have seen was the final coming of Christ in the glory of his Father; and in that case there is close connexion between the story and the verses immediately preceding (8^{38}–9^{1}). Did St Mark perhaps see the incident as at least a partial fulfilment of the promise made in 9^{1}?

Even if he did, that is of course no guarantee that the promise *originally* referred to the transfiguration. In fact it seems impossible that it could have done so for at least two reasons.

(i) However we interpret what the disciples saw, it could scarcely, in reality, have been called *the kingdom of God come with power.*

(ii) If someone says: 'So and so will happen while some of you in this very audience are still alive', he is thinking not of something that will happen a week later but of something that will happen after a lapse of a good many years when it is reasonable to suppose that some of his hearers will still be alive, while others will not.

It remains to discuss the two rather puzzling verses 5 and 6. In order to understand Peter's words it is essential to recognize that, according to St Mark, they were an *inappropriate* response to the situation on the part of one blinded by bewilderment and fear (v. 6). Seen in that light, the words may simply express a desire on Peter's part to prolong the blessedness of the experience when in fact it was God's will for Christ and the disciples that they should return into the world and enter upon the path of suffering. Certainly the last verse – always an important verse in any pericope – underlines the essentially temporary character of the episode, stressing as it does the completeness and abruptness with which the conditions of the transfiguration pass. The cloud and the two heavenly figures disappear, and Jesus stands among the disciples once more a man among men. But probably once again St Mark saw a rather more precise meaning. In contemporary Judaism the day of salvation was often pictured as a day when God would once more *pitch his tent* with his people as he had done during the forty years in the wilderness.* The Jewish Feast of Tabernacles itself had acquired an eschatological significance, not only looking back to the tent-dwelling of the wilderness days (Lev. $23^{42f.}$) but also forward to the new age when God would again 'tabernacle' with his people, and members of all nations would gather in Jerusalem to 'tabernacle' there and worship God together (Zech. 14^{16-19}). God and his people would 'tabernacle' together. The Christians too made large use of the image of tent-dwelling in their thought about the new age – cf. 2 Cor. 5^{1-4}, Rev. 21^{1-3} (literally 'the tent of God is with men') and 7^{15} and cf. *Test. Abr.*, xx. This being so, St Mark may well have understood Peter's words eschatologically – as an offer to build the sort of dwellings God and Christ were expected to share with men in the age to come. In that case what Peter was overlooking was that this scene was not the parousia, but only its foreshadowing. Before the end, there remained much to be done and much to be suffered both by Jesus and by his disciples (see e.g. Chapter 13). That suffering is not to be by-passed or evaded, as Peter here seems to think (cf. his attitude to the prediction of suffering in the previous episode). In any case, before the end comes heaven and earth must themselves pass away (13^{31}), and that makes the suggestion of building tabernacles here doubly inept.

☙

2

a high mountain: Speculation about the identity of the mountain is quite idle. Very possibly St Mark himself had no ideas on the subject. For him the significance of this trait in the story will have lain in the fact that a mountain top was traditionally the setting for theophanies and supernatural revelations – cf. e.g. Exod. 24 and 34, 1 Kings 18^{20} and $19^{8, 11}$, Matt. 28^{16}ff., Acts 1^{12}, Mark 13^{3}ff., Matt. 5^{1}, etc. Cf. 2 Pet. 1^{18} where it is called 'the holy mountain'.

4

as no fuller on earth could bleach them: A touch meant to put beyond question the wholly supernatural, divinely originated character of what happened.

* See e.g. Ezek. 37^{27}, $43^{7 \text{ and } 9}$, Joel 3^{21}, Zech. 2^{10-11}, $8^{3, 8}$, where in all cases the Greek text has reference to God's *dwelling in a tent*. The English words *tent*, *tabernacle*, and *booth* are simply variant translations for the same Greek word *skēnē*.

5
It is well that we are here: i.e. because of the opportunity of serving you and your heavenly visitors. But more probably the Greek means: *How good it is to be here!* i.e. it is an experience we should like to prolong.

7
beloved: See on 1^{11}.

9^{9-13} THE DESCENT FROM THE MOUNTAIN – A QUESTION ABOUT ELIJAH

9 *And as they were coming down the mountain, he charged them to tell no*
one what they had seen, until the Son of man should have risen from the
dead. 10 *So they kept the matter to themselves, questioning what the rising*
from the dead meant. 11 *And they asked him, 'Why do the scribes say that*
first Eli'jah must come?' 12 *And he said to them, 'Eli'jah does come first to*
restore all things; and how is it written of the Son of man, that he should
suffer many things and be treated with contempt? 13 *But I tell you that*
Eli'jah has come, and they did to him whatever they pleased, as it is written
of him.'

This passage appears to be a sort of appendix to the transfiguration story, probably pieced together by St Mark from originally independent units and designed to deal with certain questions which arose for the Church as it sought to understand the significance of its own existence and the life of Christ on which it was based. Lightfoot speaks of vv. 11–13 as constituting a first tentative effort on the part of the Church 'to construct some kind of philosophy of history, in the light of its convictions about the person and office of its Master, and of his work and its results' (*H. & I.*, p. 92).

The problem dealt with first (v. 9) – in terms of St Mark's familiar doctrine of the 'messianic secret' (see pp. 31–2) – is why so signal a vindication of Jesus' claims had so little influence during the course of his ministry, even upon his disciples. Perhaps there was some recollection in the Church that the story of the transfiguration had for long remained unknown. This particular injunction to secrecy is noteworthy for two reasons: (*a*) It would keep the secret even from the majority of those closest to Jesus; (*b*) A definite time limit is set to it, *until the Son of man should have risen from the dead.* This almost casual reference to Jesus' resurrection, with its implication of his prior death – causes bewilderment to the three disciples who, despite the teaching of $8^{31ff.}$, still cannot conceive what connexion there can be between the glorious figure they have just seen and death and resurrection. (This must be the drift of v. 10b, for belief in resurrection was so widespread among the Jews at the time that the disciples cannot be supposed to have been ignorant of the meaning of the expression in itself; it was its *application to the Son of man* which puzzled them.)

Then occurs a complete break in continuity – best explained in terms of transition to a new source (see below) – and the remaining verses deal with a difficulty which still faced the Church in the middle of the second century.* In view of Mal. 4^{4-5}, Jewish teachers held that Elijah would appear before the Messiah himself appeared. How then could it be claimed that Jesus was the Messiah if he had not been heralded by Elijah? The general tenor of Jesus' reply is clear, though the precise connexion of the various clauses in it is not (see below). If vv. 12 and 13 are a unity and are correctly translated as in the R.S.V., the connexion must be something like this:

The Jewish teachers are quite right in their interpretation of Mal. 4^{4-5} – the scripture does say that Elijah comes first. But it also says that the Messiah, when he comes, must suffer and be treated with contempt. In fact Elijah has already come (i.e. in the person of John the Baptist) and men have wreaked their wicked will on him (cf. $6^{16ff.}$). This too was foretold in scripture and so was in accordance with the will of God. And what has thus proved true already of the forerunner will prove true also of the Messiah himself. We thus have one further stage in the process of the opening of the disciples' eyes to the truth about the coming of the kingdom; cf. p. 218. However, if that is the meaning of vv. 12–13, it is as obscurely expressed in the original Greek as it is in the English, and we should not dismiss too lightly the suggestions of interpolation or dislocation referred to in the notes below.

10

they kept the matter to themselves, questioning . . . : The Greek could also

* Cf. Justin Martyr, *Dialogue with Trypho*, 49.

mean: *they observed the charge, questioning among themselves* or even possibly *they seized upon the expression*... The general sense is unaffected.

11

R.S.V. is certainly right, as against the R.V., in translating as a question.

Why is the discussion about Elijah introduced at this point? Possibly because of Elijah's appearance in v. 4 or because of the report in 8^{28} that some people identified Jesus himself with Elijah, but more probably because of the saying of Jesus in 9^{1}; it has indeed been conjectured that in St Mark's source 9^{11} followed immediately on 9^{1} and that St Mark has broken the original connexion by the insertion of the transfiguration story with its accompanying injunction to silence.

12–13

and how is it written . . . contempt?: The abruptness and apparent inconsequence of this question constitute an undeniable difficulty. It is just possible to make sense of the R.S.V. translation as it stands along the lines suggested above, or along the lines that, as the disciples have asked about an event which precedes the resurrection, Jesus draws attention to a much more important matter which precedes the resurrection. But most commentators prefer other solutions; the ones that have found most favour are:

(i) That the words were originally a marginal note to v. 13, made, on the basis of Matt. 17^{12b}, by some reader who was impressed by the parallel between the divinely ordained suffering of John and that of Jesus; in ancient MSS. such notes not infrequently found their way into the main body of the text. This is often combined with:

(ii) The suggestion of Wellhausen, who first of all discusses the logic of the question in v. 11 and takes it to be: 'If Elijah comes first and completely prepares the ground for the Son of man, how can the Son of man, when he comes, find people so unprepared for him that they reject and kill him?' Jesus' reply in v. 12a is then understood as a question which *rejects* the scribal interpretation of Elijah's coming. 'Elijah, you say, come and set everything in order? But in that case what of the predictions of the Passion? As a matter of fact Elijah has already come....'

(iii) That some dislocation of the text has occurred – e.g. C. H. Turner suggested that v. 12b originally followed immediately after v. 10.

On any view (except (ii) above) the words *restore all things* in 12a are odd, especially as in the original they are a statement of fact rather than purpose ('and *restores* all things'). However much John the Baptist might be identified with Elijah, he could hardly be said to have 'restored all things'; the words echo the Malachi passage which appears to have been extended beyond what the context here demands or allows, and, if they are original, the idea must be that if John the Baptist did not in the full sense *restore all things*, the reason must be that men violently prevented his doing so.

13
as it is written of him: The Old Testament contains no suggestion that Elijah when he returned would be rejected. Either, therefore, the reference is to some apocryphal writing then regarded as authoritative but now lost (does it also underlie Rev. $11^{6\text{ff.}}$?), or else the idea is that if the Old Testament was properly understood such a passage as 1 Kings 19^{2-10} would show that Elijah would have to suffer in his second coming as in his first (cf. the obvious parallel between Jezebel and Herodias, etc.).

The identification of John the Baptist as Elijah obviously provided an answer to one Jewish objection against Jesus' Messiahship; whether it goes back to John the Baptist himself, or even to the period of Jesus' ministry, is a much discussed question which cannot be canvassed here; the early Church itself was divided in its opinion on the matter – cf. John 1^{21}.

9^{14-29} A DUMB SPIRIT CAST OUT

14 *And when they came to the disciples, they saw a great crowd about them,*
and scribes arguing with them. 15 *And immediately all the crowd, when they*
saw him, were greatly amazed, and ran up to him and greeted him. 16 *And he*
asked them, 'What are you discussing with them?' 17 *And one of the crowd*
answered him, 'Teacher, I brought my son to you, for he has a dumb spirit;
18 *and wherever it seizes him, it dashes him down; and he foams and grinds*
his teeth and becomes rigid; and I asked your disciples to cast it out, and they
were not able.' 19 *And he answered them, 'O faithless generation, how long*
am I to be with you? How long am I to bear with you? Bring him to me.'
20 *And they brought the boy to him; and when the spirit saw him, immediately*
it convulsed the boy, and he fell on the ground and rolled about, foaming at
the mouth. 21 *And Jesus*[a] *asked his father, 'How long has he had this?' And*
he said, 'From childhood. 22 *And it has often cast him into the fire and into*
the water, to destroy him; but if you can do anything, have pity on us and
help us.' 23 *And Jesus said to him, 'If you can! All things are possible to him*

who believes.' 24 *Immediately the father of the child cried out*[b] *and said, 'I*
believe; help my unbelief!' 25 *And when Jesus saw that a crowd came running*
together, he rebuked the unclean spirit, saying to it, 'You dumb and deaf
spirit, I command you, come out of him, and never enter him again.' 26 *And*
after crying out and convulsing him terribly, it came out, and the boy was
like a corpse; so that most of them said, 'He is dead.' 27 *But Jesus took him by*
the hand and lifted him up, and he arose. 28 *And when he had entered the*
house, his disciples asked him privately, 'Why could we not cast it out?'
29 *And he said to them, 'This kind cannot be driven out by anything but*
prayer.'[c]

a Greek *he*
b Other ancient authorities add *with tears*
c Other ancient authorities add *and fasting*

We come now to a further, and final, exorcism story. To judge from the wording, the opening verse is St Mark's own composition, so he must have been responsible for placing the story in its present context, but the reasons for his decision are not altogether clear, since as we have seen (p. 37) such stories are foreign to the character of this section of the Gospel; this is in fact the only account of a mighty work it contains. Lightfoot's suggestion is probably as good as any: 'the cure of the lad with a dumb spirit is probably placed in its present position as a kind of foil to the story which immediately precedes it. It shows the same Jesus, who has just been glorified upon the mountain, once more at work among men in the plain below.'*

Perhaps too the Evangelist saw a connexion between the disciples' failure to understand the truth about Jesus, so clearly apparent in the preceding stories, and their inability to cast out an evil spirit in his name (v. 18).

As for the story itself, its present form may be due to the combination of two originally independent stories, or of two versions of a single story (see note on v. 21 below), and possibly for that reason it contains an unusual amount of detail and seems somewhat confused. There appears to be no single motif which dominates the narrative as a whole but, as it proceeds, a number of motifs emerge.

Of these the most significant concerns the necessity for *faith*. In

* *H. & I.*, p. 78. This contrast has found classic expression in Raphael's *Transfiguration*.

v. 19, Jesus' reaction to what has happened in his absence is to upbraid the whole generation for lack of faith. If the question is raised against whom this condemnation was primarily directed, whether it was the disciples, the father of the boy, or the crowd and the scribes, the clue lies in recognizing that the words are not really part of Jesus' dialogue with the father. Jesus speaks here as an incarnate deity whose human form and earthly existence are only temporary and who already has one foot in the next world;* his words are traditional, a lament such as the prophets, or even God, uttered in the Old Testament (cf. e.g. Jer. 5^{23}, 1 Kings 19^{14}, Num. 14^{27}, Deut. $32^{5,20}$) and the Evangelist will have understood them as a divine condemnation of the whole generation to which Jesus came.

St Mark does not describe the subject, or the cause, of the controversy to which he alludes in vv. 14 and 16, but no doubt he envisaged the scribes indulging in their usual captious criticism, egged on by the crowd, while the disciples, with their hardened hearts, were unable to defend their Master by either words or effective action. The very fact of their common lack of faith was further witness to Jesus' claims, for the rabbis themselves had foretold that the generation to whom the Messiah came would be marked out by its lack of faith.

If in this first half of the story it is thus shown that failure to believe in Jesus is a blameworthy, and also a paralysing, thing, it is shown in vv. 22b–24 that, if men *have* faith, there is no limit to what God will do for them. This is something the boy's father needs to learn, for the words in which he appeals for help appear to set limits on what God can or will do through Christ. He is taught otherwise, first by an explicit statement of Jesus (v. 23; cf. 10^{27} and $11^{22ff.}$) and then through the healing of his son in response to his faith, imperfect though he knows it to be.†

* Cf. Bundy pp. 311–12. It is typical of the character of this section of the Gospel that 'the expectation of the End . . . prompts or colours the exclamation' (H. G. Wood).

† In that connexion vv. 26 and 27 should be studied carefully and compared with $5^{39ff.}$ and the notes there. In the Greek of v. 27 the words translated *lifted up* and *arose* are the words normally used by the early Christians for God's 'raising' Jesus from the dead and for Jesus 'rising' from the dead; and in v. 26 the words translated *most of them* would be better translated 'most people' (see notes below). The careful wording of the two verses is hardly accidental;

The memorable, haunting cry of the father in v. 24 is in a sense the centre of the story as it now stands. Lohmeyer even suggests that Jesus is envisaged as deliberately leaving the boy wallowing in his misery until he has dealt with the lack of faith involved in the case, which is thereby shown to be the overriding issue. (If so, cf. for a partial parallel Jesus' attitude to the paralytic in 2^{5}.) It is doubtful if Lohmeyer is right in his further suggestion that the description of the father's response as a 'shout' (v. 24) is to be seen, not as a sign of human distress, but as evidence that the faith was divinely inspired. Rather the sense appears to be: 'Help me, although such belief as I have must be counted as complete unbelief in comparison with what is demanded.' So understood, the words have brought consolation, as no doubt St Mark intended them to do, to countless Christians conscious of the inadequacy of their own faith. It will be noticed that while it is the boy who is 'raised', it is the father from whom faith is demanded; this in itself should be enough to dispel the idea, if it needs dispelling, that what *the Evangelist* envisaged was any sort of auto-suggestion on the part of the patient effecting the cure by 'normal' psychological processes.* No doubt in the Church of St Mark's day it was commonly held that children of a believing household were in some sense included in the faith of their parents and could hope to enjoy the benefits of it. Cf. 1 Cor. 7^{14}, and for the general idea of participation in the faith of others, Mark 2^{5} and 1 Cor. 15^{29}.

A further motif, supplied in the last two verses, concerns the vital necessity of *prayer* for the successful performance of such exorcisms. These verses are almost universally regarded by commentators as a

* How far such categories may have a proper place in a *modern* understanding of Jesus' healing ministry is a question which lies outside the scope of a commentary such as this.

---

if men are Christians and have faith, then even after they have become corpses and 'most people' regard them as dead, the God who raised Jesus can, and will, grant life to them also. These two verses thus introduce a second motif, or at any rate an extension of the first. The 'last enemy' of mankind is death; here, if anywhere, a limitation of power might be expected to reveal itself. But even here the power of God, manifested in the resurrection of Jesus, is effective in those who 'believe' (cf. Rom. 4, especially vv. 17–20, where there is a somewhat similar play on words, Rom. $8^{35ff.}$ and John $11^{5ff.}$ especially vv. 25–27).

late addition to the story, reflecting the experience of the early Church. Neither the main body of the story itself, nor the general picture given in the Gospels, suggests that Jesus specially stressed prayer in connexion with exorcism, and the probability seems to be that the early Church, experiencing difficulty over certain types of exorcism, ascribed the failure to spiritual deficiencies on the part of the exorcists. Certain types of demon, it was held, could only be expected to yield to an exorcist who was conspicuously a man of prayer and (if the reference to *fasting* is original) a strict ascetic.

Then, although the expressions of amazement which no doubt at an earlier stage in the development of the story emphasized the supernatural character of the act have now dropped out, the repeated descriptions of the long duration and extreme seriousness of the complaint (vv. 18, 21–22, and 26), the immediate violent reaction of the demon to Jesus' presence (v. 20) and its unwilling but complete obedience to a mere word from him after it had withstood the efforts of the disciples (v. 26), all serve to emphasize the special status and messianic power of Jesus. When we discount the teaching of vv. 28–29, we can see that there may have been a stage in the development of the story at which the main emphasis lay on the contrast between Jesus and the disciples; there was an evil spirit so powerful that only the Messiah himself could suffice to dislodge it.

Finally, it has often been suggested that the story betrays a consciousness of a parallel between Jesus' descent from the Mount of Transfiguration and Moses' descent from Mount Sinai in Exod. 32–33. Both leaders descend from the mount to find that their lieutenants have been involved in controversy with the people and have been party to a general unfaithfulness; both utter condemnations of what has happened (cf. Exod. 32^{19} and 33^{5}). Moreover, Moses had in some sense been transfigured on the mount (Exod. 34^{29}), and the glory which still shone from his face when he descended made the people afraid (Exod. 34^{30}). We know that these facts were treasured in the early Church (cf. 2 Cor. $3^{7ff.}$), and if something of the sort was thought to have happened to Jesus, we might have an explanation of the otherwise motiveless 'great amazement' of the crowd in v. 15. However, the parallels between the two stories are only very general and they are not pointed by any close verbal resemblances, so readers will probably come to different conclusions, as commentators have done, about whether the Evangelist has the earlier story consciously in mind.

ꕥ

14

Some manuscripts have: *when* he *came* . . . he *saw* . . . Though this may not be the original reading, it is probable that the original form of the story presupposed a situation in which Jesus had been separated from *all* the disciples; even in the present account it is nowhere explicitly said that 'the disciples' means only the nine.

If the incident really took place in the far north, the presence of 'the scribes' in such a region seems improbable; in any case they play no real part in the story and the reference to them may well be a conventional addition which secures their explicit inclusion in the condemnation for faithlessness.

17

The symptoms described here and in the rest of the story are generally held to point to epilepsy, 'a temporary . . . inability to speak, together with insensibility towards any words addressed to him, being characteristic of an epileptic when suffering from a fit'. See further on v. 21 below.

21

Instead of performing the cure at once, as we might have expected, Jesus, apparently with the boy still wallowing in front of him, elicits from the father a second description of the illness and holds a dialogue on faith. Then, when a crowd threatens to arrive (v. 25) he performs the cure, presumably quickly, in order to avoid publicity; but the opening verses of the story give the impression that a crowd was already present. Considerations like these have led a good many scholars to the conclusion that two different stories have gone to the making of the present narrative. If so – and it seems quite likely – they have now become so closely intertwined that it is no longer possible to distinguish at all precisely the boundaries and character of each; or even to know whether, as V. T. believes, they were variant accounts of a single incident. Perhaps in one account a 'dumb spirit' (v. 17) was cast out publicly, and the emphasis lay on the contrast between Jesus and the disciples, who could not cast out the spirit (? because of their neglect of prayer).*

* See V. T. (p. 396), who thinks 28f. originally belonged with vv. 14–19. The other account, in which the disciples played no role, may have described

22
The accidents in which the boy has been involved in the course of his fits are ascribed to the direct, positive activity of the demon.

23
All things are possible to him who believes: The logical connexion might suggest that the reference is to Jesus himself, who can do anything because of his deep faith in God; but St Mark, to judge from his general attitude,* is not likely to have understood the words in that sense. He will have understood them as an exhortation to the father to have faith, the meaning being not that one who has faith will (subjectively) *regard* anything as possible, but that faith is the response in virtue of which God makes available his limitless power. (See further, p. 92.)

25
never enter him again: The boy's trouble is not continuous illness but periodic fits, so the demon must not merely leave him for the present, but must never return.

26
most of them: That must be the sense of the Greek expression (*tous pŏllous*) in the context, but since it can also mean 'the majority of people', 'people at large', the possibility of a *double entendre* cannot be ruled out. (See p. 243n.)

9^{30-32} A SECOND PREDICTION OF THE PASSION

30 *They went on from there and passed through Galilee. And he would not have any one know it;* 31 *for he was teaching his disciples, saying to them, 'The Son of man will be delivered into the hands of men, and they will kill him; and when he is killed, after three days he will rise.'* 32 *But they did not understand the saying, and they were afraid to ask him.*

* For him, the power Jesus possesses is in virtue of his status as God's son and Messiah, not in virtue of any faith relationship to God.

---

the casting out in secret of an 'unclean spirit', both deaf and dumb (v. 25), and the emphasis apparently lay on the importance and character of *faith* as exemplified in the father's reaction to Jesus (vv. 22–24).

9^{30-32}

The second of Jesus' three solemn predictions of the sufferings in store for him (cf. 8^{31} and 10^{32-34}). St Mark sets it in the context of a secret journey through Galilee, which he appears to have regarded as the beginning of Jesus' final journey to Jerusalem (cf. 9^{33}, 10^{1}, and 10^{46}), but here, as in the case of the other two predictions, there is no really essential connexion between the prediction and the surrounding events. What St Mark has in fact done – with great skill – is to distribute the three predictions through the narrative in a way that has been aptly compared to the solemn tolling of a minute bell as the party makes its way from Mount Hermon in the far north towards Jerusalem in the south. The predictions thus serve as a commentary revealing the significance of the accompanying events and also serve to assure us that, as was to be expected of the Son of God, Jesus had no illusions about the destiny in store for him, and was not surprised by it when it overtook him. The artificiality of the arrangement is further apparent from the fact (noted by Lightfoot) that the sequel to each prediction is arranged on the same basic pattern, namely (*a*) an example of the failure of the disciples to understand the prediction, (*b*) a (favourable) reference in consequence to a person or persons outside the circle of the disciples, and (*c*) appropriate teaching.* In this case the disciples' failure to understand Jesus' perfectly straightforward words seems inexplicable – except on St Mark's theory of the supernatural blinding of their eyes; and, in view of 9^{11}, their fear of asking for an explanation seems equally hard to explain. It is difficult to deny the force of B.'s words:† 'the Evangelist knew well the story of what took place at Jerusalem. When the events occurred, the disciples, taken apparently by surprise, fled. A threefold detailed explanation of what was to come could only be reconciled with this result on the theory that the disciples did not understand what they were told. Modern readers are more likely to conclude that Jesus' predictions were not as detailed as Mark describes them.'

The prediction itself is considerably shorter than the others, and in

* For a full discussion see *H. & I.*, pp. 117ff. Bultmann, who agrees with Lightfoot in regarding this section of the Gospel as a 'literary' introduction to the Passion, suggests that the three predictions of suffering may be three versions of a single statement; he points out the frequency of such threefold repetition in the Gospels, e.g. 3 temptations, 3 prayers in Gethsemane, 3 denials. See Bultmann, pp. 342–3.

† p. 168.

contrast to that in 8^{31} it does not state a law of suffering to which Jesus must conform, but simply announces as an assured fact* that he will suffer. It is probably a mistake to press too closely the differences of formulation between the three predictions, though see note below.

✠

31
delivered into the hands of men: The Greek word for *delivered* (*paradidōnai*) can be used of handing a person over to the authorities for arrest or imprisonment, so there may be a reference here to Judas' act of betrayal. But the word was a favourite one with Paul, and in view of such passages as Rom. 8^{32} or 4^{25} (literally 'was delivered for our transgressions'), we should probably find here the further idea that the whole Passion of Jesus had its ultimate ground in God's initiative and his concern for the salvation of men.† If so, the play on words *Son of man . . . men* is no doubt deliberate; in a fallen world men had become so hostile to God that when, as the culmination of his plans for their salvation, he sent to them the Man, their Saviour and ultimate model, they regarded and treated him as their worst enemy. Men and the Son of man stood on opposite sides in God's eschatological battle against the powers of evil.

9^{33-50} THE SEQUEL TO THE SECOND PREDICTION OF THE PASSION

33 *And they came to Caper'na-um: and when he was in the house he asked*
them, 'What were you discussing on the way?' 34 *But they were silent; for on*
the way they had discussed with one another who was the greatest. 35 *And he*
sat down and called the twelve; and he said to them, 'If any one would be
first, he must be last of all and servant of all.' 36 *And he took a child, and put*
him in the midst of them; and taking him in his arms, he said to them,
37 *'Whoever receives one such child* in my name *receives me; and whoever*
receives me, receives not me but him who sent me.'

* In the Greek the verb 'delivered' is in the present tense, which heightens the assurance of the statement; the suffering is as good as happening already.

† See p. 67n.

9^{33-50}

38 *John said to him, 'Teacher, we saw a man casting out demons* in your
name[a] *and we forbade him, because he was not following us.'* 39 *But Jesus*
said, 'Do not forbid him; for no one who does a mighty work in my name
will be able soon after to speak evil of me. 40 *For he that is not against us is for*
us. 41 *For truly, I say to you, whoever gives you a cup of water to drink*
because you bear the name of Christ, *will by no means lose his reward.*

42 '*Whoever* causes *one of these little ones who believe in me* to sin,[b] *it*
would be better for him if a great millstone were hung round his neck and he
were thrown into the sea. 43 *And if your hand* causes *you* to sin,[b] *cut it off;*
it is better for you to enter life maimed than with two hands to go to hell,[c]
to the unquenchable fire.[d] 45 *And if your foot* causes *you* to sin,[b] *cut it off;*
it is better for you to enter life lame than with two feet to be thrown into
hell.[c,d] 47 *And if your eye* causes *you* to sin,[b] *pluck it out; it is better for*
your to enter the kingdom of God with one eye than with two eyes to be
thrown into hell[c] 48 *where their worm does not die, and the* fire *is not*
quenched. 49 *For every one will be* salted *with* fire.[e] 50 Salt *is good; but if the*
salt *has lost its* saltness, *how will you season it? Have* salt *in yourselves, and*
be at peace with one another.'

a Other ancient authorities add *who does not follow us*
b Greek *stumble*
c Greek *Gehenna*
d Verses 44 and 46 (which are identical with verse 48) are omitted by the best ancient authorities
e Other ancient authorities add *and every sacrifice will be salted with salt*

Readers may well feel slightly bewildered after a first glance at these verses, for the material they contain is extremely diverse and the principle on which it has been collected into one section not immediately obvious. However, the problem is partly solved when we remember that what we are dealing with is the sequel to the second prediction of the Passion (see p. 248). J. H. Ropes writes:* 'The series of incidents and sayings in the last part of chapter nine . . . are not accidental in their place here, mere survivals of the crude context of an earlier source, nor are they due to a biographical motive. They are deliberately brought in by the Evangelist as part of Jesus' instruction

* *The Synoptic Gospels*, pp. 23–4.

regarding the inseparable connexion, inevitable both for leader and for followers, of sufferings with the career and the cause of the Messiah. In this situation the dispute as to who is greatest (v. 33ff.) betrays failure to understand; again, for them to reject any friends however uninstructed and slight in their attachment (v. 38ff.) is an arrogance that reveals their inadequate comprehension; what is requisite is sacrifice and self-denial, and persistence in it (vv. 43–49), and that repression of jealousy and ill-feeling (v. 50) which alone befits men who are entering on a march towards a Cross.' The section is, in fact, a commentary on the second prediction of the Passion, showing once again that the freely accepted suffering which awaits Jesus is not an accidental, isolated occurrence, but exemplifies a law of the kingdom which applies equally to all who would enter upon its life (cf. above p. 227, and also see p. 268 and p. 259n. below for the possibility that the first half of Chapter 10 was thought of by the Evangelist as continuing this commentary).

A further principle of connexion is indicated in the translation above by the printing of certain words in roman type. A study of these words will show that even where items in the section have no immediate relevance to one another from the point of view of subject-matter, certain words or phrases which they have in common – e.g. 'name', 'fire', 'salt' – provide at least a verbal link between them. Such purely verbal linkage may seem to modern readers curiously artificial, but it was a not uncommon feature in ancient writing (cf. e.g. James 1), no doubt connected with the habit of learning large blocks of material by heart – a process obviously made much easier by such verbal links. No doubt a good deal of the material in this section had already been linked in this way before it reached St Mark, in order to meet the catechetical needs of the early Church.

For our purposes this section breaks up conveniently into three divisions which will be considered separately.

33–37 THE CONTROVERSY ABOUT GREATNESS

As it stands, this episode appears to be a compilation by St Mark, and if it fails to make any very clear single impression that is because he has shown rather less than his usual skill in the compilation of his material. The first two verses serve to place the whole section (33–50) in the context of the journey through Galilee and at the same time set the scene for vv. 35–37; they must, however, be the creation of the Evangelist. Apart from the difficulty of reconciling the stay in Capernaum with a *secret* journey through Galilee (v. 30), we can hardly imagine grown men discussing their relative greatness quite in the way suggested here; and in any case the saying in v. 35 seems already to have been provided with its own introduction (v. 35a), which sorts ill with the picture in vv. 33–34. The saying itself (v. 35b) is one variant of a pronouncement frequently attributed to Jesus in the Gospels (10^{43-44}, Luke 9^{48}, Matt. 23^{11}, and cf. Luke 22^{26-27}), and it is perhaps strange that St Mark should have preferred this version of it to the one he himself gives in 10^{43-44}, which, besides being in all probability more original (see notes), is more appropriate to the present context. Literally translated, the words mean: 'If anyone wants to be great he will be last' . . . R. comments (p. 127) 'The words should not be interpreted as a threat of what will happen at the Judgement to those who have displayed the temper of ambition; but as an indication of how really to become great, and of the essence of true greatness, viz. that it consists in service.' That is probably substantially true, though we must beware of unduly modernizing the Gospels, and the possibility cannot be ruled out that the saying contained an element of threat, cf. Matt. 23^{12}, and such rabbinic sayings as: 'God will exalt him who humbles himself, God will humble him who exalts himself.'*

The introduction of the child (v. 36) would be more natural if he were used, as he is in Matthew's parallel version (Matt. 18^{3-4}), as an example for the disciples to copy. ('Except you adopt the same attitudes as this child . . .') But in the Marcan version the point lies not in the *child's* attitude, but in the attitude of the others *towards* him, the connexion presumably being that the true disciple achieves greatness not by holding great offices but by doing services to insignificant people such as the child. Such a connexion seems highly artificial in this context, and our suspicions are increased by the wording of the saying itself. What exactly is meant by 'receiving' a child – an expression as obscure in the Greek as it is in the English? St Mark presumably understood it as meaning 'show kindness to' or even possibly as referring to the reception of children in baptism; but

* For further parallels see Montefiore, *Rabbinic Literature and Gospel Teachings*, pp. 328ff.

the fact seems to be that Jesus was in the habit of describing certain of his followers as 'little ones' or 'children' and that as a consequence a certain amount of confusion arose in the tradition between sayings of his about children and sayings about disciples. If our present saying referred originally to Jesus' disciples, 'receiving' them would be a perfectly natural expression, especially as the Aramaic verb *gabbēl* meant both 'to receive' and 'to hear' in the sense of 'obey' cf. e.g. Mat. $10^{11\text{ff.}}$ (esp. v. 14) // Luke $10^{5\text{ff.}}$ (esp. vv. 8 and 10). It is noteworthy that both Matthew and Luke have versions of this saying in Jesus' charge to his disciples as he sent them out on missionary work (Matt. 10^{40}, Luke 10^{16}) – a setting which seems more likely to be original. The sense would then be fully in line with the well-attested principle of Jewish life that 'One who is sent (by a king) is as the one who sends him', and it is probably a mistake to read a 'mystical' meaning into the idea of 'receiving' Jesus and the Father. If such language were used in the fourth Gospel it would no doubt refer to receiving the in-dwelling of God's spirit through love and self-sacrifice, but such ideas are hardly present in Mark.

38–41 THE EXORCIST WHO WAS NOT A DISCIPLE

Another episode which in its present form is an artificial construction. No doubt vv. 38–39 (? and 40) were already attached to v. 37 through the verbal link *in my name* before they reached St Mark; and he has preserved the connexion and inserted them here, interpreting them as a further example of the disciples' arrogance and failure to understand. Earlier, however, emphasis will have fallen on a rather different point in the story. We know from the evidence of the magical papyri and of such passages as Acts $19^{13\text{ff.}}$ (and cf. Acts $8^{18\text{ff.}}$) that the early Christians were often faced with the problem of the pagan exorcist who successfully used the name of Jesus for purposes of exorcism, without becoming a Christian. In this story they will have found the Lord's own solution of the problem – an exceedingly tolerant solution, indeed so tolerant as to arouse some doubt of its genuineness; for if the first Christians had from the beginning had such explicit directives to tolerance, it is hard to account for the very intolerant attitude they seem often to have adopted in such cases (cf. Acts $19^{15\text{ff.}}$ and perhaps $8^{20\text{ff.}}$ and 13^{10}). It is of course possible that the question arose in Jesus' own lifetime, but it seems more probable that we are dealing with a story from the early Church; notice that the question is stated in v. 38 in terms of the right treatment of one who does not follow *the disciples.**

The point is generalized by the saying in v. 40, a proverbial saying well known in the ancient world; there is no means of telling whether it went originally with vv. 38–39 or not.

The connexion of v. 41 with vv. 38–40 appears to be through the purely verbal link 'in the name'; the thought of the verse is more akin to that of v. 37, which perhaps at some stage it immediately followed. In Matthew the saying finds a more appropriate context (and perhaps a more original form) in the discourse on the sending out of the twelve (Matt. 10^{42}). In its Marcan context it must presumably be interpreted as an example of how those who have not formally thrown in their lot with the Christians may yet be 'for them'.† The words translated *because you bear the name of Christ* are certainly an early Church formulation as they stand (see notes), but whatever the original wording may have been precisely, the question is raised why it should have been thought especially meritorious to help people because they were Christians. B. writes (p. 172): 'It is well to keep in mind that the sharpness of the distinction between Christians and outsiders represented by the motive *because you belong to Christ* is characteristic of the early Church. It was a by-product of the effort to emphasize the fellowship of Christians and to create an organization. One thinks of Paul's words, "Do good to all men, but especially to the household of faith", and similar injunctions. Organization involved the Church immediately in distinctions on the basis of membership. Such a development did not contradict the ethic of Jesus, but it certainly complicated it' – and he draws a contrast with the teaching of Matt. 5^{44-46}. There is no doubt truth in this, but will not Jesus himself have taken the view that since his followers were people who had thrown in their lot with him and were cooperating with his Father in the work of introducing the kingdom, to help them was in a special way to help forward the

* The point would be even clearer if we could follow the reading of some MSS.: *does not follow* [Jesus] *with us.*

† The whole section is especially relevant to the circumstances of a Church under persecution; perhaps we are to think here of penniless and persecuted missionaries receiving help and hospitality from benevolent non-Christians.

saving work of God? On the hope of reward as a motive for good conduct see R. Bultmann, *Jesus and the Word*, pp. 78ff.

42–50 A CATENA OF SAYINGS

Within this sub-section the links between the items are purely verbal, but (apart from some general resemblances between vv. 42 and 37) there is no verbal link between the sub-section as a whole and the two earlier ones. As we have seen, it was probably the theme of self-renunciation (vv. 43–48) which led St Mark to insert the passage at this point, the immediate connexion being effected through the contrast between the thought of service to others in v. 41 and the opposite thought of hindering or obstructing others which is stated in v. 42 in the vigorous pictorial language which was characteristic of Jesus.

For *cause to sin* (*skandalizein*), see on 6^{3} and cf. 4^{17}. The addition of *who believe in me* (not found in the independent version at Luke 17^{2}) suggests that St Mark was here thinking of simple Christians and of those who 'led them into sin' by wantonly shaking their faith. But if, as is possible, the saying originally referred to children, it 'may have emphasized the reverence due to children and the sin of leading those who were literally little ones astray' (R).*

To this warning about 'causing sin' in others is added a group of sayings about 'causes of sin' in oneself (vv. 43–48), sayings which also appear, in a slightly different version, in the Sermon on the Mount (Matt. 5^{29-30}). The aim is to impress indelibly upon us that the kingdom of God is worth any sacrifice (cf. the parables of the pearl of great price and of the hidden treasure) and the vivid details of the imagery (for which see notes) should not be overpressed, though they may perhaps to some extent reflect the old Hebrew concept of 'diffused consciousness', according to which each organ was the seat of some one of the psychological forces which go to make up the total personality. The thought here expressed in terms of sacrificing a part of the body rather than the whole life is at least closely akin to the thought expressed elsewhere under the images of taking up one's cross and of dying in order to live (cf. e.g. $8^{34ff.}$); no doubt in this context St Mark saw it as a further expression of the basic law of

* T. W. Manson suggests that in v. 41 too the reference was originally to children (*S. J.*, pp. 138–9).

the kingdom which was supremely exemplified in Jesus' recently predicted death.

The remaining three sayings (vv. 49–50) are linked to one another and to the context by purely verbal ties, without there being any real connexion. Since the original meaning will have depended in each case on the context in which the saying was spoken, it is no longer possible to know what the original meaning was, or even certainly what St Mark thought it was. In v. 49 the situation is further complicated by the fact that the MSS. offer widely divergent forms of the saying. That accepted by R.S.V. seems most likely to be original, and, since the metaphor of salt suggests the idea of purification* and fire is a frequent figure for trials and persecution, the meaning probably is that in the eschatological situation introduced by Jesus every Christian disciple must expect to have to undergo the fire of suffering and persecution as a means of his purification. In that case the further words added by some MSS. are probably a gloss based on Lev. 2^{13} and designed to make the thought clearer: '. . . just as every sacrifice is purified (salted) by salt'. However, others have understood the fire as the testing fire of the final judgement then so soon expected (cf. I Cor. $3^{12ff.}$) and the reader is warned that more than a dozen other suggestions have been made.† A judicious account of the whole matter will be found in V. T.

The last verse again is attached quite externally to v. 49, and indeed the two halves of it seem to have been originally independent. In the light of Matt. 5^{13}, v. 50a is taken by most commentators as referring to the disciples themselves. They are to season and purify the world, but if the seasoning element should lose its purifying quality, its environment cannot season it again. If the disciples lose the spirit of devotion and become proud and impure, who is to restore

* Wellhausen thinks rather of salt as a *preservative*, and speaks of a fire which at the same time purges what is bad and preserves (like salt) the essential man which is to be saved.

† One attractive suggestion, based on the evidence of some MSS., is that what v. 49 originally contained was a freely rendered continuation of the quotation from Isaiah 66^{24} begun in v. 48: . . . *and all (their) substance shall be destroyed.* Verse 49 would then, however, contain no reference to *salt*, and, as *salt* seems to be the only link with v. 50, it would be hard to see why v. 50 came to be placed where it is, unless of course we assume that it was not added till later, when the reference to *salt* had already found its way into v. 49.

them? In 50b, which may well be a later addition designed to round off the whole section by bringing it back at the end to the subject with which it started (33–34), *salt* stands not for the disciples, but for some astringent qualities they are to possess, perhaps true charity and readiness for sacrifice, or perhaps sound common sense (cf. Col. 4^{6} and also Rom. 12^{18}, 2 Cor. 13^{11}, 1 Thess. 5^{13}). The sense probably is: 'Have salt in yourselves, *and then* you will be at peace among yourselves.'

33
The question presupposes that Jesus knows by supernatural insight what had been going on in the disciples' minds; so explicitly Luke 9^{47}, but contrast Matt. 18^{1}.

34
There is some evidence that the rabbis were in the habit of discussing who would be the greatest in the new age. If the disciples' discussion is historical it must be seen in that context, but the verse reads much more like a free composition of the Evangelist designed to set the scene for what follows.

35
See further p. 280.

37
in my name: Either simply 'for my sake' or 'on the ground of my name', i.e. because of his connexion with me. Some commentators take the meaning to be 'because my name has been invoked over him (in baptism)' – cf. James 2^{7}, and commentaries on it. The artificiality of the verbal links in this section is illustrated by the fact that this phrase is used as the link between vv. 37 and 38, although in v. 38 it is employed in a quite different sense in connexion with the use of Jesus' name in exorcism.

39
It throws an interesting light on the contemporary outlook that Jesus is not represented as shocked or incredulous at the suggestion that his name could be used to effect cures in a semi-magical way unrelated to any personal knowledge of, or faith in, him.

41
because you bear the name of Christ: Literally: 'in (the) name that you are Christ's – a phrase as odd in Greek as it is in English. *Because you are*

Christ's is Pauline terminology (cf. Rom. 8^{9}, 1 Cor. 1^{12}, 3^{23}, 2 Cor. 10^{7}) and the word *Christ* is nowhere else in the Gospels or Acts used as a proper name without the article. So it seems clear that in its present form the phrase must be the work of the early Church; but no reconstruction of the original so far proposed is entirely convincing.

42
if a great millstone . . . : A Roman form of punishment, though not quite unknown among the Jews; *great millstone* is literally 'donkey millstone' and is usually explained as meaning a millstone turned by a donkey, as distinct from the lighter handmill served by a woman.

43
hell: A word with so many irrelevant associations that it is probably better to keep to the original word, *Gehenna*. This was a valley west of Jerusalem where at one time children were sacrificed to the god Moloch (2 Kings 23^{10}, Jer. 7^{31}, $19^{5f.}$, 32^{35}); after being desecrated by Josiah it came to be used as a refuse dump for Jerusalem, a fact which explains the imagery of worm and fire borrowed from Isa. 66^{24} in v. 48. The suggestion is of maggots preying on offal and fires perpetually smouldering for the destruction of refuse. Because of all its bad associations, the Jewish imagination had come to picture *Gehenna* as the place of future torment for the wicked – cf. e.g. 2 Esdras 7^{36}.

48
Whether, as many commentators believe, this addition to v. 47 is the work of St Mark or of the first compiler of the passage, or whether it goes back to Jesus himself, it is important to remember that it is not an original saying expressly designed to convey the Christian view about the fate of the 'lost' but a quotation of traditional language (Isa. 66^{24} – itself based on the imagery of the earthly *Gehenna*) designed to call up an image of utter horror. It is difficult to say just how seriously or literally such use of an accepted idea was intended, especially if the image came to Jesus' mind quite naturally on some occasion when he was teaching near *Gehenna*. Certainly it affords no ground for attributing to Jesus the later fully developed doctrines of eternal punishment. On the other hand we shall probably get nearest the *historical* truth if we heed the warning of V. T. against dismissing the words too lightly as simply picturesque metaphor.

50
lost its saltness: Strictly speaking, as an unfriendly rabbinic writer soon pointed out, salt cannot lose its salty properties in this way. But the saline deposits of the Red Sea contain a good deal beside common salt,

and so it was easy for the appearance of salt to persist after the salt had in fact been dissolved. Hence the popular view in the Palestine of the day was that reflected in this saying.

10^1–12 DIVORCE

10 *And he left there and went to the region of Judea and beyond the Jordan, and crowds gathered to him again; and again, as his custom was, he taught them.*

2 *And Pharisees came up and in order to test him asked, 'Is it lawful for a man to divorce his wife?'* 3 *He answered them, 'What did Moses command you?'* 4 *They said, 'Moses allowed a man to write a certificate of divorce, and to put her away.'* 5 *But Jesus said to them, 'For your hardness of heart he wrote you this commandment.* 6 *But from the beginning of creation, "God made them male and female."* 7 *"For this reason a man shall leave his father and mother and be joined to his wife,*[a] 8 *and the two shall become one."*[b] *So they are no longer two but one.*[b] 9 *What therefore God has joined together, let not man put asunder.'*

10 *And in the house the disciples asked him again about this matter.* 11 *And he said to them, 'Whoever divorces his wife and marries another, commits adultery against her;* 12 *and if she divorces her husband and marries another, she commits adultery.'*

a Other ancient authorities omit *and be joined to his wife*
b Greek *one flesh*

On reaching the southern limits of Galilee Jesus emerges from the privacy into which he had retired in order to teach his disciples (cf. 9^30–31), and resumes his public ministry. After a while he is asked by some Pharisees, or more probably (see notes) by some unspecified inquirers, whether it is ever lawful for a man to divorce his wife.* In that precise form the question must have originated with St Mark, or

* It is not clear why St Mark has chosen this particular point in the Gospel to introduce this debate, which seems to have little in common either with what precedes or with what follows. Lightfoot's suggestion (*G. M. M.*, p. 114n.) is surely fanciful; he sees an allusion to Israel as the bride of God and to Our Lord as the bridegroom, and writes: 'the Lord finds himself faced with the necessity of deciding whether at all costs to Himself He will maintain the union and remain faithful to His people, however they may treat Him.' Wellhausen's observation that St Mark inserts such episodes as this at various

at any rate with some group of early Christians for whom the issue was a live one. A Jew, not to say a Pharisee, would hardly have posed such a radical question; for him Deut. 24^{1-4} made clear beyond doubt that divorce *is* lawful in certain circumstances; the only question was what those circumstances are.* On this, comparatively limited, question Jewish opinion was sharply divided, and in St Matthew's version of our incident it is only that limited issue which is put to Jesus for decision.†

* This statement is hardly affected by Mal. 2^{13-16}, a passage which was as obscure to the scribes as it is to modern exegetes. Some of the rabbis certainly took it as expressing God's dislike of divorce, but by the time of Our Lord, when the Law was held in the very highest veneration, it seems extremely improbable that anyone would have thought of Malachi's words as throwing radical doubt on the clear teaching of Deut. 24 and so rendering the possibility of divorce an open question.

It is sometimes suggested that the question in v. 2 was asked by Jews who already knew of Our Lord's radical attitude towards the Law and hoped to trap him into some outright contradiction of it, for which he could be reported to the authorities. But this is pure speculation, and to those familiar with the history of the Gospel tradition, the explanation of v. 2 given above will seem preferable.

† See Matt. 19^{3} (and cf. Matt. 5^{31-32}). Although the version of the incident given there is thus more plausible from the historical point of view, St Matthew does not appear to have had any independent authority for it; he has simply recast the Marcan version in the light of his greater familiarity with the Jewish situation. We therefore have no direct evidence as to the original form of the question, a fact which should be borne in mind when the passage is being used as a basis for deciding current questions about marriage.

The Jewish difference of opinion over the legitimate grounds for divorce turned on the detailed interpretation of Deut. 24^{1}, and particularly of the phrases *find favour* and *some indecency*. The latter phrase was taken by the school of Shammai to refer only to acts of unchastity, whereas the school of Hillel gave it a wider connotation and took it to cover almost any failure on the part of the wife to satisfy her husband.

---

points in his Gospel 'for the sake of variety' states the problem rather than solving it. Probably the most we can say is that this story seemed to St Mark too important to omit and he could find no place for it in the Gospel more suitable than this; but it is certainly strange that he has put it before vv. 13–16 and vv. 17–31, both of which seem to carry on the theme of the latter part of Chapter 9 – Jesus' instruction to his disciples about the character and cost of discipleship. Could it be that the exacting new standard for the marriage relationship seemed to St Mark one aspect of the character and cost of discipleship in which the disciples needed instruction? (cf. Matt. 19^{10}).

As we should expect in a Jewish debate, the appeal is to the Old Testament Law, and it emerges that Deut. 24^{1-4} allowed divorce to the male partner provided that he safeguarded the woman's interests by giving her a 'writ of dismissal'.* Jesus, however, regards this passage as simply a concession to human sinfulness, and argues that God's original (and real) intentions in the matter are to be deduced from two other texts in the Old Testament Law, viz. Gen. 1^{27} and 2^{24}. If taken together, these reveal God's original purpose in creating the human race, as witnessed by his division of it into two sexes; he meant that each male should be united to one female in an indissoluble union. The argument is thus in essence an appeal to God's original intention in instituting marriage; in form – reasoning from one scripture to another – it is an almost exact duplicate of 7^{6-13}, and though in a very general way it might be called rabbinic, no rabbi would have interpreted one Old Testament text as flatly invalidating another. If this was what Jesus did here, the passage is reminiscent of $2^{23\text{ff.}}$ and 7^{14-23} and the argument would, if carried to its logical conclusion, cut right across the idea of the Old Testament as in all its parts the unequivocal expression of God's will.†

While most commentators interpret the passage in this sense, as an unambiguous refusal by Jesus to allow divorce in any circumstances, and that was no doubt St Mark's understanding of it as well, the matter is undeniably somewhat obscure, and several other views about it have been put forward. In particular:

(i) It has been argued that cases of adultery are entirely excluded from the argument on the grounds that they were already dealt with in Deut. 22^{22}; in that case, the exceptive clauses in Matthew (19^{9} and 5^{32}), even if added by the Evangelist, correctly interpret Jesus' meaning. It is true that, according to Abrahams's careful study (in *Studies in Pharisaism and the Gospels*, I Chapter 9), 'the death penalty was neither pronounced nor inflicted for adultery in the time of Christ', but we know that soon after the time of Christ Jewish husbands were *compelled* to divorce their wives in cases of unchastity, and so the possibility

* The purpose of this document was to enable the woman to prove that she had been formally divorced and so was free to marry another man.

† Cf. R., p. 134, n. 2: 'Jesus ... had taken up a position which virtually abrogated a Pentateuchal Law.' If St Matthew's version of the incident is secondary, the changes he introduces will have been partly due to unwillingness to admit that Our Lord would have done any such thing.

cannot be altogether ruled out that already in Christ's day divorce on this ground would have seemed so obviously right as to be beyond discussion altogether. Jesus may even have held that in such circumstances the adulterous wife had already sundered the unity and so no question of 'putting asunder' (v. 9) arose. (Cf. Montef., I, pp. 228 and 232 – his long and careful discussion of the whole passage deserves to be consulted.)

(ii) It has been suggested that teaching of this kind must be related to the eschatological perspective of the whole ministry. What Jesus proclaims is the coming of the kingdom, of a new existence before God; in such commands as these he sets forth the pure will of God in its absolute form and as such it cannot be completely fulfilled before the end, but only in the time following, in the new world of God's kingdom. For example Dibelius, who is inclined to see in v. 9 an originally independent logion, writes (*Jesus*, E.T., pp. 115–16): 'It was in this sense, for example, that Jesus forbade oaths (Matt. 5^{34}). For God's absolute will forbids man to make God the guarantor of man's statements or intentions. To what extent the state or the courts in this present world are compelled to employ such assurances as oaths – this question is not even raised. . . . in this untransformed world the pure will of God does not yet achieve its full realization. As with the oath so with divorce. . . . The fact that there are marriages in this present world that are by no means true marriages in this sense does not enter into the discussion, since the sole concern is with God's will and God's kingdom. The consequences which men draw from the fact of such marriages Jesus would judge in the same way that he judged all those ways of giving assurance by oath; they only prove that all this sort of thing "belongs to the evil [of this present world]".'*

* See further note on v. 5 below and cf. V. T., p. 421: 'His teaching gives to marriage a position of the highest dignity. This positive emphasis is His gift to the Church and the world. It is more difficult to apply His teaching to the problem of divorce in the modern world. For Christians His words are regulative, but in particular cases they need to be interpreted under the guidance of the Spirit. It cannot be assumed that the question is settled by simply quoting His words; for the record is limited to His reply to a hostile question and to detached sayings in Mark $10^{11f.}$, Matt. 5^{32}, and Luke 16^{18}. Moreover the trend of His teaching is against legalism. The exceptive clauses in Matthew represent the first stage in a process by which His sayings have been treated as enactments, *but in their original form they are operative principles all the more searching because they have this spiritual character*.' [Italics mine.]

Verses 10–12 form an appendix which depicts Jesus expounding to the disciples in private the full bearing of what he has just said in public. As we have seen, such private expositions to the disciples have been featured by St Mark since $4^{10\text{ff.}}$ (cf. $7^{17\text{ff.}}$ and $9^{28\text{f.}}$), and in this instance the synoptic parallels suggest that the exposition is built up from words which circulated originally as isolated logia. For an attempt to reconstruct the original form of these sayings in the light of the parallels see notes below.

❧

1

the region of Judea and beyond the Jordan: At this point Jesus passes from Galilee to the southern territory where his ministry was to end, but it is impossible to be sure what exact picture, if any, St Mark had formed of his movements. The variety of forms in which the MSS. give the phrase show that it was felt to be difficult, and in need of correction, from early times.

Some important MSS. – the western text – omit *and*; this is the reading of the parallel passage in Matthew (19^{1}), but the difficulty about it is that such a way of describing the district east of the Jordan (*Perea* – see map) is quite unparalleled and linguistically very odd. And Burkitt's famous attempt to explain this oddness by supposing that what we have here is a description of Jesus' arrival along the east bank as seen by Peter from the west bank is now generally, and rightly, rejected.

The reading reproduced in A.V. 'into the coasts of Judea by the farther side of Jordan' is again universally rejected as a correction by a scribe on the R.S.V. reading which he recognized to be difficult.

The difficulty of the R.S.V. reading is that it suggests a single area, whereas in fact Perea was completely separate from Judea, being under the jurisdiction of Herod Antipas while Judea was under the Roman governor Pilate. If the idea is that, after reaching Judea, Jesus deliberately crossed the Jordan to conduct a ministry in Perea, the passage would perhaps tie in with Luke 17^{11}, John 10^{40}, 11^{7}, and 11^{54}, but this hardly seems to have been St Mark's understanding. He is thinking rather of a continuous journey to Jerusalem, and if he pictured Jesus as approaching Judea along the east bank of the Jordan (? to avoid Galilee), then the areas are named in the wrong order, like Bethphage and Bethany in 11^{1} (see note there). Here, as there, the simplest thing is to assume that the Evangelist had very little knowledge of the places he is referring to, and the R.S.V. reading is probably the right one, see Introduction, p. 40.

In any case 'the statement in [v.] 1 is very indefinite, and the incidents which follow are not anchored to any particular places and strike one as simply floating traditions which could have happened anywhere' (B., p. 175).

2

Pharisees: The reference to them is omitted by a number of important MSS., probably rightly. In that case the verb is an impersonal plural of the type so common in Mark, and we should translate: 'the question was put to him. . . .'

test: The Greek word (*peirazein*) can mean simply to 'test' in the sense of seeking to elicit the truth about something or it can mean 'tempt', i.e. test in the hope of eliciting some damning admission. St Mark no doubt understood it here in the second sense – Jesus was to be brought into open conflict with the Law or discredited in the eyes of Herod; but just possibly (see above) the question which gave rise to the incident in its original form was a quite straightforward one designed to elicit Jesus' views on a much-debated question in contemporary ethics.

On the content of the question see above p. 260. It will have been a particularly pertinent one in Rome, where divorce was easy and constantly occurred, but the wording suggests that in the present form of the question it originated in *Jewish*-Christian circles, for it does not seem to contemplate a woman divorcing her husband (contrast v. 12). This was possible according to Roman Law, but not according to Jewish (see below on vv. 11–12).

3–4

Many commentators think that in an earlier form of the pericope all of this belonged to the Pharisees, as it still does in effect in Matthew.

5

hardness of heart (*sklērŏkardia*)*:* Some commentators take *hard* here to mean 'rough' or 'coarse' and think of 'the rude nature which belongs to a primitive civilization' (Gould); the implication then is that the words express a merciful concession for the woman's sake. But perhaps we should think rather of unteachableness, stubborn refusal to obey God's will as revealed in Genesis. The implication is that the Mosaic Law was in certain cases a kind of second best. The highest law could not, or would not, have been obeyed. So there was a concession made to human weakness or 'hardness'. The divorce enactment was not a law but a dispensation.

Did Jesus suppose that with his coming this dispensation lost all its validity, or did he think that where men – even the sons of the kingdom – failed to live up to the divine will in its fullness, some such dispensation was still the best way of dealing with the situation? It is difficult to say how far his view may have been influenced by his belief that this world of 'marrying and giving in marriage' had only a very short time to last (9^1 etc.). Much will depend on whether we regard vv. 11–12 as detailed legislation or whether we take it as a vivid way of expressing God's *absolute* will in this matter.

6

Some scholars translate in 6a: 'at the beginning of his book' (or 'of Genesis') and supply 'Moses wrote'; whether or not that is right, the point of the argument is not to confute 'Moses' by appealing to the direct authority of God himself, but to appeal from the concession made by 'Moses' in Deuteronomy to what 'Moses' himself had previously written in Gen. 1^{27} and 2^{24}, though see now J. Knox, *The Ethic of Jesus*, p. 68.

7

For this reason: Refers in Gen. 2^{24} to the woman's origin from Adam's rib, but by a piece of exegesis reminiscent of the rabbis Jesus makes it refer to something different – the fact (in Gen. 1^{27}) that the human race was created from the beginning in two sexes; it was because God originally made them male and female that a man will leave father and mother and cleave to his wife and the two will become one flesh. There is reason to think that Gen. 1^{27} was currently quoted in support of monogamy, as opposed to polygamy (cf. *The Zadokite Fragment*, $7^{1f.}$), but it appears to have been original to Jesus to see it as prohibiting divorce. His argument no doubt was that if marriage makes a man and his wife *one flesh*, it clearly creates a relationship between them as real and as indissoluble as that which binds a man to his relations by blood (v. 8b and cf. Gen. 29^{14}).

9

man: In antithesis to God, this could mean simply 'any human authority'; but in fact it is no doubt the husband who is contemplated, for neither in Jewish nor in Roman Law were the parties divorced by any extraneous authority; in Jewish Law the man divorced his wife, in Roman Law either party could divorce the other.

Once again the precise scope of this saying is open to dispute: cf. Montef. 'Do the words mean: "Let not man lightly separate. Let not man separate for any reason of his own"? It may be held that in the case of adultery, the union has *ipso facto* been dissolved.'

10

Most commentators regard this setting as artificial, especially in view of the different context in which the sayings appear in Matt. $5^{31f.}$ and

Luke 16^{18}; Matthew in his parallel account has no transition to a new setting at this point (Matt. 19^{8-9}).

11–12

St Mark probably understood these verses simply as crystallizing in clear-cut terms the truths inherent in vv. 2–9, though strictly interpreted they add something new. To divorce your wife is a sin, but it is not adultery; if in addition to divorcing her you marry another woman, then you add the sin of adultery to the sin of divorce.

A full understanding involves setting the verses against the background of Jewish marriage customs in the time of Christ. According to these:

(*a*) Adultery was always intercourse between a married woman and a man other than her husband. A woman could commit adultery against her husband, but a man could not commit adultery against his wife; he could only commit adultery against another married man. In view of this, the teaching in v. 11 will be seen to be strikingly novel, implying as it does that a man *can* commit adultery against his wife. That means that in respect of marriage after divorce both parties are put on a footing of complete equality. In view of the closely similar wording in Q (Luke 16^{18a}) this saying has every appearance of authenticity, except that the words *against her* (i.e. the first wife) which are lacking in Q, were probably added to make the novel teaching more precise and definite.

(*b*) According to Jewish Law a woman could not divorce her husband.* Roman law, as we have seen, was different, and it is generally agreed that if the R.S.V. reading in v. 12 is the right one, the saying must be regarded as an amplification of Jesus' original teaching designed to apply it to the circumstances of Gentile Christians.

There is, however, a well-attested reading according to which Jesus said: 'if a woman *leaves* (Greek *ĕxĕlthē* – commentators are disagreed whether this implies that she is divorced) her husband and marries another . . .' Burkitt then saw a reference by Our Lord to Herodias (6^{17}ff.) who had left her husband (? after divorce proceedings in Roman Law) in order to live with Antipas – himself a *divorcé*.

The R.S.V. reading, however, seems more likely to be original, and if so the verse must be explained as above or, just possibly, it may be a mistranslation of an Aramaic original more correctly translated in Luke 16^{18}b (so *S.J.*, pp. 136ff.).

* In certain circumstances (*not* including infidelity on his part) she could *claim* divorce, but if the husband was obstinately contumacious the claim could not be enforced. In the last resort, divorce among the Jews was always the man's act

10^{13-16} THE BLESSING OF THE CHILDREN

13 *And they were bringing children to him, that he might touch them; and*
the disciples rebuked them. 14 *But when Jesus saw it he was indignant, and*
said to them, 'Let the children come to me, do not hinder them; for to such
belongs the kingdom of God. 15 *Truly, I say to you, whoever does not receive*
the kingdom of God like a child shall not enter it.' 16 *And he took them in his*
arms and blessed them, laying his hands upon them.

A little story which has justly become famous; but like many of the vivid scenes depicted in the Gospels, it contains a good deal more than may at first appear.

Why did the disciples object to the bringing of the children? A common suggestion is that Jesus was tired and the disciples did not want him troubled further. But such biographical motifs are foreign to the Gospels, and in any case the strong word used to describe the disciples' reaction suggests that some deeper issue was at stake. Perhaps the families from which the children came were not committed to Christ (cf. the disciples' attitude in 9^{38} and Jesus' response to it), or more probably the idea is that contact with Jesus is not for those too young to make a responsible decision upon his claims (see further below). Jesus' reaction also suggests that some important matter of principle was involved, for nowhere else in the Gospels is 'indignation' (*aganaktĕō*) ascribed to him.

What does the word *such* mean in his reply? There are two possibilities:

(i) 'these and other (literal) children'. In that case cf. such passages as Ps. 8^{2}, Matt. 21^{15-16}, 11^{25}. Just as it is God's inscrutable will that the truth should be 'hidden from the wise and understanding and revealed to babes', so it is his will that those who have not yet reached 'the age of the Law' should inherit his kingdom. Alternatively, Lohmeyer has the ingenious (? over-ingenious) idea of linking the saying with 9^{1}. Since Jesus there says that a few members of his own generation will survive to see the kingdom come in power, presumably the younger generation will be *the* 'generation of the last times'. In view of that, should they be denied the attention and blessing of Jesus, the bringer of the kingdom?

(ii) The meaning may be: 'these and others who, though not literally children, share the characteristics of children', in which case we have to ask what characteristics. 'The point of the comparison is not so much the innocence and humility [or obedience] of children; it is rather the fact that children are unselfconscious, receptive, and content to be dependent upon others' care and bounty; it is in such a spirit that the kingdom must be received – it is a gift of God and not an achievement on the part of man; it must be simply accepted, inasmuch as it can never be deserved.' (R., pp. 136–7.) Such an interpretation fits well with our other information about the teaching of Jesus (cf. e.g. Luke 17^{10}, Matt. 23^{12} and 5^{5}), and v. 15 makes it clear that this was how St Mark understood the saying; indeed it was no doubt as revealing the disposition of the true disciple that he included the story in this general context which deals with the character and cost of discipleship. But since there is some doubt if v. 15 is an original part of the saying (see notes), it remains possible that (i) was the original meaning (so Bultmann).

Jesus' action in v. 16, which goes even beyond what was asked of him, emphasizes the contrast between his attitude and that of his disciples, and the verse gives a sort of pictorial expression to the truth in 14b, for the early Church certainly believed, if not that 'Jesus Himself is the Kingdom' (V. T., p. 423) at least that reception by him carries admission to the kingdom.

Finally, it should be noticed that, as described by St Mark, Jesus' action corresponds fairly closely to that of the minister at infant baptism; evidence has been collected which makes it at least plausible to suggest that the primitive Church (like the later Church) found in this story an expression of the Lord's mind on the vexed question of infant baptism. (See notes on vv. 14 and 16 below, and O. Cullmann *Baptism in the New Testament*, pp. 71ff., and A. Richardson, *An Introduction to the Theology of the New Testament*, pp. 360f.) Certainly the story gains considerably in point if read with that suggestion in mind, and it would explain why Jesus and the disciples are pictured reacting so sharply, as if to an issue of principle. It cannot be claimed, however, that scholarly opinion is united in finding such a reference here.

ꕥ

13
children: The Greek word (*paidia*) definitely means 'children' (up to twelve years) rather than 'babies', but this would not have prevented the early Church from finding the passage relevant to infant baptism. For a development in that direction cf. how Luke (18^{15}) has 'babies'.

To secure for children the 'touch' of a great or holy man is a common custom in most civilizations. Cf. 'touching' by the monarch for the 'king's evil', which persisted in England down to the time of Queen Anne.

rebuked: In Marcan usage the Greek word tends to have a solemn flavour and to presuppose really serious evil – cf. e.g. 4^{39}, 8^{32} and ^{33}, 9^{25}.

14
hinder: See Cullmann and Richardson for the suggestion that this is a deliberate allusion to the baptismal rite of the primitive Church, in which the question: 'What hinders?' was asked liturgically before the candidates were baptized.

15
Few deny the authenticity of this saying; the main reason for doubting whether this is its original setting is its incongruity as the centre-piece of a story which deals with Jesus' attitude to children, and not with children as examples to be imitated. It is a curious fact that this saying would be wholly appropriate after 9^{36}, and 9^{37} would be more appropriate here. C. H. Turner (*A New Commentary on Holy Scripture*, p. 87) suggests that the two sayings 'have suffered some confusion with one another'.

16
laying his hands upon them: An essential complement to, if not actually part of, the primitive rite of baptism. C. H. Turner says: 'It is by a true instinct that this action of Our Lord's is claimed as implying his sanction for infant baptism.'

$10^{17–31}$ RICHES AND OTHER BARRIERS TO SALVATION

[17]*And as he was setting out on his journey, a man ran up and knelt before him, and asked him, 'Good Teacher, what must I do to inherit eternal life?'* [18]*And Jesus said to him, 'Why do you call me good? No one is good but God*

alone. 19 *You know the commandments: "Do not kill, Do not commit*
adultery, Do not steal, Do not bear false witness, Do not defraud, Honour
your father and mother."' 20 *And he said to him, 'Teacher, all these I have*
observed from my youth.' 21 *And Jesus looking upon him loved him, and said*
to him, 'You lack one thing; go, sell what you have, and give to the poor,
and you will have treasure in heaven; and come, follow me.' 22 *At that saying*
his countenance fell, and he went away sorrowful; for he had great possessions.
23 *And Jesus looked around and said to his disciples, 'How hard it will be*
for those who have riches to enter the kingdom of God!' 24 *And the disciples*
were amazed at his words. But Jesus said to them again, 'Children, how hard
it is[a] *to enter the kingdom of God!* 25 *It is easier for a camel to go through the*
eye of a needle than for a rich man to enter the kingdom of God.' 26 *And they*
were exceedingly astonished, and said to him,[b] *'Then who can be saved?'*
27 *Jesus looked at them and said, 'With men it is impossible, but not with*
God; for all things are possible with God.' 28 *Peter began to say to him, 'Lo,*
we have left everything and followed you.' 29 *Jesus said, 'Truly, I say to you,*
there is no one who has left house or brothers or sisters or mother or father or
children or lands, for my sake and for the gospel, 30 *who will not receive a*
hundredfold now in this time, houses and brothers and sisters and mothers
and children and lands, with persecutions, and in the age to come eternal
life. 31 *But many that are first will be last, and the last first.'*

a Other ancient authorities add *for those who trust in riches*
b Other ancient authorities read *to one another*

The opening verse includes an unusual amount of detail, which is preserved because of the light it throws on what follows. It reveals first that the stranger was altogether too obsequious and effusive in his approach. Jesus pricks the bubble of his fulsomeness by reminding him that religion has a hard, practical side. The way to obtain eternal life is not by giving flattering titles to Jesus, but by doing the will of the Father (v. 18, Matt. 7^{21}, cf. Luke 6^{46}); for the man, as a Jew, the will of God is expressed in the Old Testament Law (here typified by the Ten Commandments) so let him get on and fulfil that (v. 19).

On the other hand, the form of the man's question in v. 17 is significant. Most Jews would never have asked such a question; they would have taken it for granted that keeping the Law was enough. This man has sincerely tried to keep the Law all his life (v. 20) and, perhaps for that very reason, has come to realize that it is not enough.

Jesus, looking at him (v. 21) and sensing his sincerity, warms to him and answers his original question with the seriousness it deserves. The man is quite right, he tells him, in suspecting that there is more in man's relationship with God than negative blamelessness with respect to the Law. The way to eternal life is to throw in one's lot with him and *follow* him in the path of Christian discipleship (v. 21); but Christian discipleship is always costly, and in this case, if the man would lay up treasure in heaven, he must sell all his possessions and give the proceeds to the poor.

It now appears that the man has many possessions (v. 22) and he cannot bring himself to accept Jesus' demand to give them up. In this, Jesus tells the disciples, he is typical of all rich people (v. 23).* They find the demands of Christian discipleship impossibly hard to accept. Riches in fact are an almost insuperable barrier to Christian discipleship and to the achievement of eternal life (vv. 23 and 25, which originally occurred together before v. 24 – see notes). Such instruction comes as a great surprise to the disciples, who have been brought up in the rabbinic teaching† that worldly wealth, though it involves great responsibility, is on the whole a sign of God's favour and makes easier the 'good works' on which salvation will depend. Jesus offers no reasons to convince them, but the reasons are not far to seek.

For a man to give away his wealth, if it is great, is terribly difficult because it means depriving himself of the resources on which he has come to rely for status, security, interest, and enjoyment in life. But that is precisely the reason why disciples of Jesus must give up wealth; for the essence of Christian faith is to put all one's trust in God and to rely on him as the sole source of security and well-being. Strictly

* Verses 23–27 form a sort of appendix to the story, in which, according to the common Marcan pattern, the meaning of what has taken place in public is further expounded to the disciples (? in private) (cf. e.g. 4^{1-9} and $4^{10ff.}$). The disciples, as usual, find this meaning hard to understand and accept (24 and 26), and this trait serves to unite the story with the general context (9^{30}–10^{31}). It will be remembered that Jesus, after a second prediction of his own Passion, is trying to open the completely blind eyes of the disciples to the fact that suffering and sacrifice will be demanded from them too.

† For rabbinic teaching on the subject see Abrahams, *Studies in Pharisaism and the Gospels*, I, pp. 113ff. At least since the time of the Psalmists there had been *some* in Israel who had been very alive to the temptations of wealth and who had sometimes almost come to make the equation: poor = good and pious; rich = sinner.

speaking, of course, it is possible to rely on God in this way without actually giving up one's earthly possessions, and in fact Jesus does not always demand the literal renunciation of property from those he calls to follow him (see further the note on v. 28). But Christians who have been allowed to keep their property are reminded by this story that to have become a disciple of Jesus – to take God seriously as the only Lord and Saviour – involves complete inner detachment from worldly things, a willingness at any moment to sacrifice one's wealth, or anything else that may be required. The last clause is important, for in a further comment on the story (v. 24, which originally followed v. 25 – see notes) Jesus draws from it an even wider moral. Riches are not the only thing from which it is hard to detach oneself; even the poor may have personal ties (cf. Luke 9^{57-62}) or other earthly resources which they find it virtually impossible to renounce. So for all – rich and poor alike – the true relationship with God, the only relationship that can be expected to survive the arrival of the kingdom, involves conditions virtually impossible of fulfilment. At this further teaching the astonishment of the disciples knows no bounds – additional evidence, in St Mark's eyes, how completely they still misunderstood the true character and cost of their calling. 'If this is the case,' they say, 'no one would ever attain salvation' (v. 26). 'Quite right,' Jesus replies, 'no one ever does on the basis of human effort; if men *are* saved, it is solely due to the grace and unlimited power of God' (v. 27). Lagrange remarks that this verse contains in germ the teaching of St Paul. From St Mark's point of view it has a further significance. In vv. 13–16 the kingdom was a gift which cannot be earned, while here the most strenuous effort is required, a contrast already noticed by Shakespeare – see King Richard II, v, 5. Such a juxtaposition was hardly accidental; both truths, St Mark believes, are vital to Christianity, and the apparent contradiction between them is resolved in this saying of Jesus that *all things are possible with God.*

One further point should perhaps be mentioned. St Matthew's rather different account of the incident (Matt. $19^{16\text{ff.}}$) is at least *capable* of interpretation along the lines of the 'double standard', i.e. that keeping the Law is sufficient of itself to secure eternal life, but 'perfection' (Matt. 19^{21}) demands the complete renunciation of property. Such an interpretation has also been proposed for St Mark's account, but, as the exposition has shown, it runs counter to his whole understanding of the story. For him the reference to the Commandments in v. 19 will have been significant as showing that Jesus was not the thorough-going opponent of the Law the Jews made him out to be; a sincere effort to obey the declared will of God is a basic element in Christian discipleship which no other element can ever render superfluous.

The teaching of v. 27 does not lead on very naturally to that of v. 28ff., which appears to connect rather with v. 21. Probably vv. 29–30 reached St Mark as an unattached saying and he felt that the story of a rich man who refused to leave everything and follow Jesus furnished a good setting for it, dealing, as it does, with the reward of those who *have* made such a sacrifice. He therefore attached it to vv. 17–27 by means of the saying attributed to Peter in v. 28, though originally it seems to have envisaged a wider circle than the twelve. There is considerable uncertainty about the original wording and meaning of v. 30; probably the R.S.V. version is the correct one, but we should perhaps punctuate differently, marking a pause after *hundredfold*, which would then govern the whole of the rest of the verse. In any case, according to a large number of commentators (see notes), the words after *hundredfold* are an interpretative addition to the saying, made by the early Christians and reflecting their experience that the fellowship they found in the Christian community more than compensated for the loss of home ties and possessions, and even for the persecutions their new faith so often entailed. (Cf. e.g. Rom. 16^{13}, Acts 2^{44} and 4^{34}, 1 Cor. 4^{15}, Philem. ^{10}.) On v. 31 see notes below.

❧

17
The first phrase, by setting the incident in the context of a journey, provides a formal link with the surrounding material.

Good: Such an address was quite contrary to the Jewish convention. As Lohmeyer says, it would almost have been tantamount to 'holy' or 'divine', and like the accompanying gestures would have seemed altogether too much for one whom the man thought of, after all, as no more than a *Teacher* (i.e. rabbi).

life = 'the kingdom of God to come' and

inherit = 'gain entrance to' were current usage among the rabbis.

18
Undeniably a very puzzling verse which has never been wholly satisfactorily explained; it has caused difficulty to Christian readers at least since the time of St Matthew, who felt obliged to alter it radically (Matt. 19^{17}). The suggestion has often been made – e.g. by the Jewish scholar Montefiore – that the words testify to a sense of sin, or at any rate sinfulness, on the part of Jesus, but even if that were true, it would not explain how, or in what sense, the words came to be included by St Mark; for certainly he, and those from whom he got the tradition, believed in the sinlessness of Jesus. How did they understand the words? One popular line of approach has been to stress that Jesus was looking at the matter from the questioner's point of view, and saying, in effect: '(Though I am good) you have no right to call me good, for, as far as you know, I am simply a man.' Though that puts the point too crudely, there is probably some truth in it, and, bearing in mind what was said about the word *good* in the last note, we shall perhaps get nearest the truth if we suppose that what alarmed and offended Jesus was the indiscriminate bandying about of divine or quasi-divine titles. Any serious religious quest must be based on the recognition that the one God is the sole norm and source of all goodness, even of the goodness of Jesus in the days of his flesh. It sorts well with this that Jesus immediately goes on to point the man to the Law as the expression of God's righteous will. (For a full discussion, with references, of the various lines of interpretation that have been proposed, see V. T., pp. 426–7.)

19
As shown in the exposition, Jesus did not suppose that the Law could supply the full answer to the man's question. His words are a challenge. Cf. the interesting parallel in *Epictetus*, I, 25, 6.: 'But lay your commands on me.' 'Why should *I* lay commands on you? Has not Zeus already laid *his* commands on you? . . . Seeing you have such commands from Zeus what sort of further commands do you want from me?'

The commandments cited are a rough summary of the so-called 'Second Table' of the Ten Commandments, the Fifth Commandment being placed last, and the Tenth summarized in the words *Do not defraud*, perhaps because fraudulence is a special temptation of the rich. No doubt these commandments were meant to typify the Law of God as a whole, but it is perhaps characteristic of Jesus' emphasis that all those actually quoted deal with man's duty to his neighbour.

21
loved him: That is the normal meaning of the Greek word (*agapaō*), but here we should perhaps think rather of some definite outward gesture

of affection – 'caressed him' or 'put his arms round him' (see Dibelius, *F. T. G.*, p. 50, n. 1 – many modern commentators take the same line).

you will have treasure in heaven: The phrase is rabbinic, and so, in one sense, is the whole saying which precedes it. According to the rabbis, God would reward righteousness with treasure in heaven (cf. e.g. *Pss. Sol.* 9^9), and in later Judaism almsgiving, for those who could afford it, had come to be regarded as a – if not indeed *the* – principal ingredient of righteousness. On the other hand, it is one thing to give regular alms out of one's income (no doubt the man did that already) and quite another to be asked to give up the sources of the income itself. And, as we have seen, even the latter demand does not stand by itself; it is the prelude to the further demand: *come, follow me.*

24
Some MSS. (the 'western text') have v. 25 before this verse, and this was probably the original order. The disciples' growing astonishment (cf. vv. 24 with 26) then corresponds to the way Jesus' insistence on the difficulty of salvation grows and widens its scope. In the R.S.V. order, v. 25, referring only to the rich, is something of an anti-climax after the general statement of v. 24. If R.S.V. order is right, the words *for a rich man* in v. 25 may be an interpolation, but there is no MS. authority for such a suggestion.

In v. 24 the western text includes the words relegated by R.S.V. to the margin. As the exposition has shown, they are a perfectly sound comment on the difficulties of the rich. If they are genuine, the passage was originally concerned exclusively with *riches* as a barrier to salvation, but a number of extremely important MSS., followed by the majority of commentators, omit them, and R.S.V. is no doubt right in doing so.

25
Sayings of other Jewish teachers have survived which speak of the impossibility of some vast object (e.g. an elephant) getting through the eye of a needle, so the comparison was clearly proverbial, and there is no substance in the suggestion that *camel* (*camēlos*) is a mistake for *camilos* ('cable'), or for the medieval fancy that there was a gate in Jerusalem, known as the needle, through which a camel might just squeeze. The fact that such minimizing interpretations have been thought up is itself an eloquent comment on the passage! The expression is of course a hyperbole meant to be memorable by reason of its very grotesqueness, but it would be a mistake on that account to ignore the utterly serious truth it expresses.

27
The wording of this verse varies a good deal in the MSS. – but the variations do not affect the general sense. Cf. Zech. 8^{6}, Gen. 18^{14}, and Job 42^{2}.

28
left everything: Used rather loosely; cf. 1^{29}, 3^{9}, $4^{1 \text{ and } 36}$, 1 Cor. 9^{5}, etc., for evidence that their separation from home and possessions was not complete. And Jesus seems to have been partly supported out of the possessions some of his women disciples were allowed to retain.

29
The absence of 'wife' from the list may well be significant. The early Christians may have regarded the marriage tie as so close (cf. above, v. 9) that nothing short of martyrdom could justify the permanent breaking of it (cf. 1 Cor. 7^{12}ff.).

and for the gospel: cf. 8^{35} – here, as there, generally agreed to be an editorial addition.

30
with persecutions: These words are added so artificially, almost as an afterthought, that most commentators regard them as a later interpolation. Some of these commentators regard the whole of the rest of the verse as an original part of Jesus' saying, but the repetition of the list seems intolerably flat, and already appeared so to St Matthew and St Luke, who both omit it. Moreover the sharp distinction between the two 'ages' seems to reflect the teaching of the early Church rather than any that Jesus is known to have given (see Dalman, *The Words of Jesus*, p. 148), and the unusual phrase *in this time* is reminiscent of Pauline phraseology – cf. Rom. 3^{26}, 8^{18}, 11^{5}, 2 Cor. 8^{14}. So Jesus' original saying probably ended at *hundredfold*.

31
A saying which circulated unattached in the early Church; each Evangelist has provided his own setting for it – cf. Matt. 20^{16} and Luke 13^{30}. Originally it may have been simply a proverbial saying about the unpredictable mutability of the human lot. In this context it is presumably to be understood either as an encouragement to the disciples (i.e. the rich and prosperous who are *first* in this world shall in many cases be *last* in the world to come, and vice versa) or as a warning to them (i.e. they, who have been called first, must not count on being first in the kingdom – cf. 35ff. below).

10^{32-52} THE THIRD PREDICTION OF THE PASSION AND ITS SEQUEL

32 *And they were on the road, going up to Jerusalem, and Jesus was walking*
ahead of them; and they were amazed, and those who followed were afraid.
And taking the twelve again, he began to tell them what was to happen to
him, 33 *saying, 'Behold, we are going up to Jerusalem; and the Son of man*
will be delivered to the chief priests and the scribes, and they will condemn
him to death, and deliver him to the Gentiles; 34 *and they will mock him, and*
spit upon him, and scourge him, and kill him; and after three days he will
rise.'

35 *And James and John, the sons of Zeb'edee, came forward to him, and said*
to him, 'Teacher, we want you to do for us whatever we ask of you.' 36 *And*
he said to them, 'What do you want me to do for you?' 37 *And they said to*
him, 'Grant us to sit, one at your right hand and one at your left, in your
glory.' 38 *But Jesus said to them, 'You do not know what you are asking. Are*
you able to drink the cup that I drink, or to be baptized with the baptism
with which I am baptized?' 39 *And they said to him, 'We are able.' And*
Jesus said to them, 'The cup that I drink you will drink; and with the baptism
with which I am baptized, you will be baptized; 40 *but to sit at my right hand*
or at my left is not mine to grant, but it is for those for whom it has been
prepared.'

41 *And when the ten heard it, they began to be indignant at James and John.*
42 *And Jesus called them to him and said to them, 'You know that those who*
are supposed to rule over the Gentiles lord it over them, and their great men
exercise authority over them. 43 *But it shall not be so among you; but whoever*
would be great among you must be your servant, 44 *and whoever would be*
first among you must be slave of all. 45 *For the Son of man also came not to*
be served but to serve, and to give his life as a ransom for many.'

46 *And they came to Jericho; and as he was leaving Jericho with his*
disciples and a great multitude, Bartimae'us, a blind beggar, the son of
Timae'us, was sitting by the roadside. 47 *And when he heard that it was Jesus*
of Nazareth, he began to cry out and say, 'Jesus, Son of David, have mercy
on me!' 48 *And many rebuked him, telling him to be silent; but he cried out all*
the more, 'Son of David, have mercy on me!' 49 *And Jesus stopped and said,*
'Call him.' And they called the blind man, saying to him, 'Take heart; rise,

he is calling you.' 50 *And throwing off his mantle he sprang up and came to*
Jesus. 51 *And Jesus said to him, 'What do you want me to do for you?' And*
the blind man said to him, 'Master,[a] *let me receive my sight.'* 52 *And Jesus*
said to him, 'Go your way; your faith has made you well.' And immediately
he received his sight and followed him on the way.

a Or *Rabbi*

32–34

For the first time Jerusalem is named as the goal of the southward journey. In St Mark's eyes Jerusalem, the eventual site of Jesus' death, was throughout the ministry the real centre of hostility to him (cf. p. 446 and note on 3^{22}); and so in these verses, where Jesus is pictured as deliberately 'setting his face to go up to Jerusalem' (Luke 9^{51}), the conscious acceptance of his messianic destiny is depicted, and it is possible that in the mind of Mark '*followed* implies a sharing of the disciples in the same, albeit with fear' (V. T. – cf. John $11^{7-8 \text{ and } 16}$). Certainly their strong emotions seem to imply that they foresaw what was involved in the journey – a strange contrast to the complete incomprehension with which St Mark usually credits them. Verse 32 would be more intelligible after vv. 33–34 which contain the third prediction of the Passion.

This prediction, which makes no reference to the other two, is much fuller than either of them and exhibits greater literary art. It has been described as 'reading like a printed programme of a Passion Play' and the six stages on the way to the Cross are clearly defined. In its present form it is regarded by almost all commentators as a 'prophecy after the event', especially as the vocabulary is characteristically Marcan. It has been noted that in this prediction Jesus appears far more active in the determination of his destiny than in the other two.

35–40

St Mark does not report the reaction of the disciples to this prediction (contrast $8^{32\text{f.}}$ and 9^{32}), but there can be little doubt that by placing immediately after it the – originally unconnected – story of the selfish request of James and John (and of the equally selfish reaction of the other ten) he intends to convey that, as usual, the disciples completely missed the point. (Cf. p. 248 for the parallel arrangement of material after the first two predictions.)

As these verses stand, there are two possible answers to the request in v. 37, one in vv. 38–40 and the other in vv. 41–45. Some think the latter more likely to be original and conclude that vv. 38–40 are a later insertion into an original unit, 35–37 and 41–45 (or 44).* This is a distinct possibility, but perhaps probability slightly favours another suggestion – that the original unit was vv. 35–40 and vv. 41–45 is an appendix to it, constructed by St Mark out of originally isolated sayings (see below).

But even in vv. 35–40 there seem to be two answers. First, v. 40 is sufficient answer in itself. It repudiates the request outright, though the present wording which is very awkward (in the Greek there is nothing corresponding to *it is*) seems to conflate two reasons for doing so. The first, and probably original, reason is that the matter lies outside the competence of Jesus, at any rate in the days of his flesh (cf. 13^{32} and Acts 1^{7}), but the last eleven words of the verse (three only in the Greek, and perhaps a later addition) suggest a different reason: places in the kingdom are awarded in accordance with the age-old decree of God who settles all things righteously and is not to be moved, like some fickle oriental despot, by individual pleas for special treatment.

A different answer is contained in vv. 38b–39, which state – or assume – (i) that priority in the kingdom is related to a martyr's death; (ii) that Jesus asked the two disciples in highly symbolic terms if they were prepared to undergo a fate like his own; (iii) that they understood him (rather surprisingly in view of such passages as 9^{32}) and expressed their willingness; (iv) that Jesus prophesied that martyrdom would in fact be their lot. The combination of (i) and (iv) should lead logically to the granting of the disciples' request, but in v. 40 this conclusion appears to be nullified. If, as many scholars accordingly believe, these verses are a secondary (though pre-Marcan) element in the story, the question why they were inserted cannot now be answered with any assurance – see notes for some possible suggestions.

In any case St Mark was no doubt untouched by these difficulties; he will have seen the incident as a sequel to vv. 33–34 – one more attempt

* So e.g. Lightfoot and Dibelius (who further suggests that the mention of particular names is a later modification of the original – cf. *M. J.*, p. 138). If this suggestion is accepted 'the failure of the sons of Zebedee is seen in an even more conspicuous light' (*H. & I.*, p. 120).

on the part of Jesus to open the blind eyes of the disciples to the meaning of his life and suffering. There is no short cut to God's favour (v. 40); for disciples, as for the master, the path to glory is through suffering (Luke 24^{26}, Acts 14^{22})* – an aspect of Jesus' teaching of great significance to the little martyr church for which the Gospel appears to have been written.

41–45

The general character of the sayings collected here makes them an appropriate enough appendix to vv. 35–40, though strictly speaking they refer to priority in the Christian community on earth, and not to pre-eminence in the future kingdom of God. The fact that St Luke has an alternative version of 42b–45a in a completely different context (Luke $22^{24\text{ff.}}$), that St Matthew gives a doublet of v. 43 at 23^{11}, and that St Mark has already used a shortened version of vv. 43–44 to form the basis of a scene very similar to this (9^{33-37} – see notes there) suggests that the sayings circulated without context and the Evangelists introduced them, in whole or part, wherever they seemed appropriate. The demand they contain for humility and self-giving is clinched in the last verse by a reference to Jesus' own life (v. 45a) and in particular to his death (v. 45b), so the passage ends, as it began, as a commentary on the meaning of Jesus' approaching Passion. Whether the reference to the Passion is original here or is the work of the Evangelist is a question which has been almost endlessly discussed and cannot be settled in the space available here. The most that can be done is to list some of the chief considerations which have been advanced for and against the originality of v. 45b. Against – and probably the majority of scholars are against – are:

(i) The Lucan version of the sayings, which appears to be derived from sources independent of Mark, has no reference to the Passion, ending instead with the words: 'But I am in the midst of you as a servant.' These words, in their complete simplicity and congruity with the thought of the preceding verses, seem more likely to be original.

* Notice that though in their context in the story the expressions 'drinking the cup' and 'undergoing the baptism' undoubtedly referred to the *martyrdom* of Jesus and the two disciples, their symbolic character made it possible to interpret them of any suffering for the faith – cf. e.g. Ps. $75^{8\text{ff.}}$, Isa. 51^{17}, Jer. 49^{12}, Pss. 42^{7}, 69^{2-15}, 124^{4-5}, and Isa. 43^{2}.

(ii) The Marcan version of the saying is out of harmony with its context. The transition from the idea of service to that of giving one's life as a ransom is really a change from one class of ideas to another.*

(iii) 'The reference to redemption occurs here only, in the Marcan record of the ministry' (*H. & I.*, p. 120, n. 3). Though Jesus may have included his death in his work of service and love for men, there is little or no evidence elsewhere in the Gospels that he thought of it in terms of sacrifice or ransom.

(iv) The general idea behind the saying is so common in early Christian writing, especially Paul's Epistles (cf. e.g. Gal. 3^{13}, Rom. 3^{24}, 1 Cor. 7^{23}), that Pauline influence might well account for its presence here. On the other side it is urged:

(i) That the link between service and vicarious suffering would be a natural one for Jesus to make if he was influenced by the conception of the servant in deutero-Isaiah, whose 'service' consisted precisely in such vicarious suffering. (Cf. the *many* of Isa. 53^{11-12} with *for many* here.)

(ii) The *ransom* image would be a natural one for anyone familiar with the Old Testament; and such passages as 4 *Macc.* 6^{29}, 17^{22}, and 2 Macc. $7^{37\text{ff.}}$ show that the idea of the martyr deaths of the righteous being accepted as compensation for the sins of the people was by no means unfamiliar at the time.

(iii) The once-popular hypothesis that St Mark was greatly influenced by Paul is now discredited, and in fact no *precise* verbal parallel to this passage can be found in Paul. 'His theology as revealed in 1 Cor. 6^{20}, 7^{23}, Gal. 1^{4}, 2^{20}, 3^{13}, 4^{5}, Rom. $3^{24\text{ff.}}$, etc., is in line with Mark 10^{45}, but reveals its distinctiveness for itself' (V. T.).

Different people will obviously evaluate these considerations differently, but since a good deal clearly turns on the possible influence upon Jesus of the suffering servant conception, it may be well to warn readers that not everything written on this subject in recent years should be accepted uncritically; a judicious examination will be found in M. D. Hooker, *Jesus and the Servant*, and see also J. Knox, *The Death of Christ.*

46–52

The healing story which follows is the last in the Gospel and has

* The idea that, by dying, Jesus was doing men the 'service' of rescuing them from otherwise unavoidable damnation presupposes a later, sophisticated atonement theology otherwise quite unattested in the Gospels.

been variously evaluated. On the one hand, some commentators, impressed by the vivid detail it contains, see it as 'an account which goes back, and owes its details, to the reminiscences of an eyewitness' (B.), and attribute its position here to the remembered connexion of the incident with Jericho. On the other hand, placed where it now is, it contributes to the general progress of the Gospel in a way which hardly seems accidental, and the special angle from which it is told suggests that it had long been used in the Church (and is being used by St Mark) as a vehicle for instruction on certain aspects of Christian discipleship. As for its position, the mention of Jericho shows that Jesus and his party are now only fifteen miles from their goal, and in fact the following episode (11^{1-10}) finds them on the outskirts of Jerusalem and opens a quite new section of the Gospel. Our story, therefore, has the dual role of concluding the present section of the Gospel (8^{27}–10^{52}) and making the transition to the next; and its character corresponds to this.

It contains the first public and unrebuked recognition of Jesus as Messiah. Hitherto only the demons and the disciples had recognized him as such, and they had been forbidden to speak of it; but now the secret seems to have leaked out, and a blind beggar hails Jesus as *Son of David.* So far from rebuking this acknowledgement of his Messiahship, Jesus actually endorses it by the performance of a miracle, and the way is prepared for the people to take up the cry in the next episode: 'Hosanna – blessed be the kingdom of our father David, that is coming' (see 11^{8-10}). On the other hand, if we look back, it can hardly be accidental that the very important section 8^{27}–10^{45}, which is concerned with Jesus' endeavour to open the eyes of his disciples to the fact and meaning of his Messiahship, is rounded off, as it was introduced (see on $8^{22\text{ff.}}$), by a story of Jesus opening a blind man's eyes. We are thereby reminded of the point of view from which the preceding section is to be understood, and are also perhaps led to contrast Bartimaeus with the disciples, who 'though they see, are blind' (cf. John 9^{35-41}). It may be too that Jesus' treatment of the blind man (v. 49) is seen as a repudiation of the attitude of his followers (v. 48), and a further object-lesson in the ideal of service he has been inculcating unsuccessfully throughout 8^{27}–10^{45} (cf. for example 9^{38} and 10^{13}).

When we come to the content of the story, we are struck by the fact – exceptional in a story of this kind – that a great deal of the interest centres not on Jesus but on the attitude and action of the blind man. The miracle is of course due to the compassion and effortless power of Jesus, which are thereby shown to be messianic and to fulfil Old Testament expectation (cf. Isa. 42^{18} and 61^{1} (LXX)), but the fact that so much attention is directed towards the blind man and his behaviour suggests that when the story was used in the early Church it was in order to hold him up as a model and encouragement to other believers and would-be believers. Aware of his blindness and consequent helplessness (and the preceding section has shown that we are all blind till Jesus opens our eyes – though the apostles, in contrast to Bartimaeus, remain obstinately unaware of their plight), when Jesus draws near he realizes that his only hope has come, and he calls on Jesus for help. His faith persists, despite all discouragement, till Jesus, through his disciples, calls him. That call and his immediate, eager response to it mean that he is 'saved' from his helpless plight, and as a result he must begin at once to 'follow' Jesus in 'the way' of Christian discipleship – a way, incidentally, which we shall see leads straight to danger and suffering at Jerusalem. That 'faith', 'save', 'follow', 'way' (cf. Acts 9^{2}, $19^{9,\,23}$, etc. for 'the way' = the Christian religion) are all used here with their full religious meanings in mind seems clear, despite the denials of some commentators.

❦

32
According to an emendation proposed by C. H. Turner, St Mark wrote: *he* (i.e. Jesus) *was amazed* – i.e. deeply shaken by the prospect of what he knew awaited him at Jerusalem.

37
The positions on either side of a ruler or host were the most honourable.

in your glory: St Matthew, probably rightly, takes this to refer to the future messianic kingdom (Matt. 20^{21}). If so, and the story is authentic, it perhaps points to a time when the disciples were expecting the imminent arrival of the kingdom. But the request could envisage equally thrones of judgement (cf. Matt. 19^{28}, Luke 22^{30}) or the glories of the messianic feast (14^{25}) and we cannot rule out the possibility that the disciples expected Jesus on his arrival at Jerusalem to inaugurate a temporary earthly paradise (see p. 44) and that the reference is to this.

38–39
As we have seen, there are a number of Old Testament passages which might have made the equation *cup* and *baptism* = *suffering* intelligible, and there is a second-century papyrus in which 'baptized' is used to mean 'overwhelmed with disasters'. However, the Old Testament contains no really exact parallels, and the imagery here seems more likely to have originated with early Christians reflecting on Christ's life and death as a whole in the light of such sayings as 14^{36} and Luke 12^{50}. In St Matthew's parallel version, 20^{23}, the reference to *baptism* is missing, and St Mark may have added it to his source to make the saying correspond more closely with the sacramental practice of the Church. The idea would be that, in the conditions of St Mark's day, to accept baptism and become a partaker of the eucharistic cup is to take a step which might well lead to martyrdom; let would-be converts count the cost!

As for the reason for the insertion of these verses into the original story, the usual assumption is that they were added at a time when the martyr deaths of the two apostles were giving rise to reflection in the Church. 'They were known to have been ambitious for high honour. Their wish is now fulfilled, but quite differently from the way they had intended . . . and the actual terms of their request have been recast in such a way as to correspond with this fulfilment [i.e. they now ask only for pre-eminence *in the next world*]. The narrator, by making Jesus say *you do not know what you are asking*, means us to understand the apostles' request as an unconscious prophecy of their own death, but Jesus interpreted to them how it would be fulfilled' (J. Weiss). This is a perfectly possible explanation, though it has to reckon with the difficulty that Christian tradition, while reporting the martyr death of James (Acts 12^{2}), ascribes to John a ripe old age and peaceful death at Ephesus. However, this tradition is not unanimous and may be inaccurate. But the difficulty is avoided by the ingenious suggestion of Lohmeyer, who thinks that the verses were inserted in the course of controversies over the leadership of the early Church. In view of the way things had developed and of such a tradition as Matt. 16^{18}, it seemed impossible that James and John were meant to be the leaders. This passage was seen as evidence that this was in accordance with the will of Jesus. But though he had not been able to offer these two primacy in the Church, he had prophesied for them the honour of a martyr death very like his own. This interpretation is very much strengthened if we follow the MSS. which punctuate the end of v. 40 differently (*allois* instead of *all'ois*), so that it means: *it has been prepared for others.*

45
The Greek is a little stronger than R.S.V. suggests. The Son of man *himself* . . . (who is by nature the greatest in the kingdom and therefore *the* example of what greatness in the kingdom implies).

a ransom: The Greek word has a variety of meanings in the Greek Old Testament, among the most important: a monetary compensation paid for a crime (e.g. Num. 35^{31-2}), or for a life that would otherwise be forfeit (e.g. Exod. 21^{30}), the money paid for the release of a captive or slave (e.g. Lev. 25^{51-2}, Isa. 45^{13}), or the equivalent accepted instead of certain sacrifices (e.g. Num. 18^{15}). The kindred verb and verbal noun (*redeem, redemption*) are used of God 'delivering' his people without any special emphasis on the idea of *ransom* in the narrow sense. In view of all that, it is probably wrong to press the word here as meaning more than 'means of deliverance' or 'redemption'.

for: The Greek word (*anti*) normally means 'instead of', 'in place of', and some commentators find that meaning here – e.g. according to V. T. the word 'suggests that in the act of deliverance "the many" not only benefit, but receive what they cannot effect'. But there are passages where the word means no more than 'on behalf of' and it is doubtful how far we should press the more exact meaning.

many: A semitic use of the word which does not necessarily envisage the exclusion of some.

46
Jericho: To the south of the ancient Israelite Jericho and to the west of the modern Rîhâ; rebuilt and adorned by Herod the Great and Archelaus, it was later the seat of a Roman garrison. (See map.)

The awkward double reference to the town probably means that the story was already associated with Jesus' departure from it when it reached St Mark, and he therefore had to introduce it with a formula getting Jesus *into* the town. How far back the connexion of the story with the town may go is a question tied up with that of the blind man's name. Bartimaeus *means* 'son of Timaeus', but the unusual way these words are introduced in the original leads commentators to regard them as a later gloss. As for the name itself, we have seen that, owing to the way the tradition was preserved, proper names stood little chance of being preserved (Introduction, p. 28), and there is a lot to be said for the view that this story referred originally to a nameless blind man who later came to be identified with Bartimaeus of Jericho, a figure well known in the early Church as one who had *followed Jesus on the way*. This is still more likely if we follow the MSS. which have '*the* blind beggar'.

47
Jesus, Son of David: In the Greek: 'son of David, Jesus'. *Son of David* is here simply a messianic title, probably without specific reference to Jesus' family descent. Although there were objections to it as a comprehensive term to describe Jesus' person (see on 12^{35}ff.), this verse is not the only evidence that the early Church valued it as a useful, and indeed vital, title, if properly understood.

50
A detail symbolizing the eager alacrity with which the call of Jesus should always be answered. In fact an oriental beggar would already have had his cloak off, spread on the ground to receive alms; some scribes who realized this altered the text to 'put on his cloak'.

52
made you well: The Greek word (*sōzein*) can refer both to healing and to 'salvation'.

on the way: Greek can = both 'along the road' and 'in the way' (of discipleship).

Mark 11-12

The Ministry in Jerusalem

With Jesus' arrival in Jerusalem the final period of his life and ministry begins. As told by Mark, the narrative of this period falls into two distinct sections:

14^{1}–16^{8}: The Passion narrative and its sequel; and

11–13: A ministry in Jerusalem and its neighbourhood which consists mainly of teaching, much of it public, and forms a prelude to the Passion narrative proper.

In fact most of the material which has been combined to make up this 'ministry' seems to have existed originally in the form of isolated units of tradition containing no indications of time or place.* So this ministry in its present form is an artificial construction by the Evangelist, and equally artificial is the distribution of it over three days (see $11^{1, 12, 19f.}$). Not only does this arrangement heavily overload the third day, but we have good reason for believing that now, if not before, Jesus spent an extended period in and near Jerusalem.†

* With regard to the sections of teaching contained in this 'ministry' Lightfoot writes (*H. & I.*, p. 81): 'Some of the teaching recorded in the last week is almost as general in character as the early Galilean teaching, and has no reference to the crisis immediately pending; some of it might have been given in early days in Capernaum as suitably as at this moment in Jerusalem.' Elsewhere Lightfoot remarks that Chapters 12 and 13 break the connexion between Chapters 11 and 14–16 and suggests that at an earlier stage in the tradition the entry into Jerusalem and the cleansing of the temple may have been vitally connected and have formed the immediate introduction to the Passion narrative. He points out that according to St Mark it is the cleansing which causes the authorities to plan Jesus' death (11^{18}) and the opening words of the Passion narrative only repeat their decision (14^{1}) (see *G. M. M.*, p. 61). If this were so, the entry into Jerusalem (11^{1-11}) would gain an even greater solemnity and significance.

† Wellhausen writes (p. 94): 'Mark's attempt to compress the sojourn [at Jerusalem] into a single week is not successful; the material resists the six-day scheme – itself somewhat precariously maintained – into which the attempt is made to force it. The associations and the connexions which, as appears from time to time, Jesus has in Jerusalem are not to be explained on the basis of earlier visits, for at that time he could not have appeared as the great prophet from Galilee; in Bethany he seems to have got together the kernel of the later Jerusalem community. And when in 14^{49} he says : "*Day after day* I was with you in the temple teaching", a teaching ministry of two days is

Some of the implications of all this will be considered below; meanwhile, if we ask the reason for St Mark's artificial chronological arrangement, the answer perhaps lies in the fact that the early Church was already celebrating an annual 'Holy Week', and St Mark wanted his account of the final period of the Lord's life (Chapters 11–16) to conform to the pattern of it. For unusually exact notes of time, see $11^{11, 20, 27}$, $14^{1, 12}$, 15^{1}, and also on 15^{25} and ^{33}.*

The first day of the scheme is occupied with:

11^{1-11} THE ENTRY INTO JERUSALEM

11 *And when they drew near to Jerusalem, to Beth'phage and Bethany, at*
the Mount of Olives, he sent two of his disciples, 2*and said to them, 'Go into*
the village opposite you, and immediately as you enter it you will find a colt
tied, on which no one has ever sat; untie it and bring it. 3*If any one says to*
you, "Why are you doing this?" say, "The Lord has need of it and will send
it back here immediately."' 4*And they went away, and found a colt tied at the*
door out in the open street; and they untied it. 5*And those who stood there*
said to them, 'What are you doing, untying the colt?' 6*And they told them*
what Jesus had said; and they let them go. 7*And they brought the colt to*
Jesus, and threw their garments on it; and he sat upon it. 8*And many spread*
their garments on the road, and others spread leafy branches which they had
cut from the fields. 9*And those who went before and those who followed cried*
out, 'Hosanna! Blessed be he who comes in the name of the Lord! 10*Blessed*
be the kingdom of our father David that is coming! Hosanna in the highest!'

* Lightfoot, on the other hand (*H. & I.*, p. 100 and n. 5), doubted whether St Mark intended any significance to be attached to the fact that his various notes of time in this part of the Gospel, do, if coordinated, amount to one week. Perhaps St Mark was not conscious of the fact, and it is later piety which has extracted a 'Holy Week' from it.

On Chapters 11–13 as a whole see further below, p. 365 and n.

---

not enough to justify the expression "day after day".' We certainly cannot rule out earlier visits of Jesus to Jerusalem (cf. e.g. John $2^{23\text{ff.}}$ and see Introduction, p. 36), and Wellhausen's argument is perhaps weaker there than it is in his last point, where it seems very strong indeed.

11[1-11]

[11]*And he entered Jerusalem, and went into the temple; and when he had looked round at everything, as it was already late, he went out to Bethany with the twelve.*

In studying this story it is particularly important to do two things which the original readers will have done automatically; to have in mind certain Old Testament and later Jewish expectations, and *not* to have at the back of one's mind impressions derived from the accounts of the incident in the other Gospels.

1–10

As we have seen, the Gospel has for some time been working up to Jesus' arrival at Jerusalem, and the original readers, for whom Jerusalem was both the holy city of God and the city which slew Jesus, are bound to have looked forward with some excitement to the account of his eventual entry into it. They will have been fully familiar with Zech. 9[9] and 14[4] and with the popular Jewish belief, based on the latter passage, that the Mount of Olives would be associated with the coming of the Messiah (cf. e.g. Josephus, *Jewish War*, II, 13, 5 and *Antiquities*, XX, 8, 6). Accordingly, the mention of the Mount of Olives in v. 1 and of *a colt . . . on which no one has ever sat* in v. 2 (cf. Zech. 9[9] 'a new (i.e. unused) colt'*) will already have told them in principle what they wanted to know. Jesus' entry into Jerusalem was the entry of the Messiah, in full conformity with Old Testament prophecy and Jewish expectation. The miraculous way – for so they will have interpreted it – in which the necessary ass's colt was waiting and Jesus knew of its whereabouts will have served only to enhance their sense of his supernatural power and mission.

But if this is the basic meaning of the story for St Mark, it will be noticed that he, in contrast to the other Evangelists, carefully avoids making the messianic character of the incident fully explicit. In his Gospel the sending for the colt is set forth without explanation, apparently as a plain narration of history; Zechariah is not quoted or referred to (contrast Matt. 21[5] and John 12[15]); the ovation comes not from a multitude, but simply from the little band with Jesus, and the words in which it finds expression befit the prophet of the coming

* That is, in the Greek version, the one with which they will have been familiar.

kingdom rather than the person of the king. (Mark 11^{9-10} should be carefully compared and contrasted with Matt. 21^{9}, Luke 19^{37-38}, and John 12^{12-13}.* Obviously St Mark's account is still dominated by his doctrine of the secret Messiahship (cf. the way the crowd in $10^{46ff.}$ took no notice of Bartimaeus' cry), but, as Lightfoot points out, this doctrine 'is here strained to breaking point', for it is difficult to see why Jesus sent for the colt and entered the city on it unless he intended to make clear the fact of his Messiahship. Pilgrims normally entered Jerusalem on foot, so, as the story stands, the fact that Jesus deliberately procured and rode an ass makes it impossible to think of him as simply a passive figure in a demonstration which was none of his doing. It is sometimes suggested that he deliberately chose this mode of self-revelation because it would be significant only to those who 'had eyes to see', and to them it would signify the 'humble' Messiah of Zechariah's prophecy, as opposed to the violent warrior-Messiah of so much contemporary expectation. In this connexion commentators sometimes quote Rabbi Joshua ben Levi (*c.* A.D. 250), who is reported as saying that if Israel was worthy, the Son of man would come 'on the clouds of heaven', but if it was not worthy, he would come 'lowly and riding upon an ass'. Against this, however, is the fact that if Jesus deliberately secured a 'new' ass's colt and rode on it from Olivet to Jerusalem amid the plaudits of his followers, he could hardly hope to hide his messianic claims from anyone who knew of the incident, and he could hardly expect them to be interpreted peaceably. It is in any case doubtful whether the Zechariah background would have been seen at the time as implying the peaceable non-violent messianic activity which modern commentators have in mind; Rabbi Joshua ben Levi will hardly have been thinking in terms of a suffering Messiah.

The question therefore arises why such a messianic demonstration seems to have produced no results, and in particular to have brought no reprisals from the authorities. A full discussion of this much-debated problem is out of the question here, but a few points relevant to a solution may be made.

* See notes below, and cf. Lightfoot's description of the acclamation in Mark as '*all but* messianic' and the words of V. T. (p. 452): 'they imply that the kingdom is near, but stop short at the use of the title "Son of David". Their words . . . are not full-throated messianic homage.'

First, various legendary traits in the story of the finding of the colt may make us wonder whether the whole incident occurred exactly as St Mark describes it, and in particular whether an ass's colt played precisely the part he assigns to it.

On the other hand, the actions and shouts of those accompanying Jesus create an impression of authenticity, because, although they conform in a general way to Zech. 9^{9a}, they include details which are not necessary, or even particularly appropriate, and so are unlikely to be the invention of the early Church.

F. C. Burkitt, who subjected these features to a careful examination (*J. T. S.*, XVII, p. 139ff.), advanced an interesting hypothesis. As the story stands, it is closely associated with the Feast of the Passover which follows five days later; but this association rests entirely on the Marcan chronological scheme which we have seen to be artificial. Accordingly, the association can be discounted, and once that is done, Burkitt found good reason for associating the incident with the Feast of Dedication, which commemorated the recleansing of the temple by Judas Maccabaeus in 165 B.C. The ceremonies at this feast were closely modelled on those of the Feast of Tabernacles, and so included the carrying of green branches by the people. The *Hallel* (Pss. 113–118) was recited, at certain points in the service the branches were waved, and then, after the appropriate sacrifice, there was a procession during which the branches were carried and the *Hosanna* from Ps. 118 was intoned; in fact the branches themselves were actually called 'Hosannas'. We have evidence that they were difficult to buy in the city itself, and if we may assume that pilgrims were in the habit of gathering them in the country as they got near the city, we seem to have a scene so like that in Mark that the resemblances can hardly be accidental.* We should then assume that as Jesus and his company approached Jerusalem on their way to the Feast of Dedication, the sight of the city and the strong emotions aroused by Jesus' announcement of the nearness of the kingdom combined to produce a spontaneous outburst of enthusiasm which naturally clothed itself in the actions and words appropriate to the coming feast. The disciples may well have expected something decisive to happen when Jesus got into

* They are even more striking if St Mark assumed what St John explicitly states (John 12^{13}): that the people carried and waved branches, as well as strewing them in the way.

the city, but their numbers were small and their words, which were simply quotations from the current liturgy, did not explicitly claim Messiahship for their Master.

Such an occurrence would not call for any action on the part of the authorities, and if it seems altogether too insignificant to account for St Mark's narrative, we may recall Lightfoot's comment (*H. & I.*, pp. 82–3): 'It must have become ever harder for the little churches to believe that this coming, so much fraught with destiny, could have passed almost unnoticed at the time; that, in Professor Burkitt's words, to contemporary observers it may not have seemed more than a ripple on the surface. Was this the day of that coming of which the prophet had asked who could endure it, and who should stand at its appearing (Mal. 3^2)?'

11

The last verse, which stands rather apart from the rest of the incident, seems to have been composed by St Mark in the interests of his time-scheme. Experts in oriental religion say that a procession such as that described in vv. 1–10 could only have ended with a ceremonial approach to the temple, and the cleansing would then have followed immediately. As it is, this visit to the temple seems entirely pointless, for the idea of Jesus 'seeing the sights' like some provincial tourist is entirely at variance with the spirit of the Gospels. No doubt in the tradition the cleansing followed at once, but if St Mark wished, in accordance with a method he uses elsewhere (see on $3^{19b\text{ff.}}$), to put the cleansing between the two parts of the withered fig tree story, he was bound to make some break, however slight, between the procession and the cleansing.

1

The geographical details make an impression of awkwardness, especially as *Bethphage* and *Bethany* are given in the reverse order to that in which travellers from Jericho would reach them. (See map and cf. Lake in *Beginnings of Christianity*, v, pp. 15–16 and pp. 474ff., for a full account of the places mentioned.) There is a good deal of variation in the MSS., and it is possible that either *Bethphage* or *Bethany* is a later insertion; however, the weight of the MS. evidence is against that being the case, and we must therefore assume that St Mark did not know the relative positions of the two villages on the Jericho road; for the possible bearing of that on the question of authorship see Introduction, p.40.

2–7
These verses are, as Lightfoot says, 'very difficult'. They remind us in a general way of 14^{12-16}, and there are parallels, some of them quite close, in the folklore of many lands. Undoubtedly St Mark understood the story as a miraculous confirmation of Jesus' powers and claims, and Wellhausen rightly protests against attempted rationalizations, e.g. that Jesus had made a previous arrangement with the owner of the colt who was already a disciple. As Klostermann remarks, it would be difficult to go into any village in the Middle East *without* finding a tethered colt; there would of course be no means of telling whether it had been ridden before, and this detail is almost universally agreed to be an embellishment designed to bring the story into closer conformity with Zech. 9^9. The idea seems to be the one, common in antiquity, that anything intended for sacred or ceremonial use should not have been used before for secular purposes. Cf. Num. 19^2, Deut. 21^3, 1 Kings 6^7, Homer, *Iliad*, VI, 94, Horace, *Epod.*, 9^{22}, etc.

3
the Lord: i.e. Jesus. The fact that the word is not used as a title for him elsewhere in Mark (or Matthew) only points to the late and exceptional character of the story; it does not justify taking the word here = 'God' or as = 'the owner of the ass'.*

The last seven words correctly translate the best-attested text. However, there is MS. authority for making the words part of Jesus' prophecy and not of the disciples' message: 'and at once he [the objector] will send it here'. That is what St Matthew wrote, and despite the balance of the present MS. evidence, it is hard to believe it was not what St Mark wrote too.

4–7
The details are repeated almost verbatim, after the fashion of folklore, because the fact that things fell out exactly as prophesied is seen as further evidence of the supernatural character of the prophecy.

4
out in the open street: Probably the correct reading of the original, which *could*, however, also mean 'at the crossroads'. If we read 'vine'

* The last is the interpretation of V.T., who suggests that the man was with Jesus and had agreed beforehand what form the message should take; but negotiations of that kind are wholly foreign to the character of such a story.

(*ampĕlou*) for 'open street' (*amphŏdou*) we get the fulfilment of Gen. 49[11] with which certain early Christian writers were familiar. But no doubt this was a refinement read into the passage after Mark's time.

8

The spreading of garments and fragrant herbs before great personages as a sign of homage is a widely attested custom, cf. e.g. 2 Kings 9[13]. For the whole scene cf. 1 Macc. 13[51].

leafy branches: Probably the correct translation here, though the Greek word normally means a litter of straw, rushes, or leaves. For 'palm branches' the only authority is John 12[13].

9–10

The words of the acclamation are not altogether easy to interpret.

The Hebrew word *Hosanna* is properly a cry for help addressed to God or the king (cf. 2 Sam. 14[4], 2 Kings 6[26]) meaning 'save now!' or 'May God save'. It will be seen, therefore, that the words in v. 9 correspond pretty closely with Ps. 118[25-26a] (where *Hosanna* is the opening word in the original). As it stands in the Psalm, v. 26a should be translated 'Blessed in the name of the Lord be he that cometh', and the words were simply a greeting to a pilgrim arriving at the temple or to anyone coming on any other religious errand. They need not, therefore, imply that Jesus was being greeted *as Messiah*, and neither need the words of v. 10; for though v. 10 gives to the word *coming* an eschatological reference, the word refers to the kingdom rather than the king; and the strange expression *Hosanna in the highest* may be interpreted in the light of Ps. 148[1] to mean: 'May God save from heaven' i.e. by some transcendent action. (It was generally believed that God himself would bring the kingdom.)

On the other hand St Mark certainly thought – and intended his readers to think – that on the lips of the disciples, the words did have messianic significance. He no doubt interpreted the words of the Psalm as meaning: 'He that cometh in the name of the Lord' i.e. the Messiah who comes in God's name, and it is possible that 'he that cometh' was already a veiled title for the expected Messiah (so Bousset; cf. Matt. 11[3], Luke 7[19], and ? Matt. 3[11]). Probably too St Mark no longer thought of *Hosanna* as a Hebrew word with a literal meaning, but simply as a term of greeting – '*Hail!*' *Hosanna in the highest* would then have meant for him 'Praise in High Heaven'. The words could not have meant that in Hebrew, so we seem once again to find ourselves pointed to a non-Palestinian author.

kingdom of our father David: A strange expression not really paralleled elsewhere. The kingdom is usually 'of God,' and 'father' normally reserved for one of the patriarchs. But this is probably not sufficient ground for doubting the authenticity of the verse, though it is true that St Matthew and St Luke both omit it.

11 12–25(26) THE FIG TREE AND THE TEMPLE

12 *On the following day, when they came from Bethany, he was hungry.*
13 *And seeing in the distance a fig tree in leaf, he went to see if he could find*
anything on it. When he came to it, he found nothing but leaves, for it was
not the season for figs. 14 *And he said to it, 'May no one ever eat fruit from*
you again.' And his disciples heard it.

15 *And they came to Jerusalem. And he entered the temple and began to*
drive out those who sold and those who bought in the temple, and he over-
turned the tables of the money-changers and the seats of those who sold
pigeons; 16 *and he would not allow any one to carry anything through the*
temple. 17 *And he taught, and said to them, 'Is it not written, "My house*
shall be called a house of prayer for all the nations"? But you have made it a
den of robbers.' 18 *And the chief priests and the scribes heard it and sought a*
way to destroy him; for they feared him, because all the multitude was
astonished at his teaching. 19 *And when evening came they*[a] *went out of the*
city.

20 *As they passed by in the morning, they saw the fig tree withered away to*
its roots. 21 *And Peter remembered and said to him, 'Master,*[b] *look! The fig*
tree which you cursed has withered.' 22 *And Jesus answered them, 'Have faith*
in God. 23 *Truly, I say to you, whoever says to this mountain, "Be taken up*
and cast into the sea," and does not doubt in his heart, but believes that what
he says will come to pass, it will be done for him. 24 *Therefore I tell you,*
whatever you ask in prayer, believe that you receive it, and you will. 25 *And*
whenever you stand praying, forgive, if you have anything against any one;
so that your Father also who is in heaven may forgive you your trespasses.'[c]

a Other ancient authorities read *he*
b Or *Rabbi*
c Other ancient authorities add verse 26, *But if you do not forgive, neither will your Father who is in heaven forgive your trespasses*

This complex consists of the story of the cleansing of the temple (vv. 15–19) sandwiched between the two parts of the story of the cursing of the fig tree (vv. 12–14 and 20–25). For St Mark's fondness for this type of arrangement see on 3^{19b}, 5^{21-43} and for his reasons for employing it here see p. 299.

As already hinted, both parts of the fig tree story seem to be an insertion into this early stage of the Jerusalem narrative, and if they are removed, along with the matter which goes with them, the connexion of material is improved and the progress of events seems more natural – the ovation (vv. 1–10), cleansing (vv. 15–19), and challenge from the authorities (vv. 27b–33) follow in rapid succession on Jesus' approach to Jerusalem. The point may be clarified by the following table (taken in the main from Bundy, p. 424):

PRIMITIVE SEQUENCE	LATER INSERTIONS
The Ovation 1–10	
	11
	12–14 Fig tree (i)
The Cleansing 15–17	
	18–19 Editorial, see below
	20–27a Fig tree (ii)
The Challenge 27b–33	

That being so, it will be more convenient for purposes of exposition to discuss both parts of the fig tree incident before dealing with the cleansing of the temple.

12–14 and 20–25

This story is one of the most difficult in the Gospels, for it 'approximates more closely than any other episode in Mark to the type of "unreasonable" miracle characteristic of the non-canonical Gospel literature' (R.: see M. R. James, *The Apocryphal New Testament*, pp. 49ff., for examples of the type of miracle referred to).

St Mark appears to have seen two meanings in it:

(i) He apparently understood it as an example of faith and prayer. As the story now stands, this meaning emerges clearly enough, but the concluding sayings (22–25) by which it is suggested were first appended to the incident by St Mark himself; and, taken by itself, the incident hardly furnishes a basis for the teaching found in these verses.

Strictly speaking, the cursing of the tree was neither an act of faith nor a prayer, and it hardly seems to exemplify the forgiving spirit demanded in v. 25.

(ii) The manner and place of its insertion strongly suggest that the story was intended to make a didactic point, the fate of the fig tree symbolizing the fate that awaited Jerusalem and the Jewish people and religion. Like the fig tree with its leaves, the Jewish people made a fine show with their numerous ceremonies and outward observances, but when the Messiah came looking for the fruit of righteousness he found none, and the result was condemnation and destruction for Judaism, as it was for the tree, Such an interpretation is strongly suggested by the parable in Luke 13^{6-9}, where the fig tree clearly represents the house of Israel, and also by such Old Testament passages as Jer. 8^{13}, Joel 1^{7}, Ezek. 17^{24}, Micah 7^{1-6}, and Hos. $9^{10, 16f.}$ Indeed in the light of these Old Testament passages, the action of Jesus here may well have been seen as a fulfilment of the scriptures.

However, none of these considerations removes the fundamental objection to the historicity of the story, which is that the action ascribed to Jesus seems completely out of character: 'It is irrational and revolting . . . and lacks any sort of moral motive or justification' (Bundy). The only way to preserve some element of historicity in the story would be to suppose that the original cursing was an act of prophetic symbolism of the type known to us from the Old Testament (cf. e.g. 2 Chron. 18^{10}, Jer. 27^{2} and $28^{10ff.}$). The Gentile world, being unfamiliar with such prophetic acts, might then have interpreted it simply as a nature miracle designed to confirm Jesus' supernatural power and status.

It seems more probable, however, either that the story was originally a parable which in the process of transmission was transformed into an actual deed of Jesus, or that some conspicuous withered tree on the road between Bethany and Jerusalem gave rise to the legend that Jesus had cursed and withered it. J. Weiss suggests that such a legend would have been especially likely to arise as events moved towards the destruction of Jerusalem in A.D. 70. The Christians may have seen the destruction of the Holy City as symbolizing a withering away of Judaism which was bound to follow on its refusal to accept Jesus, as inevitably as the destruction of the fig tree followed on its failure to satisfy his demand.

22–25

The appended instruction on prayer, and on the need for faith and the forgiving spirit in connexion with it, is made up of sayings which circulated independently in the early Church in various slightly different forms (cf. v. 23, itself based on a proverbial saying, with Matt. 21^{21} and 17^{20}, Luke 17^{6}, and 1 Cor. 13^{2}). As often in Mark (cf. e.g. $9^{42ff.}$) the connexions are artificial and mainly verbal, 'faith' (22), 'has faith' (23), 'have faith' and 'prayer' (24), 'praying' (25).

As far as the content is concerned, it is important to recognize, even in 24–25, the bold, figurative hyperbole which so often characterizes the teaching of Jesus (cf. on 10^{25}). In v. 23 he simply wishes to say, in the strongest manner possible, that by faith men can do what seems absurd or impossible; and in v. 24, although, as Montefiore says, 'a Jew of the first century must necessarily have thought about petitionary prayer very differently from ourselves' (p. 270), we can hardly suppose Jesus to have meant literally that prayers are answered simply because we believe that we have received our request, or that we can expect to receive literally 'whatever' we ask, however selfish or contrary to God's will. Perhaps v. 25 was added to guard against such a notion, but it in turn should be taken, not as laying down legalistic conditions for the efficacy of prayer, but as the other side of Jesus' teaching on the mercy and love of God; the loving-kindness of God demands that we should act likewise. R.S.V. rightly omits v. 26; it is found in a number of MSS. but is no doubt an insertion from Matt. 6^{15}.

15–17

As we have already seen, St Mark's understanding of the temple cleansing emerges in part from the way he has sandwiched it between the two parts of the fig tree story. The temple and its worship stand for Jewish life and religion; the Messiah comes to it and when he finds that the outward foliage of ceremony hides no fruit of righteousness, his only possible reaction is one of judgement and cleansing. Added solemnity attaches to the visit because it is seen as the fulfilment of Mal. 3^{1}, Zech. 14^{21}, Hos. 9^{15}, passages which all referred to God's *final* intervention in history. Jesus' action is therefore seen as that of the messianic king on his great final visit to his Father's house and people, and, as such, it embodies God's *ultimate* judgement upon the life and religion of Israel.*

The story corresponds very closely to the Old Testament prophecies, and some critics have traced its whole origin to them. Certainly it is not without its difficulties. How could one person have overcome the resistance to which this action would obviously have given rise?† Or, if we suppose that Jesus was assisted by his followers, why did the temple police or the Roman garrison do nothing to preserve the peace (contrast Acts $4^{1ff.}$), and why was the matter not raised at Jesus' trial? And how did Jesus gather an audience (v. 17) which included those responsible for the desecration of the temple?

Perhaps the most we can say is that while some definite historical incident may well underlie the story, St Mark's account is too brief and imprecise to enable us to be sure what it was, or to tell exactly what was in the mind of Jesus. It is often assumed that his anger was aroused by the greed and dishonesty of the dealers and the way they were fleecing the poor (in that case, cf. *robbers*, v. 17). But St Mark, who makes no mention of anger, says that the buyers were driven out as well as the vendors, and in any case the careful researches of I. Abrahams suggest that trading in the temple was strictly controlled and on the whole was conducted fairly and in the interests of the pilgrims (see notes).

There is still less justification in St Mark's account for the suggestion that Jesus' action expressed the old prophetic antithesis between prayer and sacrifice and was a protest against the sacrificial system as such (see further below). In fact his refusal to allow the carriage of goods through the temple precincts (v. 16) suggests a concern for the 'holiness' of the temple ceremonial and its environment fully in line with contemporary ideas on the subject (see notes). It would appear that what Jesus objected to was the 'secularization' of a place which should have been kept holy for worship.

* Cf. also V.T., p. 464: 'From the time of Ezekiel (40–48) the renewal of the temple was expected in messianic times, *v.* 1 *Enoch* $90^{28f.}$, *Ps. Sol.* $17^{30f.}$, Rev. 21^{2-5}.'

† St Mark probably thought of Jesus as exercising the supernatural power which would naturally belong to 'the Lord' when 'he suddenly comes to his temple'. R., on the other hand, says: he 'dominated the crowd of traffickers by moral and not by physical means: they simply quailed before His holy indignation'. This does not seem very convincing.

Some mention must be made of the suggestion of Lightfoot, who saw the clue to the passage in v. 17, where St Mark, alone among the Evangelists, completes the quotation from Isaiah by including the words *for all the nations*. In the passage from which the quotation comes the prophet is expressing the fairly widespread Jewish belief that when the messianic age came, redemption would be found to extend to Gentiles as well as Jews, so that Gentiles would have their share in the Jewish house of prayer. Lightfoot points out that Jesus' action is entirely confined to the so-called 'court of the Gentiles', the only part of the sacred precincts to which non-Jews were admitted (see notes). No attempt is made to interfere with the Jewish ritual and worship which were carried on in the inner enclosures; Jesus' only concern is to safeguard the rights and privileges of the Gentiles and to remove all that prevented them from worshipping in the one part of the temple open to them. The Jews allowed trading in the court of the Gentiles, and by so doing they were robbing the Gentiles even of such privileges on the threshold of the temple as had been granted to them. Must it not, therefore, be the first act of the messianic king on his arrival at the temple to restore to the Gentiles their religious rights, for surely with his coming the prophecy would be fulfilled and Jewish worship would become the universal worship?* If this interpretation is correct, Jesus' action is to be understood as the fulfilment of a further aspect of the messianic role, that of vindicating the Gentiles and gathering them into the life and worship of the people of God.

For a full statement of this interpretation see *G. M. M.*, p. 60ff.; it is at any rate an interesting possibility, though the other Evangelists did not interpret St Mark along these lines, and it must be repeated that his account is too short to allow of certainty with regard to any interpretation.

18–19

Such an action on the part of Jesus may well have provoked the hostility of the authorities, but the reaction ascribed to them here seems disproportionate to the immediate circumstances, and the verse

* Jewish universalism always took the form of expecting that non-Jews would be granted a share in a basically *Jewish* worship and bliss.

as it stands is probably a generalizing comment by St Mark designed to prepare the way for their later action.

Verse 19 is a contribution to the Marcan chronological scheme.

❧

12
The note of time marks the beginning of the second day.

13
for it was not the season for figs: This comment, added by St Mark, or possibly some later scribe, only deepens the difficulty of the story, for it makes Jesus' attitude to the tree more unreasonable than ever; he curses it for doing what it could not possibly have been expected to do. The words have never been satisfactorily explained. Are they somehow connected with St Mark's dating of the event just before Passover, or were they intended as a hint that Jesus' action was to be understood symbolically despite the reference to his hunger in v. 12? Many scholars, accepting St Mark's account and chronology as substantially accurate, have laboured to show that fruit of some sort (e.g. green knops, or late-ripening fruit from the previous season) might reasonably have been expected on a fig tree at Passover time. Only an expert on things Palestinian could rightly judge, but even if these scholars are right, does it make it any more reasonable for Jesus to have forbidden a tree to have any fruit in the future simply because it did not have any at the moment?

15
the temple: An impressive building begun by Herod the Great in 20 B.C. on the site of the ancient Temple of Solomon. The building itself stood in the midst of four concentric courts, the outermost and largest of which, known as the Court of the Gentiles, was the scene of the incident described here. Around this court ran colonnades which were a favourite resort of scribes teaching their disciples (see on 1^{22}), while on the open pavement stood the booths of traders and also, at any rate at certain seasons of the year, of money-changers. The former sold the wine, oil, salt, birds (and possibly larger animals) needed for sacrifice; the latter probably confined themselves to one particular kind of transaction, viz., changing the Greek and Roman money of the pilgrims into the Jewish or Tyrian currency in which alone the temple-dues, required annually from every male Jew, could be paid.

It is not altogether clear how all this trading was organized or who got the profits. As far as the money-changing is concerned, one ancient authority says that the bankers took the profits; according to others, they were used to defray one or other of the temple expenses. The trading may possibly have been carried on by the priests themselves, but even if not, it was controlled by them and there can be no doubt that they profited directly or indirectly from it. That they were sometimes guilty of profiteering is shown by several pieces of evidence which have survived in Jewish sources of the period before A.D. 70. But it should be added that, as so often, it was Pharisees who championed the cause of the people and complained of the priestly exactions, and Abrahams, after a careful study, doubts if we are justified in generalizing from the evidence as widely as many Christian commentators have done. Within the context of Judaism, the system was legitimate enough, and on the whole it probably proved of great assistance to the pilgrims for whose benefit it was originally devised. (See further, for full and complementary discussions: I. Abrahams, *Studies in Pharisaism and the Gospels*, I, pp. 82–9, and B., pp. 202–6.)

16
'The prohibition implies a respect for the holiness of the temple and is thoroughly Jewish in spirit' (V. T.). In support of the latter statement cf. the passage in the *Mishnah* (transl. Danby, p. 10) prohibiting anyone from entering the Temple with staff, sandals, or wallet or with dust on his feet. It would also appear that the use of the temple court as a thoroughfare (cf. old St Paul's) had already been forbidden by Jewish law, in which case Our Lord here seems to be simply reinforcing a recognized rule.

17
This verse, which combines two Old Testament quotations, Isa. 56^{7} and Jer. 7^{11}, is regarded by some critics as a later Christian comment on the cleansing. It is cut off from the action by an introductory formula, as though it were a separate unit, and it is not altogether clear to whom it is addressed. 'Them' and 'you' can hardly be the traders (see above); probably, in accordance with St Mark's understanding of the story, the words refer generally to the Jewish people and its leaders, in which case the scene must be an ideal one designed to bring out the significance of the cleansing and effect the transition to what follows. St Mark may have envisaged a session of teaching in which more was said than is recorded here. Bultmann suggests that the story of the cleansing may originally have ended with the words now preserved in John 2^{16}.

a den of robbers: Should be translated 'a brigands' cave' and probably understood in the general sense that the temple had become a meeting place of rogues.

18
The latter half of the verse is strangely phrased; fear of Jesus' popularity with the crowd seems a strange reason for wanting to destroy him; it would more naturally be a reason for not daring to arrest him as in $14^{1, 2}$.

20
in the morning: Presumably of the third day, which lasts now for two and a half chapters.

22
Have faith in God: Probably a Marcan addition (the words *in God* may be even later) to effect the transition from the story to the teaching which follows.

23
'Removing mountains' was a recognized metaphor for doing things of great difficulty; e.g. a rabbi who could explain difficult passages of scripture was known as a 'mountain-remover'.

and does not doubt in his heart: Missing in the Q version (Luke 17^{6}, Matt. 17^{20}); it sounds like a homiletical expansion.

25
stand: Standing and kneeling were both accepted positions for prayer among the Jews.

The wording of this verse is reminiscent of St Matthew's version of the Lord's Prayer (Matt. $6^{9\text{ff.}}$) and is generally taken as evidence that St Mark was familiar with that prayer. If so, however, it seems inexplicable that he does not quote it, and we cannot rule out the possibility that v. 25 like v. 26 has been inserted from, or at any rate much influenced by, Matthew 6 (cf. especially Matt. 6^{14}, the verse before the one from which v. 26 has been borrowed).

11^{27-33} THE SOURCE OF JESUS' AUTHORITY

27 *And they came again to Jerusalem. And as he was walking in the temple, the chief priests and the scribes and the elders came to him,* 28 *and they said to him, 'By what authority are you doing these things, or who gave you this authority to do them?'* 29 *Jesus said to them, 'I will ask you a question;*

answer me, and I will tell you by what authority I do these things. 30 *Was the*
baptism of John from heaven or from men? Answer me.' 31 *And they argued*
with one another, 'If we say, "From heaven," he will say, "Why then did
you not believe him?" 32 *But shall we say, "From men"?' – they were afraid*
of the people, for all held that John was a real prophet. 33 *So they answered*
Jesus, 'We do not know.' And Jesus said to them, 'Neither will I tell you by
what authority I do these things.'

This section introduces a series of four or five controversy-incidents all related to leading issues in contemporary Judaism;* the individual stories contain no indications of place or time, and according to the Marcan arrangement of them, 11^{27} sets the scene for the whole series.

The most natural interpretation of the first story, as it is now placed, is that Jesus' opponents were a delegation from the Sanhedrin (the body ultimately responsible for the temple police), sent to interrogate him about the cleansing of the temple; *these things* in v. 28 then refers back to vv. 15–19 despite the intervening incident and the intervening night (vv. 19–20). It is very possible, however, that the introductory setting to the story (v. 27) was composed by St Mark, and *these things* (v. 28) may earlier have had a different, and perhaps wider, reference. (See notes below.)

In any case, the real point of the question in v. 28 is to expose a *lack* of authority on Jesus' part. He replies with a counter-question. This was a common form of reply in rabbinic debates, but rabbinic counter-questions were normally of such definitive character as to settle the question at issue by themselves, and it may be that this story originally closed with Jesus' question in v. 30. The meaning will then have been: 'John the Baptist is a man who can point to no human authorization; but you accept him in the belief that he is a prophet sent from God. His ministry and mine are in many ways similar; why should I too not have authority direct from God?' Such a reply presupposes inquirers who accepted John's claims, as the Jewish authorities refused to do. Originally the inquirers may have been described simply as 'they' or 'some people' and then when a specific reference to the Jewish authorities was introduced, an appendix to

* These stories may already have been combined when they reached St Mark; if he was following a single source in 2^{1}–3^{6}, these stories perhaps formed a further section of it.

the story became necessary (vv. 31–33) to show how, even in their case, Jesus' reply proved effective, placing them in a dilemma which effectively prevented them from pressing their question further. No doubt the early Church will have been encouraged by this evidence of Jesus' ability to outwit and out-argue the trained experts of Judaism; when the latter had attempted to force him to declare himself, he had preserved the messianic secret without denying his Messiahship.

❧

27
The first sentence is generally agreed to be a Marcan construction designed to link 11^{27}–12^{44} with what has gone before (cf. $11^{15, 19, 20}$). On the second sentence see above; the original pericope probably began with the typical 'impersonal plural' at the beginning of v. 28 (cf. e.g 2^{3} and 7^{32}).

The three classes of people mentioned are those who made up the Sanhedrin (cf. on 8^{31}, 14^{53}, and 15^{1}), and no doubt St Mark thought of them as a deputation from that body.

28
authority: If this was the original form of the question, the reference may have been to the authority conferred by ordination as a rabbi (see on 1^{22}), or to the claim of Jesus as a religious teacher to act independently of the supreme tribunal in such matters. In Jesus' reply and the subsequent Christian understanding of the story, however, divine authority, and not legal or political right, was meant.

these things: See above. If the relation of this passage to the temple cleansing is secondary, the reference may have been to Jesus' teaching and ministry generally (so most commentators) or, according to the attractive suggestion of Bultmann, to his activity as a baptizer – cf. John 3^{22} and ^{26} and see Bultmann, p. 18, n. 2.

30
the baptism of John: No doubt this is meant to include John's activity and teaching as a whole.

from heaven: i.e. from God – a normal Jewish circumlocution to avoid mentioning the divine name.

31ff.
As thus completed, the story assumes that Jesus could foresee the inward thoughts of his adversaries and so knew that his question would prove unanswerable (cf. 2^{8}, 8^{17}, Matt. 12^{25}, and notes).

As shown above, v. 30 was probably written originally from the point of view of John's heavenly authority being acknowledged by both sides; vv. 31 and 32, however, are written from a later stand-point according to which the Jewish leaders were held to have rejected the message of John (which foretold and authenticated Jesus) and to have denied his heavenly authority. This may explain the rather surprising course their reflections take; we should have expected them to reason: 'If we say "from heaven", he will say: "so too is my authority from heaven".' The use of the expression 'believing' John (v. 31) also seems to reflect a Christian standpoint.

12^{1-12} THE PARABLE OF THE WICKED HUSBANDMEN

12 *And he began to speak to them in parables. 'A man planted a vineyard,*
and set a hedge around it, and dug a pit for the wine press, and built a tower,
and let it out to tenants and went into another country. 2 *When the time came,*
he sent a servant to the tenants, to get from them some of the fruit of the vine-
yard. 3 *And they took him and beat him, and sent him away empty-handed.*
4 *Again he sent to them another servant, and they wounded him in the head,*
and treated him shamefully. 5 *And he sent another, and him they killed; and*
so with many others, some they beat and some they killed. 6 *He had still one*
other, a beloved son; finally he sent him to them, saying, "They will respect
my son." 7 *But those tenants said to one another, "This is the heir; come, let*
us kill him, and the inheritance will be ours." 8 *And they took him and killed*
him, and cast him out of the vineyard. 9 *What will the owner of the vineyard*
do? He will come and destroy the tenants, and give the vineyard to others.
10 *Have you not read this scripture:*

> *"The very stone which the builders rejected*
> *has become the head of the corner;*
> 11 *this was the Lord's doing,*
> *and it is marvellous in our eyes"?'*

12 *And they tried to arrest him, but feared the multitude, for they perceived*
that he had told the parable against them; so they left him and went away.

In its Marcan context, this parable forms part of the controversy between Jesus and the Jewish authorities which began at 11^{27}; the setting should not be pressed, however, for 12^{1} could well be an independent beginning, perhaps originally introducing a series of parables from which St Mark has selected a single example. (Cf. the plural *parables* in v. 1.)

The parable itself has generally been taken as an allegory, the vineyard standing for Israel (cf. Isa. $5^{1ff.}$), the owner for God, the husbandmen for the Jewish authorities, the servants for the various Old Testament prophets who had been rejected and persecuted (see below), the son and heir for Jesus. As we have seen (cf. p. 130), the parables of Jesus and the Jewish rabbis were *not* allegories, and the authenticity of this parable has been widely doubted, chiefly on that ground, but also because it presupposes:

(i) that Jesus knew in advance about his death;

(ii) that he knew in advance about the fall of Jerusalem (thought to be referred to in v. 9);

(iii) that he made an open and emphatic messianic claim incompatible with his attitude in such passages as 1^{44}, 5^{43}, 7^{36}, $9^{9f.}$

A further point is that the behaviour of the characters in the story seems very improbable. What owner, for example, would keep risking his slaves, and finally risk the life of his son, in the way described here? And why did the husbandmen fail to realize that if they murdered the son they would still have to reckon with the father? The modern reader is not immediately struck by these implausibilities because he has the allegorical application in mind all the time, but to Jesus' contemporaries, who could have known nothing of this application, the story would hardly have presented itself as a credible, everyday incident such as parables normally depicted.

There can be no doubt that St Mark and his contemporaries did understand the story in this allegorical fashion, and few would deny that in its present form it contains secondary, allegorizing traits (see below); nevertheless, increased knowledge of conditions in first-century Palestine has made it possible to maintain that what we are dealing with here is essentially an authentic parable which can be reconstructed and interpreted with reasonable accuracy.

Much of Galilee in those days was parcelled out into large estates, many of them owned by foreign landlords, a fact which naturally led to a good deal of discontent among the Galilean peasants; this resentment, when combined with nationalist feeling under 'Zealot' influence, produced a chronic state of near-rebellion. If this is taken into account, and allowance is made for a number of later embellishments to the story, the basic incident, it is claimed, is intelligible enough. A foreign landlord who lives abroad (v. 1), after failing more than once to collect his rent, sends his son to act as his agent; the tenants, inspired no doubt by nationalist passions and perhaps presuming on the remoteness of the landlord, or perhaps thinking that if the son has come the father must be dead, and relying on the law of proselyte inheritance (see below), murder the son in the hope of getting possession of the property. The landlord, however, possibly with government assistance (see below), takes vigorous counteraction and the tenants are killed and dispossessed in favour of others. It is suggested that, if we allow for a little 'parabolic licence', some such event might well have occurred just about the time when Jesus told the parable, and in any case, if the story is understood in this way, very little allegorism is involved; 'the parable stands on its own feet as a dramatic story, inviting a judgement from the hearers' as parables usually do (Dodd; see below for the possibility that v. 9b is secondary). Presumably it was addressed to the leaders of the people (as St Mark implies), and the meaning will have been that since they, the tenants of God's vineyard, have been guilty of repeated rebellion against God, the vineyard is to be given to 'others' (v. 9) – that is, perhaps, on the analogy of such passages as Matt. 22^{1-10} // Luke 14^{16-24} and Matt. 5^{5}, to the 'poor'. (On the meaning of that word in such contexts see p. 271n.)

But was there originally any reference to Jesus himself? Dodd thinks there was; 'the climax of iniquity in the story suggests a similar climax in the situation to which it is applied', i.e. if Jesus told the parable towards the end of his ministry, he may well have implied that the chronic rebelliousness of the Jewish leaders, against which the parable is directed, would soon reach a climax in a murderous assault on himself, the Successor of the prophets. If the priests and scribes were known to be plotting against him, such an allusion might well have been caught by some of his hearers.

This view of the parable, first put forward by Dodd (*Parables*, pp. 124–32) and elaborated, though with some caution, by Jeremias (*P.J.* pp. 55–60), has been widely accepted in recent years, and clearly has much to commend it. On the other hand it involves a good deal of speculation, and, at any rate in Dodd's version of it, assumes that the parable was largely an allegory, even in its original form (the son = Jesus, the tenants = the Jewish authorities, the murder = the crucifixion, and so on); there is therefore something to be said for the suggestion of B. T. D. Smith (*The Parables of the Synoptic Gospels*, pp. 222ff.) that the original parable told simply of the three slaves (the number three is characteristic of the popular tale) and bore the sort of meaning suggested on p. 310 above. In the light of what happened later, the reference to the son would be a natural addition for Christians to make at a time when the parables were coming to be interpreted allegorically.*

❧

1

in parables: Often taken (here and in 3^{23}) adverbially as simply = 'parabolically'. However, this is awkward when only one parable is involved (St Matthew and St Luke both felt the difficulty) and the explanation suggested above is perhaps preferable.

The likening of Israel to a vineyard was common (cf. Isa. 5^{1}ff., Ps. 80^{8}ff., Jer. 2^{21}, and for the rabbis *Tanchuma* (Jerusalem, 1952) 151a) and is entirely credible on the lips of Jesus. The assimilation of the wording to that of Isa. $5^{1 \text{ and } 2}$ (very close in the Greek) is no doubt the work of the Evangelist, or one of his predecessors.

The various items mentioned do not suggest any allegorical application; they were all common form in the preparation of a Palestinian vineyard, the *hedge* to give protection from wild animals, the *pit* or trough to receive the juice when the grapes were trodden out in the *press* above, and the *tower* to provide shelter for the vinedressers and a point of vantage from which jackals (cf. Song of Sol. 2^{15}) and thieves could be spotted.

let it out to tenants, and went into another country: For foreign and absentee landlords see above. The leasing of vineyards in return for a fixed proportion of the produce (v. 2) was a common practice.

* The point is often made that we have no right to assert arbitrarily that Jesus *never* employed allegory – so e.g. R., p. 161, and Lagrange, who regards this parable as a *parabole-allégorie*; that is certainly true, but the present parable, even in Dodd's reconstruction of it, is allegorical to an extent not really paralleled in Jesus' other parables (cf. R.; 'an allegory rather than a parable proper'), and in view of the known tendency of the early Church to allegorize the parables, this rightly gives rise to suspicion.

2
When the time came: i.e. in the fifth year according to Lev. 19^{23-25}.

4
wounded him in the head: The commonly accepted translation of an obscure Greek expression; but Dodd translates the two verbs: 'beheaded and outraged'.

5
It is generally agreed that 5b is an embellishment added at a time when the story was beginning to be understood allegorically; the reference is to the 'many' prophetic messengers of God whom the Jews had repudiated and martyred – cf. e.g. 1 Kings 18^{13}, 22^{27}, 2 Chron. 24^{20}ff., 36^{15}ff., Neh. 9^{26}. Some think that v. 5a is also unoriginal and implies an unlikely degree of patience on the part of the owner. It may be so, though the number three is characteristic of the popular story, and there may also have been some deliberate exaggeration designed to emphasize the patience God had shown towards the Jewish leaders.

6
beloved: Or 'only' (*agapētos*) – see on 1^{11}; as shown there, the word may well have had messianic overtones, and, if so, its use here may be an additional reason for treating the introduction of the son as allegorical and secondary; on the other hand, if the son was to be mentioned he must be an 'only' son; if he had had brothers, and not been sole heir, his murder would not have done the tenants any good.

7
See above, p. 310. According to contemporary law, the estate of a proselyte who died intestate could be regarded as ownerless property and claimed by anyone, though with the proviso that a prior right belonged to a claimant already in occupation.

8
cast him out: Left him unburied, a supreme outrage in contemporary eyes. Note how St Matthew and St Luke (Matt. 21^{39}, Luke 20^{15}) by an unnatural change of order (why should the tenants 'cast him out' before 'killing' him?) assimilate the story to the facts of the crucifixion (cf. Heb. 13^{12}) and so carry the process of allegorization a stage further.

9
It was not on the whole Our Lord's habit to answer the questions to which his parables so often led up (cf. e.g. Luke 17^{9}); the Evangelists on the other hand *were* often in the habit of pointing the moral of the parables; so it is possible that 9b is a later addition of this kind. (Contrast

Matt. 21[41] where it is the *audience* who answer the question.) However, v. 9b is a natural enough conclusion to the story, and in illustration of it Dodd cites the case of Marcus Brutus who brutally enforced payment of a debt from the corporation of Salamis with the help of cavalry supplied by the governor of Cilicia (cf. Cicero, *Ad Atticum*, v, 21; vi, 1). The action is also in line with that of a king in a rabbinic parable who leased out a possession to husbandmen and when he could not secure his share of the fruits, ejected the tenants and gave the property to 'others', in this case their own children.*

to others: See p. 310 above. How St Mark understood the words it is not easy to be certain; probably he thought in terms of the status and privileges of the Old Israel, or its leaders, being transferred to the Church, the new Israel, or its leaders. That is probably also the meaning of 'nation' in Matt. 21[43].

10–11

These verses require separate consideration. While it is not unknown for a parable to end with an Old Testament quotation (there are rabbinic parallels) the question arises whether the passage cited here (Ps. 118[22-23]) would have been intelligible as the conclusion of this particular parable in its original form. It makes sense in this context only if the parable is understood as being about the 'rejection' (cf. v. 10) of Jesus, and, on the assumption that that was at most a secondary implication of the original parable, most commentators regard these verses as an addition made when the story was already interpreted allegorically. Even so, it does not necessarily follow that the passage was not cited by Our Lord himself on some other occasion; our view about that will depend on whether we think he foresaw and foretold his 'rejection' (v. 10) and subsequent vindication explicitly enough for this citation to have been understood during his lifetime. In the post-resurrection period it became a favourite quotation among the early Christians – Acts 4[11], 1 Pet. 2[7], Eph. 2[20], and cf. Rom. 9[32-33] – and no doubt figured in the 'testimony books' (for which see p. 60). Some such book is perhaps the most likely source here, at any rate for v. 11, which would have sounded a little oddly on the lips of Jesus himself.

10

the head of the corner: The Greek means either the corner-stone which

* Unless our passage is a Christianization of this rabbinic parable, which seems unlikely, its existence and that of a similar rabbinic parable (see S.-B., I, 874) are further support for the view that in some form or other the Marcan parable goes back to a Jewish *milieu*, and presumably to Our Lord.

holds the walls of a building together, or the keystone of an arch or gateway.

12

The phraseology is Marcan; throughout this part of the Gospel the Evangelist is preparing us for the dénouement.

R.S.V. covers up a certain oddness in the phrasing of the original; *but* and *so* are both 'and' in the Greek. It almost looks as if *but they feared the multitude* should come after ... *parable against them*. Some take the last seven words as the beginning of v. 13.

12^{13-17} A QUESTION ABOUT THE POLL-TAX

[13]*And they sent to him some of the Pharisees and some of the Hero'di-ans,*
to entrap him in his talk. [14]*And they came and said to him, 'Teacher, we*
know that you are true, and care for no man; for you do not regard the position
of men, but truly teach the way of God. Is it lawful to pay taxes to Caesar, or
not? [15]*Should we pay them, or should we not?' But knowing their hypocrisy,*
he said to them, 'Why put me to the test? Bring me a coin,[a] *and let me look*
at it.' [16]*And they brought one. And he said to them, 'Whose likeness and*
inscription is this?' They said to him, 'Caesar's.' [17]*Jesus said to them,*
'Render to Caesar the things that are Caesar's, and to God the things that
are God's.' And they were amazed at him.

a Greek *a denarius*

This is a typical pronouncement story; there are no indications of time or place or of the identity of the questioners (vv. 13 and ?17b are probably later additions – see below), but everything is subordinated to the pronouncement of Jesus. The question to which this provides the answer is one which will have been of burning practical importance to Jews and Jewish Christians throughout the period preceding the fall of Jerusalem; and as for Mark's Roman readers, the story will have been of great importance to them because of the possibility of interpreting it as evidence that Christianity need involve no disloyalty to the State.

The pronouncement itself is almost certainly genuine, but it needs to be set against its orginal background if it is to be properly understood. The particular tax (not *taxes* as in R.S.V.) referred to in v. 14 was a poll-tax (as distinct from property taxes or customs dues), payable, since A.D. 6, by all inhabitants of Judea, Samaria, and Idumea. It was extremely unpopular, both because it was a constant reminder of the Jews' subject status, and also because the silver coinage in which it had to be paid bore the name and image of Caesar. When the tax was first imposed a serious revolt broke out (cf. Acts 5^37), and, though this was suppressed, Josephus says it left as a continuing legacy what he calls 'the fourth philosophy of the Jews', i.e. the intense nationalism of the Zealots, who declared 'that God was their only ruler and king' and were bitterly opposed to the tax and all it stood for (Josephus' *Antiquities*, XVIII, 1, 1 and 6). It will thus be seen that the question here put to Jesus was well calculated to do him great harm, whichever way he answered it; if he advised payment of the tax he would discredit himself in the eyes of all the nationalist groups (here perhaps symbolized by *the Herodians*, v. 13); for such advice would be regarded as a betrayal of the national cause, and no one who gave it could expect much support or acceptance of his messianic claims from the crowds. If he pronounced against payment he would offend those (represented in v. 13 by the *Pharisees*) who were prepared to tolerate the *status quo*, and he might even be reported to the Romans for inciting to rebellion.

What is the meaning of Jesus' reaction to the question? It presupposes, in the first place, the normal ancient view that sovereignty was coterminous with the rights of coinage and the validity of one's money. According to ancient ideas, coins were ultimately the private property of the ruler who issued them, and whose image they bore; and the writ of a ruler ran wherever his money was *de facto* 'coin of the realm'. Accordingly, Jesus is here saying: 'Since the money you have in your possession is Caesar's (the point of getting them to produce a coin is to establish this), you implicitly acknowledge his authority and therefore you have an obligation to pay taxes to him.' (The Greek word translated *render* in v. 17 implies that the payment is a debt.)

But does not the civil obedience attested by the payment of tax conflict with the obedience which is due to God? To understand Jesus' words here we must keep in mind his conviction that the future of this world, and of the Roman empire within it, would be short; very soon the kingdom of heaven would arrive and the rule of Rome would disappear, not through man's agency but through God's. Essentially, therefore, Jesus is not enunciating any principle bearing on the problem of 'Church and State' (Dibelius, *Jesus*, E. T., pp. 114–15), he is saying simply that men's duty to Caesar does not contradict their duty to God; it is insignificant in comparison with it. Men should perform the first (without attaching to it greater importance than it really possesses), but they should concentrate above all on their relationship to the God whose coming is now so imminent. Loisy puts it well (*Évangiles synoptiques*, II, p. 336): 'Jesus emphasized the lawfulness of political power and of tribute much less than the *insignificance* of these things in comparison with the kingdom of heaven. It is implied that the kingdom of heaven is not to be established by violence . . .; in the interval before its coming one should pay to Caesar the tax which attests his sovereignty, and it would be foolish to believe that God and his reign would gain anything by the rejection of an obligation of this kind. Let the things of this world be esteemed according to the smallness of their value, and let these duties be discharged as necessity may arise; but let men know above all that the greatest thing lies elsewhere, in fidelity to the heavenly father.'

Subsequently, when the immediate pressure of eschatology was removed, the Church rightly sought a more positive doctrine of the relation between Church and State, and far more has been read into the saying than it originally meant; no doubt, as we have seen, it was because it was interpreted along the lines of St Paul's teaching in e.g. Rom. 13$^{1ff.}$ that the saying was preserved and treasured in the Rome of St Mark's day.

13

Probably St Mark thinks of *the chief priests and the scribes and the elders* (11^{27}) as still the subject; but before the passage was placed in its present context, *they sent* (literally 'send') was probably an 'impersonal plural' (see on 10^{2}). For *the Herodians* see on 3^{6}; they appear more naturally in Galilee and many scholars think that at some earlier stage of the tradition this story was located in Galilee; some take it as a continuation of the source they believe St Mark was following in 2^{1}–3^{6}. However, this introduction may be artificial and the *Herodians* may be introduced simply as typical nationalists, symbolizing one horn of the dilemma with which Jesus was to be faced (see above). The reading of one group of MSS. suggests a stage when the story began with v. 14 which ran: 'The Pharisees asked him . . .'

the Pharisees on the whole took very much the attitude in this matter which is expressed by Jesus in v. 17.

14
No doubt the point of the public compliment is to put Jesus in a position where he cannot avoid giving a direct and unequivocal answer (contrast $11^{29\text{ff.}}$) and so discrediting himself with one or other important group in the State.

true: i.e. sincere, upright.

the way of God: i.e. the way of living God demands; does it, or does it not, include paying the poll-tax?

15
knowing their hypocrisy: i.e. Jesus recognizes that the question is asked not for the sake of getting at the truth, but in order to put him in a difficulty.

a coin: Greek: *denarius*; see on 6^{37}.

let me look at it: This, and the next verse, do not imply that Jesus had never seen such a coin before. For the point of the request, see above.

16
likeness and inscription: For details and illustrations see Madden *Jewish Coinage*, p. 247, and *Hastings Dictionary of the Bible*, III, p. 424f. The emperor was Tiberius (A.D. 14–37) and the inscription will have run: *Ti(berius) Caesar divi Aug(usti) f(ilius) Augustus*, and on the reverse side *Pontif(ex)Maxim(us)*. The copper coins of smaller denominations minted locally for use in Palestine carried no images of living creatures, out of deference to Jewish susceptibilities. The poll-tax, however, had to be paid in the silver currency.

17
the things that are God's: The reference is quite general and all-inclusive.

they were amazed at him: The words of Jesus would form the best climax, and this typically Marcan ending may well be an addition to the pericope; in any case, as Klostermann says, what is regarded as so remarkable is not just the truth of the pronouncement but the way it deals with the question without giving anyone real ground for offence or complaint.

12^{18-27} A QUESTION ABOUT RESURRECTION

18 *And Sad'ducees came to him, who say that there is no resurrection; and*
they asked him a question, saying, 19 *'Teacher, Moses wrote for us that if a*
man's brother dies and leaves a wife, but leaves no child, the man[a] *must take*
the wife, and raise up children for his brother. 20 *There were seven brothers;*
the first took a wife, and when he died left no children; 21 *and the second took*
her, and died, leaving no children; and the third likewise; 22 *and the seven left*
no children. Last of all the woman also died. 23 *In the resurrection whose wife*
will she be? For the seven had her as wife.'
24 *Jesus said to them, 'Is not this why you are wrong, that you know*
neither the scriptures nor the power of God? 25 *For when they rise from the*
dead, they neither marry nor are given in marriage, but are like angels in
heaven. 26 *And as for the dead being raised, have you not read in the book of*
Moses, in the passage about the bush, how God said to him, "I am the God
of Abraham, and the God of Isaac, and the God of Jacob"? 27 *He is not God*
of the dead, but of the living; you are quite wrong.'

a Greek *his brother*

Another controversy story culminating in a pronouncement of Jesus; it has much the same characteristics as the last, and St Mark may have taken them both from some collection of controversy stories which he was using as his source at this point (see above). On the other hand he may have got this story from some other source and deliberately place it after the last story because he wanted to exhibit Our Lord as being 'put to the test' (v. 15) by – and successfully maintaining his orthodoxy against – the Sadducaic, as well as the Pharisaic, wing of contemporary Judaism.

The Sadducees in this story are the only ones mentioned in the Gospel and it is typical of a pronouncement story that all we are told about them is the bare minimum necessary for the intelligent appreciation of the incident. In fact the Sadducees were a priestly and aristocratic party from among whom the High Priest was appointed, and their attitude, in contrast to that of the popular Pharisaic party, was conservative and traditionalist. They took their stand on the Pentateuch, and though they did not, as has sometimes been suggested, deny the validity of the other Old Testament books, they did reject the various extra-canonical writings and traditions which the Pharisees and their supporters produced and accepted; and along with these they rejected the new beliefs they contained, particularly belief in eternal life, angels, spirits, and foreordination or fate (cf. Acts 23^{6-8}). The novelty of these latter beliefs, which Our Lord shared with the Pharisees, is often not sufficiently realized; apart from one or two later post-exilic passages, some of them of doubtful interpretation (cf. Dan. 12^{2}, Isa. 25^{8} and 26^{19}, Ps. $73^{24f.}$, and Job 19^{25-27}), belief in resurrection or immortality is entirely missing from the Old Testament, which knows only of a shadowy existence – it can hardly be called life – which the departed soul shares in a gloomy and desolate region known as Sheol. In accordance with their biblicist attitude, the Sadducees were unwilling to go further than this,* and they here seek to show, by methods which are typically rabbinic, that not only does the Law say nothing about resurrection, but what it *does* say – with regard to levirate marriage (see below) – is incompatible with resurrection, and thus shows that the Old Testament positively *excludes* belief in any resurrection doctrine. If Moses ordered levirate marriage he cannot have believed in the resurrection.†

Our Lord's reply is twofold:

(i) In v. 25 he argues that it is only a crude and false form of resurrection hope that is 'reduced to the absurd' by the provisions for levirate marriage. If the resurrection life is properly conceived, the alleged incompatibility disappears.

(ii) In vv. 26–27 he argues that the Law itself, if its implications are weighed, *demands* belief in the resurrection.

The reasoning in (ii) is as characteristically rabbinic as that of the Sadducees (see below) and there is some reason for thinking it reproduces a standard Pharisaic argument; many scholars regard the verses as a later addition to the original pronouncement story, which will then have ended, as such stories usually do, with a single striking and conclusive word of Jesus (v. 25).‡ However, this argument is not

* According to Josephus they would not go even so far; but Josephus was a Pharisee and is probably maligning the Sadducees.

† B., looking at the question more broadly, describes their aim as: 'to discredit Jesus by presenting one of the many complications which arise as soon as one thinks of a state or condition which will preserve all of the relationships arising during a time process' (p. 216).

‡ And one which, as Dibelius says, 'must surely have overwhelmed the Sadducees already'.

conclusive; we clearly cannot exclude the possibility that Jesus sometimes thought it right to fight his opponents with their own weapons; and of course, even if the verses are secondary, their contents can still have value – see below.

For the significance of the pronouncement to Mark's Roman readers, see note on v. 25.

ꙮ

19
See Deut. 25^{5-10}, from which this is a loose quotation. In fact the institution of levirate marriage goes back far beyond the Pentateuch to the most primitive times, when to die without issue was regarded as a terrible calamity, since anyone doing so would have no one to perform the filial duty of making offerings to propitiate his ghost. Later the custom was followed as a means of keeping property within the family (see Deuteronomy), but by Our Lord's time it had very largely fallen into abeyance. That, however, did not invalidate the Sadducees' use of it as showing that Moses had not believed in resurrection.

20ff.
The number seven is typical of such contexts – cf. e.g. Tobit 3^{8}.

24
The Greek is even less clear than the English. The meaning may be either: 'Isn't the reason why you are wrong that you do not know . . . ?' or: 'Isn't it clear from your producing such a false argument that you are in error, as the result of not knowing . . . ?'

know neither the scriptures nor the power of God: The meaning may be quite general; however great their intellectual knowledge of scripture, their moral and experimental knowledge of it is inadequate; and they do not appreciate the power of God to overcome death and bestow life. Or, if the reference is more precise, the Sadducees show that they know neither the scriptures (which prove the resurrection) nor the power of God (which makes the resurrection life quite different from, and higher than, the life of this world). In that case the second point refers forward to the argument of v. 25, the first to that of vv. 26–27.

25
The essential point is that the conditions of the resurrection life will be quite different from those of the present life, and so arguments about that life based on earthly conditions are beside the point.

Our Lord here gives his authority to one of the two attitudes current at the time with regard to the resurrection life. Popular opinion sometimes thought of it simply as a resumption, with certain modifications, of life as we know it in this world; but some striking rabbinic sayings show that at any rate a little later a view similar to that of Jesus was also current.* This saying also fits in with other indications in the Gospels that Jesus rejected the crude popular idea of Israel's reward in terms of the restoration of the ancient glories of the nation. 'The more carefully Jesus' sayings are studied, the more clear it becomes that He turned away from the series of political and temporal ideas which the popular religion of the people made so much of. This means that Jesus' idea of the Anointed One whom God would send would necessarily be different, if it remained at all, from popular and conventional ideas.' (B.)

For the condition of the angels cf. e.g. 1 *Enoch* 15^{6-7}, where angels are described as 'immortal for all generations of the world' and told 'therefore I (God) have not appointed wives for you'; and cf. Tobit 12^{19}. Our Lord is clearly thinking only of the resurrection of the righteous.

From the point of view of the later Gentile Church his statement will have been of the greatest significance as suggesting a spiritual view of the resurrection, free from the crudely materialistic traits which we know to have been a genuine stumbling-block to more spiritually minded 'Greeks'. (Cf. 1 Cor. 15, where St Paul also argues for a 'spiritual' view of the resurrection – see especially vv. 35ff.)

26–27

'The answer now passes from the *manner* to the *fact* of the resurrection of the dead' (V. T.). The argument is typical of contemporary methods of exegesis and not altogether convincing to modern ears.† The essence of it is that since, in Exod. 3^{6}, God describes himself as being

* Cf. especially the view of Rab, a third-century Babylonian teacher: 'The world to come is not like this world. In the world to come there is no eating or drinking or begetting or bargaining or envy or hate or strife; but the righteous sit with crowns on their heads and are satisfied with the glory of God's presence.' We have similar passages from an earlier period, and, as Montefiore says, there is no reason to think that such teaching would not have been acceptable to the best rabbinic contemporaries of Our Lord.

† Cf. how Rabbi Gamaliel (*c.* A.D. 90) argued to the resurrection of the dead from Deut. 11^{9} on the grounds that God there promised the three patriarchs to give the land *to them*; similarly Rabbi Johannan (*c.* 270) found evidence of eternal life for Aaron in Num. 18^{28}. The fact that in 4 *Macc.* 7^{19} and 16^{25}, Abraham, Isaac, and Jacob are described as 'not having died' but 'living unto God' (see the context) has suggested to some commentators that the argument in our text may have been a stock argument of the Pharisees.

in the present (*I am*) the God of the three patriarchs at a time when they were no longer alive according to the flesh, they must have been alive in some resurrection state. But according to the original sense of Exod. 3[6], God's words meant, not: 'I am the God with whom they *now* stand in relationship,' but 'with whom they *once* stood in relationship.' He is the one who *had been* their God when they were alive.* In any case the argument would prove only life after death, as opposed to resurrection in the strict sense.

Nevertheless, as Loisy and others have pointed out, the argument, broadly considered, may be regarded as a first-century way of expressing the consideration on which, more than any other, modern Christians base their belief in life after death. In their experience of communion with God they come to know him as a God of such goodness that, as Loisy puts it, he 'cannot have ceased to be the God of those who have served and loved Him and been the recipients of his favour'.

26

in the passage about the bush: Greek literally: 'at "the Bush"' – a customary way of referring to a particular passage, at a time when the only division of the Old Testament was into paragraphs, each with a title derived from its subject-matter. Cf. Rom. 11[2] where the Greek has 'in Elijah', i.e. 'in the passage about Elijah'.

27

you are quite wrong: V. T. describes this ending as 'impressive', and so in a way it is; it certainly serves to emphasize the utterly unjustified character of the Sadducees' attack on Jesus – see p. 318. But normal synoptic practice would lead us to expect some note of people's reaction to Jesus' words, such as St Matthew and St Luke have both felt obliged to add (cf. Matt. 22[33] and Luke 20[39–40]); perhaps the absence of any such note from St Mark is support for the view that the pericope is not reproduced here in its original form, and that 26–27 have taken the place of some ending of the normal type.

* Wellhausen dryly remarks that the Old Testament's own deduction from the words was the precise opposite of what is deduced here; from the admitted fact that God is the God of the living 'the Old Testament deduces that the dead are excluded from all relationships with him' – he cites Ps. 6[5].

12^{28-34} THE FIRST COMMANDMENT

28 *And one of the scribes came up and heard them disputing with one
another, and seeing that he answered them well, asked him, 'Which commandment is the first of all?'* 29 *Jesus answered, 'The first is, "Hear, O Israel:
The Lord our God, the Lord is one;* 30 *and you shall love the Lord your God
with all your heart, and with all your soul, and with all your mind, and with
all your strength."* 31 *The second is this, "You shall love your neighbour as
yourself." There is no other commandment greater than these.'* 32 *And the
scribe said to him, 'You are right, Teacher; you have truly said that he is one
and there is no other but he;* 33 *and to love him with all the heart, and with
all the understanding, and with all the strength, and to love one's neighbour
as oneself, is much more than all whole burnt offerings and sacrifices.'* 34 *And
when Jesus saw that he answered wisely, he said to him, 'You are not far
from the kingdom of God.' And after that no one dared to ask him any
question.*

Jesus has triumphantly answered priest, Pharisee, and Sadducee; in this fourth pronouncement story it is the turn of a *scribe* to question him. This he does, according to St Mark, in no hostile spirit (cf. especially v. 32 and contrast Matthew 22^{34-35} and Luke 10^{25}), and if the preceding incidents were derived from a collection of controversy stories, this story will hardly have found a place in it. Verses 28a and 34b are fairly clearly Marcan constructions designed to adapt the story to its present position, and no doubt the point of putting it here is to emphasize, just at the moment when the rift between Jesus and the religious leaders is reaching its climax, the essential orthodoxy of Jesus and his faithfulness to the Law. (See *H. & I.*, pp. 109 and 124.)

The value of the passage to Mark's original readers, or, for that matter, to all subsequent readers, needs no elaboration, but certain questions must be faced. If, as most scholars believe,* Luke 10^{25-28} is a variant account of this incident, the question arises whether the central saying came from Our Lord (so Mark vv. 29–31) or from the scribe himself as in Luke's version (v. 10^{27}). Some commentators, feeling how natural it would have been for the Church to claim such

* Though cf. Manson, *S. J.*, p. 259ff.

a fine creative utterance for Jesus, and detecting certain vestiges of Luke's version still surviving in Mark's (see below), prefer the Lucan account, but the majority maintain the originality of Mark's account, holding that in Luke's Gospel it has been rewritten with a view to making it a better introduction to the story of the Good Samaritan which there follows it.*

This question leads on to another, closely allied to it. Although vv. 29–31 consist almost entirely of verbatim quotations from two Old Testament passages (Deut. 6^{4-5} and Lev. 19^{18} – both fully emphasized and commented on by the rabbis) the *combination* of these two widely separated texts as taking us to the heart of religion is clearly an original and creative achievement of the highest order. Did it originate with Jesus? Even if we prefer the Marcan account to the Lucan, that is by no means certain. The same combination is found in the *Testaments of the Twelve Patriarchs* (*Dan* 5^{3} and *Issach.* 5^{2}, 7^{6}), and even if these passages are left on one side as being of Christian origin, a case can be made out for thinking that the combination was well known in the age of Our Lord and perhaps occurred, in a form similar to that found in the Christian *Didache*, in a Jewish manual for the instruction of proselytes (and cf. Philo, *De Spec. Leg.*, II, 63).

Even if that is true, however, it does not dispose of all the questions, for we have to ask what a statement such as this would mean coming from the lips of an orthodox Jew. We know of a number of attempts by rabbis before and after the time of Our Lord, to sum up in the shortest possible form the fundamental principle, or principles, of the Law, the most famous being that of Hillel (*c.* 25 B.C.): 'What you yourself hate (to be done to you), do not do to your fellow; this is the whole law; the rest is commentary; go and learn it.' Cf. also Gal. 5^{14} and Rom. 13^{9}. But as Abrahams points out† the aim of all such rabbinic attempts was to formulate the basic principle from which the rest of the Law could be deduced as a corollary (cf. Matt. 22^{40}), not to isolate certain commandments as being vital, in contrast to others which were less important or could be ignored. According to the rabbis, *all*

* It is argued that Mark's version of the story in which – most unusually – a scribe is friendly is likely to be more authentic than a version in which the incident is represented as a typical controversy between Jesus and the Jewish authorities – so e.g. Bultmann, p. 21.

† In an important essay 'The Greatest Commandment' in *Studies in Pharisaism and the Gospels*, I, 18ff.

the commandments must be kept (cf. James 2^{10}), and because the rabbinic formulations just described tended, despite their authors' intentions, to conflict with this principle, they became suspect and unpopular in many quarters; and Abrahams thinks that what the inquirer in our passage really wanted was 'an opinion as to whether Jesus did or did not share this fear of reducing the Law to fundamental rules'. The answer he received was clearly entirely satisfactory to him as an orthodox Jew and for that reason we should not perhaps too easily assume that by formulating the 'first of all commandments' (v. 28) Jesus implied any more than contemporary rabbis implied by their formulations. No doubt 'the importance of the episode from the standpoint of the Evangelist lay precisely in the fact that the Christian Church had drawn the inference which Judaism refused to draw, viz. that provided the spirit of the Law, as thus summed up, were kept, all else might be ignored,'* but how far such an attitude went back in its entirety to Jesus, as R. seems to believe, is a further question, and one too far-reaching to be decided here (such passages as Matt. 5^{17-20}, Luke 16^{17}, Matt. 23^{23}, and James 2^{10} would have to be taken into account, as well as, on the other side, Mark 7^{19}, etc.).

Likewise a full discussion of the implications of the saying is beyond the scope of a commentary such as this. As far as love towards God is concerned, it is a deceptively simple idea, only mentioned elsewhere in the Synoptic Gospels at Luke 11^{42}, and seldom referred to in other parts of the New Testament (though cf. Rom. 8^{28}, 1 Cor. 2^{9}, 8^{3}, 16^{22}, and Eph. 6^{24}); this is no doubt, as V. T. says, because the New Testament emphasis lies rather on God's prior love for man, from which man's love for God is derived and takes its character (cf. e.g. Rom. 5^{8} and 1 John 3^{16} and 4^{9-11}). 'As such it is indeed *agape*, pure self-giving, which looks neither for reward or satisfaction' (V. T.). But this is by no means the whole story – see further J. Burnaby, *Amor Dei*, A. Nygren, *Agape and Eros*, P. S. Watson, *Let God be God* (especially pp. 48–59), and G. Bornkamm, *Jesus of Nazareth*, pp. 109f.

The same writers discuss the equally complex conception of love

* R., p. 171, who goes on: 'It was in this fashion that the Christian Church, in its Gentile-Christian form, was able to reconcile in one religious system the retention as sacred Scripture of the Old Testament, in which the Law was set forth as God's revealed will for His people, with the Pauline principle that the Law nevertheless was not binding upon Christians of Gentile descent.'

for one's neighbour; in Lev. 19^{18}, where the conception stands in contrast to 'taking vengeance or bearing any grudge' against one's neighbour, the idea is clearly of a tender regard for others and a promoting of their good, as active as our promotion of our own. Probably Jesus interpreted the command in the same sort of way, except that, whereas in Leviticus *neighbour* meant simply a fellow countryman,* Jesus gave it the wider connotation it was generally taken to have in his time (see below).

A further point which is often stressed is the essential *interrelatedness* of the two commandments; true love of the neighbour springs from the love of God, and on the other hand there can be no true love of God which does not express itself in love of the neighbour. Wellhausen (p. 103) goes even further and sees the grounding of the whole matter in the monotheism proclaimed in v. 29b: 'Monotheism is no theory; it is a practical conviction; it is the spring of inward character and of our conduct to our neighbour. It is in other words, the motive of morality' (cf. V. T., p. 486, to the same effect). Of the practical truth of these contentions there will be no doubt, but perhaps a word of caution may be allowed about the danger of reading too much into the actual words of our text.

28

On linguistic grounds the first half of the verse should be regarded as a Marcan composition; perhaps as it reached St Mark the story began: 'And one came and asked him . . .'

Which commandment . . . ? As we have seen, this is a question which seems to have been debated a good deal among the scribes; the words of Hillel quoted above were spoken in answer to a similar inquiry, and it is entirely plausible that Jesus should have been asked such a question without there being any intention to trap him.

the first of all: For the meaning of this see p. 325 above.

29–30

The first part of the so-called *Shemah* (Deut. 6^{4-9}, 11^{13-21}, and Num. 15^{37-41}) which every pious Jew recites daily and which played a great part in late-Jewish piety and in rabbinic discussion. St Mark is the only Synoptist to include v. 29b, so it must remain doubtful whether the early Church saw in it the profound significance which Wellhausen

* The context makes that clear.

discovers (see above). Perhaps in a Gentile *milieu*, such as St Mark's, an emphasis on the strict monotheism of Christianity was particularly necessary; cf. 1 Cor. 8[5-6].

and with all your mind: This does not occur in the Old Testament text, though *dianoia* (mind) is often used in LXX as an alternative translation for the Hebrew word here translated *heart*. The addition no doubt emphasizes the all-embracing character of the required response.

31
Strictly speaking the inquiry concerned only *one* commandment (v. 28); perhaps the two Old Testament passages are thought of as constituting a single supreme command, or perhaps the whole of v. 28 is secondary and not perfectly adapted to the pericope it introduces.

neighbour: Whatever the meaning of the word in the original Leviticus passage, it seems clear that by Our Lord's time it was taken to include at any rate the resident aliens in Israel as well as the Israelites themselves; whether it was interpreted more widely still is disputed. Christian commentators almost always assume, on the basis of Luke 10[29-37], that Our Lord here understood it in a completely unrestricted sense, but perhaps Montefiore's caution about this deserves at least to be considered (I, 285 and II, 466–8), though see now Bornkamm, op. cit.

32ff.
These verses are found only in Mark and their presence produces the unusual result that the decisive saying of Jesus does not form the conclusion of the pericope. Those who think that in the original version of the story the decisive words were spoken by the scribe see in these verses a reminiscence of it, and they point out that Jesus' strong commendation in v. 34 would be most natural if the scribe had said something strikingly novel and bold. If we accept St Mark's version as the original one, perhaps the best explanation is that these verses were retained as driving home the complete identity of view between Jesus and this representative of orthodox Judaism.

Wellhausen comments (p. 103): '(morality,) according to . . . the scribe, belongs to the service of God and is the true way of worshipping him; it is of more value than all sacred actions which are specially rendered to God and are of no use to anyone else.' Such ideas are by no means novel – cf. e.g. 1 Sam. 15[22] and Hos. 6[6]; and there are rabbinic parallels. The words do not exclude ceremonies and sacrifice, and just how much they meant would have depended, as V. T. observes, on the tone of voice in which they were uttered. Jesus clearly found them acceptable, though the precise terms of his answer raise a problem.

Taken at their face value they seem to represent the kingdom as something already present. J. Weiss points out that there are other New Testament passages where we find the image of the kingdom as a goal towards which men must make their pilgrimage, some being nearer to it than others. But he adds (p. 175): 'that does not alter the fact that in its basic idea, the kingdom of God is something which comes down to men from on high'; and the present passage should not be pressed against the general impression of Jesus' teaching on the kingdom which St Mark gives. We cannot be sure that we are dealing with Jesus' precise words, and even if we are, they may easily mean: 'You come near to possessing the qualifications requisite for entry into the kingdom when it comes' (so R. and Montef.).

Despite their negative form, the sense of Jesus' words is no doubt to stress the scribe's *nearness* to the kingdom and we probably should not ask what he still lacked which kept him from a still closer approach (cf. 10^{17}ff.); if, however, St Mark did have any such question in mind, no doubt his answer, as Wellhausen suggests, was that what is lacking is the acknowledgement of Jesus, imitation of him, and admission to the company of his disciples (cf. Mark 10^{21} and Matt. 11^{11} // Luke 7^{28}).

34b
To be ascribed to St Mark on linguistic grounds; its purpose is to round off the series of pronouncement stories and mark a pause before the final incident in the section, in which Jesus takes the initiative; but it is only imperfectly adapted to this position, for the last incident is not such as to discourage further questions, and St Matthew and St Luke both remove it to other contexts (Matt. 22^{46}, Luke 20^{40}).

12^{35-37a} ON DAVID'S SON

35 *And as Jesus taught in the temple, he said, 'How can the scribes say that*
the Christ is the son of David? 36 *David himself, inspired by*[a] *the Holy*
Spirit, declared,

> *"The Lord said to my Lord,*
> *Sit at my right hamd,*
> *till I put thy enemies under thy feet."*

37 *David himself calls him Lord; so how is he his son?'*

a Or *himself, in*

12^{35-37a}

This originally independent pericope formed part of a loosely knit supplement to $11^{27}–12^{34}$; it is described by Manson as 'a polemical passage which has been much discussed without any very satisfactory conclusion being reached' (*T. J.*, p. 266, n. 2). Jesus now takes the initiative;* his argument, which presupposes (*a*) that the Psalms were composed by David under infallible divine guidance, and (*b*) that the particular Psalm verse quoted refers to the Messiah, has generally been supposed to be directed against various nationalistic forms of the Jewish hope prevalent at the time. According to these, the coming kingdom of God would be a restored and glorified, but still essentially nationalistic, Davidic kingdom, and correspondingly the Messiah – the head of the kingdom – would be a descendant of the Davidic line (cf. 2 Sam. 7^{12}, Jer. 30^{9}, Ezek. 34^{23}, etc.). (See Introduction, pp. 44 and 46.) Jesus points out, however, that any member of the Davidic dynasty – even the latest and most powerful – would be only David's son; David could say to him: 'You owe your position to me. You are only a member, however exalted, of a dynasty of which I am still the head.' But David in fact calls the Messiah 'Lord' – he must therefore be something altogether higher than a second David (and his kingdom must be of an altogether higher order – see *T. J.*, as above). What Jesus disclaims, on this view, is 'the Pharisees' notion of Messiahship as *determined* by sonship to David "according to the flesh", rather than by the divine sonship, or unique spiritual relation to God – which was to Jesus the basis of his own messianic vocation'. Bartlet, from whom this quotation comes, and many other commentators assume that Jesus here claims to be Messiah, and, as such, son of David (cf. e.g. Matt. 1^{1-17}, Luke 3^{23-38}, Rom. 1^{3}, 2 Tim. 2^{8}) but that he claims to be much more beside (so e.g. V. T. and also R.: 'He was indeed "Son of David", but he was only "Son of David" with a difference'). By the time the Gospel was written, Jesus' Messiahship and his Davidic descent were accepted throughout the Church, so it must have been in some such way as this that St Mark understood the passage.

But when we inquire about the original sense of the saying, certain difficulties have to be faced. In the first place, even if we suppose that Jesus in his lifetime believed himself to be Messiah, the passage seems

* Cf. 3^{1-6} where he similarly takes the initiative after a series of controversy incidents in which he has been attacked.

to conflict with the messianic secret. Even those who hold that Jesus towards the end of his ministry initiated his disciples into the secret of his Messiahship recognize that he forbade their making the fact known to others. How then would he have come to be defending his Messiahship against Jewish critics? If he was not defending or defining his own messianic role, he must have been carrying on a merely verbal exchange about a purely speculative question, and that, despite Dibelius (*F. T. G.*, p. 261), seems extremely unlikely.*

Secondly, if the argument is taken in its natural sense, it implies, not that the Messiah was *not merely* son of David, but that he was not son of David *at all*.† Accordingly, many critics have supposed that Jesus, not being in fact of Davidic descent, but having become firmly assured of his Messiahship, searched the scriptures for evidence that the Messiah would not in fact be of David's line. If it be objected that the Old Testament evidence for the Davidic descent of the Messiah was too strong for anyone to have hoped to set it aside in this fashion (cf. e.g., in addition to the passages cited above, Isa. 9^{2-7} and 11^{1-9}, Jer. $23^{5f.}$, Ps. $89^{20ff.}$), it may be replied that a number of non-Davidic 'messiahs' are known to have won widespread support, and that Jesus may have shared the view of those who expected a purely supernatural figure (the Son of man) as redeemer, and not a human figure at all (cf. how he uses *Son of man* as self-designation in preference to *Messiah* with its earthly and political associations – see on 8^{31}, pp. 224–5, 14^{62} and pp. 46–7). If, however, Jesus himself had uttered these words, it is difficult to understand how the Church so soon came to prize and proclaim his own Davidic descent, and it is probably best, with the

* See John Knox, *The Death of Christ*, p. 41.

† B. thinks this need not be so if we allow for the semitic idiom whereby *A is X rather than Y* could be expressed *A is X and not Y*. Cf. e.g. Hos. 6^6 which was held perfectly compatible with the rites of the temple because it was taken to mean 'I desire mercy more than I do sacrifice'. In accordance with this idiom the expression here might mean only: 'The Messiah is David's Lord much more than he is his son.'

In view of the use of Ps. 110^1 at Acts $2^{34f.}$ and elsewhere in the New Testament, B. thinks the superiority of the Messiah to David which made the latter call him 'Lord' was found in the fact that the Messiah was elevated after death to God's right hand and thus became a heavenly being, while David was not. This view deserves to be considered carefully, but, as B. himself says, there is no evidence for it in the present passage, in which the entire weight of the argument seems to depend on the first six words of the quotation.

majority of scholars, to regard them as an early Christian production. In that case they are probably the product either (*a*) of a party which sought to show that the Messiah was Son of man rather than son of David (perhaps as a means of countering a Jewish objection that Jesus was not of Davidic descent),* or possibly (*b*) of some hellenistic group which sought to show that Jesus was more than son of David, namely Son of God.

Some such suggestion is the more likely in view of the fact that Ps. 110[1] was well known and much used as a 'proof text' in the early Church (see above).

35–37

This is one of the sayings which was preserved with little or no biographical setting. Verse 37b is generally agreed to be part of the introduction to the next section; v. 35a presumably served to introduce this saying when it was current as an isolated unit; in the present context the words are redundant after 11[27]. No real attempt is made to link the passage with what has gone before, and it is uncertain whether, as many commentators believe, St Mark envisaged a change of scene between vv. 34 and 35.

36

David . . . Spirit: The argument is strengthened by the insistence that David's description of the Messiah as Lord has divine authority.

If the saying is authentic Jesus already regarded himself as the 'Lord' of the Psalms; the likelihood of that has been endlessly debated – cf. e.g. R., *The New Testament Doctrine of the Christ*, especially pp. 76ff. and 231ff., and on the other side Bultmann, *Theology of the New Testament*, I, 121ff. The title was certainly widely used of Jesus in the primitive Church and no doubt this passage was valued by the Evangelist as providing scriptural justification for such usage.

The view on which the argument rests, that the Psalms were written by David, though universal at the time, is erroneous. R. comments: 'it was no part of the meaning of the Incarnation that the Lord's human mind should be possessed of miraculous information about matters of historical fact.'

A similar comment may be made about the assumption that Ps. 110[1]

* If Jesus was not originally known to be of Davidic descent, such a Jewish objection could be met either, as here, by denying that Davidic descent is a necessary qualification for Messiahship, or else, as elsewhere in the New Testament, by the endeavour to provide evidence that he *was* of David's line.

refers to the Messiah; this too was probably widespread at the time, though we have no explicit evidence for it from Jewish sources till the third century. In fact, according to many modern commentators, the Psalm is of Maccabean date and the reference is to Simon Maccabeus (142 – 134 B.C.), though others assign it to the eighth or ninth century.

37
how: Probably the correct translation here of a Greek word (*pŏthĕn*) normally meaning 'whence'. The word gives no support to the suggestion of R. and others that the meaning is: 'in what sense . . . ?'

12^{37b-40} A WARNING AGAINST THE SCRIBES

And the great throng heard him gladly.
38 *And in his teaching he said, 'Beware of the scribes, who like to go about*
in long robes, and to have salutations in the market places 39 *and the best seats*
in the synagogues and the places of honour at feasts, 40 *who devour widows'*
houses and for a pretence make long prayers. They will receive the greater
condemnation.'

This section is linked to the last by means of the catchword *scribes* (see on $9^{42ff.}$, etc.), but there is also a topical connexion: the teaching of the scribes having been attacked in vv. 35–37a, their practice now comes under fire; and the upshot (especially in view of vv. 13–27) is to reinforce the lesson of vv. 1–12 that the leaders and teachers of the nation have proved unfaithful husbandmen and fully merited the condemnation which is in store for them.

The sayings themselves are generally agreed to have been excerpted by St Mark from a larger compilation similar to those underlying Matthew 23 and Luke 11^{37-52}. The general sense is clear enough, but in the light of the detailed points discussed below considerable qualifications of the general scope of the attack seem to be called for.

ꙮ

37b
the great throng: A rather unusual phrase in the Greek. Moffatt may be right in translating 'the mass of the people'.

38
go about in long robes; Most commentators agree with R.S.V. in preferring this to the alternative reading 'walk about in porticoes'; if so the reference will be to the Jewish outer garment known as the *tallith*, of which the scribes wore a distinctively large version. Properly, the time for them to wear these garments was at prayer and during the performance of certain other scribal duties, but according to this passage they were parading their piety by wearing them continually; it may be that Matt. 23^{5b} presents an alternative version of the Aramaic original behind the saying (see *S.J.*, pp. 229–31).

38–39
salutations ... feasts: The picture is of men who expect the greatest deference to be paid to them in virtue of their religious superiority. The rule was that a man should 'salaam' his superior in knowledge of the Law, though it is only fair to add that some of the most distinguished rabbis are known to have waived this right and been eager to make their salutation first (see below). In the synagogues it was becoming the custom at this time for the Elders to sit in front of, and facing, the congregation. For the importance attached to precedence at banquets cf. Luke 14^{7-11}; according to later custom it was decided in accordance with age, but in the time of Our Lord it went in accordance with learning.

40
The Greek is not grammatically connected with v. 39, and is better represented by R.V. which adds *they* at the beginning of the verse. Possibly the lack of connexion means that the verse comes from a different part of St Mark's source, and if, as the Greek allows, we add the *they* of R.V. and omit that of R.S.V., this may be a self-contained saying with no special reference to the scribes. However, St Mark is probably right in taking it to refer to them, in which case the point may be that they took large sums from credulous old women as a reward for the prolonged prayer which they professed to make on their behalf. If, however, we take the two parts of the charge in v. 40 separately, the second will be another reference to ostentatious and hypocritical exhibitions of piety,* while, as to the first, religious leaders in every

* C. F. Burney argued that the words are a rendering of an Aramaic original better translated in Matt. 23^{5} *they make their phylacteries broad* – see *S.J.*, p. 230.

age have been known to make undue use of their influence over wealthy women in the cause of religious institutions (cf. Josephus, *Antiquities*, XVII, 2, 4 and see Abrahams, *Studies in Pharisaism and the Gospels*, I. Ch. 10). We have, however, no reason to think that this or any other form of 'devouring widows' houses' was common among the scribes, and in general the passage must be regarded as altogether too sweeping and unqualified in its attack on the scribes as a class. No doubt there may have been bad scribes, but there were also a large number of very good ones. V. T. writes: 'A hostile attitude to Judaism and to the rabbis is reflected in the choice and use of these sayings, despite the probability that they represent actual utterances of Jesus.'

12$^{41-44}$ A POOR WIDOW GIVES HER ALL

[41]*And he sat down opposite the treasury, and watched the multitude putting*
money into the treasury. Many rich people put in large sums. [42]*And a poor*
widow came, and put in two copper coins, which make a penny. [43]*And he*
called his disciples to him, and said to them, 'Truly, I say to you, this poor
widow has put in more than all those who are contributing to the treasury.
[44]*For they all contributed out of their abundance; but she out of her poverty*
has put in everything she had, her whole living.'

This beautiful story is perhaps best explained as originally a Jewish parable which Jesus took over in his teaching and which was later transformed into an incident in his life. A number of quite close parallels are known from both pagan and Jewish sources, most notably the story in *Leviticus Rabba* (III, 5) of a priest who scorned a woman's offering of a handful of flour; overnight he received in a vision the rebuke: 'Despise her not; it is as though she offered her life.'

The present setting of the story may in part be due simply to the catchword *widow* (vv. 40 and 42), but a more apt position for it could hardly be imagined. Not only does it form a fitting contrast to the previous section ('In contrast to the bad scribes, who "eat" widows' property, we have now the tale of the good widow and her sacrifice' (Montefiore)), but with its teaching that the true gift is to give 'everything we have' (v. 44) it sums up what has gone before in the Gospel and makes a superb transition to the story of how Jesus 'gave everything' for men.

41
The details are even more imprecise than usual, especially as there is some uncertainty about what is meant by *the treasury*. Elsewhere the Greek word is used for the rooms or cells in which the temple valuables or deposits were stored (e.g. 1 Macc. 14^{49}, 2 Macc. 3^{6}, etc.); here it is generally taken to refer to some kind of receptacle for offerings. According to the *Mishnah* there were thirteen such receptacles (known from their shape as 'trumpets') placed round the walls of the court of women. Other suggestions, however, have been made, particularly with a view to explaining how Jesus could have known what the rich people and the poor widow gave; but even such suggestions do not explain how he knew what the widow gave was *her whole living* (v. 44), and it is probably simplest to suppose that a story related *by* Jesus (on the basis of a current Jewish parable) has been transformed into a story *about* him. In that case St Mark himself may have had no very clear idea what *treasury* was intended.

42
two copper coins: The Greek word (*lĕpton*) means literally 'a tiny thing' (cf. English 'mite') and was used for the smallest coin in circulation.

which make a penny: Literally a *quadrans*. St Mark transliterates the Latin word into Greek. The coin is often said to have circulated only in the West, and the inclusion of the explanation that the two *lepta* make a *quadrans* is held to point to Roman readers, who could not be expected to be familiar with the coinage of Palestine. However, there is evidence that the name was naturalized in Palestine through the Greek, and Cadbury shows that it is unsafe to deduce from this verse any conclusions about the Gospel's place of origin (*The Making of Luke-Acts*, p. 89 and n. 15).

Mark 13

The Future Foretold:

Suffering will lead to Glory

This chapter is the only place in the Gospel where we hear of Our Lord delivering a long, consecutive speech on a single topic.* In order to understand this unique section of the Gospel it is more than ever necessary to put ourselves in the position of the original readers in the last third of the first century. To begin with, many of the things mentioned in the chapter were known to them from bitter personal experience (e.g. vv. 6–8, 9–13, 21–22?, and 14–20) and very likely the destruction of Jerusalem and the temple were to them already things of the past; secondly they were familiar, from the Old Testament and later Jewish writings, with just the kind of speech here attributed to Our Lord. Two types of writing prepared them for it.

(*a*) *The Apocalypse* (see Introduction, p. 44). This was a literary form, very popular and widespread at the time, in which the author revealed the substance of visions which had been granted to him. Despite the highly coloured, and often rather obscure, imagery of these visions, the reader could always see in them a picture of contemporary or impending events, and the drift of the visions was to encourage him by showing that, however black things might look, they were in fact fully under the control of God, who would shortly, and dramatically, vindicate himself and his faithful servants. Apocalyptic was a means of sustaining hope and perseverance among an oppressed people during periods when *direct* reference to oppressors and their approaching downfall was dangerous or impossible. The effect of the visions was enhanced by the fact that they were almost always attributed to some great religious figure of a previous age. It

*4^{1-34}, 9^{31-50}, and 7^{1-23} provide only partial parallels, but they do help us to see St Mark's method in such cases. 'A particular saying, significant for his purpose, becomes the point of departure for a series of loosely connected logia of kindred (or supposedly kindred) nature, usually in the form of later explanation to the inner circle' (Bacon, *The Gospel of Mark*, p. 121). For any real parallel to this section of Mark we have to go to the discourses in St John's Gospel.

was thus made clear that contemporary disasters, so far from being out of God's control, had been foreseen and foretold by him many years previously; and the reader was encouraged to feel that if the prophecies of disaster had been so signally fulfilled, the prophecies of subsequent salvation would receive like fulfilment.*

(*b*) *The Farewell Discourse.* It was believed that when great religious leaders such as Jacob or Moses, Samuel or David, knew that they were about to die, they summoned their family or disciples or subjects, as the case might be, and delivered what amounted, religiously speaking, to their last will and testament. This might include a survey of the past and its lessons; it almost always included a survey of the prospects, and especially the dangers and sufferings, of the future, together with an exhortation to remain faithful and steadfast in face of them. These surveys, like the visions of the apocalyptists, were believed to depend on divine revelation and so they provided a solid ground for confidence in the period to which they referred, and the warnings they contained will have been taken very seriously.†

It is against this background that Mark 13 must be seen. Although it is commonly referred to as 'the little Apocalypse', it does not in fact correspond exactly with either of the categories just described, but combines characteristics of both.‡

* The obvious example of an apocalypse is the book of Daniel. Written in fact to bring comfort to the faithful during terrible times of persecution in the early second century B.C., it professes to reproduce (Chapters 7–12) the visions granted to a young Jew whose life is described (Chapters 1–6) as having been lived in Babylon early in the sixth century. The visions contain unmistakable allusions to Antiochus Epiphanes, the second-century oppressor of the Jews, and his miraculous overthrow is predicted.

† For examples, cf. the speeches of Jacob (Gen. 48^{21}–49), Moses (Deut. especially $31^{28\text{ff.}}$ and 32), Joshua (Joshua 23–24), Samuel (1 Sam. 12), David (1 Chron. 28–29) and Tobit (Tob $14^{3\text{ff.}}$); and for the New Testament, cf. Paul in Acts $20^{17\text{ff.}}$ (note especially v. 25). *The Assumption of Moses* and *The Testaments of the Twelve Patriarchs* are evidence for the popularity of this form at about the time when Mark was writing. In fact, needless to say, these speeches were composed long after the lifetime of the figure to whom they were attributed, though to say that is not to deny them their measure of inspiration.

‡ It has often been pointed out that, unlike the normal apocalypse, this discourse does not rest on any vision; moreover there is comparatively little fantastic imagery, and the continual tone of warning also distinguishes it from the normal apocalypse, which is concerned with encouragement and raising of hopes; Mark 13 is largely concerned with the *restraining* of them (cf. vv. 6,

The position of the discourse in the Gospel is also noteworthy. As we shall see, the subsequent chapters (14–15) already existed in some form before the Gospel was composed, so this discourse is used by Mark as the climax to that whole part of the Gospel he was responsible for composing. As such, it brings out the infinite significance the Evangelist saw in the events of the ministry. It can only be because those events are nothing less than God's final saving intervention in history that they can be expected to be followed, more or less immediately, by the end of the world and the coming of God's kingdom.

But equally the discourse has significance in relation to what follows; the section of the Gospel in which it occurs is undeniably sombre in tone (cf. e.g. the threat to Jesus implied in 12^{1-11}, 12^{12}, and 12^{13}), and this tone of sombreness and tragedy will deepen still further in the next two chapters; but just as the parabolic discourse was inserted at 4^{1-34} (see notes there) to give assurance of ultimate success despite temporary difficulties and hindrances, so this discourse, with its promise of ultimate glory and triumph, serves to set the sombreness of the Passion in its true perspective, and is meant to be kept in mind throughout our reading of the next two chapters. The suffering there described is but the path to the glory predicted here (cf. Luke 24^{26}). But, though the Evangelist, by his placing of the discourse, makes the *fact* clear, he does not establish any *organic connexion* between the suffering and the glory. Chapter 13 deals with the period after the crucifixion and in that period it predicts ultimate triumph for the Son of man, without any hint of previous suffering on his part; the crucifixion is nowhere referred to. Conversely Chapters 14–15 contain little reference to a glorious consummation in connexion with the Son of man. Lightfoot comments on these facts: 'The position of the discourse in St Mark, immediately before the Passion narrative, but

---

7, 8, 10, 21, 22, 24 and see below). Professor Dodd accordingly prefers to call it 'a *Mahnrede* ("warning speech") in apocalyptic terms rather than an apocalypse proper.' B. W. Bacon has pointed out its resemblance to 2 Thess. 2, suggesting that, just as that chapter was designed to curb over-eager expectations aroused by the events of A.D. 40 (see below), this discourse, in its present form, was designed to curb 'the fanatical apocalypticism the Evangelist expects (or knows) as an immediate sequel to the disasters of A.D. 66–70' (see *The Gospel of Mark*, Part II). On the other hand, the apocalyptic imagery it does contain, and its concern with the end of the world (especially vv. 24–27) distinguish it from most of the farewell discourses cited above.

altogether independent of it, suggests that at the time of the composition of his Gospel the Church had not yet found it possible to define satisfactorily the relationship between the crucifixion and the expected final consummation' (*H. & I.*, p. 94). For the required definition we must go to St Paul and St John and later writers.

One other feature of the discourse deserves notice – its secrecy. It is given *privately* (v. 3) to the four disciples who, according to St Mark, have been longest with Jesus. We have seen that such private expositions of public pronouncements are something of a convention in Mark (cf. e.g. $4^{10\text{ff.}}$ $7^{17\text{ff.}}$, 9^{11-13}, 10^{10-12}) and Professor Dodd notes that they are usually designed to clear up some difficulty in the public pronouncement concerned. He suggests that one purpose of the discourse here is to remove possible misunderstanding of Jesus' prophecy about the destruction of the temple (v. 2) by showing that he saw it as an integral part of the final drama and not simply 'as an impending historical event, still less an act which Jesus Himself had plotted, as His enemies alleged' (*Parables*, p. 62). There may well be truth in this, though, more generally, we should no doubt also see the discourse as an effort on the part of the Church to apply the teaching of Jesus to its present urgent and bewildering needs. The mountain (v. 3) was the traditional place of revelation, and cf. Zech. 14^4 for the Mount of Olives in particular (v. 3) as the destined scene of the apocalyptic judgement.

With regard to the authenticity and integrity of the discourse, there is a wide variety of opinion. For a long time critics generally found the basis of the chapter in an independent Jewish or Jewish-Christian apocalypse, probably composed about A.D. 40, which St Mark and his predecessors expanded with sayings derived from Our Lord and other sources. However, the precise limits of this supposed document were very variously defined, and, though the hypothesis of its existence still has many defenders, the tendency of late has been rather to suggest a number of sources for the chapter, both written and oral. This would certainly explain the inconsistencies which make it difficult to give a single coherent exposition of the discourse as a whole.* In a commentary such as this, only broad questions of

* In two notable books, *Jesus and the Future* and *A Commentary on Mark Thirteen*, Dr G. R. Beasley-Murray has indeed recently attempted to show that the chapter goes back to Jesus himself and may even have been delivered by

analysis can be considered, and the following widely accepted scheme will be followed:

1–4 Introduction to the discourse proper.

5–27 The discourse.

(i) 5–13 Miseries which will precede the last days. (*a*) vv. 5–8 which seem to go back to some Jewish, or Jewish-Christian, apocalyptic document. (*b*) vv. 9–13 a group of sayings of Jesus, in its present form compiled by the Evangelist.

(ii) 14–23 The last days. This section reproduces a pre-Marcan document, clearly distinct from: i(*a*), together with a number of additional sayings.

(iii) 24–27 The end. Another pre-Marcan document, possibly originally the continuation of: i(*a*).

28–37 A supplement, consisting of originally independent sayings designed to set all the above in its true perspective for Mark's original readers.

13 1–4 INTRODUCTION TO CHAPTER 13

13 *And as he came out of the temple, one of his disciples said to him, 'Look,*
Teacher, what wonderful stones and what wonderful buildings!' 2 *And Jesus*
said to him, 'Do you see these great buildings? There will not be left here one
stone upon another, that will not be thrown down.'
3 *And as he sat on the Mount of Olives opposite the temple, Peter and James*
and John and Andrew asked him privately, 4 *'Tell us, when will this be,*
and what will be the sign when these things are all to be accomplished?'

These verses serve as a link between the last scene and the discourse, though in fact there is something of a hiatus between vv. 4 and 5, for the saying in v. 2, and the question it provokes in v. 4, are concerned simply with the destruction of the temple, whereas the answer in 5ff. makes no explicit reference to the temple, but deals with the end of the world.*

* Cf. already in the fifth century the comment of Victor of Antioch (J. A. Cramer, *Catenae in Evang. S. Matt. et S. Marci*, p. 408): 'They asked

him, in more or less its present form, as a continuous discourse. Dr Beasley-Murray makes a number of important points, but, for all its acuteness and learning, his argument hardly carries conviction as a whole.

The section itself seems to be an artificial construction. As far as v. 1 is concerned, although Herod's temple was certainly a striking sight – 'probably the most imposing edifice of contemporary civilization' – the disciple's remark here seems, as Bultmann says: 'too obviously composed to elicit the well-known prophecy about the temple' (p. 36). As for v. 2, it is probable, as we shall see (see on 14^{57-59}), that Jesus did some time utter a prophecy of the destruction of the temple, though whether, as many scholars think, it was in this quite general form (cf. Mic. 3^{12}, Jer. $26^{6, 18}$, and the story in the *Talmud* that Rabbi Johanan ben Zakkai foretold the destruction of the temple forty years before it occurred) or whether it implied that Jesus would be the instrument of the destruction and would build a new, spiritual temple, it is impossible to say. During the siege of Jerusalem in A.D. 70 Roman soldiers set fire to the temple and it was subsequently demolished together with the rest of the city. Clearly the impact of this prophecy on the Roman Christians would be considerable, if they had just heard news of its fulfilment.

For vv. 3 and 4 see p. 342.

13^{5-13} A WARNING OF THE MISERIES WHICH WILL PRECEDE THE LAST DAYS

(*a*) 13^{5-8} *A negative reply*

[5]*And Jesus began to say to them, 'Take heed that no one leads you astray.* [6]*Many will come in my name, saying, "I am he!" and they will lead many astray.* [7]*And when you hear of wars and rumours of wars, do not be alarmed; this must take place, but the end is not yet.* [8]*For nation will rise against nation, and kingdom against kingdom; there will be earthquakes in various places, there will be famines; this is but the beginning of the sufferings.'*

Jesus foretells the occurrence of certain disastrous events; these, he says, need occasion no desperate alarm, for they all lie within the

---

one question; he answers another.' Elsewhere in Mark the formula *he began to say* introduces a speech rather than an answer to a question, for which Mark has other formulas. See *T.J.*, p. 262, n. 1.

scope of God's plan (v. 7 – see below); on the other hand, they must not be mistaken for the 'birth-pangs', the terrible sufferings which will be the *immediate* precursor of the end of the world; these they merely introduce.

Most of the disasters referred to are mentioned as divine judgements in the Old Testament and had become commonplaces in apocalyptic descriptions of the end of the world. (Cf. e.g. 1 Kings 8^{37}, Jer. $4^{11ff.}$, Ezek. 5^{12}, 2 Esdras 9^{3}, 13^{31}, $15^{14f.}$, *Sib. Orac.*, 3, 633–64, etc.) The early Christians, however, would naturally identify them with the disasters of their own day (the *wars and rumours of wars* on the eastern frontier of the Empire and in Britain, the famines and earthquake shocks we know to have occurred under Claudius and Nero, various risings in Palestine, and the like); and so they would be helped to see these latter in perspective, and warned against the various fanatics who were seeing in them the immediate inbreaking of the kingdom. Verses 5–6 clearly witness to the existence of such fanatics, but from the rather obscure wording of v. 6 it is not possible to tell exactly who they were or what they claimed (see below).

❧

5–6

This fits awkwardly with v. 4, where the question is not: 'When will you appear?' but: 'When will the temple be destroyed?'

6

come in my name, saying, 'I am he!': The last three words represent two Greek words *ego eimi* ('I am'), which in this context may possibly mean 'I am the Messiah'. We know of various individuals in first-century Palestine who collected large numbers of followers on the promise of working various marvels (cf. e.g. Judas and Theudas in Acts $5^{36f.}$), and the reference may be to them. But it is not certain that any of these made messianic claims, and certainly they did not come 'in Christ's name'.* If the passage is derived from a Jewish source, the words *in my name* must be a Christian addition; in any case their meaning presumably is that in claiming to be Messiah, these pretenders were usurping a title which belongs properly to Jesus. But this would be a very strained meaning for the phrase *in my name* (contrast 9^{39}), and the R.S.V. translation 'I am *he*' may well be the right one; in that case, there must have been pretenders, otherwise unknown to us, who actually claimed to be Jesus himself returned from on high.

* See e.g. J. Knox: *The Death of Christ*, pp. 118–19.

7–8
Two reasons are given for not being *alarmed.* The disciples are to realize that God has a plan and the disasters which surround them are a necessary part of it (this is the force of *this* (better 'these') *must take place,* cf. Dan. 2^{28} (especially in LXX) and for *must* see p. 225); on the other hand, since these disasters are not the 'birth-pangs' (see on v. 8 below), there is no call for the sort of inward agitation to be expected when the end comes. The best commentary here is 2 Thess. (especially Chapter 2), which shows that there were Christians who had been persuaded by events that the end of all things had arrived. The aim of 2 Thess. is to persuade such people that *the end is not yet,* and it is significant that in doing so it uses language closely similar to that used here; see 2 Thess. 2^{3} (cf. v. 6 here), 2^{1-2} (the Greek word for *excited* in v. 2 is the same as that translated *alarmed* here, the only other place in the New Testament where the word is used). As V. T. says: 'It is manifestly a question for consideration whether the Pauline apocalypse has affected the arrangement of Mark 13 and is in some way connected with it' (p. 505).

8
the sufferings: Literally 'the travail pangs'. The doctrine that the messianic age would come to birth through a period of woes, as a baby does (based on such passages as Isa. 26^{17}, 66^{8}, Jer. 22^{23}, Hos. 13^{13}, Mic. $4^{9f.}$), later became a commonplace with the rabbis, and there are grounds for thinking that 'birth-pangs' was already a technical term in this connexion by the time of Our Lord. If the last phrase is genuine here the emphasis must be as in R.S.V. – the disasters just described will do no more than *introduce* the 'birth-pangs' proper; but in the Greek, the passage as a whole exhibits a poetic structure which is broken by the last phrase of v. 8, which may, therefore, be a marginal gloss interpolated into the text.

(*b*) 13^{9-13} *Warning to Christians*

9 '*But take heed to yourselves; for they will deliver you up to councils; and*
you will be beaten in synagogues; and you will stand before governors and
kings for my sake, to bear testimony before them. 10 *And the gospel must*
first be preached to all nations. 11 *And when they bring you to trial and deliver*
you up, do not be anxious beforehand what you are to say; but say whatever
is given you in that hour, for it is not you who speak, but the Holy Spirit.
12 *And brother will deliver up brother to death, and the father his child, and*
children will rise against parents and have them put to death; 13 *and you will*
be hated by all for my name's sake. But he who endures to the end will be
saved.'

Having been warned about the fate in store for the world at large, and the right reaction to it, the disciples are now told of the particular things in store for them *as Christians*; they will need to keep a firm watch on themselves (v. 9a) if they are to survive it all without loss of faith, but the reward is great (v. 13b) and they here receive forewarning, guidance, and the promise of divine help (v. 11b).

Jesus may well have foretold sufferings for his followers in this sort of way (cf. e.g. $8^{34ff.}$),* but most commentators believe that, as now formulated, the passage reflects to some extent the experience of the early Church, particularly the career of St Paul and the circumstances of the Neronian persecution (see below). Certainly Mark's first readers will have seen a reference to the events of their own day and will have been helped accordingly.

The fact that the Lucan parallel (Luke 21^{12-19}) agrees closely in substance, but differs almost completely in wording, suggests that the two Evangelists are giving independent versions of an original which must have been pre-Marcan, and may possibly have been in Aramaic. Which parts of the section St Mark derived from this original is a question which depends largely on the correct punctuation of the passage, and will be discussed briefly below.

❧

9–10

The punctuation of the Greek presupposed by R.S.V. is the normally accepted one, and on the basis of it, v. 10 is commonly regarded as an insertion into the original document by St Mark or a later redactor. Verses 9 and 11 are closely connected in thought and also linked by the catchword *deliver*;† the vocabulary of v. 10 is distinctively Marcan throughout, and, as a prose sentence, the verse breaks the poetic arrangement apparent in vv. 9 and 11–13. As to the originality of the verse as a saying of Jesus, if it implies that the Gentiles are to be admitted to the

* Though whether he originally assigned them to a period after his death is another matter; cf. e.g. the discussion between Dr Beasley-Murray (*Mark Thirteen*, pp. 12ff.) and Dr C. K. Barrett (*H. S. G. T.*, pp. 154ff. and *Expository Times*, 67 (1955–6), pp. 142ff.), who thinks the original reference was to the crisis of suffering Jesus and his followers were to undergo together as a *prelude* to the crucifixion.

† This word also links v. 11 to v. 12, and may have been the basis on which the various elements of this section were originally brought together – cf. p. 251.

Church without the necessity of circumcision, it can hardly be authentic. For if any such explicit saying had been known, the early Church would hardly have been as divided as it was over the question of Gentile converts. If *first* has its normal meaning, the idea is that the gathering in of *the full number of the Gentiles* is a necessary part of God's plan before the end can come; in that case cf. St Paul e.g. in Rom. 11[25ff.]. It is less likely that *first* is here used in a non-temporal sense – 'before all things'.

It is, however, possible to punctuate the Greek differently, in which case we get a poetic structure of another sort, and a significantly different meaning, which may be conveyed roughly as follows:

> Take heed to yourselves.
> *They will deliver you to councils and to synagogues*
> *You will be beaten before (both) governors and kings*
> *You will stand, for my sake, for a testimony to them and among the nations.*
> (Wherever you find yourselves) first preach the gospel;
> Then after your arrest by the authorities have no fear, etc.

The words in italics are arranged so as to indicate their poetic structure in the original; what follows, down to the end of v. 11, provides an explanation and development of them, and then vv. 12–13a form a further poetic structure, and commentary begins again in v. 13b. Professor Kilpatrick, who has argued most strongly for this sort of interpretation,* holds that it eliminates any reference to a Gentile mission. In the third clause he takes *to them* as referring to *governors and kings*, and *among all nations* as referring to a mission *to Jews* in the various countries in which they were scattered. 'All our text need imply is a mission in the synagogues, going far and wide beyond Palestine.' It should be pointed out, however, that even if this arrangement of the passage is the correct one, the last conclusion is not necessarily entailed. It would still be possible to take v. 10a with what precedes, as Professor Kilpatrick himself recognizes. The sense would then be: 'Before you are arrested, beaten, etc., the gospel must first be preached' and, in that context, the final phrase would perhaps most naturally be interpreted in a universalist sense.

9

councils: Though the Greek word is the same as that for the *Sanhedrin*, the reference here is to local councils such as those at whose orders St Paul

* See *Studies in the Gospels*, ed. D. E. Nineham, pp. 145ff., where the case is argued on the basis of Marcan and contemporary Greek usage.

was repeatedly beaten.* Likewise each *synagogue* had its *beth din* or local court of discipline. The governors (*hēgĕmŏnĕs*) will be Roman magistrates – procurators such as Felix and Festus (Acts 23[24], 24[27]) and also proconsuls such as Sergius Paulus and Gallio (Acts 13[7f.] and [12], 18[12], 19[38]), while *kings* refers no doubt to Antipas (6[14]) and Agrippa I (Acts 25[13]) and could also include the emperor. Cf. also Ps. 119[46], which the early Christians will have seen referred to here. If the narrower meaning is accepted for each word 'there is no compelling reason to think that the historical horizon of the saying extends beyond Palestine'; but Mark's first readers, at any rate, will surely have understood the saying in the light of what St Paul and others had experienced in all parts of the empire, particularly in Rome (cf. 2 Cor. 11[23ff.], etc.).

to bear testimony before them: Literally 'for a testimony to them'. Cf. 1[44], either this should be taken as R.S.V. (when Christians are on trial their judges cannot avoid hearing testimony to Christ – cf. Acts 24[24ff.] and 26[1ff.]), or the meaning may be that the suffering of the disciples, being part of the woes before the end, will make clear to governors and kings that the end is near. (So Kilpatrick, op. cit.)

11

A saying preserved in three independent forms (cf. Luke 12[11-12] and 21[14-15]); in view of the considerable divergence between these, and the division of opinion as to which is the more original, it is unsafe to make deductions about Our Lord's teaching on the Holy Spirit, especially as one form of the saying (Luke 21[15]) omits all reference to the Spirit.

When we remember that most of the early Christians were simple and unlearned people, for whom a speech in court would have been a terrible ordeal, we realize how much such a promise will have meant to them.

12

On the basis of Mic. 7[6], the idea of family divisions as a feature of the last days had become a commonplace of apocalyptic (cf. e.g. 2 Esdras 5[9], *Jubilees* 23[19], 2 *Baruch* 70[3], and cf. Luke 12[5ff.] for the thought of Jesus). This verse is probably a secondary form of the Lucan passage, modified in the light of the Church's experience during the Neronian persecution: 'One is strongly reminded of the *delatores* of later times who laid information against Christians before the imperial authorities' (V. T. – see further on next verse). Confronted with such treachery, Mark's readers would gain comfort from the fact that it had been

* 2 Cor. 11[23-4]; in later Greek the word could mean council or assembly of any kind.

foreseen by their Lord, and indeed foretold in the Old Testament (Mic. 7^{6}; cf. the fulfilment of Ps. 119^{46} in v. 9).

13
Here again, Jesus may well have prophesied unpopularity for his followers, but if so, his words have been transposed into another key; we seem here to be in the period when Christianity is universally known in the empire and hated 'on account of the Name'; for this last cf. 1 Pet. 4^{14} and, at a rather later date, *Ep. of Polycarp* 8^{2}, Justin, 1 *Apology*, 4 and Tertullian *Apology*, 2; see also Tacitus, *Annals*, xv. 44. V. T. thinks that v. 13b also is secondary as compared with Luke 21^{19}, being 'adapted to contemporary apocalyptic' – he compares 2 Esdras 6^{25} (5^{10}).

to the end: The Greek has no article and may simply be adverbial (= 'finally', 'without breaking down'). If R.S.V. is right, the idea may possibly be that those who keep faith to the 'end' (cf. v. 7) will obtain salvation without passing through death (cf. 2 Esdras 6^{25} and 7^{27} – though cf. also Rev. 2^{10}).

With regard to vv. 9–13 as a whole, Lohmeyer and others point out that vv. 10, 11b, and 13 disturb the poetic structure of the remaining verses and regard them as additions to the original source. This consisted of three four-line strophes, and each of the additions contains an assurance calculated to help those beset by the troubles described in the preceding strophe. (For Kilpatrick's view see on vv. 9–10 above.)

13^{14-23} THE SIGN BY WHICH THE ARRIVAL OF THE LAST DAYS MAY BE KNOWN, AND A DESCRIPTION OF THE LAST DAYS

14 *'But when you see the desolating sacrilege set up where it ought not to be*
(let the reader understand), then let those who are in Judea flee to the moun-
tains; 15 *let him who is on the housetop not go down, nor enter his house, to*
take anything away; 16 *and let him who is in the field not turn back to take*
his mantle. 17 *And alas for those who are with child and for those who give*
suck in those days! 18 *Pray that it may not happen in winter.* 19 *For in those*
days there will be such tribulation as has not been from the beginning of the
creation which God created until now, and never will be. 20 *And if the Lord*
had not shortened the days, no human being would be saved; but for the
sake of the elect, whom he chose, he shortened the days. 21 *And then if any one*

says to you, "Look, here is the Christ!" or "Look, there he is!" do not believe it. [22]*False Christs and false prophets will arise and show signs and wonders, to lead astray, if possible, the elect.* [23]*But take heed; I have told you all things beforehand.'*

This passage presents the exegete with difficulties as great as any in the Gospel. Its general significance in the total scheme of the chapter is obvious enough, and is indicated in the title above. Difficulties start with the fact that what is foretold here appears to be essentially a specific *historical* situation, and not, as we might have expected, a purely supernatural event. Professor Dodd, for example, writes (*Parables*, p. 64f.): 'The tribulation in Judea is described in Mark 13^{14-20} in a fantastic context, but nevertheless in terms which suggests a historical catastrophe ... The injunction [i.e. vv. 15–16] would admirably suit a supposed situation in which ... armies are threatening Jerusalem; and the prayer that it might not happen in winter [v. 18] is appropriate to war conditions. In a purely supernatural "apocalyptic" tribulation, summer or winter would matter little!'

What then is the historical situation in mind? We may start from St Luke's version, which is clearer than St Mark's, substituting for the enigmatic allusion in v. 14a, the words (21^{20}): *But when you see Jerusalem surrounded by armies, then know that its desolation has come near.* This deviation from St Mark has generally, and probably rightly, been taken as meaning that St Luke was writing after the siege and fall of Jerusalem in A.D. 66–70 and so conformed St Mark's version of the prophecy more exactly to the events which he regarded as its fulfilment. More recently, however, it has been suggested that Jesus himself may well, in the spirit of the prophets (cf. Mic. 3^{12} and Jer. $26^{6 \text{ and } 18}$), have foretold God's judgement on Jerusalem (cf. Luke $13^{34f.}$ and $19^{41ff.}$), and may quite possibly have predicted the form the judgement would take, at any rate in the general way attributed to him in St Luke. So the view has been gaining ground in some quarters that St Luke's version of the passage may reproduce, in something like its original form, a saying of Jesus which St Mark has 'apocalypticized', possibly because more precise language would have been dangerous at Rome during a period of persecution. (So e.g. *S. J.*, p. 330, V. T., and J. A. T. Robinson, *Jesus and His Coming*, p. 122. If so, the significance of the parenthesis in v. 14 will be obvious enough; the reader is to see through the symbolic language to the original reference. In that case what St Mark has done in this section is to transform an original prediction of the fall of Jerusalem (Luke 21[20–24])* into an apocalyptic utterance, by modifying it (v. 14a), adding apocalyptic traits (vv. 19–20), and setting it in a context where it represents one phase of a developing apocalyptic scheme.

However, H. Conzelmann (*The Theology of St Luke*, pp. 125ff) and J. C. O'Neill (*The Theology of Acts*, pp. 1–4) have now presented very strong arguments against the priority of the Lucan version, and in any case the question remains why St Mark chose the particular obscure wording he has adopted in v. 14a. Clearly in mind are such passages as Dan. 11[31], 12[11], and 9[27] and 1 Macc. 1[54]† where the reference is to the profanation of the temple by Antiochus Epiphanes, who in 168 B.C. placed in it an altar (? and statue) of Olympian Zeus. But in the Greek of Mark, whereas the word for *sacrilege* is neuter, the participle (*set up*)‡ is masculine, which suggests that St Mark is thinking, not of some object, such as an altar or a statue, but of a personal being, perhaps anti-Christ or his living representative.§ Some commentators see in the phrase simply a description of Rome (cf. the use of 'Babylon' in 1 Pet. 5[13], Rev. 18[2], or *the man of lawlessness* in 2 Thess. 2[3]) 'with the suggestion that Roman might embodies satanic power and is anti-Christ' (V. T., pp. 641–2). Most scholars, however, feel that something more specific must lie behind the choice of this particular imagery, and refer

* As it reached St Mark, it may not of course have been precisely in the form in which we now have it in Luke; C. H. Dodd thinks (see *J. R. S.*, 1947, p. 47ff.) that St Mark's and St Luke's versions are variant modifications of an earlier version.

† Dr Beasley-Murray's attempt to avoid this conclusion, on textual grounds, is hardly successful.

‡ A more literal translation than that of R.S.V. would be: 'When you see the abomination of desolation standing where *he* ought not'.

§ On anti-Christ see Introduction, pp. 44–5 and cf. R., p. 187, who speaks of 'the expectation .. that shortly before the final victory of God and of His Christ the power of incarnate Evil should be manifested in the mysterious form either of a God-opposing tyrant (such as had been Antiochus Epiphanes in the second century B.C., such as the Roman Emperor had come to be for the seer of the Revelation of St John) or else of a seductive agency, the incarnation of Beliar (= "Lawlessness"), who should claim for himself the prerogatives of God (so the Pauline Apocalypse in 2 Thess. 2[3ff.]). . . . It is probable that the roots of the conception are to be found ultimately in the (originally Babylonian) legend of the battle of God with a dragon-like monster' at the time of creation.

to the events of A.D. 40 when the Emperor Caligula came within an ace of having his statue set up in the temple at Jerusalem.* Naturally, at such a time the words of Daniel's prophecy would be very much in men's minds, and it is suggested, either

(*a*) that in some places the tradition of Jesus' words was modified at that time to fit the situation (which would account for the difference between the tradition as known to St Mark and as known to St Luke), or else

(*b*) that a Jewish-Christian apocalyptic document, drawn up in A.D. 40 to encourage and advise Christians, was subsequently incorporated into the tradition of Jesus' words.† If the latter view is correct and vv. 14–23 is based on a Jewish-Christian apocalypse, there is no means of knowing how much, if any, authentic utterance of the earthly Jesus it contains.

On such questions certainty is clearly unattainable, but it is perhaps in favour of the last view that Jesus is nowhere else reported as having given detailed instructions of this sort about what his followers were to do in situations of the remote future; indeed, as we have seen, it is uncertain how far Jesus envisaged an earthly future for his followers after his death (see Barrett as above, and on the other side W. G. Kömmel, *Promise and Fulfilment*). In either case it seems strange that we have no specific reference to the temple, but only the enigmatic words *where* he *ought not to be*. Either we must suppose, with V. T., that the situation at Rome when St Mark was writing made any more explicit reference dangerous, or, perhaps more probably, that by the time St Mark wrote, the temple had been destroyed, and so a prophecy which had referred explicitly to it had to be understood as having some more general reference. (See the discussion in B. W. Bacon *The Gospel of Mark*, Part II, where it is argued that the non-fulfilment of a Christian Apocalypse composed in A.D. 40 was a continuing problem to Christian writers of the first century, and was differently dealt with, according to the varying circumstances of their day by St Paul in 2 Thessalonians, St Mark, St Matthew, and St Luke;

* For the details, and the story of how the emperor's design eventually came to nothing, see Josephus, *Jewish War*, II, 184ff.

† No doubt if it emanated from a Jewish-Christian 'seer', it was thought of from the beginning as, in a very real sense, a word of the exalted Lord.

whatever may be thought of its conclusions no reader can fail to profit from this acute and learned study.*)

ཊཊ

14
For the literal translation see p. 352n. St Mark's phrase reproduces the Greek of Dan. 9^{27} and 12^{11} with only slight variation, but in the Hebrew the emphasis is not so much on the 'desolation' of the temple in the sense of its being destroyed or deserted, as on the idea of its being horribly profaned. To anyone who was aware of this it might have seemed that the destruction of the temple in A.D. 70 hardly fulfilled the prophecy.

where it ought not to be: See p. 352n. If the Gospel appeared after the destruction of the temple in A.D. 70, the meaning will be that the man of the desolating profanation will take his stand somewhere in Palestine or Jerusalem. 'All Palestine, but especially Jerusalem, was to a Jew holy ground, where the Gentile had no right to be' (Swete).

let the reader understand: Clearly these words can never have formed part of a spoken discourse. Either we are dealing with an apocalypse which originally appeared in writing, or else the words were added by St Mark or someone who worked over the tradition before him. The meaning will depend on the general interpretation of the passage. For one interpretation see p. 352; on Bacon's view the point is to make sure the reader takes in the reinterpretation of the prophecy from Daniel; Daniel's 'abomination' is not a material object but a manifestation of the man of sin or anti-Christ (Bacon, p. 130).

reader may mean the public reader of the community, who is to explain the meaning of the allusion to his hearers.

15–16
The idea of hasty flight is vividly portrayed. The flat roof of a Palestinian house connected directly to the street by an outside staircase. For work in the fields the outer garment was laid aside (cf. Virgil *Georgics* I, 299).

* On this view St Luke's version is not a verbatim reproduction of the original, but an attempt, alternative to St Mark's, to deal with a well-known prophecy of profanation which had not been precisely fulfilled with reference to the temple. Luke regards the destruction of Jerusalem and the temple in A.D. 70 as fulfilment enough, but St Mark and St Matthew, conscious that the events of 70 had involved no actual *profanation* of the temple, believe that the prophecy had been wrongly supposed to apply to the temple and that its fulfilment still lies in the future.

17
Obviously hasty flight would be especially difficult for expectant and nursing mothers; however, in apocalyptic, the sufferings of mothers and young children figure frequently among the woes of the end (cf. e.g. 2 Esdras 5^{8} and 6^{21}); the emphasis is usually on monstrous and untimely births, and that may be in mind here.

19
Almost an exact quotation from Dan. 12^{1}. For the 'Great Tribulation' cf. e.g. *Assump. Mos.* 8^{1} and Rev. 7^{14}.

20
The idea is that, according to God's plan, the Great Tribulation has a fixed length (cf. e.g. Dan. 12^{7}); but since, if it lasted so long *no human being* would survive, God in his mercy has already decided (the force of the aorist *he shortened*) to curtail it for the sake of *the elect*, i.e. the 'remnant' of the Old Testament, those whom God has chosen to be the inheritors of the kingdom. For the idea of shortening the days cf. 2 *Baruch* 20^{1-2} and 83^{1} and *Ep. Barnabas* 4^{3}, and for *the elect* cf. 1 *Enoch* 1^{1}, 38^{2-4}, etc. – the idea has its roots in the Old Testament – e.g. Ps. 105^{6}, Isa. 42^{1}, 43^{20}, etc.

It is clear that in v. 20, and the last four words of v. 19, the perspective has widened beyond a siege of Jerusalem or any other specific historical event even if understood as a divine judgement; what is here envisaged is the end of the world.

21–23
Apparently a cento of sayings added by St Mark to reinforce the warning already given in vv. 5–6. Verse 22 may have gone originally with 20 and given one of the reasons for the 'shortening'.

Verse 21 seems to be an authentic saying, attested in a different context, and slightly different form, in Q (Luke 17^{23} // Matt. 24^{26} and cf. Luke 17^{21}).

22
Is strongly reminicent of Deut. $13^{1 \text{ and } 2}$, especially if, with many MSS., we read *give* for *show*; the vocabulary and outlook seem to be those of the later Church (see V. T. for details). In particular cf. 2 Thess. 2^{9}, of which V. T. says: 'Either this passage has directly influenced 22 or it illustrates the doctrinal and religious situation out of which both have independently emerged.'

23
Begins in the Greek: 'Do *you* take heed' – i.e. see that *you* heed what has been said in vv. 14–20 (and 22) about *the elect*.

13^{24-27}

24 '*But in those days, after that tribulation, the sun will be darkened, and the moon will not give its light,* 25 *and the stars will be falling from heaven, and the powers in the heavens will be shaken.* 26 *And then they will see the Son of man coming in clouds with great power and glory.* 27 *And then he will send out the angels, and gather his elect from the four winds, from the ends of the earth to the ends of heaven.*'

The climax of the whole apocalyptic drama is here described in language almost entirely derived from the Old Testament (see J. A. T. Robinson, op. cit., p. 56). Nearly every trait here can be paralleled several times over from known apocalypses; and on the grounds that Jesus is not otherwise known to have used the Old Testament quite in this way, or to have made apocalyptic predictions of this kind, many scholars regard these verses as largely, or wholly, secondary (Robinson, pp. 57 and 119f. and, rather more cautiously, V. T., pp. 517–19); this conclusion is strengthened if it is true that some of the Old Testament allusions depend for their point on the use of the *Greek* version.*

These verses are often regarded as part of the apocalyptic source St Mark is held to have used; V.T. makes the interesting suggestion that 5–8 + 24b–28 were originally a continuous passage (A) from some Jewish-Christian apocalypse, which St Mark has bodied out with the separate sections 9–13 (B) and 14–23 (C); certainly we now enter an atmosphere quite different from that of 14–19, where essentially *historical* events were predicted; here all is supernatural, and we hear no more of the *desolating sacrilege* or of what happens to it when the end comes.†

The repeated note of time in v. 24a is emphatic; it is only *after* the tribulation in vv. 14–23 that the end is to be expected. Had some Christians been led into premature expectation of the end? See on

* So e.g. T. F. Glasson, A. M. Hunter, Robinson, and others; Beasley-Murray, *Jesus and the Future*, 246ff., disputes it. Have scholars who deny *all* authenticity to the passage been influenced at all by the desire to dissociate Jesus from ideas and language strange to modern minds?

† Montefiore suggests that vv. 14–23 may have dated from before A.D. 70 and so had nothing to say about how the *sacrilege* was disposed of.

vv. 7–8 and also cf. e.g. Luke 19^{11b} and 2 Thess. 2. The effect of v. 24a, probably added by St Mark, is to make the portents in vv. 24b–25 *part* of the end, whereas in the source they were no doubt preliminaries to it.

ꕥ

24–25
Celestial portents are often mentioned in the Old Testament in connexion with God's future action, and the apocalyptists took them, very literally interpreted, as a regular feature of their pictures of the end – cf. e.g. 2 Esdras 5^{4}, 1 *Enoch* 80^{4-7}, *Assump. Mos.* 10^{5}, *Sib. Orac.* 3,796f.; probably here the idea is at least quasi-literal – the picture is of the general break-up of the universe.

the powers: From the *Greek* of Isa. 34^{4}; St Mark at any rate may have interpreted the word of the elemental spirits believed to inhabit and control the stars. The Hebrew of Isaiah refers only to the stars themselves.

26
The consummation of the end is described in the language of Dan. 7^{13}; whatever is meant in Daniel by *the Son of man*, here it clearly refers to a superhuman person invested with divine authority (*power*) and clothed with the power and majesty of God (*glory*); for *clouds* as betokening divine status see p.235.

they will see = (by semitic idiom) 'he will be seen'; even so, the change from second to third person in an address to disciples is strange.

27
For *angels* as messianic agents cf. 1 *Enoch* 61. Likewise, the gathering of the elect was a traditional idea, which in Jewish thought referred to the gathering of the Jews of the Dispersion to join the faithful remnant in Palestine – cf. e.g. Isa. $11^{11, 16}$, 27^{12}, Zech. 2^{6-11} and 10^{6-11}, 1 *Enoch* 57, *Pss. Sol.* 11^{3}, etc.

gather . . . from the four winds: so the *Greek* version of Zech. 2^{6}.

13^{28-37} A SUPPLEMENT – VARIOUS SAYINGS ON WATCHFULNESS

28 '*From the fig tree learn its lesson: as soon as its branch becomes tender*
and puts forth its leaves, you know that summer is near. 29 *So also, when you*
see these things taking place, *you know that he is near,* at the very gates.
30 *Truly, I say to you, this generation will not* pass away *before all* these
things take place. 31 *Heaven and earth will* pass away, *but my words will*
not pass away.
32 '*But of that day or that hour no one knows, not even the angels in heaven,*
nor the Son, but only the Father. 33 *Take heed,* watch;[a] *for you do not know*
when the time will come. 34 *It is like a man going on a journey, when he*
leaves home and puts his servants in charge, each with his work, and com-
mands the doorkeeper *to be* on the watch. 35 Watch *therefore – for you do not*
know when the master of the house will come, in the evening, or at midnight,
or at cockcrow, or in the morning – 36 *lest he come suddenly and find you*
asleep. 37 *And what I say to you I say to all:* Watch'

a Other ancient authorities add *and pray*

This consists of a number of originally separate sayings and parables included here because they all deal with the general theme of watchfulness in view of the End. Their conjunction and order in Mark appear to be based, somewhat artificially, on a series of catchwords: *these things taking place* (v. 29) – *these things take place* (v. 30); *pass away* (v. 30) – *pass away* (v. 31); *watch* (v. 33) – *on the watch* (v. 34) – *watch* (vv. 35 and 37); *at the very gates* (Greek 'doors', v. 29) – *doorkeeper* (v. 34). See on $9^{33ff.}$ for a similar sort of arrangement, which here, as there, suggests a practical, catechetical interest.

The artificiality of this addition to the discourse is brought out by the fact that the parousia, which has just been pictured (vv. 24–27) as the climax and fulfilment of the last times, is itself treated here as only a preliminary sign. The End is now said to be of completely indeterminate date (v. 32), and its only connexion with the present is the purely *moral* one that here and now men are to be continually on the watch for it. On the face of it, the outlook here seems radically different from that of the rest of the chapter; there Jesus was pictured as perfectly prepared to reveal signs by which the coming of the End might be recognized and prepared for; here he disclaims all knowledge of the time of its coming (v. 32), and the emphatic command to be continually on the watch suggests that it may come, like the returning householder (vv. 35–36), without any warning, or premonitory signs, at all.* This second attitude is the one attributed to Jesus in our other sources (cf. e.g. Matt. $24^{37ff.}$ // Luke $17^{26ff.}$, or Matt. 24^{27} // Luke 17^{24} and Luke 21^{34}), and many scholars believe it to be the one he in fact held – for details cf. Dodd, *Parables*, pp. 83f., and Manson, *T. J.*, pp. 261ff., who makes the interesting suggestion that 32–37 may represent the original answer of Jesus to the question put to him in v. 4.

ꕤ

28–29

In its present context this little parable speaks clearly enough for itself. *these things* in v. 29 must, taken naturally, include what has just been described in vv. 24–27; on the strangeness of that see p. 358 above. Even if, as is sometimes suggested, the words could be taken as referring only to the contents of vv. 6–22, it is by no means certain that the parable originally referred to the end of the world at all. Many scholars regard the explanation in v. 29 as secondary and think the original reference was to the various activities of Jesus' ministry as indications that with it the kingdom of God was already manifesting itself. Cf. e.g. *Parables*, p. 137n., *P. J.*, p. 96, and Dibelius, *Jesus* (E.T.), pp. 72–3.

29

you know: More probably imperative: 'then know'.

he: Or possibly 'it' – i.e. the kingdom of God, which will come to gladden the hearts of those who have endured through tribulation, even as summer follows the hardships of winter, cf. Luke 21^{31}.

30

Did this come originally immediately after v. 27 and form the conclusion of the discourse proper?

this generation is to be taken literally, but just possibly the saying

* It is of course possible to suppose that this uncertainty operates only within the narrow limits left open by the earlier part of the discourse; but the language of this section seems too solemn and emphatic for that – see further notes below.

referred originally to some specific event, such as the destruction of Jerusalem. However, in view of 9^{1} (see there) and Matt. 10^{23}, it more probably referred originally, as it does in effect here, to the parousia. If so it is an example of that 'foreshortening of the perspective' so frequent in the prophets. 'When the profound realities underlying a situation are depicted in the dramatic form of historical prediction, the certainty and inevitability of the spiritual processes involved are expressed in terms of the immediate imminence of the event.' (*Parables*, p. 71 – see the whole passage and cf. further on v. 32 below.)

31

For the general idea cf. e.g. Isa. 51^{6}, 34^{4}, 40^{8}, Ps. $102^{25\text{ff.}}$. The idiom is Hebraic and the meaning: 'though heaven and earth should pass away, my words will not pass away'. It has been suggested that the words originally formed the conclusion of the apocalyptic document and were spoken by its author in a state of prophetic rapture; the early Church then transferred them to the exalted Lord. Understood as words of Christ, did they, at one stage, apply to his teaching as a whole? If so, we have an absolute claim hardly paralleled outside St John's Gospel, and most commentators believe it to be an early Christian claim on Jesus' behalf – perhaps an adaptation of his saying about the Law (Matt. 5^{18}) to his own teaching.

32

A difficult verse, which has given rise to a great deal of discussion from early times. In its Marcan context, the saying means simply that, though the parousia is imminent, its precise date is not known. But the extreme solemnity of the words and the fact that *that day* seems to have been something of a Christian technical term for the Day of Judgement (cf. e.g. Luke 21^{34}, 2 Thess. 1^{10}, 2 Tim. 1^{12} and ^{18}, 4^{8}) suggest that originally this was an independent saying about the Day of Judgement,* in which case the profession of ignorance would be more absolute, and would, as we have seen, 'reflect an attitude alien to apocalyptic speculation, with its emphasis on an orderly succession of events preceding the End' (V. T., p. 523).

About the authenticity of the words directly opposing views are held by the most eminent authorities, some holding that no Christian would ever have *invented* such a self-limiting utterance to ascribe to Jesus, others doubting if Jesus ever referred to himself absolutely as *the Son* (there is no parallel in Mark, and only one doubtful one elsewhere

* It is clearly too solemn to refer simply to some specific event such as, e.g., the fall of Jerusalem.

in the Synoptic Gospels – Matt. 11^{27} ⑊ Luke 10^{22}) and stressing that the language seems to be that of the early Church.

It is perhaps not quite as difficult as some have thought to conceive situations in the early Church in which Christians might have ascribed these words to Jesus, e.g. in an attempt to deal with the non-fulfilment of (real or alleged) prophecies of Jesus about the End by trying to show that he himself had not claimed to know exactly when the End would arrive. If, however, the words are authentic, they are doubtless to be explained by the fact that, as V. T. puts it, 'it is of the glory of the Incarnation that Christ accepted those limitations of knowledge which are inseparable from a true humanity' (p. 523).

33–37

The final exhortation to watchfulness – which in v. 37 is explicitly extended beyond the circle of the four disciples to the whole Church – is reinforced by a parable. This 'parable', which in vv. 35–36 shades off into direct advice to the disciples, is generally agreed to have been put together out of parabolic material derived from various sources. Basic to it is the tradition underlying Luke $12^{35ff.}$, where, it will be noted, the master is simply attending a wedding; such a celebration might well involve a return home late at night, but no oriental traveller would return from a *journey* (v. 34) at night. The assigning of their work to the various servants, which would suit a journey situation, seems to be a reminiscence of the parable of the Talents (Matt. 25^{14-30}⑊Luke 19^{11-27}. Cf. there too a *journey*, Matt. 25^{14}) and is, on the face of it, strange here, because it seems irrelevant to the central point of the parable, which lies in the command to the porter (the central figure here? – suggested by *at the very gates* in v. 29) *to watch*. In fact, as Professor Dodd has pointed out (*Parables*, p. 164), the distinction between parable and direct teaching has worn very thin here and the figures in the parable are only thinly veiled representations of those for whom the teaching is intended.

The various implausibilities of the parable are explained if we realize that it envisages a situation somewhat like that of 2 Thessalonians; the early Christians, very conscious that their Lord is 'away' (v. 34) – perhaps for longer than they had expected (cf. Luke 19^{11-12}) – are warned to be constantly on the watch for his return, but not in any excited or impatient spirit such as would prevent them from applying themselves to the 'service' (v. 34) which has been assigned to each – cf. 2 Thess. 3^{6-13} and e.g. Eph. $4^{11ff.}$. Wellhausen suggests that this gives the clue to the section (vv. 28–37) as a whole. In view of such teaching as that reproduced in vv. 5–27, Christians had perhaps been brought to a pitch of excited expectation by the events culminating in the fall of Jerusalem in A.D. 70. These events had in fact not brought the parousia, and the expectation of it, while by no means to be abandoned, needed to be calmed and moralized. Hence the addition to the chapter of an appendix with the moral: 'Wait without impatience, but watch and be ready at every moment; for you do not know the time, and Jesus himself did not know it' (Wellhausen, p. 114). It is indeed often said that to 'be on the alert' is the unifying theme of the whole chapter (cf. vv. 5, 9, 23, 29, 33, 35, 37). In a sense this is true, but in assessing its significance we must bear in mind that the *type* of alertness called for, and the things for, or against, which it is demanded, differ from one section of the chapter to another. The unity provided by the common theme is thus somewhat artificial.

Mark 14-15

The Passion of Christ

The remainder of the Gospel (apart from the last eight verses) is generally known as the Passion narrative, i.e. the story of how Jesus came to suffer (Latin *passio* = 'suffering') and die. The designation is apt, for this part of the Gospel *is* a connected narrative in a sense in which the earlier part of the Gospel is not. Jeremias speaks in this connexion of 'a close-packed, purposeful, and coherent narrative, with precise geographical and temporal reference' (*E. W. J.*, p. 62) which contrasts sharply with the essentially independent pericopae, or small groups of pericopae, only very loosely connected, which we have encountered so far. How is the change to be explained?

To the early Christians 'the Cross' – by which they meant the death of Jesus and the events immediately connected with it – was the very centre of their faith, the central point in the whole history of God's dealings with men. (Cf. – out of innumerable examples – 1 Cor. 2^{2}, Rom. 3^{25} and 5^{8}, Phil. 2^{8}, Col. 1^{20}, 1 Pet. 1^{19}, Heb. 12^{2}.) Accordingly, from the very beginning, interest focused specially on this part of the Lord's ministry, and a need was early felt for some account of it. 'The Crucifixion had to be *pictured.* Men must see it and feel it, imaginatively entering into the sufferings of Christ and sensing the awful significance of what happened on Calvary. The story of the Passion must be told in such a fashion that the stark reality of it be felt and the full redemptive meaning of it be realized' (J. Knox, *The Death of Christ*, p. 19).

This meant that a connected account of the last part of the ministry came into being at a very early period, long before there was a comparable account of the earlier ministry; and whereas up to this point St Mark has been largely a pioneer, constructing his own narrative out of isolated stories, from this point onward he could rely on an already existing narrative, though, as we shall see, this narrative had itself been built up from separate pericopae at an earlier stage, and St Mark felt no hesitation about adding further pericopae to it.*

* The evidence for the existence of such an account is not only the different character of Mark's Gospel in Chapters 14–15, but the fact that in this section St Matthew and St Luke no longer feel free to modify St Mark to the extent that they have done earlier, and that even St John, who has felt at liberty to

If the *existence* of a pre-Marcan Passion narrative is thus fairly easily explained, a number of factors combined to give it its rather special character.

(*a*) In proclaiming as God's Son and emissary one whose life had ended in a criminal's death after due trial by a Roman court, the early Church was undoubtedly doing something extremely paradoxical.* They could have no hope of making their proclamation convincing unless they could show that, contrary to appearances, Jesus had been entirely innocent of the charges brought against him, or indeed of any others, and that in this case the Roman judge had been put under irresistible pressure to give a false verdict. To show all this a continuous and circumstantial narrative would be necessary.†

(*b*) But the question would still remain why, if Jesus was innocent and was, as the Christians claimed, God's Son, God had not intervened to prevent such injustice and suffering. The answer, according to Christian belief, was that it had been *God's express will* that his Son should accomplish his saving work by means of suffering (and for that reason Jesus had foreseen, foretold, and freely embraced such

* Just how paradoxical can be seen if we transpose the situation into modern terms and think of proclaiming as divine saviour someone who has just been hanged, after a trial at the Old Bailey in which the Archbishops of Canterbury and York were the chief witnesses for the prosecution.

† And also, sooner or later, an account of the earlier ministry which would show that Jesus' complete innocence (and his fulfilment of the Old Testament, etc. – see below) extended to that too. St Mark's Gospel, as we have seen, was very largely designed to meet this need, and from that point of view it has been well described as 'a Passion narrative with an introduction'. If Chapters 1–13 are considered in this light as an introduction to the Passion, it will be seen how appropriately St Mark has concentrated in the latter part of it – 8^{27} onward – Jesus' predictions of his Passion and explanations of its meaning.

---

rewrite the earlier history of the ministry freely, here follows the Marcan account – or some other very similar to it – fairly closely. Clearly for this section of his Gospel St Mark had the backing of a widely known, traditional, and authoritative source. Jeremias indeed points out that the assimilation of St John's Gospel to the Synoptic account, though it only becomes really exact from the story of the arrest onward, first becomes observable with the story of the entry into Jerusalem. He therefore thinks that the pre-Marcan Passion narrative began with the triumphal entry, though he admits that Mark 12–13 are insertions into it and that in its really early form it began only from the arrest – the point at which the agreement between John and the other Gospels becomes relatively close and continuous (*E. W. J.*, p. 62ff.).

suffering). But if, as was generally agreed at the time, God had revealed his intentions for the saving of the world in detail in the Old Testament, it followed that Jesus' innocent sufferings must be predicted there. Accordingly the early Christians diligently searched the Old Testament for such predictions; in doing so they had two aims:

(i) Unless such predictions could be found, they had no hope of persuading Jews that Jesus was God's Son and his sufferings God's will. For no Jew would believe that in a matter of this importance God would do anything without first having revealed it to the Old Testament writers.

(ii) If such predictions could be found, they would help to fill in gaps in the Passion narrative itself. What God had predicted he would certainly have brought to pass; of that the early Christians had no doubt. If therefore an Old Testament passage referred to the Passion of Christ, the things it predicted must have happened to Jesus, even if there was no other evidence that they had. Old Testament predictions thus became, to a certain extent, a historical source, and as Lightfoot says, they 'would be, on one side, of much greater value than the fragmentary stories of escaping young men or fearful women; for these Old Testament Passion narratives were divinely granted and attested: it stood so written' (*H. & I.*, p. 156).

Accordingly the account of Jesus' end, on which our Gospel accounts are based, was derived from historical reminiscences and Old Testament predictions in a proportion which cannot now be exactly determined,* though the matter is discussed in its relation to particular incidents in the commentary below. Meanwhile it will be realized that according to the narrative so drawn up, Jesus' last days frequently fulfilled Old Testament predictions, often in detail, and this naturally led the early communities to 'increasing confidence in the divine significance of what was also a recent historical event' (Lightfoot).

(iii) One other factor must be mentioned. Since Jesus had been innocent, his undeserved fate must have been brought about by the folly and sin of men, and accordingly the shortcomings of the various people responsible, the disciples, the Romans, the Jews and their leaders, figure large in the Passion narrative.

One point here deserves special notice. The experience of the

* Cf. J. Knox, *The Death of Christ*, p. 22.

Church, especially after A.D. 70, was that while the Jews increasingly refused to accept Christ's claims, the Romans were sometimes surprisingly friendly and Gentiles in general seemed much more inclined to believe. It was, therefore, natural to lay blame for the crucifixion exclusively on the Jews and to exonerate the Romans completely, and a steadily increasing tendency can be observed in New Testament and later Christian literature to transfer all guilt in this matter to Jewish shoulders; we shall see reason to believe that this tendency had already begun to operate before St Mark's time and has had its effect upon his account.

No doubt other factors also influenced the growth and character of the Passion narrative, but there is no space here to discuss them all or to trace the various stages by which the narrative grew up and attempt to assign each element to the stage at which it entered the narrative.*

As we shall see, the factors which controlled the character of the original narrative seem also to have controlled Mark's additions to and modifications of it. Anyone who reads through Chapters 14 and 15 with this note in mind will see that almost every item in them subserves one or other of the aims just discussed. Undeniably this means that since the selection of the material was governed almost entirely by religious and apologetic considerations, much that we should dearly like information about is passed over in silence, or referred to in such general terms that no precise picture can now be formed. For example, as we shall see, it is impossible, on the basis of Mark, to recover in any detail the historical facts about the Last Supper or about the trial, or trials, of Jesus; and though the Gospel makes it clear that Jesus' condemnation had its political side, it is no longer possible to reconstruct it.† Dibelius rightly insists more than once‡ on the general historicity of the narrative; the narrative is old, it was apparently attested in places by eyewitnesses, and many of the

* Those interested will find discussions in F. C. Grant, *The Earliest Gospel*, pp. 175ff, M. Dibelius, *F. T. G.*, 178–217 (see also his very important article in *Zeitschrift für Neutestamentliche Wissenschaft* 30 (1931), pp. 193ff., now published in *Botschaft und Geschichte*, i, pp. 248ff), Bultmann, pp. 297ff., M. Goguel in *Z. N. W.* 31 (1932), pp. 289ff. and in *Revue de l'histoire des religions* 62 (1910), pp. 165ff. and 295ff. So far as such questions are relevant to the exegesis of the Gospel, they are discussed in the commentary below.

† J. Knox, op. cit., pp. 28–9.

‡ Cf. e.g. *M. J.*, p. 145.

traits in it correspond to what we know of contemporary customs and conditions. That Jesus died by crucifixion and therefore after some sort of proceedings before Pilate, the Roman governor, hardly admits of doubt, and other features of the story also ring true; but beyond that assertion of basic historicity it is not easy to go, and the judicious words of Professor John Knox deserve to be quoted: 'I said I could promise no reconstruction of the circumstances of Jesus' crucifixion. My own conviction is that no clear picture can be drawn. We can set a kind of frame of historical possibilities within which the action of the first Good Friday occurred. But within this frame we cannot set the action with any precision or assurance. It probably belongs somewhere in the centre, midway of the several extremes' (op. cit. p. 29).

14^{1-11} THE INTRODUCTION TO THE PASSION NARRATIVE

14 *It was now two days before the Passover and the feast of Unleavened*
Bread. And the chief priests and the scribes were seeking how to arrest him by
stealth, and kill him; 2 *for they said, 'Not during the feast, lest there be a*
tumult of the people.'

3 *And while he was at Bethany in the house of Simon the leper, as he sat at*
table, a woman came with an alabaster jar of ointment of pure nard, very
costly, and she broke the jar and poured it over his head. 4 *But there were*
some who said to themselves indignantly, 'Why was the ointment thus
wasted? 5 *For this ointment might have been sold for more than three hundred*
denarii,[a] *and given to the poor.' And they reproached her.* 6 *But Jesus said,*
'Let her alone; why do you trouble her? She has done a beautiful thing to
me. 7 *For you always have the poor with you, and whenever you will, you*
can do good to them; but you will not always have me. 8 *She has done what*
she could; she has anointed my body beforehand for burying. 9 *And truly, I say*
to you, wherever the gospel is preached in the whole world, what she has
done will be told in memory of her.'

10 *Then Judas Iscariot, who was one of the twelve, went to the chief priests*
in order to betray him to them. 11 *And when they heard it they were glad, and*
promised to give him money. And he sought an opportunity to betray him.

a The denarius was worth about a shilling

This introduction is made up of two quite distinct parts:

(i) Verses 1–2 and 10–11, the introduction proper, which St Mark found as an uninterrupted whole in his source. (The word 'then' at the beginning of v. 10 is really 'and'.)

(ii) 3–9, a story which reached St Mark as an unattached pericope and which he was responsible for inserting at this point.

The two parts will be discussed separately.

(i) The purpose of this is to supply the background information without which the subsequent incidents in the Passion narrative would be unintelligible. It is entirely circumstantial;* the Jewish authorities are only very vaguely characterized, we learn nothing about where, or in what capacity, they met, nor about how or where Judas got in touch with them. Judas' motives and state of mind are left equally unexplained. The reason we are not told more is probably that the Church knew no more; indeed it is a very plausible suggestion that the Church had no *direct* information on the matter at all, and that what we have here is simply what the early Christians had been able to deduce from the subsequent course of events. It was known that the Sanhedrin had seized Jesus by a *tour de force* and that the arresting band had been able to count on the services of Judas; from these facts the previous occurrence of what is described in these verses might easily have been deduced.

However that may be, the passage is by no means entirely clear. Probably what St Mark intended to convey in vv. 1–2 was simply that the authorities, realizing that any attempt to arrest Jesus openly might provoke rioting among the crowds gathered for the feast (v. 2), decided to avoid trouble by getting hold of him secretly (v. 1). But if that was his meaning, he has expressed it very inexactly, for if the wording of v. 2 is pressed, the meaning appears to be that the authorities decided not to take action, even of a stealthy kind, during the feast. But in fact, as the sequel will show, they did act during the feast, and commentators therefore ask what made them change their minds. Was it perhaps the unexpected offer of help from Judas? That is possible, though St Mark does not seem to be aware that his narrative

* One is almost reminded of those résumés of 'what has happened so far' with which the later instalments of serial stories are introduced in periodical magazines.

implies any change of plan on the part of the authorities at that point, or indeed at any other; so perhaps the simplest explanation is that suggested above, namely that St Mark – not knowing that his every word would be subject to minute scrutiny by innumerable scholars! – expressed himself rather loosely in vv. 1–2, and really had no intention of suggesting that the authorities at any stage decided against action *of any sort* during the feast (see further below).

The point is of some importance, as we shall see presently, for if the statement in v. 2 *could* be pressed, and if, as we have suggested, it was simply a deduction by the Christians from what actually happened later, then what actually happened must have been that Jesus was arrested 'not during the feast'. But St Mark says he *was* arrested during the feast, so we should have evidence here that St Mark's source presupposed a chronology of Passion week different from the one St Mark himself gives us. In particular, if Jesus was arrested before the Passover, he cannot have celebrated the feast with his disciples, and the Last Supper cannot therefore have been a Passover meal as St Mark clearly says that it was. (See further p. 381.)

(ii) The story which St Mark has inserted here appears to have been one of the many which circulated without any indication of the point in the ministry at which it occurred; St John places it several days earlier than St Mark (John 12^{1}), and St Luke (if Luke $7^{36ff.}$ is to be regarded as a variant form of this story), at a completely different point in Jesus' career. In the form in which it reached St Mark it was located at Bethany in the house of Simon the leper – presumably a person well known in the circles in which the story grew up, since no attempt is made to identify him – but in St John's version the incident appears to take place in the house of Mary, Martha, and Lazarus (12^{1-2}). However, it matters little, for, as usual in such stories, the interest resides not in any personal details, but simply in the word or action with which Jesus responds to the situation; typically, the woman and the objectors, whose action and reaction give rise to the word of Jesus, are left completely anonymous. (Contrast the names and descriptions in John 12^{3}, Matt. 26^{8}, and Luke 7^{37}, which serve to throw into relief the comparative originality of St Mark's version.)

Originally, the words of Jesus which formed the climax of the story were probably just those reproduced in vv. 6–7a ('. . . *poor with you*', though the rest of v. 7 may have been included). In well-to-do circles at any rate, anointing the body with olive or other vegetable oils was quite customary as a means of refreshment or in connexion with a meal. But in the circles in which Jesus mainly moved it was no doubt too expensive to be common, and the reaction of the woman's critics is perfectly in character, especially as the ointment was of a very costly type and it seems to be implied that the entire flask was used. Our evidence does not suggest that Jesus is likely to have gone in very much for perfume (cf. e.g. Matt. 11^{8} // Luke 7^{25}), but he could see that the woman's action was a spontaneous expression of her sense of the honour due to him, and he objected to a criticism which would shame her for a deed of true love and devotion. The story thus throws a light both on the devotion Jesus aroused in those who heard him, and on his gracious humanity in his treatment of others.

As we shall see (15^{46} and 16^{1}), after Jesus' death no opportunity ever presented itself for the proper anointing (? embalming) of his corpse – a circumstance which apparently caused considerable distress to his intimate friends and disciples* – and to some of those who knew of this incident it came to appear as 'a kind of anticipatory rectification of the omission'. In time this interpretation of it was attributed to Jesus himself (v. 8) and the incident was associated with the last few days of his life. Verse 9 is harder to evaluate; as it stands, with its perspective of world-wide evangelism, it hardly goes back to Jesus himself, especially as the phrase 'to preach the gospel' belongs to the missionary vocabulary of the later Gentile Church. Perhaps, therefore, it is simply a later addition voicing recognition of what had in fact happened, that the incident had become an integral part of the gospel of Jesus' death as the Church proclaimed it. Possibly, however, the kernel of the saying may go back to Jesus; as the woman's name was no longer remembered, the story was not really 'a memorial of her', and it has been argued that the early Church would have been unlikely to father on Jesus a prophecy which had been only imperfectly fulfilled.

Very possibly it was yet another meaning which St Mark saw in the story that led him to place it at this precise point in his account. As we have seen earlier, the word *Messiah* means literally 'the anointed one' (i.e. in practice one whose *head* has been anointed); according to

* Cf. how the women planned to deal with the matter at the earliest possible moment (16^{1}), and the explicit, though surely unhistorical, claim in John 19^{40}.

St Mark's version of this incident (contrast the form of the story in Luke 7[38] and John 12[3]), it was precisely an anointing of Jesus' *head*, and the Evangelist may well have seen in it a token of his Messiahship. In that case, by sandwiching the story in here he has made his introduction a profound guide to the meaning of the Passion narrative. He who was the object of the guile and malice of the Jewish authorities (vv. 1–2) and of the treachery of Judas (vv. 10–11) was at the same time rightly the object of love and devotion as Messiah (vv. 3–9). St Mark 'thus puts into his readers' hands, as it were, the means whereby they may best approach and understand the narrative which follows. The Passion is the supreme act of the Messiah, and conversely the Messiahship of Jesus is the explanation of the Passion'.*

❧

1

The reason for this exact statement of time is not entirely clear, nor is its meaning. The Greek reads literally: 'after two days it was the Passover', and this may mean that the Passover would occur forty-eight hours later, or, if the reckoning is inclusive, that it would occur next day. (Cf. 8[31] where *after three days* may mean 'on the third day'). The difficulty is increased by the fact that, whereas the Romans counted their days, as we do, from midnight to midnight, the Jews reckoned from sunset to sunset, and it is not absolutely certain which reckoning St Mark, who was writing for Gentile readers, was using. The general opinion among commentators is that he was using the Jewish mode of reckoning, and this method is in any case important for the understanding of the references to the feast, which now begins to play so large a part in the story.

The Passover proper consisted of a solemn ceremonial meal eaten after sunset on the fifteenth of the Jewish month Nisan, in commemoration of the deliverance of the Jews from Egypt; the central feature of this observance was the eating of a lamb or other animal victim (to which the word *passover* could also be applied) which had been ritually slaughtered in the temple that afternoon (i.e. according to Jewish reckoning, on the afternoon of Nisan 14th). By the time of Jesus, however, the Passover rites were part of the more extended festival of Unleavened Bread, which lasted for a week. There was thus a combined festival of Passover and Unleavened Bread which could be called by either name (cf. 2 Chron. 35[17]) as it is here, though the strictly Passover rites were

* *H. & I.*, p. 141. See also the last paragraph on p. 151.

complete by the first midnight of the festival. Although Nisan 15th was the day on which the passover was eaten, and was strictly speaking, the first complete day of Unleavened Bread, no leavened bread was eaten from noon on Nisan 14th (or, in some parts, from early morning), and in practice Nisan 14th was sometimes regarded as the first day of the combined festival (though see below, p. 376). In view of all this, it will be clear why it is difficult to be sure of the exact moment Mark intended to designate in v. 1; in any case he will only have intended by his phrase to pick up the theme of the narrative – he probably did not mean that the determination to put Jesus to death was taken only two days before the Passover, cf. 3^{6} and 12^{12}. The mention of the plot here is only to set the stage for what follows. The Passover meal, originally eaten at home, was later transferred to the temple area (Deut. 16^{2}); by the time of Jesus, though it was no longer eaten in the temple, it had to be eaten in Jerusalem, a fact which explains the presence of *the people* in v. 2.

the chief priests and the scribes: No doubt the sort of people who formed the Sanhedrin are in mind, but the phrase is quite general and non-technical; 'the Jewish authorities' conveys well enough the sense intended, both here and in v. 10.

2
during the feast: It has been proposed, notably by Dr Jeremias,* to translate the Greek here 'amid the crowd'. This would make very good sense of the passage, but although the Greek word (*hĕortē*) was occasionally used to mean 'crowd' at a later date, it remains doubtful whether it had this meaning as early as St Mark's time.

3
alabaster jar: Literally: 'an alabaster', the name for a kind of globular perfume-flask without handles, often, but not always, made of alabaster.

pure nard: Nard was an unguent made from a rare Indian plant and much prized in the ancient world. 'Pure' is the most likely translation of a Greek word of uncertain meaning (*pisticŏs*).

broke the jar: probably by snapping off the neck; this detail is perhaps intended to indicate that the whole of the contents were lavished on Jesus. Some commentators, however, see the symbolism of the story peeping through here, because in Hellenistic times when a corpse had been anointed the oil flask was sometimes broken and placed in the coffin.

* *E. W. J.*, pp. 46ff.

8

The main reason for regarding this verse as an addition to the original pericope is that stories of this kind normally have a single climax in some memorable saying of Jesus, and in this case the climax seems to have been reached quite naturally in vv. 6–7 which round the incident off in a very characteristic way. But further, the point of the verse seems to be in the fact that Jesus' corpse was not anointed in the normal way at burial, and we can hardly suppose Jesus to have been aware of that in advance. There are no linguistic grounds for ascribing the verse to the early Church; the Greek is somewhat unusual, but that may well be because the verse – like much of the rest of the story, to judge from linguistic evidence – goes back to an Aramaic original.

10

one of the twelve: The Greek has '*the* one of the twelve', an expression which could be as strange in classical Greek as it is in English. Possibly there is a reference back to 3^{16-19} or possibly Judas Iscariot is being distinguished from some other well-known Judas. Other explanations have been offered, perhaps the most likely being that in the Greek of this period the article had lost its force in such an expression as this.

14^{12-16} PREPARATIONS FOR THE PASSOVER

12 *And on the first day of Unleavened Bread, when they sacrificed the passover*
lamb, his disciples said to him, 'Where will you have us go and prepare
for you to eat the passover?' 13 *And he sent two of his disciples, and said to*
them, 'Go into the city, and a man carrying a jar of water will meet you;
follow him, 14 *and wherever he enters, say to the householder, "The Teacher*
says, Where is my guest room, where I am to eat the passover with my
disciples?" 15 *And he will show you a large upper room furnished and ready;*
there prepare for us.' 16 *And the disciples set out and went to the city, and*
found it as he had told them; and they prepared the passover.

This story provides a good example of the interconnectedness of the material in the Passion narrative (see p. 365); for it could never have existed in isolation, apart from some account of the meal to which it points forward. Most commentators think that it was in fact a fairly late addition to the narrative St Mark is following in this part of his Gospel. Among the reasons are:

(*a*) The day on which the story is said to have occurred is described in a way in which no ordinary Jew of the time would have described it. While the day 'when people sacrificed the passover lamb' (v. 12), i.e. Nisan 14th, was occasionally included in the feast and so counted as 'the first day of Unleavened Bread' (see p. 374 above), this usage was confined to learned technical discussions, and the experts in such matters very much doubt if it was ever common parlance. Here, therefore, it would seem to be either a mistranslation from an Aramaic original or else the faulty expression of a non-Jewish author. The words *when they sacrificed the passover lamb* make it quite clear that St Mark was thinking of Nisan 14th; the question is whether an early tradition would have referred to that day as *the first day of Unleavened Bread*.

(*b*) Jesus' followers are described throughout this section as 'disciples', whereas in the surrounding passages (which seem to reproduce a relatively early strand of tradition) they are consistently referred to as 'the twelve' (contrast vv. 12, 13, 14, and 16 with 10, 17, and 20). This at least suggests that this section is a late-comer to its present context.

(*c*) Verse 17 knows nothing of the mission of the two disciples in v. 13; the work of preparation referred to in v. 16 would have been enough to keep them fully occupied right up to the last minute, and v. 17, if it had known of the contents of this section, would have to refer to 'the ten'.

It would seem, therefore, that vv. 12–16 were probably added after the tradition in the surrounding verses had already taken shape.

There can be no doubt that St Mark regarded the incident as evidence of supernatural foresight on the part of Jesus (and so as further proof of his Messiahship), but this particular form of foresight has numerous parallels in legends and fairy tales (cf. e.g. 1 Sam. 10, especially vv. 2, 3, and 5), and the unquestionable affinity of this story with the difficult passage 11^{1-7} also gives rise to a question.

It is of course possible to rationalize the story and suppose that Jesus' instructions were based on a prior arrangement which he had made with a householder in Jerusalem in order to keep secret till the last minute where he was going to eat the passover, and so prevent

Judas from betraying the information to the authorities. But St Mark gives no hint of any such thing, and, in view of our complete ignorance of the movements of Jesus and the disciples at this time, any such suggestion remains wholly speculative.

The age and status of this piece of tradition have been particularly closely discussed, because these verses are the only ones in the Gospel which explicitly identify the ensuing meal as a Passover celebration. If the meal was not a passover, then clearly this passage cannot be accepted as it stands.

12
when they sacrificed the passover lamb: or, to bring out the force of the Greek idiom, 'when it was customary to slaughter the passover lamb'. The Greek verb (*thuō*) can mean either 'slaughter' or 'sacrifice', and it is difficult to say how far sacrificial ideas were associated with the Passover in the time of Christ. The offering of the lamb counted as a sacrifice and the meal was a sacrificial meal, but the later tendency was very largely to subordinate the sacrificial aspect of the meal to its aspect as a commemoration of the Exodus.

13
a man carrying a jar of water: Jars, as opposed to water-bottles, were not normally carried by men in the East, so the man in question could readily have been identified; however, it is doubtful if St Mark, who viewed the incident in terms of the supernatural, envisaged the need for such mundane means of identification. Likewise he will have seen the householder's willing response as supernaturally motivated.

14
my guest room: the 'my' is rather strange; if it means any more than 'destined for me' there is perhaps a hint of messianic sovereignty in the word.

15
furnished: The Greek word (*strōnnuō*) normally means to 'spread' or 'strew' but its meaning here is not certain. English translators usually take it to mean 'provided with the necessary furniture' – particularly, divans and carpets, but it may be little more than a synonym for 'ready', or it could mean 'paved', 'floored'.

14^{17-25}

14^{17-25} THE LAST SUPPER

*17 And when it was evening he came with the twelve. 18 And as they were
at table eating, Jesus said, 'Truly, I say to you, one of you will betray me,
one who is eating with me.' 19 They began to be sorrowful, and to say to him
one after another, 'Is it I?' 20 He said to them, 'It is one of the twelve, one
who is dipping bread in the same dish with me. 21 For the Son of man goes as
it is written of him, but woe to that man by whom the Son of man is betrayed!
It would have been better for that man if he had not been born.'*

*22 And as they were eating, he took bread, and blessed, and broke it, and
gave it to them, and said, 'Take; this is my body.' 23 And he took a cup, and
when he had given thanks he gave it to them, and they all drank of it. 24 And
he said to them, 'This is my blood of the[a] covenant, which is poured out for
many. 25 Truly, I say to you, I shall not drink again of the fruit of the vine
until that day when I drink it new in the kingdom of God.'*

a Other ancient authorities insert *new*

Having described the preparations for the meal, the tradition has surprisingly little (judged by the standard of what we should like to know) to say about the meal itself. This is to be explained in the light of the considerations discussed earlier (see p. 368); the early Church was interested only in two points connected with the meal, both of practical religious significance, viz.:

(i) Jesus' foresight with regard to the traitor, and (ii) the institution of the Eucharist.

The two sections in which these two are described, (i) vv. 17–21 and (ii) vv. 22–25, did not originally stand in their present relationship to each other. The opening words of v. 22 would not have been there if the verse had originally been preceded by a section containing v. 18a, and in Luke's Gospel, which at this point may be based on a different version of the traditional Passion narrative, the two sections are arranged in a different order.

(i)

In fact vv. 17–21 did not originally presuppose vv. 12–16 (see above p. 376) or lead on to vv. 22–25, and there is nothing to tie them certainly to the Last Supper, or indeed – apart from the general tenor of the contents – to this last period of Jesus' life. But their inclusion at this point will be intelligible enough in view of what has been said earlier about the general character of the Passion narrative. For

(*a*) they show that the treachery of Judas, and the suffering to which it led, did not take Jesus by surprise. He foresaw what would happen (vv. 18 and 20) and freely accepted it (v. 21a). And he did so because –

(*b*) this also the section shows – it was in full accordance with the will of God as revealed in the Old Testament (v. 21a). No particular text from the Old Testament is cited; the point in passages such as this (cf. 1 Cor. 15^{3} and Mark 14^{49}) is not primarily to show the correspondence of particular incidents with particular Old Testament texts, but to remind the reader that the whole course of events was not just a meaningless tragedy, but a necessary, and therefore meaningful, part of 'the definite plan and foreknowledge of God'. (Acts 2^{23}; see further on 14^{49}.)

(*c*) There is a further – subtle but unmistakable – allusion to the Old Testament. The wording of v. 18b (contrast the wording in Luke 22^{21}) shows that Ps. 41^{9} (and possibly also Obad. 7 – see R.V.) is in mind (cf. John 13^{18} where the Psalm passage is actually quoted in this context). If we read St Mark's account without presuppositions derived from later versions, we shall see that according to him what Jesus does is not to reveal the identity of the traitor even in a roundabout way (Judas is not even mentioned, let alone denounced; it is not even said that the other disciples discovered who was meant – if they had, would they not have taken some action? Contrast Matt. 26^{25} and John 13^{26}), but simply to proclaim the terrible fact that, in accordance with Old Testament prediction, the one by whom the Messiah was to be betrayed would be one of his most intimate companions (as in Ps. 41, table-fellowship is the symbol for intimate relationship, which it has always been in the East). Some commentators regard vv. 18b and 20 as originally variant traditions of Jesus' words, the former designed to make clearer the Old Testament allusion.

Verse 21b is designed to make clear that, though Judas' treachery is all part of the divinely ordained plan, that does not exonerate him from responsibility and guilt (cf. e.g. Rom. $9^{19\text{ff.}}$, James $1^{13\text{ff.}}$).

As far as the historical trustworthiness of the pericope is concerned, the story clearly goes back to a fairly early stage in the formation of the tradition, as it is included by all four Evangelists at this point. On the other hand, those who doubt if Jesus referred to himself as Son of man or designated precisely twelve apostles, forthwith known as 'the twelve', cannot accept the complete authenticity of the story in its present form (vv. 20 and 21). Certainly the unusual use of *goes* in v. 21 is typically Johannine (*hypagein* in this sense of 'going' to death and through death to the Father, nowhere else in the New Testament outside John, but with him a very favourite expression. Cf. e.g. John $8^{14, 21f.}$, $13^{3, 33}$, $14^{4, 28}$); this raises a doubt, though it does not of course prove that the saying does not, in some form, go back to Jesus.

(ii)

The reasons for the quite remarkable brevity of this account have already been discussed; the tradition had no interest in the details of the meal as such, but only in its practical religious significance, i.e. as providing the title-deeds of the eucharistic rite practised in the early Church. The point was to show that the current rite had its origin in an action of Jesus himself, and so to justify it and make clear its meaning.

In the case of this particular pericope we are in an unusually favourable position, because in 1 Cor. $11^{17ff.}$ we can actually watch the process of transmission at work. The Corinthian Christians had been behaving at the Eucharist in a way which showed that they had no conception of the real meaning and seriousness of the rite (1 Cor. 11^{17-22}), so St Paul rehearses the tradition (*I received ... I delivered*, 1 Cor. 11^{23}) which traced its origin back to words and acts of Jesus, and he thereby emphasizes its solemnity (vv. 27ff.) and makes clear its meaning (v. 26, etc.). For St Paul's purpose what was needed was simply an account of just those words and actions of Jesus which formed the immediate origin of the Eucharist; and similarly here in Mark we seem to have a section dealing just with this one event, and originally unrelated to the wider context of the Passion narrative (cf. the independent introduction at the beginning of v. 22, and see above p. 378).

If so, one important conclusion follows. Although St Mark believes that this was a Passover meal (14^{12-16}), the source on which he drew in these verses gives no indication of the fact, and certainly lays no stress upon it; indeed there is nothing in it, taken by itself, even to suggest that the meal took place in Jerusalem. It would seem to follow that the pre-Marcan Church attached no great importance to the Passover character of the meal for the understanding of Jesus' action; and this conclusion is borne out by 1 Corinthians, where St Paul's tradition makes no attempt to emphasize that '*the night when he was betrayed*' (1 Cor. 11^{23}) was a Passover night. And the same is true of St John's Gospel; the Church for which it was written, while apparently having the normal understanding of the Eucharist, held that the meal in which it originated was *not* the Passover (see p. 457), a view very possibly shared by St Paul (cf. 1 Cor. 5^{7} and see p. 457). Even St Mark himself, who, as we have seen, does believe the meal to have been a Passover one, lays no emphasis on the point* and shows no sign of having thought it essential to the understanding of this section.

In order to understand how St Mark and his immediate predecessors understood the story, therefore, we must approach it without presuppositions derived from our beliefs about the *original* meaning of the event, remembering that the first readers will have brought to its interpretation the ideas associated with the celebration of the Eucharist in the Churches of their day.†

So approached, the Marcan account yields a perfectly intelligible meaning. Jesus is shortly to leave this world, and the visible union which has hitherto existed between him and his disciples will then cease, until it is finally renewed, or rather, fulfilled, when the kingdom of God comes in its fullness (v. 25). Accordingly, for the interim,‡ Jesus provides a means of invisible union with himself by investing a broken and shared loaf and a cup of wine with special significance (vv. 22–24). For St Mark and his readers it went without saying that Jesus was here instituting a sacramental rite (cf. 1 Cor. $11^{24, 25}$ which make this explicit); he made the loaf his body in the sense that those

* It is confined to three verses in the Gospel – $14^{12, 14, 16}$.

† Otto justly remarks that no one would ever explain the origin of a rite by a story whose contents were understood to contradict the current understanding of the rite (*The Kingdom of God and the Son of Man*, p. 274).

‡ For the eschatological colouring see note on v. 25.

who partake of the loaf (originally the disciples, but later all who participate in the Eucharist) participate in his body, i.e. through communion with him, and hence with one another, they share all the various benefits which the early Church associated with being 'in Christ', 'members of his body'. By his words over the cup Jesus defines the meaning of his forthcoming death as a sacrificial shedding of blood, the means of inaugurating a new covenant between God and man (v. 24); and the drinking of the wine (whether by the original disciples (v. 23) or by the later participants in the Eucharist) is the means of participating in the atoning effects of his death and in the blessings of the new covenant it inaugurates. If such ideas seem at first somewhat strange to the modern reader, he should remember in the first place that the ancient world was perfectly familiar with what the Hebrews called the *oth*, the symbolic action which announced and also effected or helped to effect that which it symbolized (cf. e.g. Ezek. 4 and $5^{1ff.}$, Jer. $19^{10ff.}$, 2 Kings 13^{14-19}). Two other ideas were equally familiar: (*a*) that whoever drinks the cup of someone enters into a communion relationship with him (cf. e.g. the ideas lying behind Ps. $16^{4f.}$ or 1 Cor. 10^{21}); and (*b*) 'that participation in consecrated food bestows a *menāth*, or *koinōnia*, a sharing in the blessing, in the possession of salvation, in the consecration, the sanctification, the holiness with which the previously secular food was sanctified'. (R. Otto, *The Kingdom of God and the Son of Man*, p. 282; the whole of this section of the book is well worth consulting, and see also V. T., p. 544, col. 2 at end.)

The above exposition has perhaps too scrupulously observed the difference between v. 22 and v. 24. It is true that in v. 22 there is nothing corresponding to the words over the cup '... *of the covenant*' and '*which is poured out for many*', and some have thought this very significant. They have argued that the non-sacrificial words over the bread (v. 22) betray the original character of the incident, which related simply to a communion. Jesus' action meant in effect: 'You are one in eating and drinking of the same loaf and cup' – and the utterance, at least that in connexion with the bread, adds the reference to Jesus – 'You are *My* body, hence one in Me.'* On this view the sacrificial interpretation was a later importation. (But see further, p. 455). This, however, is probably over-subtle. St Paul already has

* *F. T. G.*, pp. 206–7.

words of sacrificial significance over the bread (1 Cor. 11^{24}) and even if, as many scholars think, they are secondary, the very fact that it is *broken* bread to which Jesus likens his body may well have been intended to suggest the idea of sacrifice. (See *E. W. J.*, p. 145, etc.) Certainly, so far as St Mark and his readers were concerned, it is virtually impossible that they should have attached different interpretations to the two elements. So possibly we should add to the exposition of v. 22 given above these words from Dr Vincent Taylor:* '... when Jesus took a loaf, gave thanks and broke it, and gave the broken pieces to His disciples, He meant their action to be a means whereby they might share in the power of His self-offering and the virtue of his approaching death.' Even so, the word 'this' in v. 22 certainly refers to the loaf itself and not to the action of breaking it.

As St Mark's is our earliest Gospel, the question has naturally been raised how far his account of the Last Supper helps us to reconstruct what originally happened and to discover its significance for Jesus and the first disciples. That very large question would take us far beyond the confines of St Mark's Gospel, and it cannot be properly dealt with in a commentary of this sort. A short appendix is added (pp. 455ff) setting out some of the main issues involved and referring the reader to fuller discussions.

17
when it was evening: i.e. since St Mark is thinking of a Passover meal, when the sun set, Nisan 15th began, and the Passover had to be eaten.

19
Is it I? The Greek means: 'Surely it is not I?'

20
the same dish: More correctly the Greek, as given in the best MSS., means: 'in the one bowl'; the heinousness of what the traitor does is emphasized by his being one who dips in the common bowl – shares the closest possible intimacy. If this was a Passover meal, it has been suggested that the bowl will have contained the *harōseth*, a sort of fruit purée which formed part of the preliminary dish eaten before the grace over the unleavened bread and the main meal. But as we have

* V.T. p. 544.

seen, the reference here is probably quite general, and if these verses were originally separate from vv. 22–25 it is difficult to press them as describing the preliminaries to the main meal in vv. 22–24.

21

For the Son of Man . . . : The Greek word translated 'for' (*hŏti*) sometimes means 'because'; but that hardly makes sense here, and the word must mean 'that' (introducing a statement). This suggests that the saying belonged at some earlier stage to another context (? a sayings collection) in which it was preceded by a verb of saying.

as it is written of him: A general reference to Old Testament predictions which were believed to predict the suffering of Christ; there is no Old Testament passage in which suffering is directly ascribed to the Son of man.

22

bread: Better perhaps 'a loaf'. The Greek word (*artŏs*) would most naturally suggest leavened bread, but Dr Jeremias has produced abundant evidence to show that it could also mean unleavened bread. (See *E. W. J.*, pp. 37ff.)

blessed: Or 'said grace over it'. The Greek word (*eulŏgein*), when used by Jews in this sort of context, implied not so much the hallowing, or consecrating, of the bread (though doubtless that was thought to be effected indirectly), as a solemn blessing or thanking of God over the bread. The form used would be something like: 'Praised be thou, O Lord our God, king of the world, who causest bread to come forth from the earth', though Jesus may have used a slightly variant form.* This grace was said by the head of the table, and when the company had replied with an Amen, he broke a piece of the loaf for each person (at Passover it had to be at least the size of an olive) and gave or passed it to them. It will thus be seen that the action here ascribed to Jesus (both with the bread and the wine) is fully in accord with the Jewish custom of his day. It is of course possible that in the Gentile circles in which St Mark moved, the blessing had come to be understood as a direct consecration of the bread.

23

given thanks: The Greek word (*eucharistein*) seems to be used simply as an alternative translation of the same Aramaic word translated 'bless' in v. 22. At the end of the meal it was customary to say a long grace over a cup of wine. (For the threefold form used in Jesus' time, too

* See Dalman, *Jesus-Jeshua*, p. 135.

long to quote here, see *E. W. J.*, p. 111). If this was a Passover meal, the cup will have been the third cup, the so-called 'cup of blessing', but in any case, according to Jewish custom, the meal will have intervened between vv. 22 and 23 (cf. 1 Cor. 11^{25} 'after supper' and Luke 22^{20}); the fact that no one would get that impression from a simple reading of Mark shows how little concerned St Mark was with the original setting of the incident, Passover meal or not. Indeed it is difficult to think St Mark *intended* to give the impression of any gap here; and in that he was surely influenced by contemporary Christian eucharistic practice, according to which the wine immediately followed the bread as it does today.

One of the arguments for thinking the Last Supper was a Passover meal is that ordinary Jews could not often afford wine apart from Passover; on the other hand it is not certain whether in Jesus' time a common cup was used at the Passover or whether each person used an individual cup. Perhaps the emphatic words 'they drank of it every one' (so the Greek) are directed to some in the early Church who objected to drinking from a common cup at the Eucharist, or who, on conscientious grounds, were in the habit of communicating in one kind only.

24

This is my blood of the covenant: For the background see Exod. 24^{8}, Zech. 9^{11}, and cf. Heb. 9^{15}ff. The words imply reflection on the blood of the covenant at Mount Sinai, which, according to ancient Jewish interpretations, had atoning power. As the blood established the covenant of Moses, so the blood of Jesus established the new covenant (Jer. 31^{31-34}) which had as its content perfect fellowship with God (Jer. 31^{33}) founded upon God's forgiveness (Jer. 31^{34b}) in his kingdom. As Moses' sprinkling of the blood on the people ensured their participation in the blessings of the old covenant, so the disciples' drinking of the wine ensures their participation in the blessings of the new.

However, the phrase which translates literally 'the blood of me of the covenant' is very harsh in Greek and virtually impossible to retranslate into Aramaic, and if the original saying contained any reference to the covenant idea, it will have been in some such form as that given in 1 Cor. 11^{25} ('this cup means a new covenant which is to be instituted by my blood, i.e. by my death'). But there are some grounds for thinking that the covenant reference is an addition even in St Paul's version of the saying, and probably in its original form the saying contained no reference to the idea of covenant, though that of course leaves open the question whether Jesus thought of his life's work in terms of the establishing of a new covenant between God and man – an idea very prominent in St Paul's thought.

for many: Commentators often refer to Isa. 53:12, but the similarity is not really very close, and the occurrence of the words *for many* in both passages is not as significant as it might seem, for the words are a translation of a common semitic idiom. Neither Hebrew nor Aramaic has a word for 'all' in the plural, and this use of 'many' does duty instead; the meaning is not exclusive ('some, but not all') but inclusive ('all in contrast with one').

25
The ideas and vocabulary are semitic. For the final state of blessedness pictured as a banquet cf. e.g. Isa. 25:6, 1 *Enoch* 62:14, 2 *Baruch* 29:5ff., Matt. 8:11, Luke 14:15, Rev. 19:9. *Truly* (literally, amen) and '*fruit of the vine*' are both semitisms, and according to the version in some MSS. the verse contains further semitisms.

The fact that St Luke's version of this saying occurs at a different point in his account (Luke 22:16–18 – *before* the institution) suggests that it may have circulated at some time more or less independently; but that this or some similar eschatological saying was associated with the institution from the earliest times is suggested by the evidence of 1 Cor. 11, where a similar eschatological interest appears in connexion with the institution (v. 26 after vv. 23–25), and by the consistent association of eschatological expectations with the Eucharist in the early Church. Otto is no doubt right in seeing the significance of the original event as closely bound up with Jesus' expectation of the imminent kingdom of God: Jesus qualifies the disciples 'to receive his testament, not by feeding their souls, but by lifting them out of the secular sphere by the atoning power of his death, and consecrating them for the kingdom of God' (*The Kingdom of God and the Son of Man*, p. 297). Cf. also Dibelius (*F. T. G.*, p. 208): 'when the fellowship of the parousia commences this memorial table-fellowship ends.'

14:26–31 PROPHECY OF THE DISCIPLES' DENIAL

26 *And when they had sung a hymn, they went out to the Mount of Olives.*
27 *And Jesus said to them, 'You will all fall away; for it is written, "I will strike the shepherd, and the sheep will be scattered."* 28 *But after I am raised*

up, I will go before you to Galilee.' [29]*Peter said to him, 'Even though they all fall away, I will not.'* [30]*And Jesus said to him, 'Truly, I say to you, this very night, before the cock crows twice, you will deny me three times.'* [31]*But he said vehemently, 'If I must die with you, I will not deny you.' And they all said the same.*

This section (apart probably from v. 28) appears to have formed part of St Mark's source, and the reasons for its inclusion there are clear enough.

1. It provides further evidence of Jesus' foreknowledge of his sufferings (and, when v. 28 is included, of his resurrection as well); and since this foreknowledge is precise even down to details, its supernatural character is strongly suggested.

2. It shows that what happened was in accordance with Old Testament prophecy. In this particular case that would have been specially necessary, for it must have been a great problem to the early Christians (particularly in Rome) why Peter and the other apostles, who were known to them as such fearless witnesses for Christ, should have denied Jesus in the days of his flesh.

Perhaps this story was also seen as showing that the disciples' action was not a deliberate betrayal due to loss of faith in Jesus; on the contrary they believed in him enthusiastically throughout, and their denial was simply due to that 'weakness of the flesh' of which the early Church was only too aware. (Cf. v. 38 below and Rom. 7[15]ff.*).

26

sung a hymn: This detail no doubt presupposes that the Last Supper was a Passover meal, in which case the reference here will be to the second part of the Hallēl (Pss. 114–118, or 115–118) sung at the end of the Passover meal.

went out to the Mount of Olives: Deut. 16[7] was taken to mean that the

* A papyrus fragment (? of the third century) reproduces the substance of this section. It omits v. 28 and the word 'twice' in v. 30 (see below), but its evidence is exceedingly difficult to evaluate, because, apart from the difficulty of reconstructing the original wording, we cannot be sure whether the fragment comes from an early MS. of Mark or Matthew or from some early writer who may have been quoting inaccurately. See M. R. James, *The Apocryphal New Testament*, p. 25.

night of Nisan 15th should be spent in Jerusalem, but for the purposes of this regulation a district of 'greater Jerusalem' was recognized in the time of Jesus, which included Bethphage. This verse, therefore, provides no decisive objection to the identification of the Last Supper with the Passover.

Nothing is said about the movements of Judas.

27
fall away: Or 'be offended'. For the Greek word (*skandalizein*), see its use in 4^{17}, and cf. p. 166.

The Old Testament quotation is from Zech. 13^{7} though the wording seems to have been adapted (but cf. Peake's *Commentary* on the Zechariah text); perhaps the quotation was taken from a collection of Old Testament texts. For such Christian 'modification' of Old Testament passages see on 1^{2-3}.

28
On this verse, generally held to have been inserted here by St Mark, see on 16^{7}.

30
this very night: Literally 'today, this very night'; the Jewish method of reckoning is presupposed (see above p. 373) and the second phrase defines the first more precisely (cf. $1^{32, 35}$, 4^{35}, and often in Mark). The very great precision of detail in this verse may be due to later modification of the tradition; whether the inclusion of *twice* is due to such modification is hard to say. The word is missing from some MSS., but it may be original, and its omission may be due to the desire to bring Mark into line with Matthew and Luke. Cf. Matt. 26^{34} and Luke 22^{34} and see further on 14^{68} below.

before the cock crows: There is some evidence that the keeping of cocks was forbidden in Jerusalem at this time, and it is possible that 'cock-crow' was used originally simply as a proverbial expression for early morning (cf. 13^{35})* and that St Mark took it literally here and provided in the sequel for the literal crowing of a cock or cocks. Alternatively, the expression may have referred originally to the *gallicinium* ('cock-crowing'), the bugle-call for the changing of the Roman guard at the Antonia fortress in the early hours of the morning.†

* There is some evidence in classical writers for a *double* cock-crowing (i.e., presumably, one bird answering another) being used to designate early morning – cf. e.g. Aristophanes, *Eccl.* 390 f. and Juvenal, $\text{IX}^{107f.}$

† See C. H. Mayo in *J. T. S.*, XXII (1921), pp. 367ff.

14^{32-42} GETHSEMANE

*32 And they went to a place which was called Gethsem'ane; and he said to
his disciples, 'Sit here, while I pray.' 33 And he took with him Peter and
James and John, and began to be greatly distressed and troubled. 34 And he
said to them, 'My soul is very sorrowful, even to death; remain here, and
watch.'[a] 35 And going a little farther, he fell on the ground and prayed that,
if it were possible, the hour might pass from him. 36 And he said, 'Abba,
Father, all things are possible to thee; remove this cup from me; yet not what
I will, but what thou wilt.' 37 And he came and found them sleeping, and he
said to Peter, 'Simon, are you asleep? Could you not watch[a] one hour?
38 Watch[a] and pray that you may not enter into temptation; the spirit
indeed is willing, but the flesh is weak.' 39 And again he went away and
prayed, saying the same words. 40 And again he came and found them sleeping, for their eyes were very heavy; and they did not know what to answer
him. 41 And he came the third time, and said to them, 'Are you still sleeping
and taking your rest? It is enough; the hour has come; the Son of man is
betrayed into the hands of sinners. 42 Rise, let us be going; see, my betrayer is
at hand.'*

a Or *keep awake*

Opinions are sharply divided about the historical value of this section, and even as to whether it formed part of St Mark's narrative source. Some point out that such a report could well have emanated from Peter, and emphasize the unlikelihood of the Church's having invented a scene which was so damaging to the apostles and which stressed the horror and distress of Jesus (vv. 33 and 34) in contrast to the serenity with which many of the early Christian martyrs faced death; they therefore regard the verses as a (possibly slightly elaborated) historical account, of which St Luke's story (Luke 22^{40-46}) is an abbreviation. Others emphasize that there could not possibly have been any witness for a good deal of what is here described, and that no one could have known what Jesus prayed in private (v. 35). They regard the model prayer (v. 36) and the threefold structure of the incident as artificial (? cf. Peter's threefold denial), and regard the Lucan account as based on more trustworthy, though not necessarily ultimately authentic, tradition.

Confident decision is impossible, but for the purposes of interpretation, we must remember the point made by Dibelius that everything in the story as we have it must have been regarded as having positive value for apologetic or edification or it could not have retained its place in the tradition.* Probably, therefore, Jesus' distressful prayer was seen as the fulfilment of such Old Testament passages as Pss. 22^{20}, $31^{9, 10, 22}$, $69^{1f.}$ (all Psalms which have greatly influenced the Passion narrative, see p.366–7) and of Ps. $42^{5 \text{ and } 6}$, and Jonah 4^{9} quoted in v. 34 (in the Greek version the Jonah passage has almost exactly the same wording as v. 34). Also of great significance is the pointed contrast between Jesus' agonized recognition of the will of God (v. 36) and the unsuspecting sleep of the disciples who, because they were not watching, did not know that *the hour* had come (cf. $13^{32f.}$, and see the interesting remarks of Lightfoot in *G. M. M.*, pp. 52–3). R. writes: 'For the [martyr] Church of Mark's day the example of Jesus in the Garden, as contrasted with the behaviour of the three disciples, must have had special value as setting forth the spirit in which the vocation to martyrdom should be approached. The Christian witness must not presume upon the fact that his spirit is willing: he must ever be mindful also of the weakness of the flesh. It is essential therefore that he should *watch and pray*, that when the hour of trial comes he may not break down. Had Peter and the rest (it is perhaps implied) kept vigil in the Garden, they might have stood firm instead of forsaking their Lord at the time of the arrest. The parallel is perhaps intentional between St Peter's subsequent three denials and the three occasions on which in the Garden he is found to be asleep' (p. 211). Some commentators find in such considerations the clue to the origin of the story; they regard v. 38 as originally an independent logion, comparable to Mark 13^{35} or Luke 12^{37}, and see in the sleep of the apostles a rather literalistic exemplification of it. On

* He writes: 'If we consider this section in the context of the Marcan Passion we must first of all free ourselves from the prejudice which has also obscured the understanding of Jesus' last cry on the cross – as if a conscientious chronicler had narrated in this case that even Jesus, in the stress of the moment, had shown a trace of human weakness. The scene as it stands today in Mark is not meant to produce disillusionment – for then it would not have been accepted into the Gospel at all – but understanding of the revelation. Like the entire Marcan Passion its concern is soteriological, not psychological.' *F. T. G.*, E. T., p. 211, modified).

the other hand, perhaps in favour of a historical basis for the story, we know that the early Church had a tradition of Jesus having 'offered up prayers and supplications with loud cries and tears to him who was able to save him from death' before his Passion (Heb. 5[7]).

32
a place which was called Gethsemane: Only mentioned in the New Testament here and in the parallel passage Matt. 26[36]. Perhaps *place* should be translated 'a piece of land' (see R.V. marg.), and since *Gethsemane* is generally taken to mean 'an oil press',* we should probably think of an olive grove; though see John 18[1ff.]. In view of v. 26 it was presumably in the vicinity of the Mount of Olives, though if this was once an independent pericope there may originally have been no connexion between these opening words and v. 26.

33
This verse presents something of a puzzle; the special selection of the three disciples suggests the revelation of some supernatural mystery comparable to the raising of the dead (5[37]) and the transfiguration (9[2] – with v. 40 cf. 9[6], and, remarkably, Luke 9[32]). But Jesus' prayer, even understood as a fulfilment of the Old Testament, hardly constitutes a revelation of divine glory, and even the prayer the disciples do not witness. Can the idea be that if the disciples had not displayed their usual lamentable lack of faith and understanding, some revelation would have been vouchsafed to them? (Cf. John 11[40], and again see *G. M. M.*, pp. 52–3.)

greatly distressed and troubled: Hardly strong enough to do justice to the Greek, which is 'suggestive of shuddering awe'. 'The Greek words depict the greatest possible degree of infinite horror and suffering.' (Lohmeyer).

34
even to death: The meaning is 'sorrow which almost kills' or 'sorrow so great that death could be preferable'.

35
if it were possible: i.e. consistently with the fulfilment of God's will.

the hour: Cf. v. 41. When used absolutely like this, the phrase is said to mean 'the hour of fate' – a use derived from astrology. But in the early Church it became a more or less technical term for the hour of salvation,

* But see Klausner, *Jesus of Nazareth*, p. 330 and n. 5.

the moment when Jesus by his suffering won salvation for mankind. (John 17^{1} and cf. John 2^{4}, 7^{30}, 8^{20}, 12^{23}, 13^{1}, 16^{21}.) See Dan. $11^{40, 45}$ and Mark 1^{15} and 13^{32} for partial parallels, but this later Christian usage on the lips of Jesus certainly raises a question.

pass from him: i.e. without the necessity for suffering.

36
Whatever view is taken of the pericope as a whole, this verse, which repeats the substance of v. 35 in direct speech, must surely be the reverent conjecture of the early Church 'elaborating a tradition that was too meagre for its fullest religious use' (B.). Everything points to that conclusion: the fact that no witnesses were close to Jesus, the double opening (Abba = Father) which appears to have been the recognized opening of the Lord's Prayer among Greek-speaking Christians, the reminiscence of the middle petition of the Lord's Prayer, and the obviously model character of the prayer, with its clear statement of God's omnipotence; and for the *cup* see on $10^{38\text{f.}}$.

37
Simon: In view of John $21^{15\text{ff.}}$ Swete *may* be right in saying: 'for the time he is "Peter" no more; the new character which he owes to association with Jesus is in abeyance.'

38
Probably originally an independent saying (see above). If so, *temptation* (*peirasmos*, literally 'trial' or 'testing') may well refer to the eschatological trial which the faithful expected to have to face in connexion with the coming of the kingdom. (Cf. Rev. 3^{10} and Matt. 6^{13}, Luke 11^{4}, and see pp. 63–4.) In view of Luke 4^{13} and $22^{24\text{ff.}}$ it may well be that this experience of Jesus was conceived as a conflict with Satanic powers.

39
saying the same words: Absent from some MSS.; possibly a gloss. In any case, it is clear that nothing precise was known about the second prayer and rebuke, or about the third (vv. 40–41a), and the possibility cannot be ruled out that they are a development of the story, designed to emphasize the spiritual blindness of the disciples, which St Mark so constantly stresses (cf. e.g. $4^{13, 40, 41}$, $6^{50\text{ff.}}$, 7^{18}, $8^{16\text{ff.}}$, $9^{5\text{f.}}$, 10^{24}), and which he believed to be due to a supernatural 'hardening' of their hearts. (Contrast St Luke's account.)

41
It is enough: The Greek word (*apěchei*) is obscure here; the translation given (referring either to sleep or to the ironical rebuke) is as likely as

any, though the word was not often used in this sense. Some MSS. give a different reading, which might be rendered: '(You think) the End is far off? (On the contrary) the hour has struck; the Son of man...' *the Son of man is betrayed into the hands of sinners:* A saying which defines the character of Jesus' death. He dies because he is *Son of man* and he dies at the hands of Gentiles (*sinners* = Gentiles, cf. e.g. Gal. 2^{15}) because the Jews not only reject their king but themselves hand him over to the nations of the world. Lightfoot says 'this verse may with some reason be described as the most terrible in Mark' (*G. M. M.*, p. 53). As a 'Son-of-man saying' the verse is rejected by many critics, at any rate in its present form.

42
my betrayer is at hand: Is Jesus (supernaturally) aware of the traitor's approach before he actually arrives? The opening of the next verse certainly suggests that.

14^{43-52} THE ARREST

43*And immediately, while he was still speaking, Judas came, one of the*
twelve, and with him a crowd with swords and clubs, from the chief priests
and the scribes and the elders. 44*Now the betrayer had given them a sign,*
saying, 'The one I shall kiss is the man; seize him and lead him away
safely.' 45*And when he came, he went up to him at once, and said, 'Master!'*[a]
And he kissed him. 46*And they laid hands on him and seized him.* 47*But one*
of those who stood by drew his sword, and struck the slave of the high priest
and cut off his ear. 48*And Jesus said to them, 'Have you come out as against*
a robber, with swords and clubs to capture me? 49*Day after day I was with*
you in the temple teaching, and you did not seize me. But let the scriptures be
fulfilled.' 50*And they all forsook him, and fled.*
51*And a young man followed him, with nothing but a linen cloth about his*
body; and they seized him, 52*but he left the linen cloth and ran away naked.*

a Or *Rabbi*

From this point on, the agreement between John and the synoptic tradition becomes much closer than it has been earlier in the Passion narrative; apart from comparatively insignificant exceptions, the two traditions now run parallel, with very little extra material in either. For this and other reasons it seems probable that the earliest version of the traditional Passion narrative began with the arrest of Jesus.*

The introductory words of v. 43 are, on linguistic grounds, to be attributed to St Mark, and it may be that at one time the verse began with some words which formed an introduction to the primitive Passion narrative as a whole; verses 27–31 probably formed a preface to the narrative from an early stage, and v. 43 will then have picked up directly from v. 31.

In their present form (which appears to be composite – see below) vv. 43–52 serve a number of purposes in the context of the Passion narrative:

1. They emphasize the perfidious character of a traitor who would betray a friend with a kiss (vv. 44 and 45).

2. They show, on Jesus' own authority, that what happened was in accordance with Old Testament prediction (v. 49b).

3. They make plain that, despite the warlike preparations for his capture, Jesus was not a bandit, or even a revolutionary Messiah, but a peaceable teacher-Messiah, who had nothing to hide and had always carried on his work quite openly (vv. 48–49).

4. They record the fulfilment of Jesus' prophecy in v. 27, so confirming its supernatural character (v. 50).

5. They may also have been meant to hint at the existence of the eyewitness testimony on which the record was based (see on vv. 51–52).

Incidentally, they mark one more stage in the progressive dereliction and desolation of Jesus. On that motif in Mark's Passion narrative see *G. M. M.*, p. 55.

It is only fair to add that the historicity of the entire episode has been impugned by B. W. Bacon in a famous and important article in the Hibbert Journal (vol. XIX for 1920–1, pp. 476ff.) 'What did Judas betray?' on the grounds that Jesus and his movements were well known, and the authorities could easily have discovered and appre-

* See Bultmann, pp. 297ff· especially pp. 301–2, and Jeremias, *E. W. J.*, pp. 66ff., who points out that none of the brief summaries of the Passion events in the New Testament refers to any event before the arrest. Cf. e.g. Mark $10^{33f.}$ and 9^{31}, Acts 2^{23}, 7^{52}, 13^{28}, etc.

hended him quietly without the expense of 'resort to the slippery aid of hired traitors' (p. 486). The article, which deals with a number of questions connected with Marcan interpretation, is important on several counts, and readers who can should certainly consult it: but many scholars have remained unconvinced by this particular argument in it. They feel that the Jewish authorities may well have been unaware of Jesus' whereabouts when the city was so crowded for the feast, and that if Gethsemane was full of pilgrims bivouacking for the night, an unobtrusive arrest may well have depended on instant and certain recognition which would not have been easy in the dark; those in charge of the arrest may not even have known Jesus by sight. (Cf. e.g. *F. T. G.*, p. 205.)

ꭜ

43
one of the twelve: The description suggests that this section was originally independent of what precedes, since Judas has already been introduced in vv. 10–11.

crowd: Commentators often speak of a detachment of the temple police, but the Greek word (*ŏchlŏs*) suggests something less official and formal; Contrast John 18^{3} which appears – most improbably – to envisage Roman soldiers.

from the chief priests . . . : This careful designation of the Jewish authorities is no doubt meant to emphasize the joint guilt of all three elements.

45
kissed him: The gesture, like the mode of address (*Master* = rabbi), was common between rabbis and their disciples; originally, therefore, it may not have been quite so revolting a sign of betrayal as it now appears. The Greek word for *kiss* in this verse is slightly different from that in v. 44 and St Mark *may* have meant it to suggest a specially affectionate kiss, thereby setting Judas' treachery in an even blacker light. Is there also perhaps an allusion to Prov. 27^{6}?

47
The action seems inappropriate after the arrest has already been accomplished; in any case the verse is only very loosely attached to 43–46, and no doubt is an originally isolated tradition which Luke ($22^{49\text{f.}}$) and John (18^{10-11}) have inserted at a more appropriate point in the story. Clearly there was at least a mild skirmish, and Bacon and others have thought that Jesus' followers made some attempt to

resist by violence; apart from this vestige, the fact has disappeared from the tradition, together with practically all other evidence of any political or secular elements in Jesus' Messiahship. (See Bacon op. cit. – who makes some important points in this connexion.)

48–49
Also an addition to the original narrative. Jesus' words seem inappropriate addressed to the crowd (contrast Luke 22^{52}), and are generally regarded as belonging to 'an imaginative recast of the scene' (V. T.). Their point is apologetic; what Jesus objects to is not the indignity done to him, but the manner of the arrest which misrepresents his character and the character of his activities.

robber: Better 'bandit' or perhaps 'revolutionary' – 'insurrectionist'.

49
Day after day: Clearly Jesus had been in Jerusalem longer, or more often, than St Mark's account suggests.

let the scriptures be fulfilled: The Greek, which is difficult and not in St Mark's manner, has given rise to the suggestion that this may be a scribal note incorporated into the text. If it is original to St Mark, the R.S.V. translation is *probably* the correct one. Probably no particular Old Testament passage is in mind. See on p. 379, and cf. R., p. 214 '... by the time that Mark wrote, it had become a fixed dogma of the Church that all the events of the Saviour's Passion, even down to the details, happened "according to the scriptures", and the phrase *that the scriptures might be fulfilled* might be introduced even though there were no very particularly apt passage of scripture to be adduced.'

51–52
These puzzling verses fit very awkwardly on to v. 50; some copyists rewrote the Greek in order to get a smoother connexion, and Matthew and Luke both omit these verses. Speculation about the identity of the young man has been endless, and, in view of the meagreness of our information, quite profitless; it can hardly have been the Evangelist himself, as the awkward connexion proves that he is dependent on a source for the story.*

The puzzle is why the tradition should have preserved the memory of the incident. It may have been thought valuable as showing that the tradition went back to an eyewitness (especially if he was at one time readily identifiable in the Church where the tradition was preserved),

* And were the story personal reminiscence, it would not be so compressed and enigmatic; why was the young man so ill clad in the cold of a spring night?

and also, despite many commentators, it is possible that a fulfilment of Amos 2^{16} (and ? Gen. 39^{12}) was seen in the story.

14$^{53-72}$ CHRIST BEFORE THE SANHEDRIN AND PETER'S DENIAL

[53]And they led Jesus to the high priest; and all the chief priests and the
elders and the scribes were assembled. [54]And Peter had followed him at a dis-
tance, right into the courtyard of the high priest; and he was sitting with the
guards, and warming himself at the fire. [55]Now the chief priests and the whole
council sought testimony against Jesus to put him to death; but they found
none. [56]For many bore false witness against him, and their witness did not
agree. [57]And some stood up and bore false witness against him, saying,
[58]'We heard him say, "I will destroy this temple that is made with hands,
and in three days I will build another, not made with hands."' [59]Yet not even
so did their testimony agree. [60]And the high priest stood up in the midst, and
asked Jesus, 'Have you no answer to make? What is it that these men testify
against you?' [61]But he was silent and made no answer. Again the high
priest asked him, 'Are you the Christ, the Son of the Blessed?' [62]And Jesus
said, 'I am; and you will see the Son of man sitting at the right hand of
Power, and coming with the clouds of heaven.' [63]And the high priest tore his
mantle, and said, 'Why do we still need witnesses? [64]You have heard his
blasphemy. What is your decision?' And they all condemned him as deserving
death. [65]And some began to spit on him, and to cover his face, and to strike
him, saying to him, 'Prophesy!' And the guards received him with blows.

[66]And as Peter was below in the courtyard, one of the maids of the high
priest came; [67]and seeing Peter warming himself, she looked at him, and said,
'You also were with the Nazarene, Jesus.' [68]But he denied it, saying, 'I
neither know nor understand what you mean.' And he went out into the gate-
way.[a] [69]And the maid saw him, and began again to say to the bystanders,
'This man is one of them.' [70]But again he denied it. And after a little while
again the bystanders said to Peter, 'Certainly you are one of them; for you
are a Galilean.' [71]But he began to invoke a curse on himself and to swear, 'I
do not know this man of whom you speak.' [72]And immediately the cock
crowed a second time. And Peter remembered how Jesus had said to him,

'Before the cock crows twice, you will deny me three times,' And he broke down and wept.

a or *fore-court.* Other ancient authorities add *and the cock crowed*

How this section grew up it is not easy to say: vv. 66–72 no doubt formed part of the primitive Passion narrative, and in vv. 55–64 St Mark seems to be reproducing well-established popular tradition (see further, notes below); possibly v. 53 is a Marcan introduction (for v. 55 seems to be an independent opening to vv. 55–65) and v. 54 may be either the opening verse of the story of Peter's denial, separated from the rest by vv. 55–65, or a second introductory verse by St Mark. Verse 65 was originally independent, and according to some commentators really belongs to the story of the arrest. In any case, it is clear that St Mark has deliberately interwoven the story of Jesus' trial (vv. 53 and 55–65) with that of Peter's denial (vv. 54 and 66–72); for a suggestion as to his motive see below. The story of the trial will be discussed first.

This is clearly a passage of great importance, containing as it does the Christian explanation how one who had died a criminal's death could yet be proclaimed as Messiah and, as such, completely blameless. The proceedings which were the immediate cause of Jesus' death are set forth in a threefold light:

(i) They are shown as the work of the Jews. The Romans, in the person of Pilate, also played their part ($15^{2\text{ff.}}$), but the aim of this section is to show that the primary initiative and the real responsibility lay with the Jews, who through their official representatives solemnly rejected and destroyed the Messiah in full consciousness of what they were doing (see pp. 367-8 and also notes below on pp. 404-5).

(ii) They are shown as a complete perversion of justice. Although numerous irregularities were permitted at the trial in the interests of the prosecution, no efforts could produce any genuine evidence of wrong-doing on the part of Jesus (vv. 55b, 56b, 59), and in the end the authorities had to come out into the open and admit to condemning him simply for his (perfectly legitimate) claim to be Messiah (vv. 61b–64).

(iii) They were in complete accordance with the will of God as revealed in the Old Testament (cf. vv. 56, 57, 59, 61, 62, and 65, with the notes on them).

The explanation of the intertwining of this story with the story of Peter's denial lies probably in v. 62, where Jesus for the first and only time publicly proclaims his true, heavenly status and the glorious destiny awaiting him. He does this not only in the moment of his deepest humiliation and weakness, when he is completely at the mercy of his enemies, but also at the moment when he is denied and deserted by the last of his human supporters (cf. v. 29 and note that up till v. 54 Peter still 'followed Jesus' if only 'from afar'). The true character of his act is thus brought out; it is the *good confession* (1 Tim. 6[13]), the perfect manifestation of faith as St Mark understood faith, complete trust in the unaided power of God, which is *made perfect in human weakness* (2 Cor. 12[9]). We are once again reminded of the true meaning of the Passion narrative (see pp. 372f.); it is the Messiah – God's saving agent, endowed with God's invincible power – of whose rejection and ill-treatment we are reading. See *H. & I.*, pp. 150–1, *G. M. M.*, pp. 54–5, and *F. T. G.*, pp. 192–3; Dibelius rightly describes this as a 'climax in Mark's Passion narrative' and speaks of Jesus' 'glorious divine status shining out in the midst of all the abasement' in v. 62.

In itself, the story of Peter's denial raises few difficulties and most commentators believe that, though it may have been embroidered here and there, it is a piece of early tradition, going back ultimately to Peter's own reminiscence.*

As for its significance in the context of the Gospel, we have just seen how it serves as a foil to Jesus' self-revelation in v. 62, and it serves also, of course, to demonstrate the complete truth of Jesus' prophecy in 14[30]. The early Church will no doubt have preserved the story as a warning against the perils of apostasy, and at the same time it is seen as a special example of that wilful backsliding by the disciples which St Mark regards as part of the mysterious providence of God. (Cf. how it is already interpreted in that way in v. 27 where it is regarded as the fulfilment of Old Testament prophecy.) The early Church may also have found in the story encouragement for those who had shared the experience of Peter; if such a denial as this could be followed by all the saintly heroism Peter was known to the

* It is only fair to add, however, that to Bultmann it seems 'legendary and literary', and that Goguel argues at length that it is a fictitious elaboration of the saying in 14[30].

Roman Christians to have displayed later, lesser Christians who had given way under interrogation, or 'denied' their Lord in other ways, had no need to despair. Dibelius, who takes this line, thinks that originally the story must have gone closely with a post-resurrection narrative in which the risen Lord, appearing first to Peter, accepted and re-established him rather after the manner described in John 21^{15-19} (*F. T. G.*, pp. 214–16).

If the significance in the Gospel of 14^{53-72} is thus clear, the question of its *historicity* has been, and still is, the subject of lively debate. The main reasons for doubting its historicity must be briefly set out and discussed.

1. St Mark describes the trial as taking place before 'the council' (*synĕdriŏn*, v. 55), i.e. the *Sanhedrin*, an official body of seventy-one members, under the presidency of the high priest, which was the supreme judicial authority in Israel. The Tract *Sanhedrin* in the *Mishnah* sets out fully the procedure adopted in trials before this body, and a comparison of what it says with St Mark's account of the trial of Jesus reveals numerous discrepancies, many of them very considerable. Scholars assess this fact very differently. On the one hand it is pointed out that the *Mishnah* dates from long after the fall of Jerusalem and that the Tract *Sanhedrin* is the work of second-century rabbis who were writing when the Sanhedrin as a working institution had ceased to exist.* Accordingly, it is argued that their account is largely speculation, a theoretical and highly idealized construction, from which little or nothing can be deduced about the actual procedure of the council in the time of Christ. Other scholars, while allowing some weight to these contentions, point out that the rabbis always sought to base themselves on tradition, and argue therefore that though the *Mishnah* account may have been embroidered and idealized, it can still be used as evidence for the procedure actually followed by the Sanhedrin, at any rate in general terms. If so, the divergences in St Mark's account demand some sort of explanation. It is, of course, possible that in the case of Jesus the Sanhedrin flagrantly disregarded its own rules of procedure in an effort to get the prisoner condemned at all costs; but we have no reason to think the authorities

* The 'Sanhedrin' which existed at Jabne after the fall of Jerusalem was a purely academic body which exercised no practical jurisdiction.

took the matter as seriously as that would imply, or, for that matter, that they would have been ready to pervert the course of justice in this way. A more widely held view is that the normal procedure was not followed in this case *because the proceedings were not in the strict sense a trial at all* but an informal investigation preparatory to the trial proper before Pilate ($15^{2ff.}$); Grand Jury proceedings are often suggested as an analogy. Some commentators go so far as to suggest that this was St Mark's own understanding of the matter, arguing that the language of v. 64 does not suggest the formal verdict of a duly constituted court. This latter is very doubtful, however (see notes on vv. 55 and 64 below), and the opinion more usually put forward is that though the proceedings were *in fact* an informal investigation, St Mark thought of them as a trial in the strict sense. Such a mistake could easily have arisen, seeing that the early Christians can have had no direct information about what went on behind the closed doors of the high priest's house; and in any case the sort of popular tradition St Mark is here reproducing neither knew nor cared about the minutiae of legal procedure or the niceties of a trial, as opposed to a preliminary legal investigation.*

This view has the advantage of bringing St Mark's account more closely into line with that of St John, who appears to suggest that only informal investigations preceded Jesus' appearance before Pilate (cf. John $18^{13ff., 24, 28ff.}$).

2. But would members of the Sanhedrin have met, even for such informal proceedings, in the middle of Passover night or, for that matter, if St Mark's chronology of the Passion week is inaccurate, in the middle of a night just before the Passover? Certainly, despite the arguments of Jeremias (*E. W. J.*, pp. 52–3), a formal trial at such a time seems unthinkable (see notes below) and most scholars are very doubtful about the holding of even an informal investigation at such a time. St Luke says nothing of a night session of the council (Luke 22^{66} *when day came*...), and in St Mark's account the early morning session reported in 15^{1} seems to have no real point; why should the council meet *as soon as it was morning* (15^{1}) if it had already done all that is reported in 14^{53-65} during the night? Many scholars, therefore, think

* The anti-Jewish tendency discussed below might also have had its influence, cf. Goguel, *Jésus* (1950), p. 435: '*La tradition, avec sa tendance à charger les Juifs, a transformé en un jugement ce qui n'avait été qu'un avis.*'

that St Mark, knowing two accounts of the 'trial' (that reproduced in 14^{53-65} and that reproduced in 15^{1}), and perhaps having some inkling of some sort of a private inquiry immediately after the arrest (cf. John 18^{13}), wrongly understood the two accounts as referring to two different trials. (Cf. for his tendency to interpret doublets as separate incidents 6^{35-44} and 8^{1-9}).* In fact the Jewish authorities met only once, and that was in the early morning as described in 15^{1}. A further question then arises:

3. How far does 14^{53-65} give an accurate account of what took place at this early morning session? Here again expert opinion is very divided, some commentators treating St Mark's account with great respect, despite its admitted difficulties, on the grounds that accurate information might well have been forthcoming from councillors who subsequently became Christians (such as Joseph of Arimathea or Nicodemus), others dismissing this as pure speculation, and arguing, on internal evidence, that the passage represents little more than early Christian inference as to the sort of thing that must have happened. This internal evidence must be briefly reviewed.

(*a*) If false witnesses were suborned (vv. 55–59), would they not, as a matter of common prudence, have been schooled in advance, so that their witness *did* 'agree together'? Also the transition from this part of the narrative to the high priest's question in v. 61 seems impossibly abrupt.†

(*b*) According to Jewish Law neither the temple saying, even had it been proved, nor Jesus' reply to the high priest, constituted blasphemy, for which a definite railing against the divine name was essential (cf. Lev. 24^{10-23} and the *Mishnah* translated by H. Danby, p. 392). It is true that the word *blasphemy* was sometimes used in a broader sense (cf. e.g. 2^{7}, John 5^{18} and 10^{33}), but it seems unlikely that in this wide,

* See e.g. V. T. (pp. 565 and 646) who makes the point that there is nothing in the account in 53–65 to suggest a night session.

† Contrast Matt. and cf. *H. & I.*, p. 163: 'in St Mark the high priest's question about the Messiahship has no direct reference to the temple saying'. If the refounding of the temple and its worship was something generally expected of the Messiah, as is sometimes suggested, that would provide a basis of connexion, but St Mark seems to know nothing of any such expectation, and in any case says explicitly that the testimony about Jesus' threat to the temple was false (59).

non-technical, sense it could have been made the basis of a death sentence (v. 64). Cf., however, G. D. Kilpatrick in *The Trial of Jesus*.

(*c*) If Jesus was condemned for blasphemy, why did not the Jewish authorities themselves carry out the sentence and stone him to death in accordance with the Law (Lev. 24, etc.)? It has usually been held, on the basis of John 18^{31} and certain rabbinic passages, that at this period the Jews were prevented by the Romans from carrying out capital sentences, but in the last half century this view has been challenged by very eminent authorities. However, they cannot be said to have *proved* their case and the matter is still very much *sub judice*. (See e.g. G. D. Kilpatrick, op. cit., and on the other side T. A. Burkill in *Vigiliae Christianae*, x, 1956, pp. 80ff. and xii, 1958, p. 1ff.) It is of course possible that although the Jewish authorities had the right to execute Jesus themselves, they preferred a procedure which placed the responsibility and possible odium on Pilate. This raises a further issue, namely:

(*d*) the relation between these Jewish proceedings and the trial before Pilate ($15^{2ff.}$). It will hardly do to speak of Pilate's action as simply a 'confirmation' of the Jewish sentence, for in that case Jesus would presumably have died by stoning. The indisputable fact that he died by crucifixion shows that his formal trial and sentence were the work of a Roman court, for crucifixion was essentially a *Roman* penalty. What then was the point of the proceedings before the Sanhedrin? One suggestion is 'that the leaders of the Sanhedrin were entrusted with certain powers of initiative in criminal cases, including the right of arrest, the taking of evidence, and the conduct of a preliminary examination with a view to the preparation of the case for submission to the Roman procurator for formal trial' (R., p. 219). The majority of commentators, at any rate in England, interpret Mark along some such lines as these, and they may well be right; the difficulty, however, is that such an explanation does not by any means correspond with Mark's account as it stands. When the Jews bring Jesus before Pilate ($15^{1ff.}$) there is no hint that the *many charges* they bring against him (15^{3-4}) have any relation to the proceedings described in 14^{53-65}; indeed in $15^{2ff.}$ there is no reference to a previous investigation at all. And it is by no means obvious that the accusation of claiming to be king of the Jews, brought against Jesus before Pilate,

(15^2) can be identified with the *blasphemy* for which Jesus is condemned in 14^{64}.* Accordingly, the possibility cannot be ruled out that 14^{53-65} is mainly a deduction by the early Christians, 'an attempt on the part of a section of the Church, in the absence of precise information, to set forth the grounds on which the Lord was believed to have been condemned by the leaders of his nation and handed over to the procurator' (*H. & I.*, p. 142). Certainly the early Christians were regarded by their Jewish contemporaries as blasphemers for proclaiming as Messiah one who had been crucified, and so had incurred the curse of Deut. 21^{23}; the idea could therefore easily have arisen that if it was blasphemy for the Christians to claim Messiahship for the crucified Christ, it must have been blasphemy for him to have made the same claim for himself. Thus, if there was also a tradition that Jesus' saying about the temple (vv. 57–59) had played some part in his condemnation, it is easy to see how the section might have been built up, especially when we notice that some elements in the story appear to be due to Old Testament reminiscence (see notes below).

Two further points are often made in favour of the last interpretation of 53–65. The early Church, as we have seen (pp. 367–8), exhibited a steadily growing tendency to transfer the responsibility for Jesus' death from the Romans to the Jews, and so it is natural that they should have come to posit a Jewish trial, at least as formal and decisive as that before Pilate, in which the Jewish authorities incurred the responsibility for Jesus' death. Connected with this is the question of Jesus' public self-revelation in v. 62. Such a declaration – the only

* Cf. *H. & I.*, p. 148 n. 1. 'There is no satisfactory transition in St Mark from "Art thou the Christ, the Son of the Blessed?" to "Art thou the King of the Jews?" Contrast the altogether satisfactory junction achieved in St Luke by means of Luke 23^2.' Montef. (I, 355) makes a further point: '. . . if the whole object of the investigation before the Jewish court was only to formulate a charge . . . against Jesus to be sent up to the Roman authorities, the accusation in regard to the temple would be of small avail. For the Roman court would hardly consider that a man ought to be put to death who had made what a Roman judge would consider a silly prediction or boast of this kind.' Cf. Kilpatrick, op. cit., for a most interesting, though perhaps not entirely convincing, attempt to show that the temple charge was an attempt on the part of the Sadducean high priest to convince the *Pharisees* that Jesus needed to be put out of the way, while the charge of claiming to be King of the Jews (which Kilpatrick thinks is simply the blasphemy charge suitably nuanced for a Roman court) was designed to convince Pilate.

one in the Gospel – is surprising, for it runs counter to the fundamental plan of Mark's Gospel, according to which Jesus' Messiahship is a secret, except from a chosen few, until after the crucifixion. It may be, as Lightfoot and others have suggested,* that the section formed no part of the Gospel as originally written; but, however it came into the Gospel, it needs explanation.

Increasingly (and supremely in the fourth Gospel) the Jews were seen by the Christians as having deliberately rejected Christ in full knowledge of his claims and the evidence in their support (cf. e.g. John 15^{24} and 12^{37}). This is probably the point being made here; what the Sanhedrin did, it did in full awareness of the facts. In view of Jesus' solemn declaration, the scene depicts the Jews, as represented by their duly constituted leaders, deliberately and with full knowledge casting out the 'name' of Jesus and rejecting their Messiah.

Certainty with regard to these very complex and still hotly debated questions would not be claimed by any commentator, and the reader should consult the detailed notes below before attempting to arrive at a conclusion.

53

high priest: Mark nowhere mentions his name, Caiaphas.

chief priests, etc.: See notes on 8^{31} and on 14^{1}.

54

into the courtyard of the high priest: This seems to imply that the proceedings were held in the high priest's house; if a trial in the strict sense was in question, this was an irregularity, for the high priest's house was not a possible meeting place for the court. Nor could a trial involving a capital charge take place at night; such trials had to take place by day, and there had to be a second session of the court on the following day before conviction. No such trial could therefore take place before a sabbath or feast day, which would prevent the holding of a second session on the following day. It will thus be seen what very serious irregularities the Marcan narrative implies; and see further below.

guards (hypēretai): Strictly 'servants'. The high priest's attendants, perhaps including temple police.

55

the whole council: The phrase suggests that St Mark was thinking of

* Cf. *H. & I.*, p. 151, n. 1.

formal proceedings before a duly constituted court. Twenty-three members formed a quorum.

sought testimony, etc.: The picture seems to be of the authorities looking round desperately for witnesses at the last moment. This is highly unlikely; surely the 'evidence' would have been carefully prepared beforehand and the witnesses would not have been allowed to disagree. Without such preparations where would witnesses have been obtained at this hour of the night? In any case the Jewish rules regarding the appearance of witnesses and the assessment of their evidence were strict, and rigorously fair to the point of favouring the accused; for a court to have acted as both prosecutor and judge in the way suggested here would have been a gross irregularity, at any rate by the standards laid down in the later rabbinic sources.

57–59

The repetition of v. 56a in v. 57 and of v. 56b in v. 59 has led many to the view that '55f. and 57–59 may be different versions of the same tradition, stated generally in the former and particularized in the latter' (V. T., p. 566). In any case the repetition serves both to emphasize the impossibility of finding any true evidence against Jesus and to underline the fulfilment of such Old Testament passages as Pss. 27^{12}, 35^{11-12}, and 109^{2-5}. It is impossible to say how great an effect these and other Old Testament passages have had on the formulation of the story. Some, e.g. Klostermann, have regarded them as largely responsible for it.

It is not clear why St Mark represents the testimony in v. 58 as false. According to the tradition in John $2^{19ff.}$, Jesus did utter some such saying and Acts 6^{14} seems to point in the same direction. Many scholars therefore think that the saying was genuine and that it was known to have played some part in Jesus' condemnation. The reserve about it in St Mark's tradition may be partly due to the desire to make v. 62 the sole ground of Jesus' condemnation (cf. *F. T. G.*, p. 192) and partly to 'the uneasiness of primitive Christianity regarding the saying on the part of those who continued to observe the temple worship (cf. Acts 2^{46}, 3^{1-10}, $5^{20f., 42}$)' (V. T., p. 566). Perhaps in its original form the saying did not go much beyond the prediction of the temple's destruction by others, now contained in 13^{2}, but it must be admitted that in its present form it smacks of later phraseology and ideas. For the contrast *made with hands . . . not made with hands* (*cheiropoiētos – acheiropoiētos*) cf. Acts 7^{48}, 17^{24}, Heb. $9^{11 \text{ and } 24}$; the whole idea suggests the outlook of later Christians like Stephen who questioned the permanence and significance of the temple rites. The saying sets forth the risen Christ as the life of a new and spiritual temple, in contrast to the ordinances of the earlier material sanctuary (cf. John 2^{21-2}), in a way so different from what Jesus teaches elsewhere (contrast especially the cleansing of the temple 11^{15-17}) that some scholars regard it as an early Christian product, especially as the words *in three days* are such a precise reference to the resurrection.

60–61a

This connecting link between vv. 55–59 and 61b–64 is somewhat artificial; there is no reason why Jesus *should* have attempted any answer, seeing that the testimony against him had shown itself false. The point is to emphasize Jesus' silence understood as a fulfilment of Ps. 38^{12-14} and Isa. 53^{7}.

61b–64

Some scholars think that the second accusation to which the connecting link leads was originally independent of the first, so that 55–59 and 61b–64 represent alternative accounts of what happened at the trial; in that case not only is 14^{53-65} a doublet of 15^{1}, but 55ff. and 61ff. are doublets within the former passage.

61b

The high priest's question raises two problems. On the one hand a reverential circumlocution (*the Blessed* [*One*]) is used in order to avoid speaking directly of God, which is what we should expect from the high priest, but on the other hand, as the Jewish scholar Klausner points out,* the particular circumlocution used 'is not a Hebrew expression . . . it is scarcely an abbreviation of the habitual "the Holy One, blessed be he"'. Klausner therefore concludes that, for all its semitic appearance, it 'must be a later addition'. (Matthew's very semitic Gospel has not got the words, cf. 26^{63}.)

Again, the phrase *Son of God*, though early used *by Christians* as = Messiah, does not seem to have been so used by Jews in the time of Our Lord.†

The most likely explanation of all this is that, at any rate as now formulated, the high priest's question is due to the early Church.

62

Dan. 7^{13} and Ps. 110^{1}. 'Mark represents Our Lord as acknowledging His Messiahship in the same terms as those in which the earliest Church confesses it, i.e. He is the Son of man who is shortly to appear in glory to the confusion of those who condemned him' (R., p. 222).

* *Jesus of Nazareth*, p. 342.

† This is a dogmatic statement on a very complex question – see further V. T., p. 567.

As we have seen (p. 402), the rabbis of the *Mishnah* expressly require the use of the divine name for a valid condemnation on a charge of blasphemy, so this statement, with its careful circumlocution (*Power*, or rather '*the* Power', = God) ought in justice to have escaped the charge (but see below on 63f.).

I am: Some commentators prefer the reading 'you say that I am', which is still an acknowledgement of Messiahship, but perhaps implies a difference between Jesus and the high priest over the interpretation of the term. 'The word is yours.' 'Yes, if you like to put it so.'

coming: i.e. probably down to earth for the final consummation, but see T. F. Glasson, *The Second Advent*, for the view that it means coming *up*, i.e. to the Ancient of Days to receive the 'dominion, glory, and kingdom' of Dan. 7^{14}. The whole phrase is missing in Luke's parallel – 22^{69}.

63
tore his mantle: Originally a sign of passionate grief, this gesture became a formal judicial act in the case of the high priest and is closely regulated in the later law books.

63–64
The high priest's words seem to assume that blasphemy has quite evidently been committed. Commentators sometimes say that it lay not so much in Jesus' claim to Messiahship (other messianic claimants were not accused of blasphemy) as in his claim that he would sit at God's right hand in fulfilment of Dan. 7^{13-14}. But it must remain doubtful if this constituted blasphemy in the technical sense in which it was a capital offence.

64
all: if this is pressed, Joseph of Arimathea was presumably *not* present at the proceedings (see above p. 402).

as deserving death: In view of 10^{33} it is unlikely that St Mark intended this expression to be pressed as implying 'a judicial opinion or verdict rather than a sentence' (V. T., p. 570).

65
A difficult verse, though its main point is clear enough, viz. to exhibit the fulfilment of Old Testament prophesy; cf. Isa. 50^{6} and 53^{3-5}, Mic. 5^{1}, 1 Kings 22^{24}. Almost every word in the verse is taken from the Greek version of one of these passages, and very possibly the mysterious covering of the face rests on a mistranslated and misunderstood

expression in Isa. 53^3. In Luke this trait is rationalized by the addition of the question: '*Who is it that struck you?*' (22^{64}), so that the meaning becomes: 'Use your prophetic gift of second sight to tell the striker's name'. In the best MSS. of Mark, however, the question is missing, and *Prophesy!* then simply means 'Play the prophet now!' (cf. 1 Kings 22^{24}). This leaves the reference to the covering of the face without any immediate point, and some scribes, not recognizing the Old Testament allusion, omitted the words from the text. Some scholars regard them as a late insertion, but probably they are original.

Originally the verse was clearly an independent item of tradition; in its present connexion it appears to suggest that members of the Sanhedrin took the initiative in maltreating Jesus, but this is highly improbable (contrast Luke 22^{63-5}).

received him with blows: The Greek is quite as strange as its English equivalent, and the precise meaning is uncertain, but the expression is undoubtedly meant to be reminiscent of Isa. 50^6 where the same Greek word (*rhapisma*) is used for 'blow'.

68

An alternative translation would be: 'I neither know him nor have I any idea what you can mean' (C. H. Turner), but it may be that the Greek is an inaccurate translation of an Aramaic original.

Some MSS. add the words 'and a cock crowed' at the end of the verse. This and the other textual problems raised by the section are difficult. One important MS. which omits the words also omits *a second time* and *twice* in v. 72 and *twice* in v. 30; in that case all reference to a double crowing is missing and Mark is completely in line with Matthew and Luke. But most MSS. which omit the extra words in this verse retain at least one of the expressions in v. 72 and probably *a second time* at any rate is genuine there. If with R.S.V. we reject the extra words in this verse as an interpolation, but accept the expressions in v. 72 (and 30) as genuine, the meaning will presumably be that, though the cock-crow in v. 72 was the first to be heard by Peter, 'the cock had in fact crowed before and so the prophecy of v. 30 was precisely fulfilled'.*

71

invoke a curse on himself: i.e. in the event that he was not telling the truth.

72

See on v. 68, and, for the cock-crowing, on v. 30; here, as in v. 30, it

* If the reference to a *double* crowing there was simply proverbial (see p. 388 *n.*), this passage rests on an overliteral understanding of it.

may be that a popular expression for early morning, or a reference to the *gallicinium*, has been transformed into a literal cock-crowing.

broke down: The Greek word (*ĕpibalōn*) has caused difficulty from the very beginning (cf. Matt. and Luke), and its meaning cannot be certainly determined. Other suggested translations are: 'when he thought thereon ...' 'rushing outside ...' 'throwing something over his head ...', 'casting himself on the ground ...'.

15^{1-15} JESUS BEFORE PILATE

15 *And as soon as it was morning the chief priests, with the elders and*
scribes, and the whole council held a consultation; and they bound Jesus and
led him away and delivered him to Pilate. [2]*And Pilate asked him, 'Are you*
the King of the Jews?' And he answered him, 'You have said so.' [3]*And the*
chief priests accused him of many things. [4]*And Pilate again asked him, 'Have*
you no answer to make? See how many charges they bring against you.'
[5]*But Jesus made no further answer, so that Pilate wondered.*

[6]*Now at the feast he used to release for them any one prisoner whom they*
asked. [7]*And among the rebels in prison, who had committed murder in the*
insurrection, there was a man called Barab'bas. [8]*And the crowd came up and*
began to ask Pilate to do as he was wont to do for them. [9]*And he answered*
them, 'Do you want me to release for you the King of the Jews?' [10]*For he*
perceived that it was out of envy that the chief priests had delivered him up.
[11]*But the chief priests stirred up the crowd to have him release for them*
Barab'bas instead. [12]*And Pilate again said to them, 'Then what shall I do*
with the man whom you call the King of the Jews?' [13]*And they cried out*
again, 'Crucify him.' [14]*And Pilate said to them, 'Why, what evil has he*
done?' But they shouted all the more, 'Crucify him.' [15]*So Pilate, wishing*
to satisfy the crowd, released for them Barab'bas; and having scourged Jesus,
he delivered him to be crucified.

The section opens with a second meeting of the Sanhedrin, for so St Mark regarded the gathering he describes in v. 1; but the tradition embodied in the verse gives no hint of any previous meeting, and it may well be that this was the only meeting held, the tradition enshrined in 14^{53-65} representing originally a Christian reconstruction of the sort of thing it was felt must have happened at this meeting (see above pp. 401–2). If so, the detailed historical facts are beyond precise reconstruction. Some such meeting as this there must have been, for we can hardly suppose that the Roman governor took the sole initiative in arresting and trying Jesus, but we cannot be sure who called or attended the meeting (the all-inclusive lists given by St Mark in 14^{53} and 15^{1} surely reflect the early Christian desire to emphasize the wide and general Jewish responsibility for Jesus' death), or what precise charges were chosen for presentation before the governor (v. 3). Pilate would hardly have taken these charges seriously unless they had included political matter – some threat to peace and public order – and some of the Jewish leaders may, of course, have been genuinely afraid that Jesus' popularity with the crowds might produce a dangerous popular revolt. But even if the charge was political, various motives may have led to the making of it, e.g. Pharisaic horror at Jesus' laxity with regard to the Law, and scribal jealousy of an unauthorized teacher, though it is a curious fact that these motives, so very prominent earlier in the Gospel, play virtually no part in St Mark's account of the Passion* (though cf. v. 10, *out of envy*). Having formulated its charges, the meeting has Jesus bound and appears with him before Pilate (v. 1).

Although the trial before Pilate is represented as taking place out of doors (*led him away inside*, v. 16), and will certainly have been much more public than the hearing before the Jewish leaders, St Mark's account of it is by no means an eyewitness report; indeed it is not a report at all, so much as a series of traditions, each making some apologetic point about the trial. This explains why we are not told how Pilate learned the charge (in v. 2 he already knows it), and why there is no mention of a formal verdict or passing of sentence (contrast Luke 23^{24}); and it must be admitted that the undignified chaffering which takes place between the procurator and the mob (vv. 9–15) is not the only detail which can hardly be historical as it stands, however well it may reflect the essential spirit of the trial. (See further notes below.) The choice of the material which *is* included has clearly been governed by the following aims:

* The reason may well be the Christian desire to show that it was simply *as Messiah* that Jesus was put to death.

(i) To represent the *Roman* authorities as having no essential quarrel with Jesus and no fault to find with him or his movement. This point was of overwhelming importance to Christians living and evangelizing in a Roman environment, for if the imperial authorities had discovered no harm in the founder of the religion it might be assumed that his followers were harmless too. Cf. how in Acts Roman officials are repeatedly represented as finding no serious fault with the Christian movement.

The Barabbas incident has its significance for the Evangelist in this connexion. It takes the place of any reference to a formal condemnation of Jesus by Pilate and so softens the impression of the governor's attitude to Jesus; see further notes below, and cf. Loisy (*Évangiles synoptiques*, I, 103): 'The episode of Barabbas . . . is interposed in the . . . story of the trial before Pilate to make us understand that the governor did not condemn Jesus, but that he merely allowed him to be put to death in accordance with the sentence of the Sanhedrin, after having tried in vain to free him from the hatred of his enemies.' That leads on to the second aim:

(ii) To emphasize the responsibility of the Jews (vv. 11, 15a), whose hatred of Jesus was so completely unjustified that even a man like Pilate could see through it (vv. 10, 14), yet so strong and insensate that it overcame his persistent scruples (vv. 9, 12, 14, 15). Pilate acts against his better judgement; it is the Jews who must take the responsibility (cf. Matt. 27^{24-25}). This hatred was not confined to one group among the Jewish leaders (v. 1) nor even to one class among the Jews (cf. *the crowd*, vv. 11 and 15), though the leaders, and particularly the priests (v. 11) were behind the popular rejection of Jesus.

(iii) To emphasize the *silence* of Jesus which was so remarkable that Pilate 'wondered' at it (v. 5) – *thaumazein*, a word which in the Gospels has profound religious connotations – cf. e.g. 5^{20}. The early Christians were not surprised at this deep impression made on the governor,* for was not Jesus' silence all part of God's plan? Cf. Ps. 38^{12-14} and Isa. 53^{7}.

(iv) To emphasize yet again that it was *as Messiah* that Jesus was crucified. The title *King of the Jews*, not used earlier in the Gospel,

* Loisy goes so far as to say: 'the favour . . . which Pilate is thought to have shown to Jesus has its reason, according to Mark, in the silence of the accused, not in the avowal of his messianic claims' (*Évangiles synoptiques*, I, 103).

now becomes prominent by reason of its constant repetition (vv. 2, 9, 12, 18, 26, and 32), and for St Mark it was the equivalent of Messiah (cf. e.g. vv. 31–32). Modern commentators think that it was used before Pilate, instead of Messiah, because its political associations would be more obvious to a non-Jew; and certainly if the words were inscribed on the cross (v. 26) as the ground of Jesus' condemnation, they must have been understood by the Romans in a political sense. The tradition behind Mark that this form of words was used before the Romans is thus entirely plausible, but it is doubtful if St Mark was particularly interested in this nuance; for him the point was that it was not for any wrong-doing, but simply as Messiah = King of the Jews, that Jesus was crucified.

With regard to historicity, we have seen that the passage has no pretensions to be a complete or coherent report of the trial, and it would not be right to judge it as if it had. Two questions, however, do call for brief discussion.

The first concerns the character of Pilate. To judge from the fairly full information we have about him in Jewish sources, he appears to have been an 'inflexible, merciless, and obstinate' man* continually given to corruption, violence, and cruelty of every kind. Even when allowance is made for possible exaggeration in the Jewish accounts, the weakness and the scrupulous concern for justice attributed to him in our passage hardly seem compatible with the character of such a man, and most commentators think we should allow for some idealization in St Mark's account, arising out of the Christian desire to exculpate the Romans and put responsiblity on the Jews (see above, p. 368).

The second question concerns the custom of releasing a prisoner referred to in v. 6. B's comment is typical of a good deal of scholarly opinion: 'nothing is known of any such custom as is here described. That at the feast of the Passover the Roman procurators regularly released one prisoner, and that the crowds named the individual no matter what his offence had been, is not only without any attestation whatsoever, but also contrary to what we know of the spirit and manner of Roman rule over Palestine' (p. 288). It is, therefore, widely

* A quotation from a letter of Agrippa I to Caligula given in Philo, *Legatio ad Gaium* 38; cf. also Josephus, *Antiquities*, XVIII, 2, 2; 3, 1f.; 4 1f.; *Jewish War*, II, 9, 2–4.

held that the reference to a regular custom in v. 6 is an erroneous inference by the Evangelist (or his predecessors) from the particular episode in 7ff.* That the governor should have granted an amnesty *in a particular case*, however, is quite plausible, and several partial parallels are known, one of them providing a fairly close analogy to our passage.†

There are other questions connected with the Barabbas episode, but these will best be treated in the notes below. Meanwhile Lightfoot's comment on the trial scene deserves reproduction: 'If, in the absence of any eyewitness account of what happened at the trial, the earliest tradition could only infer what had passed from the obvious result, together with the public inscription on the cross, then we can understand why the writer naïvely places the question of Pilate in the forefront of the trial. He has fashioned a trial scene in the only way which was open to him; but it is faithful to the fact of chief importance.' (*H. & I.*, p. 149.)

❦

1

This 'second' meeting cannot be explained as an attempt to comply with the legal requirement described on p. 405 because the second session required by the Law had to take place on the following day, i.e., according to Jewish reckoning, after the interposition of one sunset.

held a consultation: Or perhaps: 'held a council'. This, which seems to be the correct translation of the right reading, does not suggest an adjourned meeting; in fact it implies no knowledge of any previous session. An alternative reading, which might be translated 'prepared their decision', is probably an attempt on the part of some scribe to harmonize 15^{1} with $14^{53\text{ff.}}$; St Matthew has perceived the same need – cf. 26^{66} (no reference to a conviction) and 27^{1}.

delivered (Greek – *parĕdōkan*): St Mark's repeated use of this word, particularly in the Passion narrative (cf. 9^{31}, 10^{33}, $14^{10, 11, 18, 21, 41, 42, 44}$, $15^{1, 10, 15}$), suggests to some commentators that he saw Jesus' sufferings

* Luke contains no reference to any such regular custom, if, with R.S.V., we reject Luke 23^{17} as an interpolation.

† For details of this cf. A. Deissmann, *Light from the Ancient East*, E. T., p. 269. It relates to the governor of Egypt, G. Septimius Vegetus, who released a certain Phibion with the words: 'You deserved scourging . . . but I grant you to the crowd(s).'

as fulfilling the Old Testament prophecies about God's servant who was 'delivered up according to the definite plan and foreknowledge of God' (Acts 2^{23}. Cf. Isa. 53^{6} where the Greek version has: 'The Lord delivered him [*parĕdōken*] for our sins.'). In that case, the Jews here, and Pilate in v. 15, are in some mysterious way agents of God's plan to 'deliver up' his Son for the salvation of the world.

Pilate: Although this is the first mention of his name in the Gospel, no attempt is made to explain who he was or how he came to be in Jerusalem; on this see p. 35; the readers for whom St Mark wrote were already familiar with the story and all the characters in it.

Pontius Pilatus, the fifth procurator* of Judea, was in office from A.D. 26–36. For his character see p. 413 above. The procurators' normal place of residence was Caesarea, but at Passover time they came to Jerusalem to keep order. Sometimes when in Jerusalem they lived in the palace of Herod the Great (cf. Josephus, *Jewish War*, II, 14, 8) but they may also sometimes have stayed in the fortress of Antonia on the north side of the temple court.

2

This looks like a piece of tradition originally separate from that in vv. 3–5; on the reasons for its being so awkwardly placed here, before the charges have been made, see Lightfoot as quoted above, p. 414; perhaps too there was the desire to emphasize Jesus' silence in v. 5.

Are you . . .: The Greek may suggest contemptuous emphasis on *you*.

You have said so: This enigmatic phrase has received a variety of interpretations, ranging from those which treat it as a definite affirmation, through those which take it as a qualified admission (see on 14^{62} above), to those which take it as a denial.† Most probably St Mark regarded it as non-committal, and Dibelius points out that, though it may be more or less equivalent to 'I am', in the context it serves the useful purpose of enabling the story to continue: 'With the answer "yes" the scene would come to a close, for then it would remain only for Pilate to pass judgement; "You have said so", which implies "You do well to ask", gives the possibility of a continuation of the scene' (*Zeitschrift für Neutestamentliche Wissenschaft*, 1915, p. 117).

3–5

The awkward way in which these verses are introduced suggests that

* See further Appendix B, p. 458.

† For the light shed, or not shed, by rabbinic sources, see Abrahams, *Studies in Pharisaism and the Gospels*, II, 1–3.

originally they did not go with v. 2. The tradition clearly contained no information about the precise content of the 'many charges'.

6ff.

On the improbability of the custom mentioned in v. 6 see p. 413 above; but if we cannot accept v. 6, we cannot accept v. 8 as it stands (cf. *as he was wont to do*); and there are other difficulties. Not only is it unlikely, as we have seen, that a man of Pilate's position and character would be found bandying words with a mob of subject people in the way pictured in 9ff., but the content of the dialogue presents problems; it seems to presuppose that Pilate is faced with a choice between two condemned prisoners, so that if one is released, the other must be executed (cf. *instead*, v. 11); but at the end of vv. 2–5 Jesus has not been condemned, and, as the story stands, there is nothing to prevent Pilate, if he believed in Jesus' innocence, from acquitting him and granting an amnesty to Barabbas as well.

On the other hand the story is clearly not a pure invention, and scholars have been much exercised to uncover the historical truth which lies behind it. One fact may perhaps point the way; in St Matthew's version of the story, the name of the insurrectionary is twice (27^{16} and ^{17}) given in many MSS. as *Jesus* Barabbas, and this is widely held to be the original reading. The name *Jesus* may well have stood in Mark as well, for in v. 7 the phrase translated *a man called Barabbas* is a strange one, which, as it stands, can only mean 'the one called Barabbas'; the phrase would be perfectly natural, however, if the name *Jesus* once preceded it, when the meaning would have been: 'Jesus, surnamed Barabbas' (cf. Matt. 1^{16}, 4^{18}, 10^{2}, $27^{17, 22}$). The omission of the word in our MSS. is easily explained, for although in the time of Our Lord, Jesus (= Joshua) was quite a common name (cf. Col. 4^{11}) Christians soon came to regard it as too holy for common use, and its application to a criminal would have been particularly offensive. If Barabbas was in fact called Jesus, we have a clue to the possible origin of the story. There may well have been a tradition that the populace of Jerusalem had, by its intervention with Pilate, secured the release of a condemned insurrectionary by the name of Jesus Barabbas (which, curiously enough, means 'Son of the father').* This could hardly fail to suggest the reflexion that, while they had saved Jesus the criminal, they had allowed, or even urged, the execution of Jesus the Messiah, and it is this contrast which lies at the root of our story.† How much further the coincidence in fact went and

* Barabbas is, in fact, almost impossibly odd as a semitic name, which only adds to the obscurity of the whole matter; see further pp. 418–19 below.

† So, in general, B.; cf. also R.

how far the facts have been written up in order to produce the story as we have it, it is impossible to say. As St Mark presents it, the story, as we have seen, has the effect of concealing what must have been the fact, that a Roman judge formally condemned Jesus as a criminal, and of throwing the responsibility for Jesus' death almost entirely on the Jews.

7
the insurrection: It is assumed that the readers will know what insurrection; we do not. See Introduction, p. 35.

8
If there was no regular amnesty, we can only suppose that the crowd had in fact come to plead the particular case of Barabbas and was not immediately concerned about Jesus. Their sudden appearance at this point is a little surprising, and hardly intelligible unless the trial of Jesus was in fact over; otherwise their parleying with Pilate would have interrupted him right in the middle of a trial.

11
It is not clear how the priests could have had time to influence the crowd's attitude to Jesus between the suggestion of Pilate (v. 9) and the people's reply, nor what motives they relied on to produce the change; from St Mark's standpoint, the point is to pin responsibility where he believed it belonged.

14
The Roman authority itself testifies to the groundlessness of the Jewish objections against Jesus.

15
wishing to satisfy the crowd: Pilate's repeated questions (vv. 9, 12, 14) have shown that he could see nothing worthy of death in Jesus; yet the Christians could not deny that he had in the end condemned him. These words are designed to make clear that it was simply Jewish pressure that drove him to it.

having scourged: In the Greek a single word (*phragĕllōsas*); it covers a most terrible punishment which was the normal prelude to crucifixion (cf. Josephus, *Jewish War*, II, 14, 9; V, 11, 1). The prisoner, often bound to a pillar, was beaten with leather whips loaded with bone or metal, until the flesh was exposed and lacerated. (In Luke $23^{16, 22}$, and John 19^{1} scourging seems to be seen as a separate punishment from crucifixion.)

he delivered him: For the Old Testament allusion see on v. 1; also, the use of the word relieves the Evangelist of the necessity of referring to a formal condemnation. (See Loisy, op. cit, II, 645).

15$^{16-20}$ THE MOCKERY BY THE SOLDIERS

16 *And the soldiers led him away inside the palace (that is, the praetorium);*
and they called together the whole battalion. 17 *And they clothed him in a*
purple cloak, and plaiting a crown of thorns they put it on him. 18 *And they*
began to salute him, 'Hail, King of the Jews!' 19 *And they struck his head*
with a reed, and spat upon him, and they knelt down in homage to him. 20 *And*
when they had mocked him, they stripped him of the purple cloak, and put
his own clothes on him. And they led him out to crucify him.

Many scholars believe that this story is one of St Mark's insertions into the primitive narrative. A more important question, however, concerns the character of the tradition it reproduces. Everything described here seems quite natural and in character, and a great many commentators accept the story as a straightforward report of a historical incident. Two points, however, have been raised. The first is that the story contains echoes – distant but distinct – of the suffering servant passages in Isaiah (cf. especially Isa. 50$^{6f.}$ and 53^{3,5}), and the early Church surely saw in the incident a fulfilment of those prophecies. The question then arises how far the wording and details of the story may have been influenced by the Old Testament text. The second point is more teasing. Scholars such as Frazer and Reinach have pointed out that, as the story stands, there are interesting parallels to it in the ritual followed at certain ancient festivals, notably the Roman *Saturnalia* and a Babylonian festival known as the *Sacaea*, and also in an incident recorded by Philo (*In Flaccum*, VI, 36–9 – the parallel was first noticed by Grotius in the seventeenth century) when the populace of Alexandria staged a mime in mockery of Agrippa I, who was visiting their city on his way back from Rome, where he had just been made King of Judea by Caligula. Getting hold of a half-witted Jew, they crowned him with a paper crown, clothed him with a mat for a robe, put a papyrus reed in his hand (cf. Matt. 27^{29}; this trait may just possibly have dropped out of Mark's text), provided him with a bodyguard, and then did homage to him and pretended to consult him on matters of state. It is certainly interesting that the victim's name was Carabas, and some scholars, seeing here a connexion with

Barabbas, and drawing on various parallels in world religions, have found in the story evidence of a widespread ancient ritual in which one man (known, in the rite, as *Carabas* or *Barabbas*) was treated as a mock king while another was ritually slaughtered. In the ancient world convicts were frequently forced to play the leading parts in such rituals, so the way is open for an interpretation of Jesus' Passion, and Jesus-Barabbas' release, as having taken place within the context of some such rite. (So Loisy – for a full discussion see J. G. Frazer, *The Golden Bough*[3] Part VI, pp. 412–23.) The highly speculative character of any such theories will be obvious enough, and it is fully admitted by Frazer, who in the third edition of *The Golden Bough* confesses that: 'The hypothesis ... has not been confirmed by subsequent research, and is admittedly in a high degree speculative and uncertain.' However, he continued to include it in an appendix to his work 'on the chance that, under a pile of conjectures, it contains some grain of truth which may ultimately contribute to the solution of the problem.' Such an attitude of suspended judgement seems preferable to that of most recent commentators who dismiss the parallels as pure coincidence, or at most as suggesting that 'the mock homage ... may have been determined by some hazy notion of imitating a pagan bit of ritual'.* The parallels are perhaps rather more striking than that suggests, though on the other hand, as readers who follow the matter up will discover, no explanation of the resemblances so far put forward really carries conviction. Further discussion here would be out of place, especially as St Mark was no doubt quite unaware of any such pagan parallels and they are therefore irrelevant to *his* understanding of the incident. For him it will have been one more piece of evidence – none the less cogent for being so back-handed – that it was as King of the Jews that Jesus suffered.

16

inside the palace (that is, the praetorium): The assumption is that the proceedings hitherto have taken place in the open air. The word translated *palace* (*aulē*) normally means 'courtyard', but since *praetorium*

* Moffatt in *Dictionary of Christ and the Gospels*, II, p. 757; he is in fact dismissing a rather different theory from those outlined above, the theory of Reich to the effect that there was an established popular mime called *The King with the Crown of Thorns* and that the soldiers were here treating Jesus, in mockery, as the hero of it.

(originally the general's tent in a camp) had come to mean the 'palace' or 'official residence' of a governor, no doubt the rarer meaning *palace* is the correct one here. See p. 415 above for whether the palace in question was Herod's palace or the Antonia fortress.

battalion: The Greek word (*speira*) means technically a *cohort* (i.e. two hundred to six hundred men); here presumably something more like a 'company' or 'platoon' is envisaged.

17
a purple cloak: No doubt one of the red-coloured cloaks regularly worn by the soldiers.

a crown of thorns: This will have been intended as a mock symbol of kingly, or imperial, dignity rather than as an instrument of torture.

18
Hail, King of the Jews: A parody of *Ave Caesar Imperator*? (see p. 418).

15²¹⁻³² THE CRUCIFIXION

21 *And they compelled a passer-by, Simon of Cyre'ne, who was coming in*
from the country, the father of Alexander and Rufus, to carry his cross. 22 *And*
they brought him to the place called Gol'gotha (which means the place of a
skull). 23 *And they offered him wine mingled with myrrh; but he did not take*
it. 24 *And they crucified him, and divided his garments among them, casting*
lots for them, to decide what each should take. 25 *And it was the third hour,*
when they crucified him. 26 *And the inscription of the charge against him*
read, 'The King of the Jews.' 27 *And with him they crucified two robbers, one*
on his right and one on his left.[a] 29 *And those who passed by derided him,*
wagging their heads, and saying, 'Aha! You who would destroy the temple
and build it in three days, 30 *save yourself, and come down from the cross!'*
31 *So also the chief priests mocked him to one another with the scribes,*
saying, 'He saved others; he cannot save himself. 32 *Let the Christ, the King*
of Israel, come down now from the cross, that we may see and believe.' Those
who were crucified with him also reviled him.

a Other ancient authorities insert verse 28, *And the scripture was fulfilled which says, 'He was reckoned with the transgressors'*

15^{21-32}

This section is generally agreed to comprise a brief foundation story, no doubt derived from the primitive Passion narrative, and various items of tradition which had gradually attached themselves to it. Scholars differ a good deal about precisely which verses belonged to the primitive narrative, though there is general agreement that vv. 21 (or v. 20b) to 24a were among them. In the Greek, many of the verbs* are in the historic present, and this, together with the use of short sentences connected by *and*, gives the original a sort of breathless vividness.

Note too the remarkably impersonal tone of the passage, which in fact provides the clue to its character. We get none of the personal details the passage would have been bound to contain were it an eye-witness account by some friend or disciple; nor does it contain edifying notes about the spirit in which Jesus faced his death such as later accounts often included in order to provide guidance for the martyrs in facing their deaths (cf. e.g. Luke $23^{34, 46}$ and John 19^{25-27}). St Mark's account appears to be controlled by three aims:

(i) In the reference to Simon of Cyrene, to show that the Christians had a trustworthy source of information about these events.

(ii) To emphasize once again the implacable hostility of the Jews and their leaders (vv. 29–32).

(iii) The most important aim is best given in some words of Dibelius: St Mark's narrative 'contents itself with portraying the picture of the crucified in a few verses according to the "Passion testimonies" of the Old Testament, according to Pss. 22 and 69 and Isa. 53. In the process it often touches on what actually happened, or at any rate may well have done so. But that is not its primary concern, which is rather to establish the certainty that everything took place according to the scriptures, i.e. according to the will of God, and that Jesus' enemies themselves, without knowing it, demonstrated that God's eternal counsel of salvation was here being fulfilled. Thus his being numbered among the transgressors, as well as his refreshment with a drink, the casting of lots for his garments and also the mockery of those who passed by – all these details are understood as evidence of the will of God.'†

* e.g. 'lead' (v. 20), 'compel' (v. 21), 'bring' (v. 22).

† *Jesus*, p. 118. Cf. E. T., pp. 137–8.

21
Those condemned to be crucified were normally made to carry their own crosses, or, more exactly, to carry the *patibulum* or cross-beam, the upright stake being already in position. John 19^{17} states that the usual procedure was followed in Jesus' case, but according to Mark an otherwise unknown figure, Simon of Cyrene, was 'impressed' (the precise meaning of the Greek word) by the Romans to carry it for Jesus. No explanation is given for this, but the usual assumption is that Jesus, as a result of the scourging, was incapable of carrying it himself. Simon was presumably a Jew, perhaps up on pilgrimage from Cyrene, where there was a sizeable Jewish settlement (cf. e.g. Acts 2^{10}, 6^{9}, 13^{1}).

from the country: This is sometimes translated 'from the field', and it is argued that if Simon had been working in the fields, it cannot have been the first day of Passover. However, see Jeremias *E. W. J.*, p. 51 and nn.; apart from the uncertainty about the translation, we cannot be *quite* certain that Simon was a Jew, and while perhaps 'the words would be more natural if the day of the crucifixion were not a holiday' (Montef.) they are too vague for any real weight to be laid on them in connexion with the argument about the date of the crucifixion.

the father of Alexander and Rufus: The Church for which St Mark wrote obviously knew these two so well that it needed no further account of them; very likely they were Church members. This seems to guarantee the story of Simon's having carried the cross,* and no doubt one of the reasons for preserving these personal details in the Gospel was to remind the readers that they had a trustworthy source of information about the crucifixion.

The names *Alexander* and *Rufus* were both so common that any identification of these two with others of the same name in the New Testament must remain very precarious.

22
Golgotha: The Aramaic form – which St Mark, as usual, translates – should strictly be 'Golgoltha'. The tradition which locates the place within the Church of the Holy Sepulchre cannot be traced back beyond the fourth century and is open to considerable question; other sites have been suggested in modern times, but certainty is unattainable. We cannot be sure that the 'skull-place' was a hill and there is nothing to show how it got its name. The custom at the time was not to have a

* The reason for its omission in John may be that by the time the fourth Gospel was written the claim was already being made in gnostic circles which became so prominent later that Simon changed places with Jesus and was crucified in his stead. Cf. Irenaeus *Adversus Haer.* I, xxiv, 4.

single fixed place of execution, but to execute criminals in any convenient place where they might be widely seen and provide a warning to others. Verse 29 suggests a site near a road (*those who passed by*) and no doubt it will have been just outside one of the gates of Jerusalem, probably to the north or west.

23

This verse is a little puzzling; we know that the women of Jerusalem were accustomed (on the basis of Prov. 31^{6-7}) to provide condemned criminals with drugged wine in order to dull their sensibilities and so alleviate their sufferings, and commentators generally see a reference to that custom here. If so, St Mark must be taken to mean that, as a result of refusing the opiate, Jesus endured his sufferings to the end. However, according to our information, it was *frankincense* (a substance of uncertain identity) which was mixed with wine to produce the opiate; a mixture of myrrh and wine, which was well known in antiquity, (cf. e.g. Pliny, *Natural History*, 14), would not have had any noticeably analgesic effects. Either, therefore, the myrrhed wine was originally given to Jesus as a refreshment, or St Mark is somewhat inaccurate in his details. No doubt for him the important thing was to suggest the fulfilment of the Old Testament passage (Prov. 31^{6-7}).*

24

they crucified him: For details of this form of punishment see Bible dictionaries and larger commentaries, and also J. Blinzler, *The Trial of Jesus*, pp. 246ff., and Excursus XII, p. 263ff., who gives a useful bibliography. The precise procedure varied according to circumstances, but normally, after being scourged and stripped of all his clothes (which became the perquisite of the executioners), the victim was laid on the ground while his outstretched arms were fixed to the cross-beam by either nails or thongs. Next the cross-beam was lifted up, with the body on it, and fixed either on the top of the upright (T) or across it (+), and the feet were then fastened (at this period with thongs rather than nails, despite Luke 24^{39-40}, which may have been influenced by Ps. 22^{16} – contrast John $20^{20 \text{ and } 25}$); usually a block of wood was fixed half-way up the upright to support the hanging body. Death, which was due to exhaustion, might not follow for a great many hours. Small wonder that Cicero described this as 'the most cruel and frightful of punishments' (*In Verrem*, v. 64), combining, as it did, extreme bodily pain, the tortures of hunger, thirst, heat, and insects, all endured in conditions of rigid immobility, exposure

* Matthew's version has been further influenced by the Old Testament; cf. Matt. 27^{34} and Ps. 69^{21} where the Greek has *gall*.

to the brutality of spectators, and the shame of nakedness at a time when the natural functions were beyond control. In view of all this the restraint of the Gospel tradition at this point is particularly noteworthy.

divided his garments, etc.: In the light of what was said in the last note, this is entirely plausible; but for the early Church its significance lay in its fulfilment of Ps. 22^{18}, and it is impossible to say how far that passage has influenced the Gospel tradition at this point.

25

From the point in St Mark's narrative where Jesus is finally disowned by men (see above p. 399) the time is carefully marked off in three-hour intervals ($14^{[68\,\&]\,72}$, $15^{1,\,25,\,33,\,34,\,42}$). In this instance at least, the reckoning seems artificial, for it is hardly possible that everything recounted in vv. 1–24 could have taken place in the course of a single three-hour period, and John 19^{14} clearly implies that it did not. An attractive suggestion is that the division may reflect the catechetical interests, and perhaps the liturgical practice, of the Roman Church.

A further difficulty is concealed by R.S.V., which has *when* where the original has 'and'. It is true that two clauses were sometimes put side by side where we should subordinate one of them (parataxis), and R.S.V. may therefore give the intended meaning; but the Greek, with its second reference to the crucifixion, is undoubtedly awkward, as is shown by the fact that an early scribe altered it to read: 'it was the third hour and they were guarding him' (cf. Matt. 27^{36}), and some scholars think that the second part of the verse was originally a doublet of v. 24 to which St Mark rather awkwardly prefixed his note of time.

26

After a sentence of death by crucifixion had been passed, a tablet (*titulus*) was prepared, setting out the grounds of condemnation; this was hung on the delinquent, or carried in front of him, on the way to execution, and when he was crucified it was displayed on his cross. Such a notice would contain the name of the prisoner and his place of origin (cf. Matt. 27^{37} and John 19^{19}), so the form of words in this verse cannot be complete. As to its authenticity, opinions are very divided, some scholars thinking the precise formula was known through eye-witnesses and was in fact the Christians' only certain indication of the charge on which Jesus was condemned (cf. e.g. *H. & I.*, p. 149), others holding that the Romans are unlikely to have used such a bald form of words and that St Mark's particular formulation of the charge is due once again to his desire to show that it was *as Messiah* that Jesus was executed.

'Even the Roman himself is made to preach the Gospel, inasmuch as through the inscription on the crossbeam he causes the announcement to be made that Jesus was the King of the Jews, the Messiah.'* In any case, the words, if taken in a political sense, represent well enough the grounds on which Jesus was executed. (See above pp. 368 and 413).

27
See R.S.V. margin for the verse included by some MSS. between 27 and 29; though it is almost certainly not original in the text of Mark, the significance it suggests in the crucifixion of the two robbers on either side of Jesus is the one that St Mark will have found in it – see Isa. 53^{12}.

29–32
In the nature of the case it can be taken as virtually certain that Jesus will have been subjected to taunts and insults from the bystanders much in the way described. On the other hand, the contents of these verses suggests that the Church had no precise information on the matter. What we have here is not so much an independent historical tradition as an ideal picture designed to emphasize once again the implacable hostility of the Jewish authorities and the precise conformity of what happened to Old Testament prediction. The lack of any independent tradition is suggested by the fact that the various taunts amount to no more than a repetition of the two charges (threat to the temple and claim to Messiahship) made before the Sanhedrin (14^{53-64}); and the presence of the *chief priests* and the *scribes* (v. 31) at an execution is unlikely in the extreme, especially at Passover time. Many of the details reflect certain Old Testament passages so closely (cf. Lam. 2^{15}ff., Ps. 22^{6}ff., Wisd. Sol. 2^{17}ff., and Ps. 69^{9}, which in the Greek contains the same word for *reviled* as that in v. 32 and also a reference to zeal for the temple) that these passages are generally believed to have had a good deal to do with the shaping of the story in its present form. V. T. (p. 592) makes the further suggestion that 'the account of three successive acts of railing may be catechetical, especially as no words are assigned to the crucified rebels'.

Verses 29f. and 31–32a may have reached St Mark as separate traditions.

* Dibelius, *Jesus*, p. 118. Cf. E. T., p. 138 and by all means see John 19^{19-22}.

15^{33-41} THE DEATH ON THE CROSS

33 *And when the sixth hour had come, there was darkness over the whole*
land[a] *until the ninth hour.* 34 *And at the ninth hour Jesus cried with a loud*
voice, 'E'lo-i, E'lo-i, la'ma sabach-tha'ni?' which means, 'My God, my God,
why hast thou forsaken me?' 35 *And some of the bystanders hearing it said,*
'Behold, he is calling Eli'jah.' 36 *And one ran and, filling a sponge full of*
vinegar, put it on a reed and gave it to him to drink, saying, 'Wait, let us see
whether Eli'jah will come to take him down.' 37 *And Jesus uttered a loud cry,*
and breathed his last. 38 *And the curtain of the temple was torn in two, from*
top to bottom. 39 *And when the centurion, who stood facing him, saw that*
he thus[b] *breathed his last, he said, 'Truly this man was a son of God!'*
40 *There were also women looking on from afar, among whom were Mary*
Mag'dalene, and Mary the mother of James the younger and of Joses, and
Salo'me, 41 *who, when he was in Galilee, followed him, and ministered to*
him; and also many other women who came up with him to Jerusalem.

a Or *earth*
b Other ancient authorities insert *cried out and*

In describing the death of Jesus the Evangelist includes just those circumstances which were felt to be especially important either as guaranteeing the facts (vv. 40–41) or as revealing their essential meaning and effect (vv. 33–39). For reasons which appear below, it is particularly difficult in the case of this section to decide which elements derive from the primitive Passion narrative; almost all scholars are agreed on v. 37, a great many add v. 39, and some include several other verses.

❧

33
Since earliest times (cf. Luke 23^{45} refers to an eclipse) attempts have been made to find a natural explanation for this darkness; but, however legitimate such attempts may be, they are certainly foreign to St Mark's intention, for he was clearly thinking of a miraculous portent, no doubt symbolizing the judgement of heaven on what was taking place (cf. e.g. Isa. $13^{9ff.}$ and 50^{2-3} and Jer. 15^{6-9}), and also fulfilling the prophecy of Amos 8^{9}; it was probably the latter passage which suggested the reference to *the sixth hour* (= noon), which may well, like the time

reference in v. 25, be artificial. Similar portents are said to have marked the deaths of some of the great rabbis and also the deaths of some great figures of pagan antiquity, most notably Julius Caesar.*

The R.S.V. text is to be preferred to the alternative suggested in the margin.

34–36

These verses have given rise to several much-disputed questions with regard both to interpretation and to historicity.

The words quoted in v. 34 are in Aramaic (see below on v. 35), and they can be understood in one of two ways:

(i) It is possible to take them more or less at their face value and see in them a spontaneous cry of desolation on the part of Jesus who 'felt the horror of sin so deeply that for a time the closeness of His communion with the Father was obscured' (V. T., p. 594). Supporters of this view usually add some such warning as that given by R. 'on the assumption that our Lord really uttered the words it is better to say frankly that we do not know exactly what was in His mind at the time, that we are here face to face with the supreme mystery of the Saviour's Passion' (p. 236); and the striking words of T. R. Glover are often quoted in this connexion: 'Strange to think that is the cry of the feeling of Jesus. One is almost tempted to say that there, as in a supreme instance, is measured the distance between feeling and fact. So He felt; and yet mankind has been of another mind, that there, more than in all else that He was or did, there was God' (quoted so by H. G. Wood in *Peake's Commentary*: cf. *The Jesus of History*, p. 192).

In support of this interpretation are:

(*a*) that it interprets the words straightforwardly in their most obvious sense; and

(*b*) that St Luke and St John appear to have found the words mysterious and liable to misinterpretation; both have omitted them and substituted, the one: '*Father into thy hands I commit my spirit*' (Luke 23^{46}), the other: '*It is finished*' (John 19^{30}; for the profound meaning of this see commentary on John).

On the other hand 'such a view assumes a narrator who, interested primarily in historical fact, reports faithfully for posterity a terrible and inexplicable utterance. But all our inquiry has tended to show that there was no narrator of this sort . . . the Passion narrative was written for the strengthening and edification of the Christian communities, not for their bewilderment' (Lightfoot, *H. & I.*, p. 158). This is the only

* On the ides of March an eclipse of the sun is said to have taken place 'at the sixth hour till night'. Cf. Virgil, *Georgics*, I, 463ff.

word from the cross that St Mark reports; would he have included it as the sole utterance of Jesus at the supreme moment of his life unless he had found it full of positive meaning and edification for his readers? Had he, like St Luke and St John, taken it as a cry of despair, would he not have regarded it as a mistaken tradition and left it out, as they do?

(ii) Consequently many modern scholars adopt a quite different interpretation, which rests on the fact that the words are a quotation from Ps. 22[1]. Taken as a whole, this Psalm is anything but a cry of despair; it is the prayer of a righteous sufferer who yet trusts fully in the love and protection of God and is confident of being vindicated by him (cf. especially vv. 19–26, particularly vv. 24 and 26). There is some evidence that among the ancient Jews the opening words of this Psalm were interpreted in the light of the rest of it and recognized as an effective form of prayer for help in time of trouble,* and according to many commentators, that is the way St Mark understood the words here. He saw Jesus as taking on his lips the inspired utterance of Jewish piety and making his own the Psalmist's expression of complete faith and confidence in God.

To judge by their use of Ps. 22, the early Christians found the meaning of the Passion revealed there more than in any other single passage of scripture;† Jesus was for them the suffering figure depicted in the Psalm. What more natural then than that he should have taken its words on his lips in the central crisis of his Passion? By so doing he had stamped with his own authority the early Christian understanding of his suffering as the fulfilment of the Old Testament, rooted in the will of God. Such considerations inevitably raise a question about the authenticity of the saying, and some commentators think that the early Christians attributed to Jesus the opening words of their favourite Passion Psalm in an attempt to give content to the *loud cry* (v. 37) he was known to have uttered at the last. Certainly, if we follow this second line of interpretation, we can no longer use the well-known argument (cf. e.g. Schmiedel in *Encyclopedia Biblica*, col. 1881) that the early Church would never have ascribed a cry of despair to Jesus without the strongest historical warrant; and probably the question of historicity must remain an open one, though it is obviously linked with the question of

* Cf. the *Midrash* quoted by Dalman in *Jesus-Jeshua*, p. 206.

† Cf. e.g. B. (p. 298): 'Jesus was mocked with wagging heads and taunting words as in vv. 6–8 [of Ps. 22]. Verses 14–15 describe the dissolution which comes with approaching death. Verse 15 mentions particularly the sufferings of thirst. Verse 16 mentions the piercing of hands and feet. Verse 18 states that the garments of the righteous one are divided among his enemies. The psalm was thus almost a portrayal of the Passion.'

vv. 35–36, for which see below. If the second interpretation does give the original intention, the words were early misunderstood as simply a cry of dereliction; we have seen how St Luke and St John omitted them, and, presumably for the same reason, an early scribe sought to soften the words in Mark by writing: 'Why didst thou reproach me?' i.e. 'Why didst thou give me over to reproach?' It should be added, however, that one or two scholars expert in such matters regard that as the original reading. (Cf. e.g. C. H. Turner in *J. T. S.*, XXIX, p. 12).

35–36
For the early Church the significant thing about this incident will have been its fulfilment of Ps. 69^{21b}. Historically, difficulties have been felt about it on the grounds that only Jews could have made or understood the cruel joke about Elijah, whereas the *vinegar* of v. 36 presumably refers to the executioners' *posca* – a mixture of water, vinegar, and egg commonly drunk by Roman soldiers – and no Jew would have been allowed to approach the cross or dispense the soldiers' drink. Such questions lay far from the minds of the early Christians, and it is impossible to resolve them on the basis of the story as they preserved it with the sole aim of emphasizing the fulfilment of scripture and the unrepentant malice of the Jews. Possibly two originally independent traditions (vv. 35 + 36b and 36a) have been combined at some stage. If the story in v. 36a has a historical kernel, the action of the Roman soldier was no doubt meant kindly (and the implication is that Jesus accepted the drink), though St Mark, interpreting it in the light of Ps. 22, sees it as a further piece of ill-usage.

35
he is calling Elijah: Such a misunderstanding – even if deliberate – would have been impossible unless the words in v. 34 had been spoken in Hebrew rather than in Aramaic as Mark has it. (Cf. Matthew's hybrid version in which the vital words appear in Hebrew.) Probably at an earlier stage the story had been in Hebrew but this was changed by someone who knew that Aramaic was the language normally spoken in Jesus' time.

Elijah was the recognized forerunner and helper of the Messiah, but, more important in this connexion, he was popularly believed to appear for the assistance of good people in trouble. (Cf. Edersheim, *Life and Times of Jesus the Messiah*, vol. II, appendix viii.)

36
Wait: Perhaps rather strong; the Greek word is little more than an auxiliary: 'So let us see . . .'

37
uttered a loud cry: It would be unusual for anyone after crucifixion to have the strength for such a cry, and perhaps for that reason this cry impressed the onlookers and so was specially noted; or perhaps, since the tradition so stresses it (cf. Heb. 5^{7}), it is mentioned because regarded as fulfilling such passages as Ps. 31^{22} or 39^{12}. Cf. Dibelius: 'Not in spite of the fact that he cries out, but because he cries out, Jesus is the one who is fulfilling the divine will' (*Jesus*, E. T., p. 131).

38
It is impossible to be certain whether the *curtain* is the one before the Holy Place or that before the Holy of Holies (cf. Exod, 26^{31}ff. and Lev. 21^{23}). In either case, its tearing at the very moment when Jesus died is seen as symbolizing the effect and implications of his death. Either the meaning is that the temple (perhaps representing the Jewish nation) mourns over its own now certain destruction, or over the coming destruction of the Jewish State;* or, perhaps more probably, the veil-rending signifies the removal through Christ's death of some hitherto impassable barrier, most likely the barrier between God and man so strongly emphasized in Jewish religion (cf. Heb. $9^{1-12, 24-28}$, 10^{19-25} and 6^{19} and see Lighfoot, *G. M. M.*, pp. 55–6). It is just possible in view of Eph. 2^{14-15} that there is a reference to the removal of the barrier between Jew and Gentile.

39
If v. 38 represents the significance of Jesus' death for the *Jewish* world, this verse gives the *Gentile* acknowledgement of its significance. For St Mark at any rate the centurion's words meant not *a son of God* (R.S.V.)† but '*the* Son of God' (the Greek can mean either, but compare how R.S.V. translates the same expression at 1^{1} – the New English Bible is surely wrong in perpetuating the translation here 'a son of God'). So what we have here is not simply a case of an executioner being won over to the side of a martyr (which often occurs in the martyrologies and is all that Luke sees here – Luke 23^{47}), but a much greater miracle, the conversion of an unbeliever by the dying Saviour. There are two points:

(*a*) It was a *Gentile* who was thus converted. 'The first Gentile was

* This is the interpretation of the early Christian *Clementine Recognitions* I, 41, and compare the Jewish story to the effect that: 'Forty years before the fall of the temple (i.e. A.D. 30) the temple doors opened of their own accord, until Rabbi Johanan ben Zakkai rebuked them saying: "O Temple, Temple, why troublest thou thyself? I know that thine end is near".' Some scholars have seen here part of the origin of our story. Cf. e.g. *F. T. G.*, p. 195.

† More recent editions of R.S.V. translate correctly *the Son of God.*

converted and in his word the Gentiles make their response to the death of Jesus' (*F. T. G.*, p. 195).

(*b*) 'The reader is meant to infer from the centurion's words that this heathen was brought to believe in the divine sonship of Jesus *precisely by his death*. He stands thus at the close of the Gospel as the prototype and forerunner of the countless multitudes of heathen who shall be converted by the message of the crucified' (J. Weiss, *Die Schriften des Neuen Testaments*, I, 205).

In a very real sense this verse rounds off not only the crucifixion narrative but the whole Gospel; the divine sonship of Jesus, revealed in the prologue as the key to the understanding of the Gospel, solemnly reaffirmed in the middle of the Gospel in connexion with the disciples' confession at Caesarea Philippi, is now, as the result of Jesus' death, publicly proclaimed by a Gentile, and that in terms which go beyond Peter's confession at Caesarea Philippi and had appeared to the high priest so exalted as to constitute blasphemy. (Cf. *H. & I.*, pp. 84–5.)

40–41

The women, who have not hitherto played much part in the Gospel, appear somewhat abruptly, and B. W. Bacon argued that from 15^{40} to 16^{8} St Mark was able to draw on the special source of Luke. The women are introduced here in order to prepare the way for v. 47 and $16^{1ff.}$, and also no doubt in order to hint that the Christian account of the crucifixion went back to trustworthy first-hand testimony (cf. on 14^{51-2} and 15^{21}). The modest claims made on behalf of the women (*looking on from afar*, v. 40) lead many commentators to trust the tradition, at any rate that contained in vv. 40–41a; contrast the claim of John's Passion narrative that Christian witnesses were present at the foot of the cross, whereas, in fact, 'it is intrinsically improbable that friends and relations of Jesus would be allowed to stand near the Cross' (Barrett, *St John*, p. 98).

Magdalene, i.e. belonging to Magdala (*el Mejdel*) on the west side of the Sea of Galilee. See further Luke 8^{1-3}, which, besides giving further information about Mary Magdalene, suggests that such women as these accompanied Jesus during his ministry and helped to support him. Montef. remarks (I, 389) that 'in Jesus' attitude towards women we have a highly original and significant feature of his life and teaching'. There is no ground for identifying Mary Magdalene with the woman referred to in Luke 7^{37}.

St Mark's references to the other *Mary* are a little puzzling, because the Greek in v. 47 and 16^{1}, if taken by itself, would naturally mean the *daughter* of Joses and of James, and the present verse could be translated:

'Mary the daughter of James the younger and the mother of Joses'. However, as the text stands, R.S.V. is presumably correct.

James the younger and *Joses* (Matt: Joseph), like Alexander and Rufus in v. 21, were obviously too well known in Mark's Church to need description, and so we have no means of identifying them. *The younger* is literally 'the small (one)' and distinguishes him from some namesake (? the son of Zebedee) in respect of either stature or age or importance. His identification with *James the son of Alphaeus* (3^{18}) may be correct, but is pure speculation.

Salome appears to be identified by St Matthew as 'the mother of the sons of Zebedee' (27^{56}).

15^{42-47} THE BURIAL

42 *And when evening had come, since it was the day of Preparation, that is,*
the day before the sabbath, 43 *Joseph of Arimathe'a, a respected member of the*
council, who was also himself looking for the kingdom of God, took courage
and went to Pilate, and asked for the body of Jesus. 44 *And Pilate wondered*
if he were already dead; and summoning the centurion, he asked him
whether he was already dead.[a] 45 *And when he learned from the centurion that*
he was already dead, he granted the body to Joseph. 46 *And he bought a linen*
shroud, and taking him down, wrapped him in the linen shroud and laid
him in a tomb which had been hewn out of the rock; and he rolled a stone
against the door of the tomb. 47 *Mary Mag'dalene and Mary the mother of*
Joses saw where he was laid.

a Other ancient authorities read *whether he had been some time dead*

The story of Jesus' burial was important in the early Church on two counts: first as establishing that he had really been dead (cf. 'corpse' in v. 45), and so had really risen from the dead; and secondly, from the point of view of the tradition about the empty tomb, it was important as establishing that the women who later found the tomb empty had not gone to the wrong tomb, but to the one in which they had themselves seen the body placed. Loisy writes: 'All the details of the story [of the entombment] . . . are conceived in view of the discovery of the empty tomb. Mark would impress upon our notice that the same people who saw the entombment saw also the empty tomb' (*Évangiles synoptiques*, II, p. 707). This obvious connexion with the later story of the empty tomb has made some scholars suspicious of the present account (cf. e.g. *M. J.*, p. 182), but most commentators accept at any rate the basic facts of the story, arguing that Christians would have been unlikely to invent a tradition in which Jesus receives hurried burial from a pious Jew, and his own followers have no part in the proceedings (contrast the elaborations of the scene in later Christian tradition). There is clearly real force in this, though scholarly opinion has perhaps been a little inclined to overlook the possible influence of the Old Testament on the story and to underestimate some of the difficulties. (See below.)

42

The chronological indications here are distinctly puzzling. If *evening* (i.e. 6 p.m.) had really come, then it was no longer Preparation but already sabbath;* in order to make sense of the verse, commentators usually suppose that St Mark was in fact thinking of an earlier hour (about 4 p.m.). In that case we must suppose either that St Mark was not acquainted with the correct terminology, or more probably that he wrote as he did under the influence of his artificial three-hour time scheme.†

Even so there is a difficulty, for the assumption of the verse seems to be that there was a hurry to get things done on the Preparation which could not be done on the sabbath; but according to St Mark's chronology of the Passion, *the day of Preparation* was that year the feast of the Passover, and the prohibitions with regard to Passover were pretty nearly as strict as those relating to the sabbath. So, especially in view of the purchase in v. 46 (see below), commentators usually assume that this section comes from a tradition which did not identify the day of the crucifixion with the Passover (see pp. 371, 377, 381). But neither, be it noted, does it say anything about the *following* day (the sabbath) being Passover, so it cannot be taken to support the Johannine chronology. Small wonder the Jewish scholar Montefiore describes it as 'all most obscure and peculiar' (I, 393). Perhaps the simplest explanation is that the story originates from a cycle of tradition which knew of *no chronological* tie-up between the crucifixion and the Passover.

* It will be remembered that the Jewish day began at sundown.

† See on 15^{25}; *evening* would be three hours after the *ninth hour*, v. 34.

Preparation: St Mark correctly interprets this technical term as = Friday, the day before the sabbath; the Greek word (*Paraskeuē*) is still the name for Friday in the Christian East.

43
Joseph of Arimathea: Apart from this incident, an entirely unknown figure; if he subsequently became a Christian, he does not appear to have been a particularly well-known one, so there would have been no obvious reason for attributing the burial of Jesus to him unless he had in fact been responsible for it. The location of *Arimathea* is uncertain; perhaps it is the *Ramathaim* of 1 Macc. 11^{34}, rather than the *Ramathaim-zophim* of 1 Sam. 1^{1}; the Greek suggests not so much that he lived there as that it was his place of origin.

a respected member of the council: This translation begs some questions. The Greek noun *bouleutēs* was not a technical expression among the Jews; it is usually taken here to imply membership of the Sanhedrin (as R.S.V.), but Mark's Roman readers would think immediately of a Roman senator, and may not have taken the word, when applied to a Jew, to mean any more than a man of high official standing. The adjective (*euschēmōn*), when used in such a context, would have meant properly 'of good social position' (cf. A.V. *an honourable counsellor*), but it was popularly used to mean 'rich'. So St Matthew (27^{57}) understood it here, probably rightly, and we should surely see some influence of Isa. 53^{9} on our passage.*

looking for the kingdom of God: This was later taken to mean that he was expecting the kingdom to be brought *by Jesus* and that he was a disciple (cf. Matt. 27^{57}). St Mark may have meant it so, but originally it need only have meant that he, like so many of the Pharisees, lived in lively expectation of a fulfilment of Israel's messianic hopes; his action in burying Jesus may have been simply due to a desire to fulfil the Law, which demanded the burial of one who had been hanged before nightfall, since the body, if left on the tree, would cause defilement (Deut. 21^{23}). According to Jewish custom, the dead were always buried on the day of death, if it was at all possible, and the Jews were particularly scrupulous about such matters (cf. the Book of Tobit). In the absence of relatives or friends, it was a work of merit to arrange for the burial of a body and, at any rate a little later, charitable societies existed for the express purpose of burying those who died unattended. Josephus writes: 'The Jews are so careful about funeral rites that even criminals who have been sentenced to crucifixion are taken down and

* Isa. 53 was another of the favourite 'Passion passages' of the early Church.

buried before sunset' (*Jewish War*, IV, 5, 2). It would thus have been entirely natural for a pious Jew of means to arrange for the burial of Jesus without being, in any strict sense, his disciple, and Acts 13^{29} perhaps suggests that that is what happened. The normal Roman custom was to leave the bodies of the crucified on the cross until they decayed, but there is some evidence that from the time of Augustus they sometimes granted them to the relatives and friends, if they chose to apply for them. In any case, a concession may well have been made in this matter to Jewish sensibilities; the words *took courage* (i.e. 'screwed up his courage') suggest that Joseph was very conscious of asking a favour.

44–45
The verses are omitted by both St Matthew and St Luke; the change of subject between vv. 45 and 46 is very abrupt, whereas v. 46 follows quite naturally from v. 43. On these and certain other, linguistic, grounds, some scholars have regarded them as a later addition to the original tradition.

45
the body: The Greek says quite unequivocally 'the corpse'; it is a pity R.S.V. mistranslates and so misses something of St Mark's stark insistence on the reality of Jesus' death.

46
The buying of a shroud, while not perhaps quite impossible on the Passover (cf. *E. W. J.*, pp. 51–2), is certainly very much more natural if the day in question was not a Passover. Note the absence of anointing, and contrast John $19^{39\text{ff.}}$; St Mark is quite clear that no anointing took place – 16^{1} and cf. (p. 372). The details of the tomb are natural enough; the Jews buried their dead outside the city walls in individual tombs, cut out of the rock or formed by natural caves. Bodies were placed in recesses or on shelves or slabs of stone, and the entrance was closed either with a rectangular block of stone (sometimes hinged like a door), or with a rounded stone fitted in a groove, which could be rolled back at need, but was too heavy to be casually tampered with. Nevertheless we cannot rule out the influence on the description of such passages as Isa. 22^{16} and 33^{16} (LXX), which, like Isa. 53^{9}, no doubt appeared to the early Church to be fulfilled in this incident.

47
It is generally agreed that this verse was not originally part of the story; for the reasons which led to its addition here see above pp. 432–3.

saw: Greek '*were watching*'; the imperfect perhaps suggests that they had remained all the time at the place from which they saw the crucifixion.

Mark $16^{1ff.}$

The Resurrection

The ending of the Gospel

The interpretation of these verses necessarily presupposes some answer to the question whether they were originally intended as the conclusion of the Gospel; so this is perhaps the place for such brief discussion of this complicated question as is possible in a book of this sort. The question has been called 'the greatest of all literary mysteries' and it is so finely balanced that scholarly opinion is radically divided upon it.

The undisputed facts are that everything which follows 16[8] in any surviving MS. can confidently be declared non-Marcan on grounds of attestation, style, and content; thus the Gospel in the earliest form in which we can trace it ended at 16[8]. Moreover the evidence of both St Matthew and St Luke shows that it ended there in the versions of it known to them* and it must, therefore, have done the same in the common original from which their respective versions were copied. We are thus taken back to a period only a few years at most after St Mark wrote the Gospel.

The obvious conclusion from all this would be that 16[8] was, and was meant to be, the concluding verse of the Gospel; and a considerable, and perhaps increasing, number of scholars accept that conclusion. But it is open to a number of serious objections, notably:

(i) As an ending to a Gospel the section, and particularly the last verse, seems singularly inappropriate. The essence of a Gospel was that it was a proclamation of the *good news* of what God had accomplished in Christ (cf. Mark 1[1]). Now the last two chapters of Mark have been very sombre indeed, and while it is true that this section makes clear the fact of the resurrection, it does so in a brief, allusive, and muted way which hardly succeeds in redressing the balance or leaving the reader with a final impression of joyous victory and reversal of disaster.

* The grounds for this assertion must be discovered from commentaries on the other two Gospels – they cannot be given here; suffice it to say that virtually no reputable scholar would wish to deny the statement so far as Luke is concerned, and practically none nowadays in the case of Matthew.

That verse 8 should be the conclusion of the whole matter is a particular stumbling-block in this connexion.

The other Gospels emphasize the point by contrast. They all include post-resurrection appearances which rivet on the imagination the reversal of Jesus' fate and the fact of his risen life; and the fact that more than one continuator tried his hand at extending Mark shows that early Christian sentiment felt his Gospel ought to have ended in a similar way. What possible reason could St Mark himself have had for feeling differently?

(ii) The final words of v. 8, which are strange enough in English, are even more difficult in the Greek. The sentence ends with an extremely weak word (the enclitic *gar*) which is not normally used as the last word of a sentence, let alone a book.* Recent investigation has shown that this difficulty is not perhaps quite as great as was at one time thought. In such Greek as Mark's, the word was sometimes used to end a sentence, and even a paragraph, though it must be admitted that no real parallel has yet been discovered to its use as the last word of a whole book.

(iii) If St Mark did end intentionally at 16^{8}, he left a number of loose ends in his Gospel; in particular 14^{28} and 16^{7} seem to point forward to an appearance to the disciples in Galilee, and the special mention of Peter's name in the latter verse might suggest an appearance to him alone. In any case Peter's position raises something of a problem. 'One has difficulty in believing that the Evangelist intended to close his work leaving the chief apostle of the circumcision in the status of one who denied his Lord with curses' (B. – and contrast John 21^{15-19}).

For such reasons it is generally argued either that St Mark intended to write more, but was prevented by illness or arrest from doing so, or else that he did in fact write more and that the remaining part of his MS. was somehow lost or destroyed. Both these hypotheses, however, involve acute difficulties. With regard to the first, it is a well-nigh incredible coincidence that at the moment when he was forced

* *Gar* is usually translated 'for', as in R.S.V. here, but in Greek it always follows the word it governs, and the linguistic difficulty might be clearer to English readers if we translated: 'they were afraid, you see', which gives just the inconclusive abruptness of St Mark's original. It is sometimes also claimed that the Greek word used for 'were afraid' (*phŏbeisthai*) would have had to be followed by some object or explanatory clause; this however is not a point of substance; cf. for St Mark's own usage of this word, 10^{32}.

to break off, Mark had reached just such a point in his work that it could plausibly be regarded as the point at which he *meant* to break off;* and in any case on this hypothesis 'the disciple who gave his work to the world would surely have added a fitting termination' (Salmon). The first of these difficulties applies, *mutatis mutandis*, to the second hypothesis, and it is not the only objection; it is true that the outside leaf of a MS. did sometimes get lost or damaged in the way suggested, but in the case of a much-copied MS. such as St Mark's, we have to ask why the missing passage, when it got lost from one copy, was not supplied from another; and if the answer is that the accident occurred so early that there was still only a single copy, then why did not St Mark himself, or one of his fellows, make good the defect?

It will be clear that in the present state of knowledge no completely satisfactory solution of this problem is possible. Those who defend the text as it stands rightly point out that St Mark is the earliest of the Evangelists and that his work has a right to be considered by and for itself without constant reference to, and comparison with, the work of his successors; because *they* felt it appropriate to end their Gospels in a certain way, it does not necessarily follow that St Mark felt the same. If we consider Mark 16^{1-8} on its own merits in this way, the claim runs, it can be seen to be a perfectly legitimate ending to a Gospel. It makes the essential point of Jesus' resurrection with all necessary emphasis, and shows, in the reaction of the women (v. 8), the amazement and holy awe which the news of the resurrection must always arouse in those who really understand its import.†

How far this view of 16^{1-8} is justified the reader will perhaps be able to judge for himself from the exposition below, which, not without considerable hesitation, is based upon it. He should, however, be

* If he had had to stop even one word sooner (in the Greek) the Gospel would have been demonstrably unfinished.

† See R. H. Lightfoot, *G. M. M.*, Chapter VII, and *Locality and Doctrine in the Gospels*, especially Chapter I; also A. M. Farrer, *The Glass of Vision*, pp. 136ff. In his later book, *St Matthew and St Mark*, Chapter IX, Dr Farrer slightly modifies his earlier position, holding that Mark's Gospel originally contained one further sentence after 16^{8}; it was, he suggests: *But Jesus sent forth his disciples to preach the Gospel unto all nations.* The continuators had to remove this sentence in order to get back to a suitable point of attachment for their continuations, and so it got lost; later scribes sometimes detected and omitted the work of the continuators, but they had no means of recovering the missing sentence.

warned of one important criticism of this view. If St Mark did intentionally end his Gospel with this paragraph, he was certainly behaving with considerable literary sophistication and making great demands on the understanding of his readers, whom he expected to find the whole of the resurrection gospel in his eight allusive and enigmatic verses. In that case, he would in fact have hit on a way of ending his book which just happens to 'suit the technique of a highly sophisticated type of modern literature'. W. L. Knox has shown that such a subtle way of ending a book would have been quite without parallel in contemporary literature and so would argue a quite remarkable originality and unconventionality on the part of the Evangelist. As we have seen, there has been an increasing tendency in recent years to stress the individuality and originality of St Mark as an author, but the fact that we have been able to reconstruct so much of the history of the pre-Marcan tradition argues very definite limits to that originality, and Knox makes a telling point when he says that to have ended the Gospel in this way would imply in the Evangelist 'a degree of originality which would invalidate the whole method of form-criticism'.*

16^{1-8} THE WOMEN AT THE TOMB

16 *And when the sabbath was past, Mary Mag'dalene, and Mary the mother
of James, and Salo'me, bought spices, so that they might go and anoint him.*
2 *And very early on the first day of the week they went to the tomb when the
sun had risen.* 3 *And they were saying to one another, 'Who will roll away
the stone for us from the door of the tomb?'* 4 *And looking up, they saw that
the stone was rolled back; for it was very large.* 5 *And entering the tomb, they
saw a young man sitting on the right side, dressed in a white robe; and they
were amazed.* 6 *And he said to them, 'Do not be amazed; you seek Jesus of
Nazareth, who was crucified. He has risen, he is not here; see the place where
they laid him.* 7 *But go, tell his disciples and Peter that he is going before you
to Galilee; there you will see him, as he told you.'* 8 *And they went out and
fled from the tomb; for trembling and astonishment had come upon them;
and they said nothing to any one, for they were afraid.*

* From an article in the *Harvard Theological Review*, 35 (1942), pp. 13–23, from which the previous quotation is also taken.

16^{1-8}

Though clearly based on traditional material, this section more than most owes its final form and wording to the Evangelist; in particular the introduction of v. 7 into the context may be due to him (see below).

The very purpose of the women's visit and also the question in v. 3 emphasize their utter unpreparedness for what they found, and so serve to underline the dramatic reversal it involves. Its numinous character as 'the greatest and final manifestation of the divine activity' is clearly brought out in the very forceful expressions used to describe the tongue-tied awe it inspired in the women (vv. 5, 6, 8).

ꙮ

1

when the sabbath was past: i.e. the women buy the spices after sundown on the Saturday evening for use first thing on the Sunday morning.

Mary Magdalene, etc.: The repetition of the women's names, as if they had not been mentioned in the previous verse, is strange, especially as the second Mary, who was described in 15^{47} as the mother (or daughter) of Joses (and in 15^{40} as the mother of James the Less and Joses) is here described simply as the mother (or daughter) of James. The difficulty is avoided if we follow a group of MSS. which pass straight from 15^{47} to 16^{1b}, but this reading is probably a correction by some scribe who was conscious of the difficulty in the full text, and we should accept the latter as original. The fact no doubt is that the tradition reproduced in this section was originally entirely independent of that in 15^{42-47} (? and did not know of any connexion between Mary and Joses).

so that they might go and anoint him: A visit by the women at this point is entirely natural, especially as we know that in Palestine the relatives and friends of a dead person were in the habit of visiting the grave for three days after the burial. The motive suggested for the visit, however, is surprising. Quite apart from the question raised in v. 3, it is hard to credit the women with the intention of going to anoint a body a day and two nights after death, and most commentators echo the comment of Montef. (I, 401): 'The cause assigned for their visit to the grave is very unlikely.' However, as B. adds: 'it must be admitted that those who first collected the Christian tradition were more familiar with Jewish burial customs and attitudes than we are, and in the absence of further data the Gospel statements . . . must be taken as evidence that this motive was possible' (p. 306). According to St Mark, the body of Jesus was in fact never anointed after death (contrast John 19^{40}); for the importance attached to this in certain circles see p. 372.

2

very early: The Greek word would most naturally imply a time round 4 a.m. and has been thought to clash with the last five words of the verse; but it is quite in St Mark's manner to qualify a vague note of time with a more precise one, and if there is any slight inconsistency it may be due to St Mark's desire to make clear to Gentile readers, whose day began at sunrise, that Jesus rose on the *third* day.

the first day of the week: i.e. Sunday, the first day of the *Jewish* week.

3

It may seem strange that this question did not occur earlier seeing that two of the women had already watched the burial (cf. 15^{46}b).

The Marcan tradition clearly knew nothing of any sealing or guarding of the tomb such as that described in Matt. 27^{62-66}; note that St Matthew, consistently with what he has said in that passage, does not credit the women with any intention of entering the tomb (28^{1}).

4

for it was very large: These words would come more naturally after verse 3, and some MSS. place them there; probably, however, their present position is the original one and they should be understood as a loose way of expressing the implied thought that the rolling away of the stone was something very portentous and remarkable.

This part of the narrative is curiously reminiscent of Gen. $29^{2\text{ff.}}$; cf. especially 29^{2}b with the second half of this verse.

5

a young man . . . in a white robe: Undoubtedly an angelic being is meant; for *young man* as a designation of an angel see 2 Macc. 3^{26} and ^{33} and Josephus, *Antiquities*, v, 8, 2, and cf. Rev. 7^{9} and $^{13\text{f.}}$ for the wearing of *white robes* by heavenly beings. R. writes: 'The modern mind must make its count as best it can with the supernatural; the earliest Church believed in the objective reality of angels, as it believed in the objective reality of demons, and what Mark wishes to describe is the annunciation of the resurrection of Jesus to the women by the message of an angel' (p. 243). In this case the problem is accentuated by the fact that the angel uses human speech and the words attributed to him reflect the Marcan vocabulary and correspond to the usage of Paul and the early Church (for details see V. T., ad loc.) Since the vocabulary of v. 5 is also characteristically Marcan, many readers will probably sympathize with the conclusion of V. T. that: 'it is probable that Mark's description is imaginative; he picturesquely describes what he believes happened'.*

amazed: Here and in v. 6 translates a rare Greek word (*ĕkthambeisthai*), used only by St Mark in the New Testament; it expresses a strong feeling of awe and agitation in face of the numinous (cf. 9^{15} and 14^{33}); 'shuddering awe' (R).

6

see the place where they laid him: i.e. presumably the shelf or slab on which the body had been laid; for there is little to be said for Kirsopp Lake's rationalizing suggestion that the women approached the wrong tomb and were redirected in these words by a *young man* who happened to be standing by. (See *The Historical Evidence for the Resurrection of Jesus Christ*, especially pp. 68f. and 250ff.)

7

This verse has occasioned a great deal of discussion. It must be considered along with 14^{28}, to which it refers back (*as he told you*), and the first question that arises is the meaning of the Greek word (*proagein*) translated in both verses 'go before'.

(i) The usual view is that in both verses the word means 'go before' in the sense of proceeding to some place independently of someone else and arriving there before them. This is undoubtedly a possible meaning of the word (cf. Matt. 14^{22}, Mark 6^{45}, Matt. 21^{31}), and if it is the sense here, the angel's words mean simply that, if the disciples go to Galilee, they will find that Jesus is already there and they will be able to 'see' him in the sort of way described in Matt. 28^{16-20}.† In favour of this interpretation is the fact that St Matthew understood St Mark in this way (cf. Matt. 28^{16}), but against it is the fact that if it is correct, 14^{28} seems to have no real relevance to its context, and commentators can only say that St Mark introduced it there, very awkwardly, simply in order to prepare the way for 16^{7}.

(ii) On the other hand, if the word is taken in its other possible sense (cf. e.g. Mark 10^{32}, Matt. 2^{9}) of placing oneself at the head of others and leading them, then 14^{28} makes an excellent connexion with 14^{27}: when the shepherd is smitten the flock will be scattered, but then, after

*p. 607; cf. also p. 603, where he speaks of 'a dramatic representation due to the exercise of reverent historical imagination, in this respect more like the Johannine narratives than those familiar to us in Mark'.

† It should be noted that in that passage of Matthew we are dealing, not so much with a post-resurrection appearance in the ordinary sense, as with the disciples 'seeing' Jesus as the Lord of all power, who will be present with them until the end of the ages in the universal mission to which he now commissions them. See C. F. Evans, *J. T. S.*, April 1954, p. 16.

his resurrection, Jesus will reconstitute his community and lead them to Galilee.

In view of the fact that the word here is in the present tense and of the words *there you will see him*, it seems clear that St Mark took the word here (and presumably in 14^{28}) in the first sense,* but many scholars think that in doing so he was mistaken; they believe that he misunderstood the word in 14^{28} and that the insertion of the present verse – or at any rate of the words *there you will see him* – are the result of that misunderstanding.

If the word originally bore the second meaning, the question is why the first act of the risen Lord should be to collect his followers and 'lead them into Galilee'. One answer is that he expected (or, if the words are not his own, the early Christians expected) that the kingdom of God would come as soon as they arrived there (cf., e.g. J. Weiss, *The History of Primitive Christianity*, I, 18). Another answer is that Galilee stands in the saying as a symbol for the Gentiles (cf. e.g. Matt. 4^{15} and Isa. 9^{1}) and the meaning is that as the result of Jesus' death God's saving activity is made available to the Gentiles (cf. for that 15^{37-39}) and the risen Christ will lead his followers out among them in a world-wide evangelistic mission.† If the latter view seems perhaps a little fanciful, that of J. Weiss should not be too lightly dismissed, and a brief reference must also be made to another view in some ways akin to it. According to this, the Marcan tradition shows that Galilee had for Jesus and his earliest followers a special status as the holy place *par excellence*, whereas Jerusalem was the source of opposition and unbelief. Consequently, it was there they expected the parousia to take place, and the meaning of these verses (however exactly *proagein* is understood) is that when they reached Galilee the disciples would 'see' Jesus in the sense of beholding him in all the splendour of his parousia appearance. (For this sense of 'see' cf. John $16^{16, 17, 19}$, I John 3^{2}, Rev. 1^{7}, 22^{4}, and especially *Test. Zeb.* 9^{8}.) This interpretation rests on a number of arguments not specifically related to these two verses and cannot be discussed here; it is part of a general thesis which has not on the whole commended itself to scholars, at any rate in its entirety, but readers should consult E. Lohmeyer, *Galiläa und Jerusalem* (1936); R. H. Lightfoot, *Locality and Doctrine in the Gospels* (1938); and F. C. Grant, *The Earliest Gospel* (1943, chapter VI); and cf. the criticisms in V. T., pp. 549 and 608.

* On either view the implication is that the disciples are still in or near Jerusalem, but there is no real conflict between this and 14^{50}.

† See E. C. Hoskyns in *Theology*, September 1923, and C. F. Evans in *J. T. S.*, April 1954, pp. 3–18.

and Peter: Singled out presumably either as the one who had denied his Lord – the breach is not final – or as the disciple in whom the Roman Church was specially interested.

Most commentators think the verse was inserted into the tradition by St Mark; apart from the point raised above, this has the advantage that if v. 7 is later, v. 8 refers to the announcement of the resurrection in v. 6. 'There is then no longer any need to ask why the message to the disciples and to Peter was not delivered, while the reference to the silence of the women is apologetic' (V. T., see below).

8

The interpretation here depends to some extent on whether the verse was intended as the conclusion of the Gospel. If not, the women's fear calls for no special comment – presumably the sequel explained how they overcame it and delivered their message, though one of the difficulties about the supposed lost ending is that the Greek here would naturally mean: 'they kept their experience to themselves', 'they said nothing to anyone about what they had seen and heard', rather than 'they did not (for the time being) deliver their message', and so it is not easy to see, after this very definite and solemn statement (in the Greek it is very emphatic), how a transition could have been effected to any scene of the sort depicted in the other Gospels. And it is noteworthy that St Matthew and St Luke, in the process of adding their respective post-resurrection stories, have had to omit this reference to the women's silence altogether.*

On the assumption that this verse was meant as the conclusion of the Gospel, commentators usually suppose that the emphasis on the women's fear and silence was intended to serve an apologetic purpose; in the earliest period, they say, belief in the resurrection had been based on appearances of the risen Lord, and not on the fact of the empty tomb (cf. e.g. 1 Cor. 15^{3}ff.), and the silence of the women here is meant to explain why so decisive a piece of evidence had been so long in gaining currency. It is hard to deny all truth in this, but, as K. Lake has shown, St Paul's silence does not necessarily imply that he was ignorant of the tradition of the empty tomb, and Lightfoot may well be right in suggesting that the Evangelist's real purpose here was 'to emphasize human inadequacy, lack of understanding, and weakness in the presence of supreme divine action and its meaning' (*G. M. M.*, p. 92). The women's profound emotion is described in order to bring out the

* Cf. the very interesting article by J. M. Creed in *J. T. S.*, XXXI (1929–30), pp. 175ff. who, on these grounds, criticizes the reconstruction of the 'lost ending' by C. H. Turner in the S.P.C.K. one-volume Bible commentary.

overwhelming and sheerly supernatural character of that to which it was the response (cf. e.g. 4^{41}, 6^{50}, 9^{15}), and perhaps to suggest to the reader that if he has even begun to understand the full significance of what had occurred, he too will be bound to respond with amazement and godly fear. (Cf. Phil. 2^{12}, Heb. 12^{28}, 1 Pet. 1^{17}, and the very striking conclusion to Lightfoot's essay in *G. M. M.*, p. 97). St Mark may well have felt that the actual events of the resurrection and the risen appearances did not lend themselves to narration in a book (see *G. M. M.*, p. 96 and cf. 2 Cor. 12^{4}), while all that flowed from them his original readers already knew from their own experience. The ending of a book like St Mark's is bound to present a problem,* and if 16^{8} was St Mark's ending, it was certainly abrupt; but, as interpreted above, it clearly makes a powerful ending to the individual section. Is it impossible as the ending of a whole Gospel?†

Many attempts have been made to see what light this Gospel throws on the origins of the resurrection belief of the early Church, and which if any, of the later appearance narratives it presupposes or supports. Reconstructions of the supposed lost ending are too speculative to form a secure basis of argument in this connexion, and probably all we can say is that St Mark clearly attests belief in the bodily resurrection of Jesus, but probably did not think that the experience of the women which he describes was the *original* basis of that belief. The idea of 'appearances' of the Lord to the disciples after the resurrection is clearly familiar to him (16^{7} and cf. 14^{28}), and probably he thought of these as being vouchsafed to Peter and the other disciples (? separately – cf. 1 Cor. 15^{5} with Mark 16^{7}) in Galilee (14^{28}, 16^{7}) rather than Jerusalem. (Or are we to discount any such inference from v. 7 in view of the fact that in v. 8 the women fail to deliver their message? If so, St Mark probably thought of the appearances taking place in Jerusalem, though of this we cannot be sure.) For an interesting, though necessarily speculative, reconstruction of the events, see R., p. 271.

* Cf. C. F. Evans, 'the end of St Mark's gospel . . . is no isolated problem, for eloquent perorations are reserved either for those who believe optimistically that they have the answers, or for those who believe cynically that there are no answers to have; perorations are debarred to those for whom God's act is the last word' (op. cit., pp. 17–18).

† If the last eleven words of the verse could be regarded as an apologetic addition, perhaps Lightfoot's view and the apologetic interpretation could be combined.

16^{9-20} A SECOND-CENTURY APPENDIX TO THE GOSPEL

*9 Now when he rose early on the first day of the week, he appeared first to
Mary Magdalene, from whom he had cast out seven demons. 10 She went
and told those who had been with him, as they mourned and wept. 11 But when
they heard that he was alive and had been seen by her, they would not believe
it.*

*12 After this he appeared in another form to two of them, as they were
walking into the country. 13 And they went back and told the rest, but they did
not believe them.*

*14 Afterward he appeared to the eleven themselves as they sat at table;
and he upbraided them for their unbelief and hardness of heart, because they
had not believed those who saw him after he had risen. 15 And he said to them,
'Go into all the world and preach the gospel to the whole creation. 16 He who
believes and is baptized will be saved; but he who does not believe will be
condemned. 17 And these signs will accompany those who believe: in my
name they will cast out demons; they will speak in new tongues; 18 they will
pick up serpents, and if they drink any deadly thing, it will not hurt them;
they will lay their hands on the sick; and they will recover.'*

*19 So then the Lord Jesus, after he had spoken to them, was taken up into
heaven, and sat down at the right hand of God. 20 And they went forth and
preached everywhere, while the Lord worked with them and confirmed the
message by the signs that attended it. Amen.*

Although these verses appear in most of the extant MSS. of Mark, R.S.V. is certainly right in treating them as spurious and relegating them to the margin. The great Roman Catholic scholar Lagrange is quite clear that though 'canonically authentic' (i.e. part of the canon of Holy Scripture), they are not authentic in a literary sense (i.e. not the work of St Mark). The reasons for this view – in which all other scholars concur – are basically three:

(i) Some of our best MSS. of Mark end at 16^8; other MSS. agree with them in omitting vv. 9–20, but have the alternative ending given below. (Yet others, representing a late tradition, contain both endings, often introducing this one with the words: 'This also is current.')

(ii) The great fourth-century scholars, Eusebius and Jerome, testify that the verses were wanting in all the best Greek MSS. known to them, and they are quoted only once (or possibly twice) in the whole of Christian literature down to A.D. 325.

(iii) Most decisively of all, the style and vocabulary of the verses, which smack of the second century, are completely different from those of St Mark.

The passage cannot be dated exactly; it had become accepted as part of Mark's Gospel by about A.D. 180, when Irenaeus quotes it as such; and if some words in Justin's *Apol.* are taken from it, it must have been known about A.D. 140, though not necessarily as part of Mark's Gospel. It is also possible that Tatian's *Diatessaron*, which appeared about the same time, included it. It cannot, therefore, have originated much later than the earlier part of the second century, and it can hardly be much earlier, to judge from its vocabulary and ideas and the knowledge it betrays of the later Gospels and Acts (see below).

Its authorship is completely uncertain, for the statement in a tenth-century MS. attributing it to the presbyter Aristion (presumably the one mentioned by Papias as an early disciple of the Lord) must be treated with the greatest reserve.

With regard to the general character and purpose of the verses, they fit on so awkwardly to 16^8 that they can hardly have been composed originally as a continuation of the Gospel; more probably they were compiled for catechetical use at a time when there was no other document giving a succinct account of all the known appearances of the risen Lord. They have thus been well described as 'a sort of compendium of the proofs and promises of the resurrected Lord, made up some time after the beginning of the second century' (B.).

Even a cursory reading will make clear that the passage is not composed of traditional pericopes such as we have encountered in the Gospel proper, but of brief résumés of stories and sayings already reported more fully in other written sources, particularly Luke and Acts. The emphasis and point of view reflect the conditions and needs of the post-apostolic Church, especially the need for unhesitating faith in the gospel of the risen Christ on the basis of the reports of the original witnesses.

9–11
The appearance to Mary – cf. Luke 8^2, and there are a few touches from Luke 24. Many scholars refer also to John 20^{11}ff. but it is not certain whether the author knew the Johannine literature, and Streeter thought the appearance to Mary was derived from oral tradition or deduced from Matt. 28^9ff.

9
This clearly does not presuppose vv. 5–8. The resurrection is treated *de novo*; *he* (i.e. Jesus, though we are not told so) does not link naturally with anything in the preceding verses; and Mary Magdalene is introduced as though she had not been mentioned before.

11
Cf. Luke 24^{11}.

12–13
The appearance to two travellers – Luke 24^{13-35}.

in another form: This may mean 'in a different form from that in which he had appeared to Mary', or possibly, from the fact that the two travellers had not at first recognized Jesus (Luke $24^{16, 31}$), our author inferred that he had assumed a heavenly form. He may have been thinking of the way in which the risen Christ appeared and disappeared in spite of closed doors. (Cf. Luke 24^{31}, John $20^{19, 26}$).

13
Contrast Luke 24^{33-35}.

14–18
The appearance to the eleven – cf. Luke 24^{41-43}.

The author sees the disciples' attitude as typifying that of many in his own day; for that reason he describes it – and Jesus' upbraiding of it – in severer terms than any that St Mark uses with reference to the disciples. The verse shows what supreme importance he attached to the acceptance of the tradition about the resurrection.

For the additional passage inserted here in one MS. see below.

15–16
These sayings come very abruptly after the severe rebuke in the last verse.

15
Cf. Matt. 28^{19}, Luke 24^{47}, Acts 1^8, Mark 13^{10}. Clearly a saying current in a Gentile Church. 'Admirably expressing the spirit of Christianity, no more than Matt. 28^{18}f. is it an actual saying of Jesus; otherwise the

controversy culminating in the Council of Jerusalem (Acts 15) would not have been possible' (V. T.)

the whole creation: As often = 'all mankind'.

17–18

The argument to the truth of Christianity from the ability of the Christians to work miracles is typical of second-century apologetic. All the 'signs' referred to can be documented from the New Testament (cf. e.g. Mark $9^{38ff.}$, 1 Cor. 14, Acts $2^{4ff.}$, 10^{46}, $28^{3ff.}$, 1 Cor. $12^{9, 28}$, Acts 5^{12}, 9^{12}, 28^{8}, James 5^{14-15}) except the drinking of poison with impunity; for that cf. the case of Justus Barsabbas quoted from Papias (*c.* A.D. 130) by Eusebius (*Hist. Eccl.*, 3, 39, 9.), and also cf. *Acts of John*, M. R. James, p. 263, and Theophylact, in Swete, *St Mark*, 406.

'Here, without doubt, is the atmosphere of A.D. 100–140' (V. T.).

19–20

The Ascension and Heavenly Session.

In the Greek the effect is to distinguish what happened to Jesus from what happened to the eleven, though it is made clear that from his heavenly throne the risen Christ continues to guide and help his followers, cf. Heb. 2^{3-4}. For the heavenly session – a favourite theme in early Christianity – cf. Ps. 110^{1}.

A LATER EXPANSION OF THIS APPENDIX

After v. 14 one Greek MS. of the fifth century includes an additional passage which is also quoted in part by Jerome as being in some of the MSS. with which he was familiar. It is often referred to as the *Freer Logion*, from the name of the American who originally owned the MS. (W) in which it appears. The Greek, which in one place has to be restored on the basis of the quotation in Jerome, and is in any case not entirely clear, must have meant something like this:

And they replied saying, This age of lawlessness and unbelief is under Satan, who by means of evil spirits prevents the true power of God from being apprehended; therefore reveal thy righteousness now. They were speaking to Christ, and Christ said to them in reply: The limit of the years of the authority of Satan has expired, but other terrible things are coming, even for sinners on whose behalf I was delivered over to death, that they might turn to the truth and sin no more, in order that they may inherit the spiritual and incorruptible glory of righteousness, which is in heaven.

The words *they were speaking to Christ* seem to show that the passage was not originally composed for its present setting; no doubt it is an extract from some longer document, and was inserted here because it was felt that the *unbelief and hardness of heart* of the apostles (v. 14) needed softening and explaining. The explanation the apostles give, and their demand for an immediate parousia, suggest the second, or even third, century, rather than the period immediately after the resurrection (cf. 2 Pet. 3^{3-4}). In reply they are assured that the limits of Satan's domination have been reached (is there allusion to some special time of difficulty through which the second-century Church had been passing?) though *terrible things* (? persecution or ? the messianic woes) have still to be faced.

AN ALTERNATIVE ENDING TO THE GOSPEL

Other ancient authorities add after verse 8 the following: *But they reported briefly to Peter and those with him all that they had been told. And after this, Jesus himself sent out by means of them, from east to west, the sacred and imperishable proclamation of eternal salvation.*

These words are found in quite a number of MSS. and versions, sometimes instead of, sometimes as a preface to, the longer appendix. Unlike the latter, this ending was clearly composed for its present position, presumably by someone who felt that 16^{8} could not have been intended as the end of the Gospel. He took the last words of v. 8 to mean that the women made no *public* announcement but hurried to give their message to the disciples (on the improbability of that see on 16^{8} above). The phraseology of the second sentence suggests a date when the Gospel had already spread over a large part of the Roman world, including the west, and perhaps suggests a Roman origin for the passage (cf. 1 *Clem.* v, 6 written from Rome *c.* A.D. 96). Marcan authorship is completely ruled out on linguistic grounds.

Appendix A

ST MARK'S ACCOUNT OF THE LAST SUPPER

To what extent does Mark's account enable us to discover what actually happened and what significance Jesus originally attached to it?

A serious attempt to answer that question would involve a close comparison of Mark's account with I Cor. 11²³ff. and Luke 22¹⁴ff. and a consideration of the information to be found in John; needless to say, each of these sources raises critical problems of its own. All that can be done here is to list some of the main issues involved in the settlement of the question.*

1. It has been thought that the eucharistic sacramentalism underlying the New Testament accounts of the Last Supper is foreign to Jewish thought and practice and bespeaks the influence of Hellenistic religious practice, which, if not wholly responsible for the story, has at any rate changed it beyond hope of recognition. This change, it is suggested, went hand in hand with a process by which the original 'bread-breaking' of the earliest Church (cf. Acts $2^{42, 46}$, $20^{7, 11}$), which was just a continuation of the ordinary meals of fellowship which the disciples shared with Jesus, marked by a joyful sense of his presence and a confident expectation of his speedy return (and involving no wine drinking), was transformed into the sacramentally efficacious memorial of his sacrificial death presupposed by the New Testament accounts of the Last Supper.

Theories of this sort found a great champion in H. Lietzmann, whose book on the subject is in process of appearing in English.† While they certainly cannot be totally rejected out of hand, more recent investigation has robbed them of a good deal of the popularity they once enjoyed.

* In addition to the works quoted elsewhere cf. A. J. B. Higgins, *The Lord's Supper in the New Testament.*

† *Mass and Lord's Supper*, translated by Dorothea Reeve, Leidén. Six fascicules out of nine have appeared.

2. Apart from the semitisms noted in the commentary as pointing to a Palestinian origin for the story, we have seen that the words and actions attributed to Jesus fit very readily into the setting of a Jewish meal, and Dr Jeremias has shown that, if the meal was a Passover one, Jesus' words of interpretation are the more natural, since Passover devotions had to be taken by the person presiding, just before the eating of the lamb, and they had to include an interpretation of the various elements of the meal: the unleavened bread was a symbol of past misery, the bitter herbs a symbol of slavery, the lamb a reminder of God's 'passing over' Egypt, and so on. This means that, even if the Last Supper was not itself a Passover meal, there would have been nothing essentially strange to a Jewish company in the head of the table offering an interpretation of certain elements in the meal.

3. But would Jesus have offered *that* particular interpretation? Here we come to a more general question which will no doubt continue to occasion wide difference of opinion; its final settlement would involve reference to all sorts of wider questions concerning Jesus' self-understanding – whether he consciously intended to found a Church, and so on – but certain more specific considerations may be mentioned here:

Scholars influenced by the Enlightenment have found it impossible to conceive of a humble and enlightened human being claiming that his particular death was the necessary condition for the reconciliation of God and man, and it must be admitted that the idea is not without its difficulties, especially in view of the fact that elsewhere in the Gospel Jesus hardly appears to attach sacrificial significance to his death. (See Goguel, *Jésus* (1950), p. 352.)

But, quite apart from the question whether Jesus is adequately described as 'a humble human being', however 'enlightened', he must not be detached from the thinking of his time. The Jews of the period were preoccupied with the question of the means available for the atonement of sins, and among the many means recognized, the deaths of individuals, particularly righteous individuals and martyrs, figured quite prominently. (Cf. 2 Macc. $7^{37ff.}$, 4 Macc. 6^{29} and 17^{22}, and the other evidence collected by Jeremias, p. 151; see also the contribution by Dr C. K. Barrett to *New Testament Essays*, ed. A. J. B. Higgins, pp. 1–18.) In view of all this, quite apart from the question of Jesus' supposed self-identification with the 'suffering servant' of Isaiah, Dr Jeremias goes so far as to say that 'it is unthinkable for Jesus not to have thought about the atoning effect of his death' (p. 152). And, if that is granted, there is perhaps not very much greater difficulty in supposing that he envisaged participation in the atoning effects of his death being mediated through more or less sacramental channels. (On this see Otto, *The Kingdom of God and the Son of Man*, especially pp. 306ff.)

4. Partly in the belief that such a sacrificial interpretation by Jesus would have been even more natural in a Passover setting,* vigorous attempts have been made, particularly by Dr Jeremias, to uphold Mark's identification of the Last Supper as a Passover meal, despite the fact that explicit statements to that effect are confined to three verses in the Gospel ($14^{12, 14, 16}$), and that St John's Gospel clearly implies the contrary (John 18^{28} – the Passover is still in the future the day *after* the Last Supper; cf. also 1 Cor. 5^{7}, which *may* imply that Christ was already being crucified at the time when the Passover lambs were being slaughtered on Nisan 14th). As we have seen, Dr Jeremias has shown that the details in our accounts of the Last Supper would fit very intelligibly into the framework of a Passover meal, and he has proved that a number of objections formerly advanced against the Passover identification are groundless (for these see commentary). His view, however, can only be upheld by postulating a remarkable coincidence of exceptional circumstances,† and the

* It is argued that though the Passover of later times was not regarded as expiatory, the blood of the original paschal lambs it commemorates was regarded as having redemptive effect, and that what Jesus said about this in the course of the meal (see above p. 456) may well have paved the way for the interpretations of the bread and the wine, which in our highly selective reports of the Supper appear unduly isolated.

† In particular the considerable amount of activity ascribed to the members of the Sanhedrin is hard to credit in the middle of the feast, and, when all allowance has been made for the Church's selective interest in telling the story, a Passover without mention of the lamb is rather like Hamlet without the Prince of Denmark. We must also remember the early Church's failure to stress – or even remember – the Passover character of the Last Supper; had it been a Passover, we should have expected an annual commemoration of it by the first followers of Jesus rather than the weekly, or even more frequent, Eucharists they in fact held. And from the history of the Quartodeciman controversy it becomes clear that one party of early Christians believed their conviction that Jesus was crucified on Nisan 14th to rest on ancient, and even eyewitness, testimony.

majority of scholars have remained on the whole unconvinced by his arguments; but the significance of the point should not be exaggerated. Much of the atmosphere, and even the detail, described by Jeremias might have attached to the meal even if it was not an actual Passover meal.

We seem, therefore, justified in saying that, though Mark's account is compressed, highly selective,* and no doubt influenced by current eucharistic practice (which may in its turn owe something to Hellenistic influences), there are no decisive grounds for denying that the Eucharist could have had its origin in some such scene (apart, possibly, from its Passover character) as Mark depicts. More than that, having regard to the way the material was preserved, we can hardly say.

* In particular Mark's Gospel fails to bring out, what is probably the case, that from one point of view the Last Supper and the early Eucharists were continuations of a series of common meals Our Lord had been in the habit of holding with his disciples (and possibly with a wider circle of followers – see above on the miraculous feedings), which had foreshadowed and anticipated the ultimate (table) fellowship of the eagerly awaited kingdom of God.

Appendix B

Attention may be drawn to two articles which have appeared since the first edition of this commentary:

(1) On Mark 4[35-41] see now Professor G. Bornkamm, in *Tradition and Interpretation in Matthew*, by G. Bornkamm, G. Barth and H. J. Held, (S.C.M. 1963) pp. 53–4. He restates clearly the view of Dibelius on this passage, which differs from that offered in the commentary. However, he adduces no new arguments in favour of this view and, in the light of what is said on pp. 146–7 of the commentary, it does not seem very plausible.

(2) In connexion with Mark 15′, see now J. Vardaman in *J. B. L.* LXXXI, Part I (March 1962), pp. 70–71. He prints and discusses the text of an inscription which suggests that, at any rate at one stage of his career, Pilate was known as *prefect*. However, in view of the statements by Tacitus (*Ann.* XV, 44) and Josephus (*Jewish War* II, 9, 2) it seems clear that *procurator* was his official title during some part of his career.

Indexes

Index of References

THE BIBLE

Old Testament

INDEX OF REFERENCES

Apocrypha

New Testament

ST MATTHEW

ST JOHN

ACTS

NON-BIBLICAL JEWISH WRITINGS

INDEX OF REFERENCES

OTHER ANCIENT WRITINGS

EARLY CHRISTIAN WRITINGS

Index of Authors

(In the case of authors consistently quoted, the references given are not exhaustive)

Index of Subjects